The Industrial Relations Research Association

gratefully acknowledges the

Edna McConnell Clark Foundation

for its support of this volume.

INDUSTRIAL RELATIONS RESEARCH
ASSOCIATION SERIES

Nonstandard Work
The Nature and Challenges of Changing Employment Arrangements

EDITED BY

Françoise Carré, Marianne A. Ferber, Lonnie Golden,
and Stephen A. Herzenberg

First Edition

Library of Congress Catalog Card Number: 50-13564

ISBN 0-913447-80-3

INDUSTRIAL RELATIONS RESEARCH ASSOCIATION SERIES:
   Proceedings of the Annual Meeting
   Annual Research Volume
   Membership Directory (every fourth year)
   IRRA Newsletter (published quarterly)
   Perspectives on Work (published periodically)

Inquiries and other communications regarding membership, meetings, publications,
and general affairs of the Association, as well as notice of address changes should be
addressed to the IRRA national office.

INDUSTRIAL RELATIONS RESEARCH ASSOCIATION
University of Illinois at Urbana-Champaign
121 Labor and Industrial Relations Building
504 East Armory Avenue
Champaign, IL 61820 USA
Phone: 217/333-0072
Fax: 217/265-5130
Email: irra@uiuc.edu

CONTENTS

INTRODUCTION 1
Françoise Carré, Marianne A. Ferber, Lonnie Golden
and Stephen A. Herzenberg

SECTION I: Trends and Patterns in Employment Arrangements
CHAPTER 1—Is "Standard Employment" Still What It Used to Be? 21
Annette Bernhardt and Dave E. Marcotte

CHAPTER 2—Definition, Composition, and Economic
Consequences of the Nonstandard Workforce 41
Anne E. Polivka, Sharon R. Cohany, and Steven Hipple

CHAPTER 3—Limits to Market-Mediated Employment:
From Deconstruction to Reconstruction
of Internal Labor Markets 95
Philip Moss, Harold Salzman, and Chris Tilly

SECTION II: Explanations of Increases in
Nonstandard Work Arrangements
CHAPTER 4—The Evolution of the Demand for Temporary Help
Supply Employment in the United States 123
Marcello Estevão and Saul Lach

CHAPTER 5—Organization Size and Flexible Staffing
Arrangements in the United States 145
Arne L. Kalleberg and Jeremy Reynolds

SECTION III: Consequences of Nonstandard Work
CHAPTER 6—Nonstandard and Contingent Employment:
Contrasts by Job Type, Industry, and Occupation... 167
Dale Belman and Lonnie Golden

CHAPTER 7—The Effects of Part-Time and Self-Employment
on Wages and Benefits: Differences by
Race/Ethnicity and Gender 213
Marianne A. Ferber and Jane Waldfogel

iii

CHAPTER 8—The Bottom-Line Impact of Nonstandard Jobs
on Companies' Profitability and Productivity....... 235
Shulamit Kahn

SECTION IV: Responses to Nonstandard Work Arrangements
and to "Labor Market Churning"

CHAPTER 9—HR Strategy and Nonstandard Work:
Dualism versus True Mobility.................. 267
Charles Heckscher

CHAPTER 10—Historical Perspectives on Representing
Nonstandard Workers........................ 291
Dorothy Sue Cobble and Leah F. Vosko

CHAPTER 11—Looking for Leverage in a Fluid World:
Innovative Responses to Temporary and
Contracted Work........................... 313
Françoise Carré and Pamela Joshi

CHAPTER 12—Building "Jobs with a Future" in Wisconsin:
Lessons from Dane County................... 341
Laura Dresser

CHAPTER 13—Labor in the New Economy:
Lessons from Labor Organizing in Silicon Valley .. 361
Chris Benner and Amy Dean

CHAPTER 14—CWA's Organizing Strategies:
Transforming Contract Work into Union Jobs..... 377
Virginia L. duRivage

CHAPTER 15—New Thinking on Worker Groups' Role
in a Flexible Economy 393
Sara Horowitz

CHAPTER 16—Nonstandard Employment and the
Structure of Postindustrial Labor Markets 399
Stephen A. Herzenberg, John A. Alic, and Howard Wial

Nonstandard Work: The Nature and Challenges of Changing Employment Arrangements

Françoise Carré
Radcliffe Public Policy Center, Harvard University

Marianne A. Ferber
University of Illinois, Urbana-Champaign

Lonnie Golden
Penn State University, Delaware County

Stephen A. Herzenberg
The Keystone Research Center

Since the founding of the Industrial Relations Research Association (IRRA), its members—institutionalists and labor economists alike—have been primarily preoccupied with "standard" labor–management relations. In this prototypical relationship, a firm and a worker have a mutually beneficial, long-term attachment. Workers enjoy employment security, benefits, training, and sometimes career mobility. Employers' investment in workers' good will and on-the-job training results in greater productivity and hence higher returns. During the three decades after World War II, a time when standard employment relationships came to be regarded as the norm, labor productivity and workers' real incomes doubled. During the 1980s and 1990s, however, hallmark features of the postwar social contract, including long-term mutual attachments and well-structured internal labor markets, have been fading.

This volume, intended for practitioners, policy makers, and the general public as well as academics and researchers, is about the observed decline of the standard employment relationship and the emerging new employment arrangements. During the 1990s, these developments received extensive publicity. Prime examples are the *Business Week*

1

cover titled "The End of the Job," the *New York Times* series "The Downsizing of America," and corporate leaders at AT&T declaring that "we are all contingent workers now." Through this cacophony and the convictions of many ordinary people that the economy's tectonic plates were shifting, questioning academic voices, wondering what and how much had really changed, were only faintly heard. The popular perception of a sea change may be in part the result of the rising proportion of working women who are seeking standard employment arrangements, not just a declining availability of such jobs. Further, even if just a relatively small share of jobs in every organization is becoming "contingent" or downsized, the fear that "it may happen to me" may nonetheless be widespread. Finally, as cynics have pointed out, it was only when job instability began to affect managers and professionals with high public profiles, including journalists, that the problem received much attention in the popular press.

There is a good deal of disagreement among researchers not only about the extent of the changes but about their advantages and disadvantages for workers, employers, and the economy. One reason for this is that even researchers are rarely dispassionate concerning these matters. We freely admit that this is also true of the editors of this volume. Keeping this in mind, we have made a special effort to include scholars and practitioners who represent a wide spectrum of views. This is true both of those who analyze the evidence concerning the extent of nonstandard arrangements, their causes, and their consequences and those who offer suggestions for policies intended to improve their outcomes. Another source of disagreement is the great diversity within and among the newly emerging employment arrangements, which makes sweeping generalizations misleading.

Scope of Volume and Explanation of Terminology

Each section of the volume addresses one of the following broad questions: (1) Is there evidence that employment relations have changed, in the sense that "standard" work arrangements are being recast so that they more closely resemble nonstandard arrangements and/or are becoming relatively less prevalent? (2) What has changed about the nature of firms, workers, and labor markets in the late 20th century that may be giving rise to new arrangements now? (3) To what extent do various nonstandard arrangements adequately meet the needs of workers, employers, and the overall economy? (4) To the extent that changing employment relations have led to some needs of workers being less adequately met, what new institutions might be constructed to better meet the needs of workers, employers, communities, and the economy? The papers in the first section present an overview of the changing nature of standard jobs and patterns in nonstandard jobs, including their occupational composition and the gender, race, and age of the people who fill them. Together, these chapters make it clear that the situation concerning nonstandard employment is very complex, in part because of the substantial differences among the various types of nonstandard jobs. In the second section, the potential causes of these developments are explored. In the third section, the effects of various nonstandard work arrangements both on workers' careers, earnings, and benefits and on firms and their financial performance are examined. In the fourth and final section, authors propose a broad range of programs and innovative institutions intended to address many of the negative consequences of nonstandard jobs. Taken together, the essays in this volume, by authors from a variety of fields with diverse analytical approaches as well as value judgments, provide few definitive answers to the controversies concerning nonstandard employment. However, by delving deeply into these questions, they provide nourishing food for thought for future researchers. Their thorough research, knowledge of workers' needs, and thoughtful recommendations will also assist policy makers and activists in their efforts to reverse, or at least mitigate, some of the undesirable outcomes of nonstandard work.

Before turning to a more detailed examination of the substantive issues discussed in this volume, a few words about terminology are in order. A wide range of terms has been used to describe the various forms of what we refer to as *nonstandard* employment. They run the gamut, including *flexible, market-mediated, nontraditional, alternative, atypical, contingent, just-in-time, marginal, precarious, disposable,* and *secondary.* As might be expected, the positive or negative connotations of the chosen term often reflect observers' normative perceptions. Views of such arrangements range from seeing them as free-market innovations that liberate both employers and workers from the straitjacket of standardized employment to seeing them as a means for exploiting workers and undermining their living standards as well as the health of the economy and, in the long run, of the organizations that employ them.

Using the term *nonstandard,* favored in this volume, we hope to avoid such value-laden connotations. *Nonstandard* merely defines employment relationships that do not fit the conception of what, at least for some decades after World War II, were considered standard. The term is not, however, unambiguous. For instance, it is not clear whether to consider all high-turnover or informal employment as not "standard." At one time, such jobs might have been classified as *secondary* by proponents of segmented or dual labor market theories (Doeringer and Piore 1971; Piore 1971) because such jobs lack internal labor market features such as opportunities for training, promotion, and rising wages with increased tenure or seniority. A second ambiguity stems from the fact that many self-employed independent contractors, freelancers, and even some temporary workers have jobs with multiple clients and thus tend to have reasonably steady work and earnings (Carnoy, Castells, and Benner 1997). They are clearly in a different labor market situation than low-wage, low-status temporaries or casual day laborers, who often can find work only for a limited number of hours each week and/or a small number of weeks during the year, usually at relatively low rates of pay. These ambiguities underscore how much heterogeneity there is among (and even within) the varieties of nonstandard employment arrangements. In any case, because the typical employment relationship in what might be termed the New Deal system of industrial relations is now breaking down, it is likely that at some future point the terms *standard* and *nonstandard* may be redefined or fall out of use.

Although the papers in this volume address only the situation in the United States, the issue of nonstandard employment is by no means unique to this country. In fact, employment relationships in the European Union (EU) appear to be undergoing transformations not unlike those found here. At the same time, the levels and types of what is usually referred to there as *atypical* employment differ from those in the United States, in ways that reflect both legal differences and the greater formality of employment relations in the EU. For example, many EU countries promote job security for workers with indefinite employment contracts by requiring "just cause" discharge, advance notice of layoffs, and severance pay. Although some have argued that employers may use fixed-term contracts to avoid these restrictions (see Büchteman 1993), the situation in the EU contrasts with that in the United States, where even standard workers have little statutory protection, except for those covered by collective bargaining contracts and in some instances by certain personnel policies and procedures or those who can bring court cases under the "implicit contract" exceptions to the employment-at-will legal standard. There are, however, also differences in the proportions and growth rates of various kinds of atypical employment among the EU countries, as would be expected in view of the significant variations in laws and institutions from one to the other. For example, the share of all employees on fixed-term contracts rose considerably in France and Spain but then declined when protections for standard workers were loosened (Meulders, Plasman, and Plasman 1994; de Grip, Hoevenberg, and Willems 1997; Walwei 1998).

Trends and Patterns in Employment Arrangements

As already suggested, there continues to be disagreement among researchers concerning whether we are witnessing a fundamental change in the nature of work or in the employment contract. Many observers have suggested that such a transformation is indeed occurring (duRivage 1986; Agassi and Heycock 1989; Christensen 1989; Appelbaum 1992; Carré 1992; Warme, Lundy, and Lundy 1992; Houseman 1994). Others who are primarily concerned about the impact on duration patterns for all jobs do not find the evidence convincing that standard jobs are to any great extent being replaced by jobs that are less secure or that they offer less career mobility, benefit coverage, and social protection (Farber 1995; Diebold, Neumark, and Polsky 1997; Allen, Clark, and Schieber 1998). Among the possible reasons why definitive answers to these questions have been difficult to find are that such trends have developed only relatively recently, that they still involve only a modest share of the total labor force, and that these trends have shown themselves to be neither unidirectional nor irreversible.

Annette Bernhardt and Dave Marcotte examine whether the standard employment relationship is changing by reviewing research on trends in four defining characteristics of that relationship: (1) tenure; (2) the extent to which wages are sheltered from market fluctuations and are instead determined by administrative rules tied to job classifications and rank; (3) upward mobility within the firm, including the dependence of wages on seniority and promotions; and (4) the availability of company-sponsored health and pension benefits. They conclude that the contours of the standard employment relationship have indeed changed. Job stability has declined mildly overall but strongly among workers who are young, have no postsecondary education, or are African American. Quantitative evidence about the weakening of wage-setting institutions and qualitative research on industries and firms indicate that wages are increasingly set in external rather than internal labor markets, at least for some groups of workers. There is less upward mobility, and it has also become significantly more unequal. Finally, health and pension benefit coverage has declined along with declining commitments between firms and workers.

Anne Polivka, Sharon Cohany, and Steven Hipple present an overview of the patterns and trends in nonstandard employment and describe its composition by gender, race/ethnicity, marital/parental status, age, and level of education. Using data from the February 1995 and February 1997 Contingent Work and Alternative Work Arrangement Supplements to the Current Population Survey (CPS), they divide the sample of workers into eight mutually exclusive categories of alternative jobs. They estimate the number of workers in each category, the extent to which workers in these jobs experience lower average earnings, employee benefit coverage, and whether such workers are satisfied with their alternative work arrangement or would prefer a standard job. With the important exceptions of independent contract workers, the self-employed, and some directly hired temporary workers, those who hold alternative jobs tend to be disproportionately younger, female, African American, unmarried, and less (or very highly) educated and most often reside in central cities or other high-poverty areas. Workers in all eight nonstandard arrangements are less likely to be offered health insurance coverage and are also less likely to be covered regardless of the source of such insurance. Agency and direct-hire temporary workers generally experience a disadvantage relative to regular full-time employees in their hourly earnings rate and job stability. The authors conclude that not all nonstandard jobs are of poor quality.

Philip Moss, Harold Salzman, and Chris Tilly locate nonstandard employment in the broad context of employment structures within firms, most notably the move away from vertical integration and the devolution of internal labor markets. Specifically, they examine recent restructuring in insurance and electronics manufacturing. These two sectors offer rich opportunities for studying internal labor markets. Examining them leads the authors to believe that the demise of internal labor markets is not a foregone conclusion, because workers' desire for job stability and employers' need for a reliable source of skilled labor provide powerful counterforces to the professed desire for flexibility and cost reduction. The authors use four company case studies to illustrate how companies have encountered limits to the devolution of internal labor markets and the accompanying use of nonstandard work and outsourcing. The authors argue that the varied patterns observed as companies engage in restructuring, including the often-observed deconstruction of internal labor markets, may be only one stage in an ongoing process leading to changed employment relationships but not necessarily the end of long-term employment with rising pay profiles and opportunities for promotion.

Explanations of Increases in Nonstandard Work Arrangements

Next we turn to the question of why employment arrangements are changing at this particular time. What was different about firms, workers, and labor markets in the late 20th century that caused these changes, and why were they concentrated in particular sectors? Once again, there are no simple answers. Some observers have suggested that the expansion of retail trade and many services has greatly contributed to the growth of nonstandard employment, just as it explained most of the increase in part-time work during earlier decades. Marcello Estevão and Saul Lach, who focus on the explosion of temporary help service (THS) employment since the middle 1980s, show that THS hires have grown in virtually every sector of private industry. Their evidence includes original estimates of the number of THS workers hired by employers in eight detailed manufacturing industries. The only difference between the manufacturing and the service sector patterns is that in the latter the increase was accompanied by a large rise in direct hires of temporaries, while in the former there was a decline in direct hiring from the peak it had reached in 1989. The authors conclude that almost all of the growth in THS employment is attributable to a change in the hiring behavior of firms within all industries, rather than to the growth of jobs in industries that tend to hire more THS workers.

Unlike Estevão and Lach, who examine the representation of nonstandard workers by industry, Arne Kalleberg and Jeremy Reynolds are interested in differences by organization size. They analyze data gathered from a 1997 national survey of about 1,000 establishments, including information regarding the extent to which they used seven different categories of flexible staffing arrangements and the main reasons why firms rely on such hires. They expect larger firms to be relatively more likely, on balance, to employ such workers as a way of circumventing negative consequences of size, such as bureaucratization and unionization. A test of their hypothesis confirms that this is the case, although small firms are also very likely to employ workers in nonstandard arrangements, and they are more likely to employ workers in at least some of these categories. For example, while large firms use more direct-hire temporary workers and on-site temporary agency workers, small establishments use more on-call workers and off-site contractors, and both types of firms use more part-timers than medium-sized establishments.

Consequences of Nonstandard Work

Just as there is uncertainty about whether there has been substantial dilution of standard employment and about the extent of the growth of nonstandard jobs, so there is little agreement about the consequences of nonstandard employment. Many neoclassical economists have great faith in the efficacy of the labor market and tend to hold sanguine views about outcomes not only for employers but also for workers. They regard the effects of recent changes in standard employment as, at worst, no more than inconsequential shifts in employment patterns. As for nonstandard employment, they emphasize that a wider variety of arrangements allows a better match between the increasingly heterogeneous preferences of workers and the varied requirements of firms (e.g., Abraham 1988; Kosters 1995; Segal and Sullivan 1995; Barkhume 1996; Danner 1996). Any deterioration in wages, benefits, and advancement opportunities for workers is presumed to be offset by compensating differentials, such as greater flexibility or enhanced ability to coordinate work with family obligations. Firms are assumed to benefit as a result of restraining their labor costs and gaining flexibility in labor deployment. Other researchers hold less sanguine views about the operation of the labor market, and their investigations show that some flexible employment arrangements are clearly less advantageous for workers than regular full-time employment would have been (e.g., Loveman and Tilly 1988; Büchteman and Quack 1990; Burtless 1990; Warme, Lundy, and Lundy 1992; Devine 1994; Hipple and Stewart 1996a, 1996b; Nollen 1996; Kalleberg et al. 1997; Segal and Sullivan 1997).

Dale Belman and Lonnie Golden use the February 1997 CPS supplement to analyze the nature of nonstandard jobs through the lens of industry and occupation, first by examining the extent to which such jobs are concentrated in various industrial and occupational sectors. They find that the chances a given worker will be employed in either a nonstandard or a contingent job—one that lacks an explicit or implicit contract for long-term employment—are significantly greater in a few industries and occupations. They also find that all nonstandard and contingent workers have significantly less access to employee benefit coverage, in addition to their greater job insecurity. Many of them also receive lower wages than otherwise similar standard or noncontingent workers in the same industry and occupation. Independent contract and contract firm workers, as well as the self-employed, however, appear to get no such wage penalty, and it is not unusual for them to get a wage premium. Thus, the heterogeneity makes it difficult to draw general conclusions concerning the overall effect of nonstandard jobs on the economic well-being of workers. The results imply that the creation of nonstandard jobs by employers is being driven in large part by economic incentives faced by employers, such as the cost savings realized by avoiding payments for employee benefits.

To resolve the previously discussed differences about the advantages and disadvantages of nonstandard employment for workers, further research is necessary. For one, relatively little empirical work has been done to date concerning possible differences in outcomes of nonstandard employment for workers by gender, race/ethnicity, or level of education and skills. Even less is known about the longer-term effects, either on workers who remain in such jobs or on the many workers who eventually move into standard jobs. Some of these questions are addressed by Marianne Ferber and Jane Waldfogel. Their study focuses on part-time and self-employment because the necessary longitudinal data were available only for these two groups. Their results show that both types of employment tend to have negative effects on wages and benefits in the long run and in the current period for men as well as women, except that current self-employment is associated with higher wages for men. At the same time, the effects are not uniform for blacks, Hispanics, and whites, nor are they the same for all types of benefits. The results suggest that nonstandard employment may have cumulative, not only immediate, effects but that these effects tend to differ by demographic group.

Very little research has focused on the effects that hiring nonstandard workers has on employers, perhaps because of the widely held belief that employers would not choose to create nonstandard employment arrangements if they did not expect them to increase their profits. This does not mean, however, that their expectations will necessarily prove to be correct, especially in the long run. A few researchers have noted that a less motivated, committed, or unstable workforce may instead lower labor productivity (Granrose and Appelbaum 1986; Doeringer et al. 1991; Nulty 1993).

Shulamit Kahn uses a two-stage approach to investigate this issue. First, she presents information gathered from interviews with executives in order to learn whether they thought that their companies experienced changes in either productivity or profitability after hiring more temporary workers. This information is then complemented by statistical analysis of aggregate industry data to determine whether an industry's use of nonstandard workers is associated with past, current, or future productivity and profitability. Her effort demonstrates how extraordinarily difficult it is to obtain definitive answers to the question whether such employment arrangements improve productivity and even more whether they improve profitability. Therefore, it remains unclear whether employers have really benefited from the changes so many of them have recently adopted. This may well help to explain why Moss, Salzman, and Tilly (this volume) found that some businesses are reversing their policies.

Responses to Nonstandard Work Arrangements and to "Labor Market Churning"

The papers in the first three sections of this volume explore recent changes in the labor market and their effects on employers and particularly on workers. Some of the essays in the final section also begin by analyzing the current situation, but all go on to present examples of practical responses to the problems faced by workers as a result of these changes. As already noted, the difficulties workers confront include job instability, low wages, lack of benefits, absence of training and skill acquisition programs, and lack of some basic worker protections such as unemployment insurance and sick leave. Many of the authors concentrate on workers with the fewest skills and the lowest wages, whose problems are most acute. The focus of these essays on practical responses to nonstandard arrangements from labor, community groups, and sometimes businesses reflects the current political reality that there are virtually no prospects for federal or state policy action to improve either benefit coverage, opportunities for representation, or job quality for workers in nonstandard arrangements.

Charles Heckscher considers the development of nonstandard jobs part of a larger transformation away from organizing economic activity around large, bureaucratic firms and toward a new approach based on networks that aims for fluidity and innovation. He notes that in human resource management there is a tension between managers' encouragement of mobility in general and their attempts to discourage it among their most talented employees. This tension gives rise to a free-agent mentality among some employees and a deep resentment of free agents among others. Since the "best" employees are deluged with enticements to move on to something better, while the rest flounder, the employees the companies most want to keep have the least incentive to be loyal—and vice versa. One result of this situation is dualism within organizations, where the employees who perform most highly receive disproportionately large rewards. Another result is misunderstanding and mistrust, which undermine the collaboration particularly vital to a healthy knowledge-based organization. The underlying problem is that while a human resource management strategy that emphasizes networking as the best way to organize economic activity has rhetorical appeal, the approach that relies on the bureaucratic firm continues to be the dominant reality, buttressed by law and institutions. As a consequence, a new employment system has not yet made much progress against the tremendous inertia of the existing order. Heckscher suggests that the solution is to be found in new structures and incremental steps that would bring about progress toward "true mobility," which will satisfy both employers' increasing need for highly skilled labor to conduct project-based work and workers' need for security.

Dorothy Sue Cobble and Leah Vosko put nonstandard arrangements into historical context. They observe that the majority of jobs prior to the New Deal exhibited many of the characteristics of contemporary nonstandard arrangements. They often were part-time or temporary, lacked guaranteed income and benefit coverage, and entailed a loose and/or triangulated relationship between employer and worker. Thus, nonstandard arrangements are neither atypical nor new, and lessons can be drawn from the responses of worker organizations in the past, particularly the varied ways they chose to define who was an employee. In those days, workers formed unions on an occupational basis in recognition of the instability and ambiguity of employment relationships. These unions sought control over the labor supply but also assumed "management" functions. The authors argue that to address contemporary nonstandard employment, particularly independent contracting and triangulated arrangements, unions must once again have the ability to behave like professional organizations, for example by setting performance standards and disciplining workers. They then examine historical examples of unions that dealt with contract work, which relied upon members to regulate work effort and prevent "sweating" and at times had extensive internal debates as to who was an employer and who was a worker. They conclude that workers may be better off if unions have the right to decide this issue for themselves.

Françoise Carré and Pamela Joshi examine responses from labor unions, community groups, and businesses to the challenges posed by nonstandard arrangements. They focus on the workers who are either employed by temporary-staffing companies, short-term hires, or contractor employees and those who suffer the greatest penalties for being in nonstandard employment. Although the authors recognize that this is a heterogeneous group, they argue that these workers face many of the same problems, including difficulties in obtaining access to benefits and gaining representation. Hence, the varied "bottom-up" responses they examine have broad policy relevance. The authors collected case study information in 1996–97 on 32 cases of creative innovations developed to address worker needs. While the strategies used are wide ranging, they fall into three broad categories: improving "job brokering" through intermediaries, setting minimum standards for compensation and labor protections, and public information and legislative strategies. From these innovations the authors draw insights on the elements needed for future policy formulation.

The authors of the next four papers discuss specific programs with which they are personally associated. Laura Dresser describes a recent effort to build multiemployer career ladders in three major sectors (manufacturing, health care, and finance and insurance) in Dane County, Wisconsin. This project was the result of the discovery by members of the Dane County Economic Summit Council that, despite the low unemployment rate in that area in the mid-1990s, many young workers were mired in dead-end jobs in small service establishments. Subsequently, they decided to ask the Center on Wisconsin Strategy (COWS) at the University of Wisconsin–Madison to conduct an analysis of the regional economy and particularly of the labor market. Upon completion of this investigation, COWS recommended the building of industry training partnerships and career ladders in the hope not only that this would improve the situation for low-wage workers but that firms would come to see that this program also helps them to improve their training and skill development programs. To date, COWS has experienced both successes and frustrations. Dresser concentrates on the lessons to be learned from two years of its operation.

Chris Benner and Amy Dean focus on existing challenges and attempted solutions in Silicon Valley, a region with an economic base that relies primarily on advanced technologies and is well known for being at the cutting edge of technological innovation and economic transformation. Employment arrangements evolve rapidly there, job turnover is high, subcontracting chains are complex, and nonstandard arrangements are more common than in other regions. These conditions have resulted in growing insecurity for many workers, particularly those who lack skills and social networks. This environment requires a change in conceptions of worker representation and protection. The authors report on the comprehensive approach taken by the South Bay Central Labor Council and Working Partnerships USA, a labor-led community coalition that promotes an active labor role in shaping the regional economy and body politic, explores new forms of worker representation and job ladders across work sites and employers, conducts policy research, and promotes leadership development. Working Partnerships has developed representation structures through the Temporary Worker Employment Project, which includes a membership organization with an advocacy agenda. Their aims are to raise employment standards in the temporary help and staffing industry; to create a temporary-staffing service that is an alternative to conventional, for-profit companies; and to facilitate the establishment of regional skill standards and access to training for clerical and administrative occupations. The authors also advocate access to health insurance and pension for all employees.

Virginia duRivage examines innovations undertaken by the Communications Workers of America (CWA) to address nonstandard employment. This union of over 600,000 members represents workers in a broad range of technologically advanced trades, from telecommunications, printing and publishing, and the media to passenger services. In recent years, the combined effects of subcontracting, industry mergers, and competition in telecommunications in particular have created an employment structure where an aging core of union workers is surrounded by a ring of nonunion, often temporary or contract workers employed in AT&T subsidiaries, regional Bell companies, and companies established since the breakup of AT&T. Meanwhile, nonstandard arrangements have increased within the unionized sector as well. CWA has found that the phenomenal growth of subcontracting and competition has weakened the effectiveness of traditional union approaches such as negotiating contracts that limit the use of nonstandard employment. DuRivage reports on promising new experiments by CWA: the development of and experimentation with employment centers, union-run alternatives to temporary-staffing services, and new forms of organizing, including efforts to represent high-tech "permatemps" at Microsoft Corporation. The chapter identifies challenges that the union has faced within the union, the workforce, and the business partners in running these centers. Regarding new forms of organizing, the union has had promising results from neutrality contract provisions that guarantee neutrality in organizing campaigns in companies that AT&T acquires and its wholly owned subsidiaries. The union has also helped with the formation of the Washington Alliance of Technology Workers (WashTech), a union-affiliated worker association seeking to represent an estimated 6,100 agency temporaries hired by Microsoft. The effort targets the software manufacturer as well as the temporary-staffing agencies that payroll these workers. The association has a legislative strategy at the state level and also seeks to form a National Labor Relations Board–recognized bargaining unit for these workers.

Sara Horowitz argues that new forms of worker organization and representation that mirror the decentralized and interconnected organization of businesses are needed to address the issues faced by nonstandard workers. This is particularly true for independent contractors and freelancers, who are not considered employees by businesses or under the law. These workers need not only representation but access to affordable health care and pension plans and an end to disadvantaged treatment in the tax code. Horowitz focuses on the role of Working Today, an organization that, since 1995, has built a network of 25 associations representing 92,000 workers. It also has individual members who are nonstandard workers. The voluntary associations that join Working Today, such as the New York New Media Association, perform some of the functions for workers that craft unions performed in the past. These functions include gaining control over the labor supply, securing deals for material supplies, ensuring "fair" prices for their products, and building community among workers. Working Today is also trying to bring together the voluntary associations around common, long-term projects, such as the establishment of an experimental Portable Benefit Fund. This plan, to be launched in the spring of 2000, will test the viability of a fund for delivering quality portable health insurance at an affordable price. If the demonstration is successful, it will be a model for other organizations and unions to establish similar funds. Through these activities, Working Today hopes to encourage the building of a network of structures that will offer independent contractors and other nonstandard workers greater security, community, and, importantly, more political clout.

Stephen Herzenberg, John Alic, and Howard Wial situate the phenomenon of nonstandard work within a new theory of the structure of the American labor market, which they introduce and briefly contrast with earlier structural labor market theories, including dual labor market theory. They divide the labor market into four work systems, which differ in how production is organized and performance regulated: tightly constrained work systems, such as assembly-line jobs (an estimated 5% of jobs); unrationalized labor-intensive systems, such as janitorial jobs (a quarter of all jobs); semiautonomous systems, including jobs in which significant attachment exists between worker and firm (30% of jobs); and high-skill autonomous systems, in which employees substantially self-regulate their work practices (about 40% of jobs). The authors attribute the increase in nonstandard jobs, defined in terms of limited job security and prospects for advancement, largely as a result of expansion in the employment share of work systems that most readily accommodate nonstandard work (especially unrationalized labor-intensive). It is also viewed as the consequence of a fall in the share of the work systems that are least open to nonstandard work (especially semiautonomous work systems). In addition to clarifying the reasons for increases in nonstandard employment, the authors use their theory to identify changes in labor market institutions needed so that more workers will be able to enjoy the benefits associated in the past with standard employment. They point to the need for institutions that promote the reorganization of unrationalized jobs into semiautonomous or high-skill autonomous jobs. They also point to the need for multifirm job ladders that allow workers to advance out of unrationalized and semiautonomous work systems and that can smooth transitions across employers for workers in semiautonomous jobs. Pointing to examples of innovative labor market institutions, including several profiled in other chapters in this volume, the authors argue that the necessary labor market reconstruction can be achieved. The volume thus ends on an optimistic note with the suggestion that it is possible to close the gap between workers' aspirations and economic opportunities by expanding the latter instead of diminishing the former.

Conclusions and Directions for Future Research on Nonstandard Work Arrangements

The four broad questions around which this volume is organized have been addressed at some length and have provided a great deal of information. This does not mean, however, that they were answered definitively. In sum, the picture that emerges is that employment arrangements clearly are changing and that at least some "standard" work arrangements may be both becoming relatively less pervasive and tending to more closely resemble nonstandard jobs. In addition, the evolving nature of firms and labor markets, as well as the labor force, in the late 20th century may have given rise to new employment arrangements that may come to resemble those of the pre–New Deal era but for the most part are likely to be new. Virtually all of the emerging forms of nonstandard arrangements, however, compare unfavorably with standard employment and internal labor markets in meeting the needs of workers for security and rising living standards. Further, employers are finding that, in many cases, nonstandard work arrangements and the breakdown of internal labor markets simply replace old inadequacies with new ones. Thus, it is not surprising that employees and some employers are searching for innovative, often collective efforts by various private-sector organizations that are experimenting with the construction of new labor market institutions intended to help meet the needs of workers, employers, communities, and the economy.

To probe deeper into issues that remain unresolved, new research is needed, including empirical analysis of whether standard and nonstandard jobs are becoming less distinct and theoretical analysis of the distinction itself and of new ways of distinguishing jobs. Unresolved issues also include the questions of precisely what the most important factors are that motivate employers to create nonstandard jobs and what the role of the burgeoning for-profit labor market intermediaries is in promoting greater employer use of such jobs.

In the traditions of the IRRA, the research in this volume attempts to document key trends in employment arrangements and search for new labor market structures that promote greater stability, shared prosperity, and opportunities for the workers to achieve their aspirations. Only a few other generalizations are warranted about all the papers in this volume. They all recognize that nonstandard jobs are not identical and that not all workers in nonstandard jobs have the same problems, and they all recognize that some types of nonstandard employment arrangements have not proved particularly beneficial for employers either.

The responses and solutions proposed by essays in this volume point mainly to unions, community groups, or employer associations as catalysts for change rather than to government policy action. While there may be differences among authors in perspectives on the role of government policy, this shared emphasis reflects in part the singularity of the United States among economically advanced nations in the limited role that government plays in directly providing for the needs of workers, most notably where health care coverage is concerned. It also reflects an adaptation to the recent political climate, which has led few to expect significant federal and state action in this arena. Nevertheless, there has been activity in the policy sphere to improve access to benefits and to limit the routine use of nonstandard work. For one, there continue to be proposals for federal legislation prohibiting the differential treatment of part-time and other nonstandard workers vis-à-vis standard workers with regard to provision of benefits. Also, a number of state legislatures have been considering bills to establish minimum labor standards for the temporary-staffing industry and to mandate benefit coverage for nonstandard workers. Yet few have been enacted. This political climate has led authors to look at "bottom-up" responses.

The important role that government, the courts, and unions could play even under existing labor law in curbing the use of nonstandard arrangements was not a focus in this volume, mainly because these issues have been addressed in considerable depth elsewhere (e.g., Carnevale, Jennings, and Eisenmann 1998; duRivage, Carré, and Tilly 1998; Gonos 1998; Autor 2000). The recent series of court cases against Microsoft Corporation have raised problems for the company's systematic, high-volume, and long-term use of independent contractors and temporary-staffing-agency workers, the so-called permatemps (duRivage, this volume). Most recently, public pressures from the permatemps themselves, who organized into WashTech, an association affiliated with the Communications Workers of America, have compelled a change in company policy away from the routine "rollover" of temporary assignments and their successive renewals over long periods of time. This has opened the door for 5,500 to 6,000 permatemps to apply for 3,000 standard jobs in the corporation's Seattle headquarters. In the traditional collective bargaining arena, the Teamsters union ran a successful strike against United Parcel Service in 1997. One of their goals was to limit the use of part-time and temporary hires and allow workers in these arrangements to bid for standard jobs.

Taken together, the papers included in the volume make it clear that the labor market is characterized by newer versions of familiar problems: pockets of underemployment, unevenly distributed rewards, and inadequate job security for many workers. Yet there is no implication that these problems are inevitable or that future developments are predetermined. The problems may, in fact, be remedied by some combination of the following: the more widespread adoption of human resource practices that emphasize retention and internal flexibility over lean and "flexible" staffing; the use of collective bargaining processes to prevent exclusion of certain workers and nonstandard jobs from the bargaining unit, a greater sense of collective responsibility by public officials for ensuring more equal opportunity and more equitable outcomes; and, importantly, organized efforts to build new institutions for nonstandard as well as standard jobs that successfully replicate the advantages of internal labor markets for low-wage workers by establishing networks across firms, occupations, industries, and regions. Further research that sheds more light on the extent to which employment relationships have changed; the reasons why they have changed; and their effects on workers, employers, and the economy will make it easier to find new ways to meet the needs of all those who are disadvantaged by the emerging forms of employment.

References

Abraham, Katherine G. 1988. "Flexible Staffing Arrangements in Employers' Short-Term Adjustment Strategies." In Robert A. Hart, ed., *Employment, Unemployment and Labor Utilization*. Boston: Unwin Hyman, pp. 288–311.

Agassi, Judith Buber, and Stephen Heycock, eds. 1989. *The Redesign of Working Time: Promise or Threat?* Berlin: Ed. Sigma.

Allen, Steven G., Robert L. Clark, and Sylvester J. Schieber. 1998. *Has Job Security Vanished in Large Corporations?* NBER Working Paper No. 6966. Cambridge, MA: National Bureau of Economic Research.

Appelbaum, Eileen. 1992. "Structural Change and the Growth of Part-Time and Temporary Employment." In Virginia L. duRivage, ed., *New Policies for the Part-Time and Contingent Workforce*. Armonk, NY: M. E. Sharpe, pp. 1–14.

Autor, David. 2000. *Outsourcing at Will: Unjust Dismissal Doctrine and the Growth of Temporary Help Employment*. NBER Working Paper No. 7557. Cambridge, MA: National Bureau of Economic Research.

Barkhume, Anthony. 1996. "The Price of Temporary Help Services and Growth of Temporary Work." Unpublished paper, U.S. Department of Labor, February.

Büchteman, Christoph, ed. 1993. *Employment Security and Labor Market Behavior.* Cornell International and Labor Relations Report No. 23. Ithaca, NY: ILR Press.

Büchteman, Christoph, and S. Quack. 1990. "How Precarious Is 'Non-Standard' Employment? Evidence for West Germany." *Cambridge Journal of Economics,* Vol. 14, pp. 315–329.

Burtless, Gary, ed. 1990. *A Future of Lousy Jobs: The Changing Structure of U.S. Wages*. Washington, DC: Brookings Institution.

Carnevale, Anthony, Lynn Jennings, and James Eisenmann. 1998. "Contingent Workers and Employment Law." In Kathleen Barker and Kathleen Christensen, eds., *Contingent Work: American Employment Relations in Transition*. Ithaca, NY: Cornell University Press, pp. 281–305.

Carnoy, Martin, Manuel Castells, and Chris Benner. 1997. "Labour Markets and Employment Practices in the Age of Flexibility: A Case Study of Silicon Valley." *International Labour Review,* Vol. 136, no. 1 (Spring), pp. 27–48.

Carré, Françoise J. 1992. "Temporary Employment in the Eighties." In Virginia L. duRivage, ed., *New Policies for the Part-Time and Contingent Workforce*. Armonk, NY: M. E. Sharp, pp. 45–87.

Christensen, Kathleen. 1989. "Women and Contingent Work." In D. S. Eitzen and Maxine Baca-Zinn, eds., *The Reshaping of America*. Englewood Cliffs, NJ: Prentice-Hall, pp. 73–80.

Danner, Donald. 1996. "The Flexible Work Force." *Journal of Labor Research,* Vol. 17, no. 4 (Fall), pp. 523–524.

de Grip, A., J. Hoevenberg, and E. Willems. 1997. "Atypical Employment in the European Union." *International Labour Review,* Vol. 136, no. 1 (Spring), pp. 49–71.

Devine, Theresa. 1994. "Characteristics of Self-Employed Women in the United States." *Monthly Labor Review,* Vol. 117, no. 3 (March), pp. 20–24.

Diebold, Francis X., David Neumark, and Daniel Polsky. 1997. "Job Stability in the United States." *Journal of Labor Economics*, Vol. 15, no. 2 (April), pp. 206–233.

Doeringer, Peter B., Kathleen Christensen, Patricia M. Flynn, Douglas T. Hall, Harry C. Katz, Jeffrey H. Keefe, Christopher J. Ruhm, Andrew M. Sum, and Michael Useem, eds. 1991. *Turbulence in the American Workplace*. New York: Oxford University Press.

Doeringer, Peter B., and Michael Piore. 1971. *Internal Labor Markets and Manpower Analysis*. Lexington, MA: D. C. Heath.

duRivage, Virginia L. 1986. *Working at the Margins: Part-Time and Temporary Workers in the United States*. Cleveland, OH: 9to5, National Association of Working Women.

duRivage, Virginia L., Françoise Carré, and Chris Tilly. 1998. "Making Labor Law Work for Part-Time and Contingent Workers." In Kathleen Barker and Kathleen Christensen, eds., *Contingent Work: American Employment Relations in Transition*. Ithaca, NY: Cornell University Press, pp. 103–125.

Farber, Henry S. 1995. *Are Lifetime Jobs Disappearing? Job Duration in the United States: 1973–1993*. NBER Working Paper No. 5014, February. Cambridge, MA: National Bureau of Economic Research.

Gonos, George. 1998. "The Interaction between Market Incentives and Government Actions." In Kathleen Barker and Kathleen Christensen, eds., *Contingent Work: American Employment Relations in Transition*. Ithaca, NY: Cornell University Press, pp. 170–194.

Granrose, Cherylin S., and Eileen Appelbaum. 1986. "The Efficiency of Temporary Help and Part-Time Employment." *Personnel Administrator*, Vol. 31, no. 1 (January), pp. 71–82.

Hipple, Steven, and Jay Stewart. 1996a. "Earnings and Benefits of Contingent and Noncontingent Workers." *Monthly Labor Review*, Vol. 119, no. 10 (October), pp. 22–30.

Hipple, Steven, and Jay Stewart. 1996b. "Earnings and Benefits of Workers in Alternative Work Arrangements." *Monthly Labor Review*, Vol. 119, no. 10 (October), pp. 46–54.

Houseman, Susan N. 1994. *Job Security vs. Labor Market Flexibility: Is There a Tradeoff?* Kalamazoo, MI: W. E. Upjohn Institute.

Kalleberg, Arne L., Edith Rasell, Ken Hudson, David Webster, Barbara F. Reskin, Naomi Cassirer, and Eileen Appelbaum. 1997. *Nonstandard Work, Substandard Jobs. Flexible Work Arrangements in the U.S.* Washington, DC: Economic Policy Institute.

Kosters, Marvin. 1995. "Part-Time Pay." *Journal of Labor Research*, Vol. 16, no. 3 (Summer), pp. 263–274.

Loveman, Gary, and Chris Tilly. 1988. "Good Jobs or Bad Jobs: What Does the Evidence Say?" *New England Economic Review*, January/February, pp. 46–65.

Meulders, D., O. Plasman, and R. Plasman. 1994. *Atypical Employment in the EC*. Aldershot, Hampshire: Dartmouth Publishing.

Nollen, Stanley D. 1996. "Negative Aspects of Temporary Employment." *Journal of Labor Research*, Vol. 17, no. 4 (Fall), pp. 567–581.

Nulty, Leslie. 1993. "Comments." In Dorothy Sue Cobble, ed., *Women and Unions: Forging a Partnership*. Ithaca, NY: ILR Press, pp. 197–200.

Piore, Michael. 1971. "The Dual Labor Market: Theory and Implications." In David
    M. Gordon, ed., *Problems in Political Economy: An Urban Perspective.* Lexing-
    ton, MA: D. C. Heath.
Segal, Lewis, and Daniel Sullivan. 1995. "The Temporary Labor Force." *Economic
    Perspectives,* Vol. 19, no. 2 (March–April), pp. 2–19.
Segal, Lewis M., and Daniel G. Sullivan. 1997. "The Growth of Temporary Services
    Work." *Journal of Economic Perspectives,* Vol. 11, no. 2 (Spring), pp. 117–136.
Walwei, Ulrich. 1998. "Flexibility of Employment Relationships: Possibilities and
    Limits." In T. Donley and M. Oppenheimer, eds., *International Review of Public
    Policy,* Vol. 10, pp. 35–50.
Warme, Barbara D., Katherina L. P. Lundy, and Larry A. Lundy, eds. 1992. *Working
    Part-Time: Risks and Opportunities.* New York: Praeger.

CHAPTER 1

Is "Standard Employment" Still What It Used to Be?

ANNETTE BERNHARDT
University of Wisconsin-Madison

DAVE E. MARCOTTE
University of Maryland Baltimore County

Introduction

When the United States emerged from recession in 1991, the economy began what has been a remarkable expansion, characterized by low unemployment and steady growth. But this expansion has been accompanied by continuing reports of restructuring and workforce reduction at the country's bedrock firms. These reports followed on the heels of a decade in which the number of well-paid manufacturing jobs declined, inequality increased, and contingent employment grew.

The result has been increased public anxiety about the future of work. This was exemplified by the *Time* magazine cover story "Whatever Happened to the Great American Job?" in 1993 ("Jobs" 1993) and the *New York Times* series on "The Downsizing of America" in 1996. More recently, *Newsweek* ran a special issue titled "Your Next Job" (McGinn and McCormick 1999), a sort of worker's guide to jobs in the new millennium. The article focused on computer programmers, managerial consultants, and independent contractors who hop from employer to employer, project to project, and manage their own careers.

The common theme underlying these accounts is that the very nature of the American workplace has changed. Employment is being portrayed as more tenuous and entailing fewer reciprocal obligations between firms and workers—with workers building their careers by moving across organizations instead of within them and being responsible for their own skill development and advancement. If true, such an externalization of work raises important challenges to current labor market policies and institutions.

In this chapter, we look at whether the evidence squares with public perception: Does recent research support the view that the standard employment relationship is changing, and if so, how? To answer this question, we draw on the framework of internal labor markets as a way of conceptualizing standard employment and identifying any divergence from it over the past 30 years. While internal labor markets have been variously characterized, they generally include (1) a long-term employment relationship; (2) wages that are sheltered from market wage fluctuations and are instead determined by administrative rules tied to job classifications and rank; (3) upward mobility within the firm, so that wages rise with seniority and promotions; and (4) company-sponsored benefits (Doeringer and Piore 1971; Dunlop 1964).

This is clearly a complex structure. As a result, identifying any deterioration of internal labor markets is a challenging task for researchers. A complete analysis would require longitudinal, nationally representative data on both firms and workers over the past two or three decades. Ideally, such data would include information about firm characteristics, organizational and occupational structure, promotions, workers' wages, tenure, demographics, and so forth. Existing data fall far short of this ideal in terms of the quality and breadth of information and the consistency of measures over time.

Nevertheless, researchers from a variety of disciplines have tried to test for changes along each of the four preceding dimensions that characterize standard employment. We review research on job stability, wage setting, upward mobility, and benefit coverage.[1] We do not attempt to cover all of the research on these topics. Our goal is instead to provide an overview of conceptual approaches and findings, giving particular attention to those areas where research has not been conclusive and where new questions have arisen. The citations provided should enable readers to pursue specific issues in more detail.

Has Job Stability Declined?

We begin by reviewing the research concerning job stability, one of the key tests of trends in standard employment. If internal labor markets are being dismantled via practices such as downsizing, subcontracting, and greater use of contingent workers, then we would expect job tenure to grow shorter and job stability to decline. Despite the public perception that job instability is growing, empirical documentation of this "fact" has been elusive, in part because of severe data and measurement problems. Even so, as we reach the end of the 1990s, researchers are beginning to gain a better understanding of initial confusion and discord on the subject, as well as the trends in job stability themselves. The resulting picture is not as dire as initially depicted, but it makes clear that the issue of job stability is worthy of continued policy and analytical attention.

The Essential Findings

Our reading of the evidence accumulated to date is that there has been a moderate decline in job stability in the United States, although the extent and timing of that decline over the past three decades are not clear.[2] It appears that during the 1990s we witnessed a decline in job stability, perhaps due to exceptionally high rates of job separations in the early years of the decade, the period when concern about downsizing emerged. Evidence on trends in the 1980s and 1970s is mixed and highly sensitive to data and measurement choices.

It is also clear, however, that the mild decline in overall job stability hides as much as it reveals. The observed changes in aggregate stability are composites of very different trends for different groups of workers. One might in fact argue that we are observing primarily a redistribution, rather than wholesale decline, of stable jobs. In particular, that redistribution has reduced the stability of jobs held by men, young adults, African Americans, and less-educated workers:

- Because of growing female attachment to the labor force during the last 30 years, voluntary quits have declined among women, *ceteris paribus* increasing job stability. This also means that male workers have faced growing competition for long-term jobs. Nearly every study has found some evidence of stability declines for men, even as there appeared to be no decline (and sometimes even an increase) for women.

- Young men appear to have been hit particularly hard since the 1970s, a consistent finding across a number of studies. In the 1990s, older workers have also been affected (especially those over 50).

- Black workers have experienced the most substantial decline in job stability during the last three decades.

- Declines in job stability have been concentrated among workers with a high school education or less.

Given the initial press coverage of job stability trends, these findings are ironic. The cover photograph on the *Time* magazine issue that reported on "The Great American Job" was emblematic of the thrust of the media coverage ("Jobs" 1993). The photograph was of a middle-aged white man at the peak of his professional career. Looking at the evidence now, the photograph should more appropriately have been of a young, working-class, black man.

Reasons for Disagreements about Job Stability

While a fairly clear picture of trends in instability is starting to emerge, debate continues concerning the timing and magnitude of those trends. Conflicting findings can be traced to differences in methodology, data, and interpretation.

1. *Population:* Trends in job stability vary by demographic group. Some of the apparently conflicting findings in the literature have resulted from differences in the population under consideration. For example, Bernhardt et al. (1999), Marcotte (1999), and Monks and Pizer (1998) found evidence of a general decline in stability for the samples they studied. However, each of these authors relied on samples of young workers. Other researchers analyzing similar periods but using broader samples have found less evidence of such a decline (Jaeger and Stevens 1999).

2. *Data issues:* Limitations in data quality and coverage have been the most serious barrier to developing reliable measures of job stability. Researchers have used data mainly from the Current Population Survey (CPS),[3] the Panel Study of Income Dynamics (PSID), and the National Longitudinal Surveys (NLS). Each of these data sets has problems.

Most important, the CPS changed the wording of a key question about job stability in the early 1980s. That change likely led to a bias against finding a decline in job stability between the 1970s and the 1980s (Jaeger and Stevens 1999; Marcotte 1995). In the PSID—a longitudinal series that spans the 1970s, 1980s, and 1990s—information about job tenure is not available between 1978 and 1980 for either some or all of the sample. Moreover, in 1984 the PSID changed the wording of questions about length of time with employer. This change likely caused a bias in favor of finding a decline in job stability (Polsky 1999). Finally, while the NLS data have many advantages—they go back to 1966 and include excellent work history information—they are limited to young adults and cannot speak to trends in the general population of workers. High attrition rates for nonwhite respondents also mean that the NLS data can only reliably be used to analyze trends for white workers (Bernhardt et al. 1999).

These shortcomings mean that developing a comprehensive picture of job stability requires care. For example, Jaeger and Stevens (1999) carried out an extensive comparison across PSID and CPS data. They found that both data sets yield comparable estimates beginning in the mid-1980s, with each showing small declines in stability. However, estimates for the 1970s differ, with the CPS showing smaller declines than the PSID. The authors concluded that the estimates based on the CPS prior to the 1980s are less reliable because of the problems with that data set.

3. *End points:* Another complication is the impact of researchers' choice of end points. Based on the literature as a whole, it appears that a mild decline in stability between the 1970s and 1980s abated after 1988 and perhaps even briefly reversed itself. But then after 1991, job stability again began to fall. As a result, researchers' choices of end points have affected their conclusions.[4] For example, Marcotte (1994) found evidence of a sizable decline in job stability using the PSID from 1976 to 1988. In a later paper using data through 1992, he found somewhat smaller declines (Marcotte 1999). Polsky (1999) found no sizable decline in job stability using the same data set, and Jaeger and Stevens (1999) suggest that this is partly a function of Polsky's end point of 1991. Diebold, Neumark, and Polsky (1997) find no general decline in job stability using CPS data for 1979, 1983, 1987, and 1991. Neumark, Polsky, and Hansen (1999) update that work using data through 1995 and do find some evidence of a decline in job stability.

4. *Voluntary versus involuntary job changes:* The distinction between involuntary job loss and voluntary job changing is also important. Studies that focus primarily on job loss find relatively large changes over time (Boisjoly, Duncan, and Smeeding 1998; Farber 1997). Studies that consider all types of job changing find smaller differences (Neumark and Polsky 1998).[5] This is consistent with the notion that during times of relatively high layoffs, workers are less likely to quit their jobs. Indeed, one might anticipate that differences in the cyclical behavior of quits and layoffs would obscure any overall trend. Beyond creating complications for researchers, differences in patterns of voluntary and involuntary turnover have different welfare and policy implications. If changes in job stability were primarily due to increases in involuntary separations, we would have greater concern about the impact on workers' well-being: displaced workers often suffer substantial income losses. However, even increases in voluntary quits would be cause for concern if they stemmed from diminished prospects for advancement within firms.

5. *Is the glass half empty or half full?* Finally, it is important to appreciate that empirical evidence can be (and has been) interpreted differently by different researchers. Perhaps the best-known debate over interpretation of recent trends in job stability is the exchange between

Diebold, Neumark, and Polsky (1996) and Swinnerton and Wial (1996). This exchange raised a series of technical issues about how to measure job stability, but having resolved them, the authors were still unable to agree on the implications of their estimates. Diebold, Neumark, and Polsky concluded that the observed declines in job stability are "negligible" and that "there appears to be no case for concluding that there have been wholesale declines in job stability [between 1983 and 1991]" (p. 352). Swinnerton and Wial, on the other hand, contended that significant declines in job stability have indeed occurred, though they "do not know whether this decline qualifies as 'wholesale'" (p. 355).

Five years after that exchange, differences in interpretation persist. In part, these differences arise because it is not always clear whether a change in job stability that is statistically significant but small in magnitude is substantively meaningful. As an example, consider Jaeger and Stevens (1999) who found "little evidence in either data set of a trend in the share of employed individuals with one year or less of tenure." Yet they do estimate statistically significant increases in these short-tenure jobs, using both the CPS and PSID, between the early to mid-1970s and the mid-1990s. To be sure, their point estimates of the per-year increase in low-tenure probabilities look small. Yet when calculated over the full time span, the implication of their estimates is that, for male workers, the probability of being in a short-tenure job rose from just less than .20 in the mid-1970s to roughly .23 to .25 in the mid-1990s.

In our view, it is not clear how one ought to interpret estimates of trends in job instability. Minor declines in the rate at which workers retain their jobs may reflect only minor changes in the employment contract. On the other hand, even small changes in retention rates in any one year can be cumulative over time and could significantly affect the formation of long-term employment relationships.

Finally, researchers may differ in how they frame the question of job stability from the outset, and this has important consequences. In a recent paper, Allen, Clark, and Schieber (1999) examined whether job stability has declined in large corporations. Using a sample of 51 large firms, they analyzed changes in the distribution of tenure over five years during the early 1990s. They found no substantial changes in the distribution of tenure within those firms and concluded that there is no evidence that midcareer employees have been singled out for downsizing. This is an interesting and useful finding. But the authors then went on to infer that job stability has not declined in large firms in the early 1990s. This conclusion does not follow: if a firm suddenly laid off a large portion of its workforce, with laid-off and retained workers having the same tenure distribution, then the overall distribution of tenure within the firm would remain unchanged, though clearly job stability has fallen. And in fact, 63% of the firms in Allen et al.'s sample downsized during the five-year period, totaling a loss of 19.5% of the starting workforce in those firms.

This is an extreme example, but it does underscore the point that differences in interpretations and definitions have contributed to the lack of consensus in this research area.

How Wages Are Set

Job stability is not the only characteristic of internal labor markets. Equally important is the characteristic that wages are sheltered from the external market and are instead set according to employers' administrative rules. These rules determine how pay varies based on job classification, rank, and the qualifications of the incumbent worker. If there has indeed been a move away from these "implicit shielding agreements" in recent years, this should have affected the wage structure.

In research on wage setting, data limitations are especially acute. Personnel records at the firm level are few and far between, are limited in the occupations they cover, and rarely span more than a few years. Thus, researchers have had to resort to indirect measures, and even these have been difficult to construct with standard data.

Quantitative Evidence

Bertrand (1999) analyzed whether increases in foreign competition have changed wage setting in a manner consistent with a departure from internal labor markets. She began with the observation that in an internal labor market, wages should be sensitive to external conditions when workers are hired but not sensitive to them after that, since the firm's own compensation rules then take over. In an open "spot" market, by contrast, wages should be more sensitive to current conditions and less sensitive to those that prevailed at the time of hire. Consistent with these standard descriptions, Baker and Holmstrom (1995) found that new cohorts entering an internal labor market may have different starting wage levels because of prevailing economic conditions but thereafter experience roughly the same incremental wage progression as other cohorts, unaffected by external shocks. Bertrand's strategy, therefore, is to identify changes in wage setting by testing for changes in the relative sensitivity of workers' wages to external economic conditions.

Bertrand examined the manufacturing sector using individual, corporate, and industry data from 1976 to 1992.[6] She estimated several models and found evidence that the traditional employment relationship has changed. First, rising import competition at the industry level increases the sensitivity of workers' wages to the current unemployment rate but decreases sensitivity to the unemployment rate that prevailed when the workers were hired. Thus, the globalization of trade does appear to have moved employers toward a spot market and away from internal labor markets, at least in manufacturing. Bertrand then took the analysis one step further to elucidate the mechanism behind this relationship. She showed that declines in corporate returns increase the sensitivity of wages to current labor market conditions, especially in vulnerable, highly indebted industries. Her interpretation was that intense competition lowers firms' earnings and shortens corporate time horizons, thus increasing firms' preferences for wage flexibility.

These findings echo the prevailing popular account of the impact of globalization. Groshen and Levine (1998), however, do not reach the same conclusion. Using a unique data set, they found little change in employers' wage-setting policies over the past four decades. The data were drawn from a survey of 228 midwestern employers, conducted annually from 1956 to 1996, with information on job titles and salaries.[7] The survey was limited to "staff occupations," which included office, maintenance, technical, supervisory, and professional jobs but not production, frontline, or direct supervisory jobs. Since the authors wanted to focus only on changes in the occupational wage structure itself (not changes in the allocation of workers across that structure), they controlled for employment levels by giving each job type a weight of 1. As a result, no account is taken of practices that might change the distribution of workers across occupations and therefore across wage levels.[8]

Not surprisingly, these data show growing wage inequality from the 1970s onward, in line with trends in the larger economy.[9] But this growth was driven primarily by rising occupational differentials, which in Groshen and Levine's (1998) framework capture rising returns to human capital. Much less change is found in two firm-based differentials that measure internal labor market wage-setting practices: (1) the extent to which firms pay all employees, on average, more or less than the market wage and (2) the extent to which firms pay a subset of employees particularly well or poorly relative to both their occupation and the firm's average salary. Analyzing trends in these two differentials, Groshen and Levine found a strengthening of internal labor markets in the 1960s, some weakening in the 1970s, but not much change during the 1980s and 1990s. The authors did find indirect evidence of a rise in outsourcing and subcontracting: high-wage employers had a higher proportion of high-wage occupations, suggesting a shedding of low-wage occupations to outside firms and subcontractors.

The disagreement between Bertrand's (1999) and Groshen and Levine's (1998) studies may be caused not only by their different samples, but also by the measures and methods used in both papers, which are open to a number of criticisms. Future research should pursue the type of innovative research designs present in these two studies, with close attention to sample definition and measurement. There is also the broader issue of how to interpret findings on trends in wage setting. It may be that access to internal labor markets increasingly is differentially distributed across different groups of workers. If so, the disagreement between the two studies may not be as strong as it appears. Groshen and Levine's rising wage differences between occupations may reflect a growing segmentation between skilled workers who still enjoy the benefits of internal labor markets and unskilled workers who are increasingly exposed to the open labor market. This would mean that employers are indeed seeking greater wage flexibility, as Bertrand found, but mainly for workers in lower-skill occupations (who have seen declining demand for their skills but who have also lost substantial bargaining power over the past three decades).

Less complicated evidence on the increase in wage inequality that started in the mid-1970s can be found in Dinardo, Fortin, and Lemieux (1996). The authors considered the effect of two institutional factors—the minimum wage and unionization levels—as well as shifts in supply and demand.[10] Using CPS data from 1979 to 1988, they identified significant institutional effects that were of a magnitude similar to neoclassical effects. They estimated that the stagnation of the minimum wage during the 1980s contributed 24.8% of the rise in inequality for men and 30.2% for women. The decline in unionization also had a significant effect for men (14.3%) but not for women, who have historically had low union representation and have not been hit by deunionization as hard as men. In short, the growing polarization of the American wage structure has in part been driven by the decline of two institutions that have traditionally imposed nonmarket restrictions on wage setting.[11] The tie to a dismantling of internal labor markets is especially strong in the case of unions, as these played a critical role in negotiating the wage and seniority rules that we have come to regard as the cornerstones of the insulated employment relationship.

Qualitative Evidence

Researchers have also conducted industry and firm case studies to examine trends in wage-setting behavior. Much of this work takes a broader perspective, where trends in wage inequality are seen as part of an unfolding system of industrial relations and economic institutions (Cappelli et al. 1997; Herzenberg, Alic, and Wial 1998). These studies often focus on service industries (which have historically been neglected) and explicitly ask how economic restructuring has affected job quality. In the process, a surprising consensus has emerged on changes in the structure of internal labor markets.

Generally, this literature suggests that deregulation, market saturation, industry consolidation, and deunionization have transformed the nature of the workplace in the service sector. Service firms are strategically stratifying their customer markets based on price, quality, and level of customization and customer service, resulting in a similar stratification of service work and the wages associated with each submarket. This trend has been found in industries as diverse as retail trade, information technology, financial services, airlines, insurance, and telecommunications.[12]

The outcome for workers has been not just a polarization in wages but also a splitting of some of the paths that previously connected jobs and created careers. For example, different department stores now specialize in either high-income, middle-income, or mass markets, resulting in less-varied jobs and less-elaborate career ladders within any one store. In addition, managers are increasingly hired from the outside. Such restructuring means fewer opportunities for frontline sales workers to move up to management, merchandise buying, or high-ticket commissioned sales. Service firms are also adopting closer relationships with suppliers, relying more on subcontracted work and centralizing their operations. One result is that entry-level jobs are increasingly consolidated into centers that are geographically or organizationally separate from higher-tier jobs (e.g., customer service phone representatives or temporary workers in health care). Banking is a particularly stark example, with the emergence of large check-processing and phone centers far removed from the regional branch system. Even the branch system itself has begun to be dismantled with the growing practice of hiring manager and platform workers externally (rather than promoting tellers).

Further, although there is no doubt that new information technology has had a pronounced impact on many of these industries (McConnell

1996), it cannot alone account for the preceding trends. Detailed analyses show that the same technology often increases skill requirements in some parts of the organization while decreasing them in others.[13] Thus, restructuring and technology interact to produce different outcomes for workers, even within a single industry and a single firm (Hunter and Lafkas 1999).

In sum, this research suggests that, in the service sector at least, recent changes in domestic competition and firm strategies are yielding a very complex segmentation, both internal and external to firms. The polarization of wages reflects this segmentation. Moreover, there are also long-term effects on worker mobility, to which we now turn.

Trends in Upward Mobility

At root, one of the main concerns about changes in "standard employment" has to do with the opportunities for workers to build a career and achieve a living wage over the long run. This means that we cannot assess the fate of workers in the postindustrial economy simply from cross-sectional data on wages and job stability. We also need evidence on trends in long-term mobility (Gottschalk 1997). Ultimately, it is a question of whether we are seeing the emergence of a more meritocratic labor market in which advancement is based on skill rather than seniority, or a more segmented labor market in which some groups of workers are increasingly cut off from movement into core jobs (Freeman 1997; Noyelle 1990).

Directly answering this question would require analysis of the processes that govern individuals' mobility within firms—screening, hiring, training, and promotion—as well as across firms. Absent this type of data over time, researchers have had to rely on very basic indicators of upward mobility, the primary one being wage growth over individuals' life spans.

The consensus is that *inequality* in long-term wage growth has increased since the 1970s by roughly 30% to 40%.[14] This finding holds across a variety of data sets (CPS, PSID, NLS), for different samples, and using a variety of methods.[15] At the same time, *average* wage growth has deteriorated as well. In combination, these two trends paint a discouraging picture. For example, among men who turned 21 during 1985–1991, fewer than one quarter had attained earnings higher than twice the poverty line by age 27, as compared with 55% of those turning 21 between 1970 and 1974 (Duncan, Boisjoly, and Smeeding 1996). Similarly, Bernhardt et al. (1998) compared two NLS cohorts of young white men, one of which entered the labor market in the early 1970s and the other in the 1980s. They found that average wage growth between the ages of 16 and 36 was $8.65 for the earlier cohort but only $6.69 for the recent cohort (in 1992 dollars). Moreover, the percentage of workers experiencing no wage growth rose from 1.7% to 7.2%, respectively. And while workers with less education have clearly suffered most from these trends, even workers at the high end of the skills distribution have seen growing dispersion in their long-term prospects.

This evidence is consistent with a dismantling of internal labor markets but does not prove it. Deteriorating wage growth for some groups of workers may simply reflect their lack of skills, both measured and unmeasured, without any changes in long-term commitments on the part of employers. Even if we could link slower wage growth to more frequent job changes, the cause could still be insufficient skills. Note that the ambiguity holds in the opposite direction as well. Internal labor markets could decline without any effect on upward mobility, if workers are able to construct "multiemployer careers" and generate solid wage growth as they hop from one employer to another.

Wage stability is a more direct measure of internal labor markets than is upward mobility; within firms, wild fluctuations in wages from one year to the next are unlikely. Gottschalk and Moffitt (1994) conducted the first analysis of this issue, using PSID data on white men for the years 1970–1978 and 1979–1987. They found that the increase in inequality over the two decades was driven in roughly equal parts by an increase in long-term earnings inequality and by an increase in short-term earnings instability. Subsequent analyses have reached mixed conclusions, and the disagreements hinge on how long-term and short-term earnings are defined. Thus, Haider (1997), using a similar sample but a different model, found that earnings instability increased primarily during the 1970s, whereas long-term earnings inequality dominated the 1980s. Bernhardt et al. (1998) used data on two NLS cohorts of workers and found that most of the aggregate increase in inequality stemmed from growing inequality in long-run wage growth. More research is needed before agreement can be reached on the precise magnitude and timing of these developments.

There is, however, agreement that upward mobility appears to have both stagnated and become significantly more unequal. While not direct proof of a breakdown of internal labor markets, this does suggest that the issue deserves to be investigated further. As it stands, rising returns to education explain at best half of the growing inequality in upward mobility. Rather than putting all the blame on "unobservable skills," we might also think about the role of unmeasured characteristics of firms and labor market institutions. Even the effect of education might be reexamined. If firms are less willing to provide training for their entry-level workers without a college education, and if those workers' mobility paths are being constrained by decisions about how to organize the workplace, then trends in their wage growth tell us something about changes to the traditional employment relationship. This is especially true if such business strategies are not completely driven by the dictates of high technology and global competition but are also the result of a changed institutional environment.

Benefit Coverage

In no small part, the advantages of standard employment have included nonwage benefits. Those benefits, among many others, include employer-subsidized health insurance and employer or union provision of pension benefits. If the standard employment relationship is weakening, firms might be less willing or less able to offer workers such benefits.

While such a change clearly raises urgent policy issues, this topic has only recently received attention. The emerging research shows that the coverage and quality of nonwage benefits have, in fact, deteriorated. First, the share of workers covered by employer-provided health insurance is declining. Farber and Levy (1998) analyzed trends in health insurance coverage between 1988 and 1997, using CPS data. Overall, coverage rates during that period fell from 69.1% to 64.5%.[16] The decline was not driven by a fall in the number of firms offering health insurance to employees but rather by a growth in the number of workers within firms who either were ineligible to participate or chose not to do so. The former, the authors concluded, is consistent with an increasing tendency for firms to provide benefits only to a core group of employees. The growing proportion of workers covered under a spouse's plan helps to explain the declining take-up rate but accounts for only part of it.

Second, pension benefits are also changing in a manner consistent with a decline in internal labor markets. Far and away the dominant trend in employer-provided pension coverage in the United States has been a substitution of defined-contribution plans (which make a specified contribution to an employee's pension) for defined-benefit plans (which guarantee a specified benefit at retirement).[17] The percentage of workers who participate in defined-benefit plans fell from 39% in 1975 to 24% in 1994 (U.S. Department of Labor 1998), with a concurrent shift toward defined-contribution plans (Papke 1996).

The reasons for this shift away from traditional pension plans are not fully understood. It may be due to attempts by firms to reduce costs. It may also be due to the declining power of labor unions, which tend to prefer defined-benefit coverage for members, and movement of employment away from industries that have traditionally provided such coverage (Gustman and Steinmeier 1992). But there is also evidence that employees are increasingly opting for defined-contribution plans (Kruse 1995). More research needs to be done to understand the changing motivations of both employers and employees. However, it is clear that workers and firms are behaving in a way that is consistent with declining commitments to one another.

Conclusion

At the close of the 20th century, there is a strong conviction among Americans that the nature of work is being transformed. In this chapter, we reviewed a broad array of research that investigates trends in job stability, sheltered wages, upward mobility, and company-sponsored benefits. The evidence, although not conclusive, suggests that the contours of the standard employment relationship have indeed changed. Job stability has declined mildly overall but more strongly among workers who are young, have no postsecondary education, are male, or are African American. Quantitative evidence on the weakening of wage-setting institutions and qualitative research on industries and firms indicate that wages are increasingly set in external rather than internal labor markets, at least for some groups of workers. Upward mobility has stagnated and also has become significantly more unequal, quite possibly as a result of restructuring. Finally, health and pension benefit coverages have changed in ways consistent with declining commitments between firms and workers.

At the same time, these findings do not support the dramatic sea change that is routinely depicted in the popular press. This had led some researchers to argue that public anxiety is exaggerated and misplaced. We are reluctant to abandon public perception so quickly, because work on this subject is still in its early stages and data and measurement problems have been severe.

It is also likely that the public "reads the evidence" differently than do academics. The latter typically focus on single indicators of the employment relationship, most often in isolation from one another.

Some of those indicators show strong changes; others do not. But the public may well be viewing them all as part of one package. Thus, the stagnation in real wages; the steep rise in wage inequality; reports of downsizing, outsourcing, and temporary work; and the recent increase in uninsured workers all coalesce into a single dominant impression, that work in America is no longer what it once was. For a working-class family that now needs two full-time incomes in order to run its household, disentangling what has and has not changed may not be all that relevant.

Equally important, researchers need to recognize that changes in standard employment are not uniformly felt. To wit, it is becoming clear that workers at the low end of the wage distribution have been the ones most affected by the restructuring of work and production. Looking only at average trends obscures the *distributional* effects of restructuring, which may actually be much more important. We will not understand either restructuring itself or the uneasiness it has generated among workers until we recognize that this is the case.

A final and frustrating challenge faces researchers and interested readers alike. Because of the amount of time required for data collection and analysis, researchers have often had too little to contribute to national debate during the past three decades. Public perceptions are rooted in the experiences of today's economy, whereas researchers' analyses have necessarily been based on data that are neither current nor comprehensive enough. This has made it difficult to fully sort out short-term fluctuations from long-term trends. Only by waiting for data that are richer, more accurate, and longer in scope will we gain a better understanding of the extent to which standard employment is changing.

Notes

[1] Research on contingent and part-time work is taken up elsewhere in this volume. We also do not consider trends in training in this paper since the literature is vast and has been thoroughly reviewed by others. See Bishop (1997).

[2] A brief history of research on trends in job instability reads as follows. First, it appeared that jobs were becoming less stable across the board. Just a few years later, it was concluded that the initial findings were wrong, that instead there were no major declines in job stability. Now, however, it does seem that there have been important changes in job stability, though not as large or pervasive as initially thought. The interested reader should consult Jaeger and Stevens (1999) for details.

[3] Various researchers have used data from the tenure, displaced worker, contingent worker, and employee benefits supplements.

[4] Of course, end points are dictated by availability of data.

[5] This compositional change is confirmed by Monks and Pizer (1998), who found that the overall decline in job stability they observed is disproportionately due to an increase in involuntary job loss.

[6] Note, however, that data limitations mean that the models could not be estimated at the firm level; instead, corporate information is aggregated to the industry level, where all of Bertrand's variation in competitive environment resides.

[7] It should be stressed that the sample of employers is not random: they tend to be larger and older than average, and earnings and occupations tend to be higher and wage variation lower. The sample does, however, cover a wide range of industries and in several other respects (e.g., failure rates) seems to be relatively representative.

[8] Such changes include, for example, increased use of contingent or part-time workers and increases in the external hiring of skilled workers.

[9] This increase holds both within and between firms. Yet Davis and Haltiwanger (1991) found that within-plant wage variance grew faster than between-plant variance in the manufacturing sector, and O'Shaughnessy, Levine, and Cappelli (1999) found the opposite in their study of managerial pay practices.

[10] For a review of quantitative labor economics research that addresses institutional effects, see Fortin and Lemieux (1997).

[11] Deunionization and the minimum wage are only the most obvious institutional causes. Researchers are beginning to explore other candidates, such as government deregulation and the changing structure of financial markets and of the stock market (Appelbaum and Berg 1996; Christopherson 2000).

[12] For a broad overview of this field, see Batt (1998). Recent papers in this field include Bailey and Bernhardt (1997), Batt and Keefe (1998), Bernhardt and Slater (1998), Colclough and Tolbert (1992), Garson (1988), Hunter (1999), Keltner and Finegold (1999), and MacDonald and Siranni (1996).

[13] For reviews, see Cappelli (1996) and Moss (forthcoming).

[14] We use *mobility* here to refer to *absolute mobility*, or real earnings growth over time. Some of the studies listed in note 15 examine relative mobility (e.g., the probability of moving from one quintile in the earnings distribution to another) but then combine findings on this measure with the overall trend in the earnings distribution itself; the resulting findings therefore comment on absolute mobility as well.

[15] See Bernhardt et al. (1998); Buchinsky and Hunt (1996); Duncan, Boisjoly, and Smeeding (1996); Gittleman and Joyce (1996); Gottschalk and Moffitt (1994); Haider (1997); and McMurrer and Sawhill (1998).

[16] We do not attempt here to account for changes in the price or quality of health insurance benefits over time. Note, however, that while employers' health spending rose as a portion of total compensation in the 1980s, it has fallen since 1993 (EBRI 1998).

[17] See Mitchell and Schieber (1998). Although some studies have suggested that there has been a wholesale decline in the share of workers who are given the opportunity to participate in employer-provided pension benefits plans (Orr 1996), most studies have found little overall decline.

References

Allen, Steven G., Robert L. Clark, and Sylvester J. Schieber. 1999. *Has Job Security Vanished in Large Corporations?* NBER Working Paper No. 6966. Cambridge, MA: National Bureau of Economic Research.

Appelbaum, Eileen, and Peter Berg. 1996. "Financial Market Constraints and Business Strategy in the USA." In Jonathan Michie and John Grieve Smith, eds., *Creating Industrial Capacity: Towards Full Employment.* Cambridge: Oxford University Press, pp. 192–221.

Bailey, Thomas, and Annette Bernhardt. 1997. "In Search of the High Road in a Low-Wage Industry." *Politics and Society,* Vol. 25, no. 2, pp. 179–201.

Baker, George, and Bengt Holmstrom. 1995. "Internal Labor Markets: Too Many Theories, Too Few Facts." *American Economic Review: Papers and Proceedings,* Vol. 85, no. 2, pp. 255–259.

Batt, Rosemary. 1998. "The Changing Nature of Work in Services." Manuscript prepared for the Committee for the Enhancement of Human Performance, National Research Council. Ithaca: New York State School of Industrial Relations, Cornell University.

Batt, Rosemary, and Jeffrey Keefe. 1998. "Human Resource and Employment Practices in Telecommunications Services, 1980–1998." Report to the New American Realities Committee, National Planning Association.

Bernhardt, Annette, Martina Morris, Mark Handcock, and Marc Scott. 1998. *Inequality and Mobility: Trends in Wage Growth for Young Adults.* Institute on Education and the Economy Working Paper No. 7. New York: Teachers College, Columbia University.

Bernhardt, Annette, Martina Morris, Mark Handcock, and Marc Scott. 1999. "Trends in Job Instability and Wages for Young Adult Men." *Journal of Labor Economics,* Part 2, Vol. 17, no. 4, pp. S65–S90.

Bernhardt, Annette, and Douglas Slater. 1998. "What Technology Can and Cannot Do: A Case Study in Banking." *Industrial Relations Research Association Series: Proceedings of the Fiftieth Annual Meeting,* Vol. 1, pp. 118–125.

Bertrand, Marianne. 1999. *From the Invisible Handshake to the Invisible Hand? How Import Competition Changes the Employment Relationship.* NBER Working Paper No. 6900. Cambridge, MA: National Bureau of Economic Research.

Bishop, John H. 1997. "What We Know about Employer-Provided Training: A Review of the Literature." *Research in Labor Economics,* Vol. 16, pp. 19–87.

Boisjoly, Johanne, Greg Duncan, and Timothy Smeeding. 1998. "The Shifting Incidence of Involuntary Job Losses from 1968 to 1992." *Industrial Relations,* Vol. 37, no. 2, pp. 207–231.

Buchinsky, Moshe, and Jennifer Hunt. 1996. *Wage Mobility in the United States.* NBER Working Paper No. 5455. Cambridge, MA: National Bureau of Economic Research.

Cappelli, Peter. 1996. "Technology and Skill Requirements: Implications for Establishment Wage Structures." *New England Economic Review* (May/June), pp. 139–154.

Cappelli, Peter, Laurie Bassi, Harry Katz, David Knoke, Paul Osterman, and Michael Useem. 1997. *Change at Work.* New York: Oxford University Press.

Christopherson, Susan. 2000. "The Institutional Edge: How Capital Market Rules Influence Work Organization and Competitive Advantage." Forthcoming in *Economic Geography.*

Colclough, Glenna, and Charles M. Tolbert. 1992. *Work in the Fast Lane: Flexibility, Divisions of Labor, and Inequality in High-Tech Industries.* New York: SUNY.

Davis, Steve, and John K. Haltiwanger. 1991. "Wage Dispersion between and within U.S. Manufacturing Plants." *Brookings Papers on Economic Activity,* Washington, DC: Brookings Institution, pp. 115–200.

Diebold, Francis X., David Neumark, and Daniel Polsky. 1996. "Comment on Kenneth A. Swinnerton and Howard Wial, 'Is Job Stability Declining in the U.S. Economy?'" *Industrial and Labor Relations Review,* Vol. 49, no. 2, pp. 348–352.

Diebold, Francis X., David Neumark, and Daniel Polsky. 1997. "Job Stability in the United States." *Journal of Labor Economics,* Vol. 15, no. 2, pp. 206–233.

Dinardo, John, Nicole Fortin, and Thomas Lemieux. 1996. "Labor Market Institutions and the Distribution of Wages, 1973–1992: A Semiparametric Approach." *Econometrica,* Vol. 64, no. 5, pp. 1001–1044.

Doeringer, Peter B., and Michael J. Piore. 1971. *Internal Labor Markets and Manpower Analysis.* Lexington, MA: Heath Lexington.

"The Downsizing of America" [series]. 1996. *New York Times,* March 3–March 9.

Duncan, Greg, Johanne Boisjoly, and Timothy Smeeding. 1996. "Economic Mobility of Young Workers in the 1970s and 1980s." *Demography,* Vol. 33, no. 4, pp. 497–509.

Dunlop, John. 1964. *The Theory of Wage Determination.* London: Macmillan.

Employee Benefits Research Institute (EBRI). 1998. "Features of Employment-Based Health Plans." *EBRI Issue Brief,* no. 201.

Farber, Henry. 1997. "The Changing Face of Job Loss in the United States, 1981–1995." *Brookings Papers on Economic Activity: Microeconomics,* Washington, DC: Brookings Institution, pp. 55–128.

Farber, Henry, and Helen Levy. 1998. *Recent Trends in Employer-Sponsored Health Insurance Coverage: Are Bad Jobs Getting Worse?* NBER Working Paper No. 6709. Cambridge, MA: National Bureau of Economic Research.

Fortin, Nicole, and Thomas Lemieux. 1997. "Institutional Changes and Rising Wage Inequality: Is There a Linkage?" *Journal of Economic Perspectives,* Vol. 11, no. 2, pp. 75–96.

Freeman, Richard B. 1997. "Solving the New Inequality." *Boston Review,* Vol. 21, no. 6, pp. 3–10.

Garson, Barbara. 1988. *The Electronic Sweatshop.* New York: Penguin Books.

Gittleman, Maury, and Mary Joyce. 1996. "Earnings Mobility and Long-Run Inequality: An Analysis Using Matched CPS Data." *Industrial Relations,* Vol. 35, no. 2, pp. 180–196.

Gottschalk, Peter. 1997. "Inequality, Income Growth, and Mobility: The Basic Facts." *Journal of Economic Perspectives,* Vol. 11, no. 2, pp. 21–40.

Gottschalk, Peter, and Robert Moffitt. 1994. "The Growth of Earnings Instability in the U.S. Labor Market." *Brookings Papers on Economic Activity,* Vol. 2, Washington, DC: Brookings Institution, pp. 217–272.

Groshen, Erica L., and David I. Levine. 1998. *The Rise and Decline (?) of U.S. Internal Labor Markets.* Research Paper No. 9819. New York: Federal Reserve Bank of New York.

Gustman, Alan L., and Thomas L. Steinmeier. 1992. "The Stampede toward Defined Contribution Pension Plans: Fact or Fiction? *Industrial Relations,* Vol. 31, no. 2, pp. 361–369.

Haider, Steven. 1997. "Earnings Instability and Earning Inequality of Males in the United States: 1967–1991." Manuscript, University of Michigan, Ann Arbor.

Herzenberg, Steven, John Alic, and Howard Wial. 1998. *New Rules for a New Economy*. Ithaca, NY: Cornell University Press.

Hunter, Larry W. 1999. "Transforming Retail Banking: Inclusion and Segmentation in Service Work." In Peter Cappelli, ed., *Employment Practices and Business Strategy*. New York: Oxford, pp. 153–192.

Hunter, Larry W., and John J. Lafkas. 1999. *Opening the Box: Information Technology, Work Practices, and Wages*. Working Paper, Wharton Financial Institutions Center. Philadelphia: Wharton School.

Jaeger, David A., and Ann Huff Stevens. 1999. "Is Job Stability in the United States Falling? Reconciling Trends in the Current Population Survey and the Panel Study of Income Dynamics." *Journal of Labor Economics*, Part 2, Vol. 17, no. 4, pp. S1–S28.

"Jobs in an Age of Insecurity." 1993. *Time*, November 22, pp. 32–40.

Keltner, Brent, and David Finegold. 1999. "Changing Employment Relations in the U.S. Banking Industry." In Marino Regini, Jim Kitay, and Martin Baethge, eds., *From Tellers to Sellers: Changing Employment Relations in Banks*. Cambridge, MA: MIT Press.

Kruse, Douglas L. 1995. "Pension Substitution in the 1980s: Why the Shift toward Defined Contribution?" *Industrial Relations*, Vol. 34, no. 2, pp. 218–241.

MacDonald, Cameron L., and Carmen Siranni, eds. 1996. *Working in the Service Society*. Philadelphia: Temple University Press.

Marcotte, Dave E. 1994. "The Declining Stability of Employment in the U.S.: 1976–1988." Ph.D. Diss., University of Maryland, School of Public Affairs.

Marcotte, Dave E. 1995. "Declining Job Stability: What We Know and What It Means." *Journal of Policy Analysis and Management*, Vol. 14, no. 4, pp. 590–598.

Marcotte, Dave E. 1999. "Has Job Stability Declined? Evidence from the Panel Study of Income Dynamics." *American Journal of Economics and Sociology*, Vol. 58, no. 2, pp. 189–208.

McConnell, Sheila. 1996. "The Role of Computers in Reshaping the Work Force." *Monthly Labor Review*, Vol. 119, no. 8, pp. 3–5.

McGinn, Daniel, and John McCormick. 1999. "Your Next Job." *Newsweek*, February 1, pp. 42–46.

McMurrer, Daniel P., and Isabel V. Sawhill. 1998. *Getting Ahead: Economic and Social Mobility in the United States*. Washington, DC: Urban Institute Press.

Mitchell, Olivia S., and Sylvester J. Schieber, eds. 1998. *Living with Defined Contribution Pensions: Remaking Responsibility for Retirement*. Philadelphia: University of Pennsylvania Press.

Monks, James, and Steven Pizer. 1998. "Trends in Voluntary and Involuntary Job Turnover." *Industrial Relations*, Vol. 37, no. 4, pp. 440–459.

Moss, Philip. Forthcoming. "Earnings Inequality and the Quality of Jobs." In William Lazonick and Mary O'Sullivan, eds., *Corporate Governance and Sustainable Prosperity*. New York: Macmillan, St. Martin's Press.

Neumark, David, and Daniel Polsky. 1998. "Changes in Job Stability and Job Security: Anecdotes and Evidence." Paper presented at the American Economics Association meetings, Chicago, IL.

Neumark, David, Daniel Polsky, and Daniel Hansen. 1999. "Has Job Stability Declined Yet? New Evidence for the 1990s." *Journal of Labor Economics*, Part 2, Vol. 17, no. 4, pp. S29–S64.

Noyelle, Thierry. 1990. "Toward a New Labor Market Segmentation." In Thierry Noyelle, ed., *Skills, Wages, and Productivity in the Service Economy*. San Francisco: Westview, pp. 212–224.

Orr, Douglas V. 1996. "The Rise of Contingent Employment and the Decline of Pension Coverage." *Review of Radical Political Economics*, Vol. 28, no. 3, pp. 126–134.

O'Shaughnessy, K. C., David I. Levine, and Peter Cappelli. 1999. *Changes in Managerial Pay Structures 1986–1992 and Rising Returns to Skill*. Institute of Industrial Relations Working Paper No. 67. Berkeley: Institute of Industrial Relations, University of California.

Papke, Leslie. 1996. *Are 401(K) Plans Replacing Other Employer-Provided Pensions? Evidence from Panel Data*. NBER Working Paper No. 5736. Cambridge, MA: National Bureau of Economic Research.

Polsky, Daniel. 1999. "Changes in the Consequences of Job Separations in the U.S. Economy." *Industrial and Labor Relations Review*, Vol. 52, no. 4, pp. 565–580.

Swinnerton, Kenneth A., and Howard Wial. 1996. "Is Job Stability Declining in the U.S. Economy? Reply to Diebold, Neumark, and Polsky." *Industrial and Labor Relations Review*, Vol. 49, no. 2, pp. 352–355.

U.S. Department of Labor. 1998. *Private Pension Plan Bulletin* (No. 7). Washington, DC: Pension and Welfare Benefits Administration, Office of Policy and Research.

CHAPTER 2

Definition, Composition, and Economic Consequences of the Nonstandard Workforce

ANNE E. POLIVKA, SHARON R. COHANY, AND STEVEN HIPPLE
Bureau of Labor Statistics

Agency temporaries, independent contractors, on-call workers, contract company workers, part-timers: these workers are commonly viewed as unwilling participants in a purported movement toward a disposable workforce characterized by "bad jobs" with lower pay, fewer benefits, and less stability than "regular" jobs. The purpose of this chapter is to explore some of these notions surrounding so-called "nonstandard" employment and to examine whether these work arrangements really should be lumped into a single category of bad jobs.[1]

Using data from the February 1995 and February 1997 Contingent and Alternative Work Arrangement supplements to the Current Population Survey (CPS), we examined workers in eight mutually exclusive groups. The first section of this chapter provides a definition of each group and examines the incidence of workers in each arrangement. The second section reviews research that directly examines whether workers in nonstandard arrangements are in less stable jobs. The third section tries to determine whether these workers are fundamentally different from regular full-time workers or whether they are simply in different types of jobs. The paper concludes with an examination of the effect of nonstandard staffing arrangements on workers' earnings, health insurance coverage, and satisfaction with their arrangement.

Nonstandard Work Arrangements: Data Source, Definitions, and Incidence

The data used in this analysis are primarily from supplements to the CPS. The CPS is a monthly survey of some 50,000 households whose answers to a set of "basic" questions are the primary source of data on the labor force.[2] In February 1995 and again in February 1997, supplemental questions were asked about contingent and alternative work arrangements.[3] Based on responses to the basic and supplemental questions, workers age 16 and older were classified into eight mutually exclusive groups that add up to total employment (excluding unpaid family workers, a very small category). The eight groups are

- Agency temporaries
- On-call workers
- Contract company workers
- Direct-hire temporary workers
- Independent contractors
- Regular self-employed (excluding independent contractors)
- Regular part-time workers
- Regular full-time workers

The first six categories include both part-time and full-time workers. Individuals were classified as *agency temporaries* if they were paid by a temporary help agency. (Thus, these estimates include the small number of permanent staff of these agencies.[4]) *On-call workers* were hired directly by an organization but worked only on an as-needed basis when called to do so. Occupations that often include on-call workers are substitute teachers, construction workers, and some types of hospital workers.

Individuals were classified as *contract company workers* if they were employed by a company that contracted out their services, if they were usually assigned to only one customer, and if they generally worked at the customer's work site. The intent was to identify individuals whose employment was intermediated through a contract company. Consequently, the requirements to have only one customer and to work on the customer's premises were imposed to avoid counting individuals whose employers simply did business with other companies under contract (such as advertising agencies, military equipment manufacturers, law firms, or think tanks). Examples of contract company workers include computer programmers, food service workers, and security guards. A small number of individuals were reported to be both on-call and contract company workers; they were classified as on-call workers.

Direct-hire temporaries are individuals who were in a job temporarily for an economic reason and who were hired directly by a company rather than through a staffing intermediary. Because the supplements did not include a specific question concerning direct-hire temporaries, we constructed this category based on a series of questions in the supplement.[5] Specifically, we classified individuals as direct-hire temporaries if they indicated that their job was temporary or that they could not stay in their job for as long as they wished for any of the following reasons: they were working only until a specific project was completed, they were temporarily replacing another worker, they were hired for a fixed period of time, their job was seasonal, or they expected to work for less than a year because they said the job was temporary.

Independent contractors include all those identified in the supplement as independent contractors, consultants, or freelance workers, regardless of whether they were identified as wage and salary workers or self-employed in the basic monthly questionnaire. The self-employed were asked if they were independent contractors in order to distinguish the self-employed— both incorporated and unincorporated—who considered themselves to be independent contractors, consultants, or freelance workers from the self-employed who were business operators, such as shop owners or restaurateurs. Among those identified as independent contractors in 1997, approximately 88% were identified as self-employed in the monthly questionnaire, while 12% were identified as wage and salary workers. Conversely, about half of the self-employed—incorporated and unincorporated combined— identified themselves as independent contractors.

The category of *regular self-employed* includes those who were identified as self-employed (incorporated and unincorporated) in the main questionnaire who were not independent contractors. This category of regular self-employed differs from official Bureau of Labor Statistics (BLS) estimates of the self-employed in two respects: first, it excludes independent contractors; second, it includes both the incorporated and unincorporated. Official BLS estimates of the self-employed include only the unincorporated.

Regular part-time workers are individuals who are not in one of the other categories and who usually work less than 35 hours per week. *Regular full-time workers* are individuals who are not in one of the other categories and who usually work 35 hours or more per week.

Table 1 presents the employment distribution by arrangement for February 1995 and February 1997. Only the percentages for contract company workers, regular full-time workers, and the regular self-employed were significantly different between the two years.[6] The category of regular self-employed was the only one to experience a statistically significant decrease, falling from 5.9% to 5.1%. The absolute number of these workers declined from 7.3 million to 6.5 million.

TABLE 1

Workers in Employment Arrangements as a Percentage of Total
Employment, February 1995 and February 1997

| Type of employment arrangement | Percentage of total employed | |
	1995	1997
Agency temporaries	0.96	1.03
On-call workers	1.69	1.60
Direct-hire temporaries	2.75	2.57
Contract company workers	0.48	0.60
Independent contractors	6.74	6.67
Regular self-employed	5.89	5.14
Regular part-time	13.65	13.64
Regular full-time	67.85	68.75

At 8.5 million in 1997, independent contractors constituted the largest group of nonstandard workers. Their proportion of the employed remained the same between 1995 and 1997, at 6.7%. The second largest group of workers who might be thought of as nonstandard was direct-hire temporaries. In 1997, 3.3 million workers were classified as direct-hire temporaries, accounting for 2.6% of the employed. Another group of workers closely associated in the public's mind with short-term employment is agency temporaries. It is interesting to note that, despite the media attention given to this group, they still constitute a small proportion of all employment, approximately 1% in both 1995 and 1997. In fact, direct-hire temporaries were almost three times more prevalent than agency temporaries.

Contract company workers as a proportion of the employed grew by 25% between 1995 and 1997, a much larger rate of growth than overall employment. However, it should be pointed out that contract workers constitute a very small group (588,000, or 0.6% of the employed, in 1997); thus, a small change in the level translated into a relatively large proportional change. The final group of workers who might be thought of as nonstandard is on-call workers. In 1997, about 1.6% of those employed worked solely on call.

When added together, those not in regular positions—agency temporaries, on-call workers, direct-hire temporaries, contract company workers, and independent contractors—constituted about 12.5% of the employed in both February 1995 and February 1997. If regular self-employed and regular part-time workers are included, the proportion of workers who were not in regular full-time positions fell from 32.2% in 1995 to 31.3% in 1997, in contrast to the popular perception of burgeoning nonstandard work arrangements. Meanwhile, the proportion of the employed that were regular full-time workers increased from 67.9% to 68.8%. This increase is largely attributable to the decline in regular self-employment.

Review of a Study of the Effect of Flexible Staffing Arrangements on Job Security

The terms *flexible staffing arrangement, nonstandard work,* and *contingent work* all have been used to describe any position other than regular full-time work.[7] Conceptually, there is nothing that ties such arrangements together except that they are not what is often considered the norm. Yet for many, there is an implicit assumption that they are less economically secure and have less stability than regular full-time employment. In fact, Audrey Freedman (1985) coined the phrase "contingent work" to refer specifically to "conditional and transitory employment arrangements as initiated by a need for labor—usually because a company has an increased demand for a particular service or a product or technology, at a particular place, at a specific time." For many, nonstandard or contingent work has come to represent a just-in-time workforce, the human resource equivalent of just-in-time inventories (Brophy 1987; Carnevale 1994; Castro 1993; Schellenbarger 1995; U.S. Senate Committee on Labor Resources 1993). However, other researchers have concluded that nonstandard jobs are not necessarily unstable or insecure, nor is a full-time regular position necessarily a guarantee of lifetime employment (Cohany 1998; Hipple 1998).

By exploiting the longitudinal component of the CPS, Houseman and Polivka (1999) used the most direct way to examine the effect of nonstandard work arrangements on job security. Given the rotation pattern of the CPS, half of the households interviewed in February 1995 were interviewed again in February 1996, when a supplement on job tenure was administered. Therefore, it is possible to use these combined data sets to estimate whether, one year later, individuals in the various arrangements had the same employer, had a different employer, were unemployed, or were not in the labor force.

Houseman and Polivka (1999) found, even when controlling for personal and job characteristics, job histories, and wages, that agency temporaries, on-call workers, direct-hire temporaries, contract company workers, and regular part-time workers were more likely than regular full-time workers to have changed employers or become unemployed over the course of a year. Further, on-call workers, direct-hire temporaries, and regular part-time workers were more likely to have involuntarily dropped out of the labor market (that is, they were not in the labor force but wanted to work) than were regular full-time workers. On the other hand, there was little evidence that independent contractors or the regular self-employed experienced any more job instability than did regular full-time workers.

Further, even among the less stable arrangements, there was considerable variation, with regular part-time being the most stable and agency temporaries being the least stable. Moreover, the simple descriptive statistics presented in Houseman and Polivka (1999) indicate that the majority of those in nonstandard arrangements had the same employer a year later. Specifically, 52.0% of on-call workers, 52.3% of direct-hire temporaries, 60.2% of contract company workers, and 58.7% of regular part-time workers still had the same employer after one year, compared with 83.3% of regular full-time workers. Moreover, the higher rates of separation among workers in nonstandard arrangements are explained in part by the relatively large number of workers who voluntarily drop out of the labor force. Consequently, while there is compelling evidence that some nonstandard work arrangements are less stable than regular full-time employment, BLS's measures of contingency—which are based on workers' expected job tenure—probably provide a better measure of worker insecurity and the temporary nature of particular jobs than nonstandard arrangements do.[8]

Characteristics of Those in Flexible Staffing Arrangements

In addition to concern about the prevalence of the various work arrangements, there is interest in the characteristics of workers in each arrangement. This section presents simple descriptive statistics, followed by a probit analysis of the effect of personal characteristics on the probability of being in a particular type of arrangement, and concludes with a descriptive analysis of the occupation and industry composition of the various types of employment.

Descriptive Statistics

Age. One of the most noticeable differences among the various arrangements in both 1995 and 1997 was in the age distribution of the workers. Agency temporaries, direct-hire temporaries, contract company workers, and part-time workers tended to be younger than regular full-time workers. Direct-hire temporaries and part-timers were the youngest groups, with nearly 40% under the age of 25, compared with about 10% of regular full-time workers (see table 2). In contrast, independent contractors and regular self-employed workers were older than regular full-time workers, on average.

Gender. Most of the arrangements that had an overrepresentation of younger workers also had an overrepresentation of women. The proportion of workers who were female exceeded that of regular full-time workers in four arrangements: agency temporaries, on-call workers, direct-hire temporaries, and regular part-time workers. The most male-dominant arrangement was contract company employment, but independent contractors and the regular self-employed also were more likely to be male than were regular full-time workers.

Race. Agency temporaries were much more likely to be black than were regular full-time workers (more than 21% compared with less than 12%) in both years. Contract company workers were somewhat more likely to be black than were regular full-time workers in 1997 but not in 1995, suggesting that the growth in this group was disproportionately among blacks. On the other hand, direct-hire temporaries and part-time workers were slightly less likely to be black than were regular full-time workers, with the difference being larger in 1997. Blacks and those of other nonwhite races also were underrepresented among independent contractors and the self-employed.[9] In both years, more than 90% of these groups were white, compared with around 84% of regular full-time workers.

Education. There were significant differences among the various employment arrangements with regard to educational attainment. Generally, regular part-time workers, agency temporaries, and on-call workers were less educated than their regular full-time counterparts, with the differences being most dramatic for regular part-time and on-call workers. In both 1995 and 1997, approximately one out of four regular part-time workers and one out of five on-call workers had not completed high school, compared with only one in ten regular full-time workers.

In contrast, direct-hire temporaries were more likely to be on either end of the educational spectrum. In both 1995 and 1997, almost 16% of direct hires had not completed high school, compared with approximately 10% of regular full-time workers. At the same time, more than 13% of direct-hire temporaries had earned an advanced degree, compared with about 9% of regular full-time workers.

TABLE 2a

Workers by Employment Arrangement and Selected Characteristics, February 1995

Characteristic	Agency temporaries	On-call workers	Direct-hire temporaries	Contract company workers	Independent contractors	Regular self-employed	Regular part-time	Regular full-time
Age								
Total, 16 years and older								
Thousands	1,181	2,078	3,393	588	8,309	7,256	16,810	83,600
Percent	100.0	100.0	100.0	100.0	100.0	100.0	100.0	100.0
16 to 19 years	5.28	7.94	13.65	2.64	1.51	1.86	21.00	1.36
20 to 24 years	19.72	12.55	23.31	13.68	2.37	2.39	17.06	9.35
25 to 34 years	34.12	24.61	23.33	38.67	19.72	16.35	17.65	29.20
35 to 54 years	33.34	39.35	30.39	34.15	56.06	54.72	29.15	50.39
55 to 64 years	5.72	9.20	6.15	7.17	13.61	15.18	8.35	8.64
65 years and older	1.81	6.36	3.17	3.68	6.73	9.50	6.79	1.05
Mean age (in years)	34.79	38.45	33.77	36.74	44.52	45.92	35.53	39.11
Sex								
Men	47.20	50.14	47.39	70.95	67.33	61.11	30.10	56.91
Women	52.80	49.86	52.61	29.05	32.67	38.89	69.90	43.09
Race and Hispanic origin								
White	72.73	83.98	83.38	83.46	92.31	93.79	85.74	84.25
Black	21.76	11.01	10.86	10.74	5.00	2.73	10.44	11.75
Other	5.51	5.01	5.76	5.79	2.68	3.47	3.82	4.00
Hispanic	11.32	12.48	10.18	8.59	5.19	4.92	8.42	8.92

Educational attainment								
Less than a high school diploma	15.51	18.98	15.78	10.47	10.44	10.52	24.57	9.89
High school graduates, no college	32.74	33.05	22.95	26.52	28.37	31.44	28.32	33.35
Some college, no degree	32.87	29.70	33.02	32.48	27.42	27.55	33.74	29.20
Bachelor's degree	16.30	14.59	14.90	19.26	21.38	18.64	9.99	18.38
Advanced degree	2.59	3.68	13.35	11.28	12.39	11.85	3.37	9.19
Marital status								
Married	42.92	54.99	41.81	56.19	71.61	79.34	45.92	62.68
Not married	57.08	45.01	58.19	43.81	28.39	20.66	54.08	37.32
School enrollment								
Enrolled	5.19	8.92	25.36	3.14	1.47	2.02	28.12	1.40
Not enrolled	94.81	91.08	74.64	96.86	98.53	97.98	71.88	98.60
Region								
Northeast	15.87	17.53	20.38	15.66	19.37	14.42	20.41	18.47
South	32.43	32.44	30.38	40.02	32.90	34.45	31.39	36.56
Midwest	27.45	21.87	23.61	19.44	20.39	27.94	27.71	24.29
West	24.25	28.15	25.63	24.89	27.33	23.20	20.50	20.68
Area								
Central city	38.89	28.19	29.67	33.64	25.75	20.25	27.41	28.85
Suburbs	50.37	52.19	48.91	56.30	54.35	46.63	51.53	51.69
Rural	10.75	19.62	21.42	10.06	19.90	33.13	21.06	19.46
Poverty	18.92	19.61	17.07	20.31	9.96	11.02	14.64	13.24
Nonpoverty	81.08	80.39	82.93	79.69	90.04	88.98	85.36	86.76

TABLE 2b

Workers by Employment Arrangement and Selected Characteristics, February 1997

Characteristic	Agency temporaries	On-call workers	Direct-hire temporaries	Contract company workers	Independent contractors	Regular self-employed	Regular part-time	Regular full-time
Age								
Total, 16 years and older								
Thousands	1,300	2,023	3,263	763	8,456	6,510	17,290	87,140
Percent	100.0	100.0	100.0	100.0	100.0	100.0	100.0	100.0
16 to 19 years	6.09	9.52	16.02	2.04	0.77	0.50	21.68	1.58
20 to 24 years	16.49	12.01	20.58	8.62	2.44	2.43	16.34	8.69
25 to 34 years	30.26	22.56	23.47	34.69	18.31	15.66	18.08	27.63
35 to 54 years	37.68	39.79	30.10	44.68	57.56	54.36	28.83	52.12
55 to 64 years	6.67	9.72	6.66	7.82	13.87	17.20	8.15	8.92
65 years and older	2.81	6.40	3.18	2.16	7.04	9.85	6.93	1.06
Mean age (in years)	36.30	38.63	33.91	38.06	44.83	47.04	35.58	39.45
Sex								
Men	44.71	49.59	48.07	69.95	66.61	61.64	29.86	56.73
Women	55.29	50.41	51.93	30.05	33.39	38.36	70.14	43.27
Race and Hispanic origin								
White	75.08	89.23	81.03	80.78	90.66	92.41	87.27	83.87
Black	21.30	7.69	10.32	13.69	5.30	3.33	9.33	11.83
Other	3.62	3.08	8.65	5.53	4.03	4.26	3.39	4.29
Hispanic	12.28	13.55	11.43	6.72	7.25	4.20	8.33	10.15

Educational attainment								
Less than a high school diploma	13.26	20.23	15.83	8.80	9.35	10.20	23.79	10.30
High school graduates, no college	31.69	27.42	20.63	36.70	29.83	30.71	29.80	33.55
Some college, no degree	36.53	30.33	32.26	24.36	26.69	24.94	33.04	28.12
Bachelor's degree	14.69	17.05	17.44	19.70	20.65	19.97	10.07	18.92
Advanced degree	3.82	4.98	13.83	10.44	13.48	14.18	3.30	9.12
Marital status								
Married	42.08	52.85	40.42	61.34	70.36	79.62	45.40	61.83
Not married	57.92	47.15	59.58	38.66	29.64	20.38	54.60	38.17
School enrollment								
Enrolled	3.63	10.70	27.42	2.77	0.99	0.66	29.25	1.42
Not enrolled	96.37	89.30	72.58	97.23	99.01	99.34	70.75	98.58
Region								
Northeast	15.97	16.45	20.36	12.19	16.29	16.98	21.43	18.72
South	33.97	32.56	30.01	37.30	34.71	34.02	28.13	35.90
Midwest	26.11	22.19	21.33	29.72	20.39	26.71	28.65	24.62
West	23.95	28.80	28.30	20.79	28.61	22.29	21.79	20.76
Area								
Central city	38.21	28.93	32.83	27.54	27.65	22.32	27.55	29.50
Suburbs	49.51	51.08	49.27	59.62	54.88	49.35	53.17	52.28
Rural	12.28	19.99	17.91	12.84	17.48	28.32	19.29	18.21
Poverty	21.13	16.43	18.18	18.60	11.94	12.82	15.66	15.14
Nonpoverty	78.87	83.57	81.82	81.40	88.06	87.18	84.34	84.86

Among contract company workers, a slightly higher proportion had a bachelor's or advanced degree than did regular full-time workers; however, the pattern in the other education categories was not as clear, perhaps due to the small number of individuals in this arrangement. Finally, independent contractors and the regular self-employed were more concentrated at the upper end of the educational spectrum than were regular full-time workers.

School enrollment. The levels of educational attainment reported in table 2 are not necessarily the final levels of education individuals will obtain, since these estimates include individuals who are still in school. Consequently, the lower levels of educational attainment in some of the nonstandard arrangements may be partially associated with higher levels of school enrollment. Compared with regular full-time workers, the proportion enrolled in school was higher for agency temporaries, on-call workers, direct-hire temporaries, and regular part-time workers. School enrollment was particularly high among direct-hire temporaries and regular part-time workers, whose enrollment rates were about 20 times the rate for regular full-time workers. Only independent contractors and regular self-employed workers (who tend to be older than other workers) had lower rates of school enrollment, on average, than regular full-time workers.

Marital status. Independent contractors and the regular self-employed are the only groups of workers whose marriage rates are higher than those of regular full-time workers. In both 1995 and 1997, around 70% of independent contractors and almost 80% of regular self-employed workers were married, compared with about 62% of regular full-time workers. In contrast, no more than 46% of agency temporaries, direct-hire temporaries, and regular part-time workers were married, while about 54% of on-call workers were married. As with education, however, marital status could be partially confounded by other factors, such as age.

Neighborhoods. Agency temporaries and contract company workers were less likely to live in a rural area in 1995 compared with regular full-time workers, while agency temporaries, contract company workers, and direct-hire temporaries were more likely to live in a central city. These three groups also were more likely to live in neighborhoods designated as poverty areas. In contrast, regular self-employed workers (a category that includes farmers) were nearly twice as likely to live in a rural area as were regular full-time workers; the self-employed, along with independent contractors, were also less likely to live in a poverty area. The findings concerning agency temporaries and contract company workers suggest that employment intermediaries need to be in areas where there is a critical mass of potential workers and jobs to be filled. The findings are also consistent with the notion that employment intermediaries perform useful screening and networking functions, which may be less needed in rural areas where employers and potential employees are more familiar with one another.

In summary, characteristics of workers vary considerably by employment arrangement. The self-employed and independent contractors appear to be relatively advantaged. They were more likely to be married, middle-aged, and male, to have higher levels of education, and to live in a nonpoverty area. In contrast, agency temporaries, direct-hire temporaries, and regular part-time workers were younger and more likely to be female, and to live in a poverty area than were regular full-time workers. However, even in the arrangements that had more disadvantaged workers, there were substantial differences in the characteristics of the workers, especially with regard to education and race.

Probit Estimates

In the previous section, we compared selected characteristics of workers in nonstandard employment with those of regular full-time workers. However, it is also interesting to examine the effect of specific characteristics on the probability of being in a particular work arrangement, controlling for other characteristics. To address this issue, we estimated probit models.

Estimates for Men and Women Combined

Table 3 shows the estimates of the probability of individuals being in each employment arrangement compared with the probability of being a regular full-time worker, obtained by using a series of probit models. The 0, 1 response variables were defined to be 0 for regular full-time workers and 1 for each of the other categories, respectively.[10] The bracketed terms below the coefficient estimates in table 3 are the derivatives of the probability of being in the specified employment arrangement with respect to a change in the explanatory variable, evaluated at the mean of the explanatory variable.[11]

The probit models include controls for age, age-squared, gender, race, ethnicity, educational attainment, marital status, school enrollment, region, population density, and poverty area. The excluded categories with respect to race, educational attainment, region, and population

Table 3a-1
Probit Estimates of the Probability of Being in Specified Arrangement Compared with a Regular Full-Time Arrangement, February 1995[1]

Characteristic	Agency temporaries	On-call workers	Direct-hire temporaries	Contract company workers	Independent contractors	Regular self-employed	Regular part-time
Both Sexes							
Age	-0.054***	-0.064***	-0.078***	-0.059***	0.001	-0.021***	-0.125***
	[-0.002]	[-0.003]	[-0.005]	[-0.001]	[0.0001]	[-0.003]	[-0.026]
Age squared	0.00055***	0.00081***	0.00089***	0.00065***	0.00021***	0.0005***	0.0015***
	[0.00002]	[0.00004]	[0.00006]	[0.00001]	[0.00003]	[0.00006]	[0.0003]
Female	0.156***	0.134***	0.157***	-0.229***	-0.207***	-0.041*	0.779***
	[0.005]	[0.007]	[0.011]	[-0.004]	[-0.030]	[-0.005]	[0.166]
Black	0.249***	-0.026	0.031	-0.119	0.393***	-0.578***	-0.055
	[0.009]	[-0.001]	[0.002]	[-0.002]	[-0.047]	[-0.051]	[-0.011]
Other	0.127	0.024	0.086	0.104	-0.260***	-0.046	-0.040
	[0.004]	[0.001]	[0.006]	[0.002]	[-0.033]	[-0.006]	[-0.008]
Hispanic	-0.0160	0.014	-0.00067	-0.178	-0.301***	-0.220***	-0.059
	[-0.0004]	[0.001]	[-0.00005]	[0.002]	[-0.037]	[-0.024]	[-0.012]
Less than high school diploma	0.172***	0.198***	0.226***	0.0341	0.107***	0.024	0.322***
	[0.006]	[0.012]	[0.018]	[0.0006]	[0.017]	[0.003]	[0.076]
Some college, no degree	0.019	-0.025	0.030	0.115*	0.043*	0.030	-0.0019
	[0.001]	[-0.001]	[0.002]	[0.002]	[0.007]	[0.004]	[-0.0003]
Bachelor's degree	-0.033	-0.066	0.102**	0.108	0.129***	0.081*	-0.175***
	[-0.001]	[-0.003]	[0.007]	[0.002]	[0.020]	[0.011]	[-0.034]
Advanced degree	-0.343***	-0.328***	0.475***	0.198**	0.100***	0.088**	-0.316***
	[-0.007]	[-0.013]	[0.045]	[0.004]	[0.016]	[0.012]	[-0.056]

Married	-0.144°°°	-0.007	-0.092°°°	-0.032	0.090°°°	0.115°°°
	[-0.004]	[-0.0004]	[-0.006]	[-0.001]	[0.013]	[0.024]
Enrolled	0.185	0.694°°°	1.361°°°	0.0261	0.406°°°	1.593°°°
	[0.007]	[0.067]	[0.258]	[0.0004]	[0.078]	[0.531]
South	-0.039	-0.071	-0.126°°°	0.102	-0.028	-0.216°°°
	[-0.001]	[-0.004]	[-0.008]	[0.002]	[-0.005]	[-0.043]
Midwest	0.108°	-0.023	-0.062	-0.00171	-0.112°°°	-0.058°°
	[0.003]	[-0.001]	[-0.004]	[-0.00002]	[-0.016]	[-0.012]
West	0.090	0.131°°°	0.094°°	0.115	0.173°°°	-0.070°°
	[0.003]	[0.007]	[0.006]	[0.002]	[0.027]	[-0.014]
Central city	0.039	-0.072°	-0.044	-0.0227	-0.016	-0.028
	[0.001]	[-0.003]	[-0.003]	[-0.0004]	[-0.002]	[-0.006]
Rural	-0.246°°°	-0.031	0.091°°	-0.328°°°	-0.00360	-0.0018
	[-0.006]	[-0.001]	[0.006]	[-0.004]	[0.00001]	[-0.0001]
Poverty	0.079	0.177°°°	0.111°°	0.275°°°	-0.026	0.084°°°
	[0.002]	[0.010]	[0.008]	[0.006]	[-0.004]	[0.018]

† All models also include an intercept. Excluded categories include white, high school graduate, suburb, and Northeast. All estimates were calculated using supplement weights. Standard errors for the coefficient estimates were calculated using pseudo-cluster and strata codes to account for the complex sample design of the CPS. The bracketed terms are the derivatives of the probability of being in the specified employment arrangement with respect to a change in the explanatory variable, evaluated at the mean of the explanatory variable.

° significance of the coefficient estimate at the .10 level
°° significance of the coefficient estimate at the .05 level
°°° significance of the coefficient estimate at the .01 level

Table 3a-2
Probit Estimates of the Probability of Being in Specified Arrangement Compared with a Regular Full-Time Arrangement, February 1995†

Characteristic	Agency temporaries	On-call workers	Direct-hire temporaries	Contract company workers	Independent contractors	Regular self-employed	Regular part-time
Men							
Age	-0.064***	-0.057***	-0.076***	-0.063***	0.0055	-0.016**	-0.158***
	[-0.001]	[-0.002]	[-0.004]	[-0.001]	[0.0009]	[-0.002]	[-0.017]
Age squared	0.00070***	0.00074***	0.00092***	0.00070***	0.00019***	0.0004***	0.0020***
	[0.00002]	[0.00003]	[0.0001]	[0.00001]	[0.00003]	[0.00007]	[0.0002]
Black	0.349***	0.032	0.043	-0.082	-0.404***	-0.583***	0.100*
	[0.011]	[0.001]	[0.002]	[-0.002]	[-0.055]	[0.054]	[0.012]
Other	0.154	0.055	0.145*	0.194	-0.289***	-0.015	-0.0006
	[0.004]	[0.002]	[0.009]	[0.005]	[-0.041]	[-0.002]	[-0.0001]
Hispanic	0.122	0.087	0.034	-0.176	-0.267***	-0.156**	0.048
	[0.003]	[0.004]	[0.002]	[-0.003]	[-0.039]	[-0.019]	[0.005]
Less than high school diploma	0.134	0.220***	0.164*	-0.0026	0.057	-0.022	0.374***
	[0.003]	[0.011]	[0.010]	[-0.00006]	[0.010]	[-0.003]	[0.050]
Some college, no degree	0.062	-0.050	0.057	0.180**	0.015	0.0052	0.120***
	[0.001]	[-0.002]	[0.003]	[0.004]	[0.003]	[0.0008]	[0.014]
Bachelor's degree	-0.031	-0.351***	0.043	0.051	0.129***	0.165***	-0.058
	[-0.0007]	[-0.011]	[0.002]	[0.001]	[0.023]	[0.023]	[-0.006]
Advanced degree	-0.205	-0.471***	0.464***	0.209*	0.063	0.228***	-0.050
	[-0.004]	[-0.013]	[0.038]	[0.005]	[0.011]	[0.034]	[-0.005]

Married	-0.280***	-0.187***	-0.210***	-0.0053	-0.040	0.088***	-0.390***
	[-0.007]	[-0.008]	[-0.013]	[-0.0001]	[-0.007]	[0.011]	[-0.047]
Enrolled	0.305*	0.669***	1.331***	0.00240	0.342**	0.851***	1.674***
	[0.010]	[0.054]	[0.228]	[0.00005]	[0.071]	[0.190]	[0.444]
South	-0.095	-0.105	-0.184***	0.052	-0.036	0.069*	-0.176***
	[-0.002]	[-0.004]	[-0.010]	[0.001]	[-0.007]	[0.009]	[-0.018]
Midwest	0.0157	-0.031	-0.152**	-0.0219	-0.122***	0.069	-0.099**
	[0.0004]	[-0.001]	[-0.008]	[-0.0005]	[-0.020]	[0.009]	[-0.010]
West	-0.0418	0.134*	0.032	0.083	0.107***	0.133***	-0.055
	[-0.0009]	[0.006]	[0.002]	[0.002]	[0.018]	[0.018]	[-0.006]
Central city	0.058	-0.071	-0.104**	0.037	-0.028	-0.042	0.091**
	[0.001]	[-0.003]	[-0.006]	[0.0008]	[-0.005]	[-0.005]	[0.010]
Rural	-0.176**	-0.069	0.127**	-0.193**	0.044	0.320***	-0.086*
	[-0.004]	[-0.003]	[0.008]	[-0.004]	[0.008]	[0.048]	[0.010]
Poverty	0.122	0.182**	0.150**	0.231**	0.007	-0.049	0.087*
	[0.003]	[0.009]	[0.009]	[0.006]	[0.001]	[-0.006]	[0.010]

† All models also include an intercept. Excluded categories include white, high school graduate, suburb, and Northeast. All estimates were calculated using supplement weights. Standard errors for the coefficient estimates were calculated using pseudo-cluster and strata codes to account for the complex sample design of the CPS. The bracketed terms are the derivatives of the probability of being in the specified employment arrangement with respect to a change in the explanatory variable, evaluated at the mean of the explanatory variable.

° significance of the coefficient estimate at the .10 level
°° significance of the coefficient estimate at the .05 level
°°° significance of the coefficient estimate at the .01 level

Table 3a-3

Probit Estimates of the Probability of Being in Specified Arrangement Compared with a Regular Full-Time Arrangement, February 1995[†]

Characteristic	Agency temporaries	On-call workers	Direct-hire temporaries	Contract company workers	Independent contractors	Regular self-employed	Regular part-time
Women							
Age	-0.041°°° [-0.001]	-0.068°°° [-0.004]	-0.076°°° [-0.006]	-0.0487°° [-0.0005]	-0.0015 [-0.0002]	-0.021°° [-0.002]	-0.101°°° [-0.031]
Age squared	0.00038°° [0.00001]	0.00087°°° [0.00005]	0.0083°°° [0.00006]	0.000490°°° [0.000004]	0.0002 [0.00002]	0.00045°°° [0.00005]	0.0013°°° [0.0004]
Black	0.163° [0.007]	-0.077 [-0.004]	0.021 [0.002]	-0.221 [-0.002]	-0.361°°° [-0.035]	-0.556°°° [-0.044]	-0.107°°° [-0.031]
Other	0.090 [0.004]	-0.021 [-0.001]	0.018 [0.001]	-0.204 [-0.001]	-0.215°° [-0.022]	-0.098 [-0.010]	-0.072 [-0.021]
Hispanic	-0.169 [-0.005]	-0.129 [-0.007]	-0.025 [-0.002]	-0.194 [-0.001]	-0.344°°° [-0.033]	-0.310°°° [-0.028]	-0.083° [-0.024]
Less than high school diploma	0.224°° [0.010]	0.109 [0.007]	0.306°°° [0.030]	0.159 [0.002]	0.214°°° [0.029]	0.120 [0.015]	0.315°°° [0.104]
Some college, no degree	-0.007 [-0.0003]	0.018 [0.001]	0.0089 [0.0007]	-0.0376 [-0.0003]	0.089°° [0.011]	0.060 [0.007]	-0.037 [-0.011]
Bachelor's degree	-0.029 [-0.001]	-0.147°° [0.009]	0.150°° [0.013]	0.198 [0.002]	0.120°° [0.015]	-0.055 [-0.006]	-0.216°°° [-0.062]
Advanced degree	-0.470°°° [-0.011]	-0.191°° [-0.009]	0.485°°° [0.054]	0.168 [0.002]	0.171°°° [0.023]	-0.195°°° [-0.019]	-0.431°°° [-0.112]

Married	-0.039	0.162°°°	0.00046	-0.119	0.266°°°	0.535°°°	0.341°°°
	[-0.001]	[0.009]	[0.00003]	[-0.001]	[0.031]	[0.056]	[0.102]
Enrolled	0.036	0.781°°°	1.396°°°	0.0367	0.490°°°	0.331°°	1.422°°°
	[0.001]	[0.091]	[0.293]	[0.0004]	[0.083]	[0.050]	[0.520]
South	0.0069	-0.040	-0.061	0.210°	-0.019	0.0906°	-0.235°°°
	[0.0003]	[-0.002]	[-0.005]	[0.002]	[-0.003]	[0.0099]	[-0.070]
Midwest	0.189°°	-0.020	0.032	0.0295	-0.095°°	0.164°°°	-0.038
	[0.008]	[-0.001]	[0.003]	[0.0003]	[-0.011]	[0.019]	[-0.012]
West	0.205°°	0.117°	0.159°°	0.183	0.279°°°	0.292°°°	-0.078°°
	[0.008]	[0.007]	[0.014]	[0.002]	[0.037]	[0.037]	[-0.024]
Central city	0.0208	-0.069	0.0108	-0.150	-0.000500	-0.046	-0.092°°°
	[0.0008]	[-0.004]	[0.0008]	[-0.001]	[-0.000004]	[-0.005]	[-0.027]
Rural	-0.329°°°	-0.0031	0.050	-0.774°°°	-0.096°°	0.265°°°	-0.042
	[-0.010]	[-0.0002]	[0.004]	[-0.004]	[-0.011]	[0.033]	[-0.012]
Poverty	0.040	0.174°°	0.074	0.399°°°	-0.097	-0.011	0.092°°°
	[0.001]	[0.011]	[0.006]	[0.006]	[-0.011]	[-0.001]	[0.028]

[†] All models also include an intercept. Excluded categories include white, high school graduate, suburb, and Northeast. All estimates were calculated using supplement weights. Standard errors for the coefficient estimates were calculated using pseudo-cluster and strata codes to account for the complex sample design of the CPS. The bracketed terms are the derivatives of the probability of being in the specified employment arrangement with respect to a change in the explanatory variable, evaluated at the mean of the explanatory variable.

° significance of the coefficient estimate at the .10 level
°° significance of the coefficient estimate at the .05 level
°°° significance of the coefficient estimate at the .01 level

Table 3b-1

Probit Estimates of the Probability of Being in Specified Arrangement Compared with a Regular Full-Time Arrangement, February 1997[†]

Characteristic	Agency temporaries	On-call workers	Direct-hire temporaries	Contract company workers	Independent contractors	Regular self-employed	Regular part-time
Both Sexes							
Age	-0.059***	-0.062***	-0.076***	-0.0170	0.0036	-0.025***	-0.123***
	[-0.002]	[-0.003]	[-0.005]	[-0.0004]	[0.0005]	[-0.003]	[-0.025]
Age squared	0.0065***	0.00078***	0.00088***	0.000173	0.00018***	0.00054***	0.00149***
	[0.00002]	[0.00003]	[0.00005]	[0.000003]	[0.00003]	[0.00006]	[0.00030]
Female	0.184***	0.141***	0.140***	-0.212***	-0.194***	-0.053**	0.805***
	[0.006]	[0.007]	[0.008]	[-0.004]	[-0.028]	[-0.006]	[0.167]
Black	0.203***	-0.198***	-0.018	0.0385	-0.367***	-0.525***	-0.148***
	[0.006]	[-0.008]	[-0.001]	[0.0009]	[-0.044]	[-0.042]	[-0.028]
Other	-0.039	-0.195**	0.287***	0.083	-0.135**	-0.057	-0.138***
	[-0.001]	[-0.008]	[0.022]	[0.002]	[-0.018]	[-0.006]	[-0.026]
Hispanic	0.0267	0.0018	0.017	-0.183	-0.208***	-0.351***	-0.205***
	[0.0009]	[0.0001]	[0.001]	[-0.003]	[-0.027]	[-0.031]	[-0.037]
Less than high school diploma	0.098	0.283***	0.182***	-0.094	-0.010	0.037	0.273***
	[0.003]	[0.017]	[0.012]	[-0.002]	[-0.001]	[0.004]	[0.062]
Some college, no degree	0.123**	0.074*	0.096**	-0.100	0.028	0.027	-0.018
	[0.004]	[0.004]	[0.006]	[-0.002]	[0.004]	[0.003]	[-0.004]
Bachelor's degree	-0.047	0.051	0.189***	-0.0191	0.083***	0.096***	-0.229***
	[-0.001]	[0.002]	[0.013]	[-0.0004]	[0.013]	[0.011]	[-0.042]
Advanced degree	-0.194**	-0.134*	0.513***	0.0187	0.127***	0.194***	-0.365***
	[-0.005]	[-0.006]	[0.046]	[0.0004]	[0.020]	[0.024]	[-0.061]

Married	-0.181***	-0.028	-0.080**	0.0088	0.071***	0.145***
	[-0.006]	[-0.001]	[-0.005]	[0.0002]	[0.010]	[0.029]
Enrolled	-0.0060	0.735***	1.41***	0.202	0.209**	1.627***
	[0.0001]	[0.070]	[0.259]	[0.006]	[0.035]	[0.539]
South	0.007	-0.0181	-0.148***	0.186**	0.112***	-0.291***
	[0.0002]	[-0.0008]	[-0.008]	[0.004]	[0.017]	[-0.056]
Midwest	0.094	-0.013	-0.175***	0.242***	-0.019	-0.087***
	[0.003]	[-0.001]	[-0.010]	[0.006]	[-0.003]	[-0.017]
West	0.108	0.170***	0.071	0.181**	0.281***	-0.059**
	[0.004]	[0.009]	[0.004]	[0.004]	[0.046]	[-0.012]
Central city	0.0225	-0.021	0.0055	-0.110	-0.0040	-0.023
	[0.0007]	[-0.001]	[0.0003]	[-0.002]	[-0.0004]	[-0.005]
Rural	-0.175***	0.050	0.058	-0.234***	0.240***	-0.026
	[-0.005]	[0.002]	[0.004]	[-0.004]	[0.030]	[-0.005]
Poverty	0.063	0.031	0.070	0.161**	0.009	0.080***
	[0.002]	[0.002]	[0.004]	[0.004]	[0.001]	[0.017]

[†] All models also include an intercept. Excluded categories include white, high school graduate, suburb, and Northeast. All estimates were calculated using supplement weights. Standard errors for the coefficient estimates were calculated using pseudo-cluster and strata codes to account for the complex sample design of the CPS. The bracketed terms are the derivatives of the probability of being in the specified employment arrangement with respect to a change in the explanatory variable, evaluated at the mean of the explanatory variable.

* significance of the coefficient estimate at the .10 level
** significance of the coefficient estimate at the .05 level
*** significance of the coefficient estimate at the .01 level

Table 3b-2
Probit Estimates of the Probability of Being in Specified Arrangement Compared with a Regular Full-Time Arrangement, February 1997†

Characteristic	Agency temporaries	On-call workers	Direct-hire temporaries	Contract company workers	Independent contractors	Regular self-employed	Regular part-time
Men							
Age	-0.073***	-0.053***	-0.091***	-0.0238	0.015**	-0.025***	-0.166***
	[-0.002]	[-0.002]	[-0.005]	[-0.0006]	[0.003]	[-0.003]	[-0.017]
Age squared	0.00083***	0.00067***	0.00107***	0.000222	0.00096	0.00056***	0.0021***
	[0.00002]	[0.00003]	[0.00005]	[0.000006]	[0.00002]	[0.00007]	[0.0002]
Black	0.305**	-0.225**	0.070	0.151	-0.344***	-0.534***	0.083
	[0.009]	[-0.008]	[0.004]	[0.004]	[-0.047]	[-0.045]	[0.009]
Other	-0.0352	-0.116	0.286***	0.110	-0.168**	-0.017	0.040
	[-0.0010]	[-0.004]	[0.019]	[0.003]	[-0.025]	[-0.002]	[0.004]
Hispanic	0.054	0.061	0.034	-0.412***	-0.236***	-0.307***	-0.125*
	[0.001]	[0.003]	[0.002]	[-0.007]	[-0.034]	[-0.030]	[-0.012]
Less than high school diploma	0.148	0.267***	0.138*	-0.164	-0.034	0.022	0.265***
	[0.004]	[0.013]	[0.008]	[-0.004]	[-0.005]	[0.003]	[0.032]
Some college, no degree	0.120**	0.024	0.105*	-0.041	-0.008	0.047	0.077
	[0.005]	[0.0010]	[0.006]	[-0.001]	[-0.001]	[0.006]	[0.008]
Bachelor's degree	0.072	-0.134*	0.212***	-0.0036	0.051	0.176***	-0.058
	[0.002]	[-0.005]	[0.012]	[-0.0009]	[0.009]	[0.023]	[-0.006]
Advanced degree	0.045	-0.240*	0.580***	0.108	0.111*	0.352***	-0.131*
	[0.001]	[-0.008]	[0.047]	[0.003]	[0.019]	[0.052]	[-0.012]

Married	-0.349°°° [-0.009]	-0.189°°° [-0.008]	-0.182°°° [-0.010]	0.0067 [0.0002]	-0.048 [-0.008]	-0.339°°° [-0.038]
Enrolled	0.0333 [0.0008]	0.719°° [0.060]	1.235°°° [0.185]	0.183 [0.006]	0.149 [0.027]	1.692°°° [0.440]
South	0.102 [0.002]	-0.007 [-0.0003]	-0.092 [-0.005]	0.184°° [0.005]	0.170°°° [0.029]	-0.255°°° [-0.025]
Midwest	0.196°° [0.005]	0.026 [0.001]	-0.203°°° [-0.009]	0.177° [0.005]	0.007 [0.001]	-0.125°°° [-0.012]
West	0.192°° [0.005]	0.151°° [0.007]	0.148°° [0.008]	0.188° [0.005]	0.308°°° [0.057]	-0.015 [-0.001]
Central city	0.0275 [0.0006]	-0.066 [-0.003]	0.000091 [0.000005]	-0.084 [-0.002]	0.006 [0.001]	0.048 [0.005]
Rural	-0.231°° [-0.004]	0.036 [0.001]	0.086 [0.005]	-0.203°° [-0.004]	0.026 [0.004]	-0.0081 [-0.0008]
Poverty	0.118 [0.003]	0.045 [0.002]	0.0052 [0.0003]	0.195°° [0.006]	0.032 [0.005]	0.102°° [0.011]

† All models also include an intercept. Excluded categories include white, high school graduate, suburb, and Northeast. All estimates were calculated using supplement weights. Standard errors for the coefficient estimates were calculated using pseudo-cluster and strata codes to account for the complex sample design of the CPS. The bracketed terms are the derivatives of the probability of being in the specified employment arrangement with respect to a change in the explanatory variable, evaluated at the mean of the explanatory variable.

° significance of the coefficient estimate at the .10 level
°° significance of the coefficient estimate at the .05 level
°°° significance of the coefficient estimate at the .01 level

Table 3b-3
Probit Estimates of the Probability of Being in Specified Arrangement Compared with a Regular Full-Time Arrangement, February 1997†

Characteristic	Agency temporaries	On-call workers	Direct-hire temporaries	Contract company workers	Independent contractors	Regular self-employed	Regular part-time
Women							
Age	-0.045°°°	-0.067°°°	-0.056°°°	-0.00152	-0.009	-0.019°°	-0.092°°°
	[-0.002]	[-0.004]	[-0.004]	[-0.00002]	[-0.001]	[-0.002]	[-0.028]
Age squared	0.00048°°°	0.00086°°°	0.00063°°°	0.000438	0.00027°°°	0.00045°°°	0.0011°°°
	[0.00002]	[0.00005]	[0.00004]	[0.000001]	[0.00003]	[0.00004]	[0.0003]
Black	0.140°	-0.160°	-0.087	-0.224	-0.391°°°	-0.509°°°	-0.218°°°
	[0.007]	[-0.008]	[-0.006]	[-0.003]	[-0.038]	[-0.037]	[-0.061]
Other	-0.076	-0.290°	0.280°°°	-0.00232	-0.097	-0.133	-0.272°°°
	[-0.003]	[-0.012]	[0.025]	[-0.00003]	[-0.011]	[-0.012]	[-0.073]
Hispanic	0.0119	-0.080	0.0083	0.143	-0.132°	-0.414°°°	-0.234°°°
	[0.0005]	[-0.004]	[0.0006]	[0.002]	[-0.015]	[-0.031]	[-0.065]
Less than high school diploma	0.064	0.276°°°	0.253°°°	0.067	0.050	0.099	0.296°°°
	[0.003]	[0.019]	[0.022]	[0.001]	[0.006]	[0.010]	[0.096]
Some college, no degree	0.069	0.140°°	0.096°	-0.221°°	0.087°°	0.0071	-0.056
	[0.003]	[0.008]	[0.007]	[-0.003]	[0.011]	[0.0007]	[-0.017]
Bachelor's degree	-0.129°	0.208°°°	0.181°°°	-0.0236	0.127°°°	-0.016	-0.297°°°
	[-0.005]	[0.013]	[0.014]	[-0.0003]	[0.016]	[-0.002]	[-0.082]
Advanced degree	-0.433°°°	-0.021	0.448°°°	-0.178	0.152°°	-0.105	-0.490°°°
	[-0.013]	[-0.001]	[0.044]	[-0.002]	[0.020]	[-0.010]	[-0.123]

Married	-0.051	0.134***	0.0087	0.0316	0.213***	0.462***	0.345***
	[-0.002]	[0.007]	[0.0006]	[0.0005]	[0.026]	[0.044]	[0.101]
Enrolled	-0.049	0.789***	1.586***	0.032	0.267*	0.304	1.459***
	[-0.002]	[0.087]	[0.345]	[0.007]	[0.040]	[0.038]	[0.531]
South	-0.074	-0.041	-0.207***	0.180	0.020	-0.019	-0.316***
	[-0.003]	[-0.002]	[-0.014]	[0.003]	[0.002]	[-0.002]	[-0.091]
Midwest	0.0144	-0.057	-0.159**	0.365***	-0.060	0.056	-0.072**
	[0.0006]	[-0.003]	[-0.010]	[0.007]	[-0.007]	[0.006]	[-0.021]
West	0.040	0.187**	-0.019	0.158	0.239***	0.158***	-0.084**
	[0.002]	[0.011]	[-0.001]	[0.003]	[0.033]	[0.017]	[-0.025]
Central city	0.0185	0.024	0.014	-0.163*	0.015	-0.0060	-0.060**
	[0.0008]	[0.001]	[0.001]	[-0.002]	[0.002]	[-0.0006]	[-0.018]
Rural	-0.123	0.051	0.029	-0.301**	-0.132***	0.220***	-0.032
	[-0.005]	[0.003]	[0.002]	[-0.004]	[-0.015]	[0.024]	[-0.010]
Poverty	0.0110	0.021	0.140**	0.101	-0.075	0.109*	0.073**
	[0.0005]	[0.001]	[0.011]	[0.002]	[-0.009]	[0.012]	[0.022]

† All models also include an intercept. Excluded categories include white, high school graduate, suburb, and Northeast. All estimates were calculated using supplement weights. Standard errors for the coefficient estimates were calculated using pseudo-cluster and strata codes to account for the complex sample design of the CPS. The bracketed terms are the derivatives of the probability of being in the specified employment arrangement with respect to a change in the explanatory variable, evaluated at the mean of the explanatory variable.

* significance of the coefficient estimate at the .10 level
** significance of the coefficient estimate at the .05 level
*** significance of the coefficient estimate at the .01 level

density are white, high school diploma, Northeast, and suburb, respectively. Since testing indicated that the proportions of those employed in various work arrangements were statistically different between 1995 and 1997, as were the effects of several characteristics on the probability of being in a specific arrangement, analyses for 1995 and 1997 were conducted separately.

Many of the probit estimates mirror the descriptive statistics. For instance, school enrollment was one of the strongest predictors of being in a nonstandard arrangement. In the probit models for both 1995 and 1997, being enrolled in school increased the probability of being an on-call worker by about 7 percentage points, a direct-hire temporary by almost 26 percentage points, and a regular part-time worker by more than 53 percentage points. In addition, when other factors were controlled for, being in school even increased the probability of being an independent contractor in both 1995 and 1997 and a regular self-employed worker in 1995, which somewhat contradicts the descriptive statistics.

The probit estimates of the effects of race, age, and gender on the probability of being in the various arrangements also tend to be consistent with the descriptive statistics. The only major exceptions were that, when other factors were controlled for, in 1995, being black did not have a statistically significant effect on the probability of being an on-call or regular part-time worker, while in 1997, it significantly decreased these probabilities. These findings suggest that, as the economy improved between 1995 and 1997, blacks may have moved into regular full-time positions and out of potentially less desirable part-time or on-call jobs. Alternatively, as the economy improved, some nonstandard positions, especially regular part-time jobs, may have been converted to regular full-time jobs.

The effect of age on the probability of being a contract company worker displayed the reverse pattern, being significant in 1995 but not in 1997. Our finding that contract company workers were significantly younger in 1995 but not in 1997 suggests that the growth in contract company employment was disproportionately among older workers.

Even where there was particular concern over confounding influences, the probit estimates were fairly consistent with the descriptive statistics. The estimates in table 3 indicate that, even when age, school enrollment, and other factors are controlled for, on-call and regular part-time workers were more likely to be found among the ranks of the least educated. In 1995, not having completed high school increased the probability of being an on-call worker by more than 1 percentage point and of being a regular part-time worker by almost 8 percentage points, while having an advanced degree significantly decreased the probability of being in either category. The pattern for agency temporaries was similar, although the effect was not as strong.

Also as seen in the descriptive statistics, the probit estimates show that the educational attainment of direct-hire temporaries was bifurcated; that is, compared with regular full-time workers, direct-hire temporaries were more concentrated at both ends of the educational spectrum. Not having completed high school increased the probability of being a direct-hire temporary by more than 1 percentage point in both 1995 and 1997, while having an advanced degree increased this probability by almost 5 percentage points. Independent contractors and the regular self-employed were disproportionately on the upper end of the educational spectrum. In both 1995 and 1997, having a bachelor's or advanced degree increased the probability of being an independent contractor or a regular self-employed worker, even when controlling for other characteristics. Further, the effect of having an advanced degree on the probability of being a regular self-employed worker was significantly larger in 1997 than in 1995, suggesting that the decline in regular self-employment during this period was among those with less education.

Finally, living in a poverty area significantly increased the probability of being a regular part-time worker in both 1995 and 1997, while it had no statistically significant effect on the probability of being an independent contractor or a regular self-employed worker, once other characteristics were controlled for. Living in a poverty area also significantly increased the probability of being a direct-hire temporary or an on-call worker in 1995 but not in 1997, which may be the result of a strengthening economy.

Estimates for Men and Women Separately

Statistical testing revealed significant differences by gender in the effect of individual characteristics on the probability of being in a specific work arrangement that could not simply be absorbed by the inclusion of a gender dummy variable. Therefore, we estimated separate probit models for men and women. Salient findings include the fact that black women were significantly less likely to be regular part-time workers than were white women in both 1995 and 1997, while black men were significantly more likely to be regular part-time workers than were white men in 1995.

As would be expected, marriage also affected women and men differently. For women, being married significantly increased the probability of working part time or on call, whereas for men, being married
reduced the probability of working in these arrangements. Married men
also were significantly less likely to be agency temporaries or direct-hire
temporaries, but for women, being married had no statistically significant effect on working in these arrangements. Both husbands and wives
were more likely to be self-employed than single people, but somewhat
surprisingly, this effect was larger for women than for men. Also, the
effect of education was not always the same for women and men. Highly
educated women were less likely to be self-employed, at least in 1995,
compared with high school graduates, while the opposite was true for
men in both 1995 and 1997.

Industry and Occupation Estimates

The personal characteristics of workers have been examined through
the use of descriptive statistics and probit estimates. In addition, the CPS
allows us to look at the occupations and industries of workers in the various arrangements.[12] Not surprisingly, given the diversity of the categories
under study, the kind of work done by people in the different employment arrangements varied considerably. As table 4 shows, independent
contractors were more likely to be in executive, administrative, and managerial; professional specialty; and sales jobs compared with regular full-
time workers, while the regular self-employed were overrepresented in
managerial, sales, and farming jobs. Direct-hire temporaries were more
likely than regular full-time workers to be in professional, clerical, and
service occupations, while agency temporaries were found disproportionately in clerical and machine operator positions, and on-call and contract
company workers were overrepresented in professional and service
fields. Compared with regular full-time workers, those with regular part-
time jobs were more likely to hold sales, service, and laborer jobs.

The industry distributions of those in nonstandard arrangements also
revealed some interesting variations. For instance, about 28% of agency
temporaries, but only 7% of direct-hire temporaries, worked in manufacturing in 1997. The services and construction industries combined
accounted for about three fifths of independent contractors, while services and retail trade accounted for about three fifths of the regular self-
employed. The proportion of on-call workers and direct-hire temporaries
in services alone was about one-and-a-half times that of regular full-time
workers. Clearly, the diverse occupational and industry distributions of

TABLE 4a

Workers by Employment Arrangement, Occupation, and Industry, February 1995

Occupation and industry	Agency temporaries	On-call workers	Direct-hire temporaries	Contract company workers	Independent contractors	Regular self-employed	Regular part-time	Regular full-time
Occupation								
Total, 16 years and older								
Thousands	1,181	2,078	3,393	588	8,309	7,256	16,810	83,600
Percent	100.0	100.0	100.0	100.0	100.0	100.0	100.0	100.0
Executive, administrative, and managerial	6.50	2.88	7.95	6.37	18.56	22.82	4.18	14.97
Professional specialty	8.29	20.91	25.27	27.78	16.29	11.41	10.76	15.35
Technicians and related support	3.71	1.54	2.90	7.58	1.10	0.54	3.02	3.68
Sales occupations	2.60	5.93	6.34	2.76	18.75	19.39	18.80	9.80
Administrative support, including clerical	30.50	9.51	18.73	4.66	3.83	8.33	18.13	16.07
Services	9.01	19.69	16.28	27.63	10.60	9.10	30.29	10.50
Protective services	1.46	2.81	1.83	17.19	0.14	0.06	1.08	2.09
Services, excluding protective	7.55	16.88	14.45	10.44	10.46	9.04	29.21	8.41
Precision, production, craft, and repair	5.60	14.33	7.72	11.74	19.21	6.61	2.42	12.01
Machine operators	18.41	2.78	5.42	2.06	1.94	1.58	2.31	8.00
Transportation and material moving	2.99	8.46	3.34	4.30	3.74	1.81	2.75	4.53
Handlers, equipment cleaners, helpers, and laborers	11.80	9.23	3.89	4.14	0.84	0.62	6.03	3.76
Farming, forestry, and fishing	1.04	4.73	2.17	0.98	5.14	17.80	1.32	1.33
Industry								
Total, 16 years and older								
Thousands	1,181	2,078	3,393	588	8,309	7,256	16,810	83,600
Percent	100.0	100.0	100.0	100.0	100.0	100.0	100.0	100.0
Agriculture, forestry, and fisheries	0.33	4.52	2.12	0.33	5.26	19.36	1.29	1.27

TABLE 4a (*Continued*)

Workers by Employment Arrangement, Occupation, and Industry, February 1995

Occupation and industry	Agency temporaries	On-call workers	Direct-hire temporaries	Contract company workers	Independent contractors	Regular self-employed	Regular part-time	Regular full-time
Industry (*Continued*)								
Mining	0.19	0.50	0.35	2.60	0.21	0.26	0.10	0.71
Construction	2.75	15.61	7.42	7.09	21.23	4.84	1.59	4.75
Manufacturing	32.51	5.74	9.90	17.76	4.98	7.38	4.32	21.84
Durable goods	19.97	2.98	5.62	10.50	2.76	4.02	1.62	12.91
Nondurable goods	12.54	2.76	4.28	7.26	2.22	3.36	2.70	8.93
Transportation	3.39	7.13	1.80	4.73	4.42	2.82	2.78	4.98
Communications and public utilities	3.88	1.35	2.45	7.73	0.57	0.51	0.56	3.47
Wholesale trade	2.78	2.10	1.48	2.31	3.34	6.08	1.63	4.30
Retail trade	5.04	11.92	10.84	3.39	9.83	20.23	38.71	13.23
Finance, insurance, and real estate	7.19	1.67	2.60	6.82	9.57	6.16	4.39	7.04
Services	39.56	46.63	55.13	35.25	40.34	32.35	43.12	31.85
Business, auto, and repair services	23.38	5.90	2.38	9.65	12.85	8.23	4.06	4.50
Personal services	2.87	5.16	7.10	3.14	7.23	5.74	5.57	2.24
Entertainment and recreation services	0.64	2.42	2.88	0.50	2.54	1.35	2.76	1.12
Professional services	12.67	33.15	42.77	21.96	17.72	17.03	30.73	23.99
Hospitals	0.83	3.76	2.52	3.98	0.22	0.06	4.83	4.57
Health services, excluding hospitals	4.17	6.22	2.26	5.06	2.94	4.78	7.52	4.47
Educational services	2.26	16.80	31.41	4.60	1.40	0.96	10.23	8.62
Social services	1.51	3.21	3.18	2.23	2.92	4.87	3.80	1.91
Other professional services	3.90	3.16	3.40	6.09	10.24	6.36	4.35	4.42
Public administration	1.23	2.82	5.90	11.32	0.25	—	1.51	6.57
Data not available	1.17	—	—	0.68	—	—	—	—

Note: Dash equals zero.

TABLE 4b

Workers by Employment Arrangement, Occupation, and Industry, February 1997

Occupation and industry	Agency temporaries	On-call workers	Direct-hire temporaries	Contract company workers	Independent contractors	Regular self-employed	Regular part-time	Regular full-time
Occupation								
Total, 16 years and older								
Thousands	1,300	2,023	3,263	763	8,456	6,510	17,290	87,140
Percent	100.0	100.0	100.0	100.0	100.0	100.0	100.0	100.0
Executive, administrative, and managerial	6.93	2.68	7.59	8.55	20.72	24.13	4.50	15.55
Professional specialty	6.61	20.89	26.49	20.31	17.93	12.96	10.81	15.97
Technicians and related support	5.77	4.00	3.23	6.83	0.77	0.71	2.79	3.72
Sales occupations	1.66	6.63	5.30	2.95	17.87	20.69	19.14	9.77
Administrative support, including clerical	34.09	8.61	20.22	5.48	3.88	5.36	19.13	15.08
Services	9.04	20.17	15.21	28.37	9.11	10.05	28.77	10.60
Protective services	0.98	2.82	1.44	13.08	0.28	—	0.94	2.02
Services, excluding protective	8.06	17.35	13.77	15.29	8.83	10.05	27.83	8.58
Precision, production, craft, and repair	5.17	14.97	8.64	19.65	17.89	7.53	2.79	12.00
Machine operators	17.06	2.24	4.01	1.84	1.59	1.70	2.34	7.89
Transportation and material moving	3.49	8.46	1.64	2.54	4.36	1.58	2.63	4.60
Handlers, equipment cleaners, helpers, and laborers	8.58	8.58	4.78	3.27	0.82	0.57	5.94	3.43
Farming, forestry, and fishing	1.62	2.77	2.90	0.21	5.07	14.73	1.16	1.40
Industry								
Total, 16 years and older								
Thousands	1,300	2,023	3,263	763	8,456	6,510	17,290	87,140
Percent	100.0	100.0	100.0	100.0	100.0	100.0	100.0	100.0
Agriculture	—	3.32	2.56	0.21	5.99	15.56	1.43	1.32

TABLE 4b (Continued)

Workers by Employment Arrangement, Occupation, and Industry, February 1997

Occupation and industry	Agency temporaries	On-call workers	Direct-hire temporaries	Contract company workers	Independent contractors	Regular self-employed	Regular part-time	Regular full-time
Industry (Continued)								
Mining	0.63	0.38	0.35	1.94	0.19	0.19	0.02	0.64
Construction	2.19	15.88	8.75	4.94	20.75	5.62	2.17	5.30
Manufacturing	27.70	5.32	7.15	19.49	4.75	6.33	4.45	21.36
Durable goods	17.22	1.54	3.31	11.46	3.00	4.12	1.99	13.13
Nondurable goods	10.48	3.78	3.84	8.03	1.75	2.21	2.46	8.23
Transportation	2.58	6.21	2.07	5.84	4.64	3.20	3.15	4.95
Communications and public utilities	2.96	1.92	1.47	6.40	0.45	0.46	0.64	3.18
Wholesale trade	4.03	1.72	1.18	1.55	3.52	5.13	1.62	4.44
Retail trade	3.45	12.35	10.28	6.71	10.05	21.02	37.42	13.15
Finance, insurance, and real estate	7.63	1.55	2.55	7.91	8.42	5.44	4.60	6.96
Services	37.81	47.52	57.51	28.10	41.09	37.05	42.87	32.97
Business, auto, and repair services	23.27	5.80	2.97	6.56	13.69	9.56	4.30	5.36
Personal services	1.82	6.05	6.01	3.20	6.09	5.96	4.99	2.33
Entertainment and recreation services	0.77	2.76	2.98	0.78	2.74	2.05	2.90	1.30
Professional services	11.95	32.91	45.55	17.56	18.57	19.48	30.68	23.98
Hospitals	1.10	6.95	4.32	2.91	0.25	0.09	4.69	4.59
Health services, excluding hospitals	3.29	5.31	2.66	4.26	3.68	5.96	7.38	4.74
Educational services	1.53	17.32	31.47	5.06	1.16	0.68	10.33	8.37
Social services	1.02	1.23	2.73	2.29	2.46	6.10	3.84	2.08
Other professional services	4.98	2.10	4.37	3.04	11.02	6.65	4.44	4.20
Public administration	0.03	3.84	6.15	13.95	0.16	—	1.62	5.72
Data not available	11.02	—	—	2.97	—	—	—	—

Note: Dash equals zero.

workers in the various nonstandard arrangements reinforce the dangers of generalizing about these workers.

Earnings

Descriptive Statistics: Means and Selected Deciles

As already noted, there is a great deal of interest in the economic well-being of workers in nonstandard arrangements, and attention often focuses on how much these individuals earn. Table 5 contains the mean and median as well as the 90th and 10th percentiles of hourly earnings (in 1997 dollars) of workers in the eight employment arrangements.[13] An examination of these estimates reveals that, in both 1995 and 1997, hourly earnings of agency temporaries, on-call workers, direct-hire temporaries, and regular part-time workers were significantly lower than the earnings of regular full-time workers in terms of all four measures.

In contrast, regular self-employed workers and independent contractors had significantly higher mean hourly wages than regular full-time workers, and independent contractors also had higher median hourly wages. Both also had earnings distributions that were much more dispersed than that of regular full-time workers. For these nonstandard arrangements, the ratios of the ninth decile earnings to the first decile earnings—the 90/10 ratios, a measure of earnings dispersion—were 8.00 and 9.76 for the self-employed and independent contractors, respectively, in 1997, compared with 4.00 for regular full-time workers. For the regular self-employed and independent contractors, the first deciles of hourly earnings were slightly lower than that for regular full-time workers, but the ninth deciles were more than one-and-a-half times greater.

Agency temporaries and regular part-time workers, on the other hand, had less dispersed earnings compared with regular full-time workers. In 1997, the 90/10 ratio for agency temporaries was 3.47 and for part-time workers it was 3.16, compared with 4.0 for regular full-time workers. The smaller 90/10 ratios, combined with the lower means and medians, indicate that agency temporaries and part-time workers fairly uniformly earned less than regular full-time workers. Only contract company workers had mean and median hourly earnings that were not significantly different from the earnings of regular full-time workers.

Regression Results

Given the wide variation in the characteristics of workers in nonstandard arrangements, it is possible that some of the differences in earnings

Table 5

Mean, Median, and Selected Deciles of Real Hourly Earnings by Employment Arrangement, February 1995 and February 1997[†]

Earnings measures	Agency temporaries	On-call workers	Direct-hire temporaries	Contract company workers	Independent contractors	Regular self-employed	Regular part-time	Regular full-time
1995								
Mean	$9.16	$11.76	$10.76	$13.83	$17.68	$16.66	$9.16	$14.28
	(.325)	(.411)	(.270)	(.601)	(.316)	(.333)	(.241)	(.145)
Median	7.37	8.43	7.87	11.33	13.16	11.81	6.32	11.97
Ninth decile	16.20	22.22	21.06	26.97	36.86	35.90	15.89	24.91
First decile	5.00	4.58	4.48	5.32	4.96	4.30	4.48	6.32
1997								
Mean	10.39	11.96	11.19	15.44	19.66	18.84	8.78	14.52
	(.424)	(.495)	(.307)	(.680)	(.401)	(.491)	(.188)	(.142)
Median	7.92	8.57	8.00	12.05	13.00	11.54	6.50	12.02
Ninth decile	18.00	21.42	22.50	30.00	40.00	40.00	15.00	25.00
First decile	5.19	4.81	4.75	5.50	5.00	4.10	4.75	6.25

[†] Hourly earnings were calculated for all workers and converted to 1997 dollars using the February 1997 CPI-U as a deflator. Hourly earnings were restricted to between $2.00 and $150.00. All estimates were calculated using supplement weights, where the weights for regular part-time and regular full-time workers were inflated since earnings were collected only for the quarter of these workers in outgoing rotations. The parenthetical terms are standard errors, which were calculated using pseudo-cluster and strata codes to account for the complex sample design of the CPS.

noted previously may be due to the characteristics of the workers filling the jobs rather than the arrangements themselves. To control for the effects of observed differences among workers, multivariate analysis was conducted. Table 6 reports the results for 1995 and 1997 of ordinary least-squares regression models where the dependent variable is the real hourly wage.[14] In each model, controls were included for age, age squared, gender, race, ethnicity, marital status, school enrollment, educational attainment, region, poverty area, population density, industry (19 categories), occupation (9 categories), tenure with the employer, and tenure squared.[15] The analysis also included 0, 1 dummy variables for each nonstandard arrangement, where the omitted category was regular full-time workers. For the other categorical variables, the excluded categories were white, high school diploma, Northeast, suburb, nondurable manufacturing, and machine operators.

The coefficient estimates revealed that in both years agency temporaries, regular part-time workers, and direct-hire temporaries earned significantly less than regular full-time workers, even when other factors were controlled for. Specifically, in 1995, agency temporaries on average earned $1.30 per hour less, regular part-time workers earned $0.49 less, and direct-hire temporaries earned $0.46 less than did regular full-time workers. Agency temporaries and direct-hire temporaries earned more in 1997 than they did in 1995; however, when other factors were controlled for, the differences in real earnings were not statistically significant.

Independent contractors earned significantly more than regular full-time workers in 1995 and 1997, as did the regular self-employed in 1997, even when controlling for other characteristics. Both independent contractors and regular self-employed workers earned significantly more in 1997 than in 1995, which suggests that the decline in the number of regular self-employed (observed in table 1) was among the least financially successful.

Similar to the self-employed, contract company workers earned significantly more than regular full-time workers in 1997 when other factors were controlled for, while the difference was not statistically significant in 1995. Contract company workers' higher earnings in 1997 suggest that at least part of the growth in this arrangement was among comparatively high earners.

Somewhat surprisingly, and contrary to the simple means and medians, hourly earnings of on-call workers were not statistically different from the earnings of regular full-time workers. This finding indicates

TABLE 6

OLS Earnings Regressions of Mean Real Hourly Earnings,
February 1995 and February 1997[1]

Characteristic	Real hourly earnings	
	1995	1997
Agency temporaries	-1.299°°°	-0.790°°°
	(0.309)	(0.391)
On-call workers	0.443	0.051
	(0.393)	(0.464)
Direct-hire temporaries	-0.461°	-0.555°
	(0.272)	(0.330)
Contract company workers	-0.376	1.157°°
	(0.502)	(0.558)
Independent contractors	1.355°°°	3.289°°°
	(0.339)	(0.414)
Regular self-employed	0.537	2.883°°°
	(0.377)	(0.501)
Regular part-time	-0.486°	-0.840°°°
	(0.289)	(0.230)
Age	0.301°°°	0.342°°°
	(0.039)	(0.040)
Age squared	-0.0030°°°	-0.0038°°°
	(0.0005)	(0.0005)
Female	-2.335°°°	-2.509°°°
	(0.169)	(0.185)
Black	-1.023°°°	-0.913°°°
	(0.253)	(0.234)
Other	-0.512°	-0.776°°
	(0.273)	(0.342)
Hispanic	-1.316°°°	-1.090°°°
	(0.225)	(0.279)
Less than high school diploma	-1.020°°°	-1.208°°°
	(0.186)	(0.179)
Some college, no degree	0.966°°°	0.978°°°
	(0.152)	(0.171)
Bachelor's degree	4.480°°°	4.281°°°
	(0.300)	(0.291)
Advanced degree	8.488°°°	8.281°°°
	(0.530)	(0.490)
Married	0.636°°°	1.005°°°
	(0.179)	(0.172)
Enrolled	0.355	0.496°
	(0.266)	(0.256)
Tenure	0.346°°°	0.297°°°
	(0.032)	(0.031)

TABLE 6 (Continued)

OLS Earnings Regressions of Mean Real Hourly Earnings,
February 1995 and February 1997[†]

	Real hourly earnings	
Characteristic	1995	1997
Tenure squared	-0.004°°°	-0.003°°°
	(0.001)	(0.001)
South	-1.058°°°	-1.319°°°
	(0.228)	(0.257)
Midwest	-0.977°°°	-0.768°°°
	(0.246)	(0.278)
West	0.130	-0.138
	(0.260)	(0.286)
Central city	-0.573°°°	-0.298
	(0.185)	(0.217)
Rural	-1.645°°°	-1.958°°°
	(0.200)	(0.167)

[†] The dependent variable was hourly earnings in 1997 dollars. Both specifications include an intercept and controls for industry and occupation. Excluded categories include white, high school graduate, suburb, Northeast, regular full-time worker, industry, and occupation. All estimates were calculated using supplement weights adjusted for missing earnings data and nonresponse to the tenure question. The numbers in parentheses are standard errors, which were calculated using pseudo-cluster and strata codes to account for the complex sample design of the CPS.

° significance of the coefficient estimate at the .10 level
°° significance of the coefficient estimate at the .05 level
°°° significance of the coefficient estimate at the .01 level

that it was not the on-call arrangement per se that led to lower wages for on-call workers but rather some combination of the occupation, industry, and personal characteristics of these workers.

Other differences that are not accounted for in our regressions could influence wages. These include firm-specific factors, personal tastes, and other unobserved characteristics that might influence who is in these arrangements.[16] Nevertheless, the estimates presented in table 6 indicate that when many characteristics are controlled for agency temporaries, regular part-time workers, and direct-hire temporaries still earned less than regular full-time workers. On the other end of the spectrum, independent contractors, along with regular self-employed and contract company workers in 1997, earned significantly more than regular full-time workers.

Health Insurance

Another important measure of economic well-being and security is health insurance coverage.[17] From a worker's perspective, having health insurance coverage is likely to be more important than the source. Indeed, if individuals are covered through a family member's health plan or another affiliation, they may be willing to trade health insurance provided by their employer for higher wages. From the employers' perspective, however, the key issue is whether the company itself is providing health insurance, as that affects the costs of employee compensation, retention, and recruitment.

To address both sides of the issue, we estimated the proportion of individuals in each arrangement who are covered by health insurance, regardless of the source, as well as the proportion who do or could receive health insurance directly from their employers.[18] We refer to the former as being covered by health insurance and the latter as being offered health insurance. Table 7 contains estimates of the coverage and offer rates, with no controls for workers' characteristics. Table 8 contains probit estimates of the probabilities of being covered by health insurance from any source and of being offered health insurance by one's employer. Each probit model includes controls for age, gender, race, ethnicity, educational attainment, marital status, school enrollment, region, population density, occupation (11 categories), and industry (19 categories). Dummy variables, defined with respect to regular full-time workers, are included for all applicable work arrangements.

The coverage model is estimated for all workers, but the offer model is restricted to wage and salary workers. Excluded are all the regular self-employed and the vast majority of independent contractors who are self-employed, for whom obtaining health insurance through their "employer" means they obtain it on their own.[19] Another specification of the offer probit model includes hourly earnings as a control variable in order to see whether there was some trade-off between wages and the offer of health insurance benefits or whether, instead, workers with low wages also had low benefits. Both the simple proportions and the probit models were calculated separately for 1995 and 1997.

Proportions

In both years, individuals in every nonstandard work arrangement were less likely at a statistically significant level to be covered by health insurance from any source than were regular full-time workers. For instance, 48.2% of agency temporaries and 68.5% of on-call workers had

TABLE 7

Proportion of Workers with Health Insurance Coverage by Employment Arrangement, February 1995 and February 1997

Type of employment arrangement	February 1995		February 1997	
	% with health insurance coverage	% offered health insurance by their employer[a]	% with health insurance coverage	% offered health insurance by their employer[a]
Agency temporaries	45.48	21.51	48.15	25.80
On-call workers	64.80	28.02	68.51	32.65
Direct-hire temporaries	73.34	41.26	74.12	39.53
Contract company workers	73.76	65.73	83.10	72.85
Independent contractors	74.10	([b])	74.64	([b])
Regular self-employed	82.61	([c])	82.30	([c])
Regular part-time	75.50	36.46	77.06	34.92
Regular full-time	87.68	85.58	87.59	85.75

[a] Individuals who have health insurance from their employers or could have participated in employer-provided health insurance. Sample was restricted to wage and salary employees.

[b] Not reported due to the selective subsample imposed by restricting the sample to wage and salary workers.

[c] Not applicable.

TABLE 8

Probit Estimates of the Probability of a Specified Arrangement Having Health Insurance Coverage, February 1995 and February 1997[a]

Characteristic	Covered by health insurance from any source		Offered health insurance by their employer[b]			
	1995	1997	1995	1997	1995 including earnings	1997 including earnings
Agency temporaries	-1.240*** [-0.395]	-1.210*** [-0.380]	-1.881*** [-0.652]	-1.804*** [-0.633]	-1.867*** [-0.649]	-1.751*** [-0.618]
On-call workers	-0.695*** [-0.187]	-0.635*** [-0.165]	-1.551*** [-0.558]	-1.481*** [-0.535]	-1.555*** [-0.558]	-1.466*** [-0.526]
Direct-hire temporaries	-0.646*** [-0.170]	-0.639*** [-0.165]	-1.280*** [-0.463]	-1.329*** [-0.480]	-1.368*** [-0.493]	-1.309*** [-0.468]
Contract company workers	-0.588*** [-0.153]	-0.351*** [-0.080]	-0.742*** [-0.256]	-0.623*** [-0.209]	-0.682*** [-0.230]	-0.645*** [-0.212]
Independent contractors	-0.601*** [-0.151]	-0.578*** [-0.142]	(c)	(c)	(c)	(c)
Regular self-employed	-0.379*** [-0.087]	-0.417*** [-0.096]	(c)	(c)	(c)	(c)
Regular part-time	-0.408*** [-0.092]	-0.392*** [-0.087]	-1.137*** [-0.391]	-1.202*** [-0.413]	-1.126*** [-0.384]	-1.213*** [-0.410]
Age	0.021*** [0.004]	0.017*** [0.003]	0.005*** [0.001]	0.005*** [0.001]	0.0029* [0.0008]	0.005*** [0.001]
Female	0.031 [0.006]	0.029 [0.005]	-0.122*** [-0.034]	-0.075*** [-0.020]	-0.093** [-0.025]	-0.030 [-0.008]
Black	-0.161*** [-0.033]	-0.146*** [-0.029]	0.092*** [0.024]	0.090*** [0.024]	0.059 [0.015]	0.092 [0.023]
Other	-0.283***	-0.261***	-0.038	-0.014	0.039	-0.021

	(1)	(2)	(3)	(4)	(5)	(6)
(previous row SE)	[-0.063]	[-0.056]	[-0.011]	[-0.004]	[0.010]	[-0.006]
Hispanic	-0.481°°°	-0.567°°°	-0.271°°°	-0.221°°°	-0.188°°°	-0.240°°°
	[-0.115]	[-0.137]	[-0.081]	[-0.065]	[-0.054]	[-0.068]
Less than a high school diploma	-0.310°°°	-0.253°°°	-0.253°°°	-0.273°°°	-0.178°°°	-0.294°°°
	[-0.068]	[-0.053]	[-0.075]	[-0.080]	[-0.051]	[-0.084]
Some college, no degree	0.117°°°	0.121°°°	0.095°°°	0.133°°°	0.047	0.146°°°
	[0.022]	[0.022]	[0.026]	[0.035]	[0.012]	[0.037]
Bachelor's degree	0.403°°°	0.381°°°	0.260°°°	0.270°°°	0.184°°°	0.186°°°
	[0.065]	[0.061]	[0.066]	[0.067]	[0.046]	[0.046]
Advanced degree	0.564°°°	0.494°°°	0.361°°°	0.439°°°	0.137	0.277°°°
	[0.080]	[0.071]	[0.086]	[0.100]	[0.035]	[0.064]
Married	0.397°°°	0.438°°°	0.080°°°	0.124°°°	0.013	0.098°°°
	[0.080]	[0.087]	[0.022]	[0.034]	[0.003]	[0.026]
Enrolled	0.978°°°	0.889°°°	-0.421°°°	0.411°°°	-0.456°°°	-0.298°°°
	[0.107]	[0.100]	[-0.133]	[-0.128]	[-0.143]	[-0.087]
Central city	-0.158°°°	-0.165°°°	-0.014	-0.062	0.038	-0.085°°
	[-0.031]	[-0.032]	[-0.004]	[-0.017]	[-0.010]	[-0.023]
Rural	-0.176°°°	-0.144°°°	-0.165°°°	-0.159°°°	-0.120°°	-0.063
	[-0.036]	[-0.028]	[-0.047]	[-0.045]	[-0.033]	[-0.017]
Hourly earnings	(c)	(c)	(c)	(c)	0.023°°°	0.032°°°
	(c)	(c)	(c)	(c)	[0.006]	[0.008]

a All models include an intercept and controls for industry and occupation. Excluded categories include white, high school graduate, suburb, Northeast, and regular full-time workers. All estimates were calculated using supplement weights. The weights for specifications using earnings data were adjusted to account for missing earnings data. The bracketed terms are the derivatives of the probability of having health insurance with respect to a change in the explanatory variable, evaluated at the mean of the explanatory variable. Standard errors for the coefficient estimates were calculated using pseudo-cluster and strata codes to account for the complex sample design of the CPS.

b Individuals who have health insurance from their employers or could have participated in employer-provided health insurance. Sample was restricted to wage and salary employees.

c Not applicable.

° significance of the coefficient estimate at the .10 level

°° significance of the coefficient estimate at the .05 level

°°° significance of the coefficient estimate at the .01 level

health insurance from any source in 1997, compared with 87.6% of regular full-time workers. The arrangement with the coverage rate consistently closest to that of regular full-time workers was regular self-employment (table 7).

The vast majority of regular full-time workers with health insurance were able to receive it from their employers. In contrast, only 25.8% of agency temporaries, 32.6% of on-call workers, 39.5% of direct-hire temporaries, and 34.9% of regular part-time workers were offered health insurance by their employers in 1997.[20] In general, the offer rates for nonstandard workers increased between 1995 and 1997, although the only statistically significant difference was for on-call workers.[21]

In sum, the estimates in table 7 indicate that individuals in nonstandard work arrangements were less likely both to be covered by health insurance from any source and to be offered health insurance by their employer. However, without controlling for other factors, it is difficult to discern whether these lower rates are the result of the arrangements themselves or a function of workers' occupations, industries, and personal characteristics. To disentangle these factors, we turn to the probit estimates.

Probit Estimates

The probit estimates in the first two columns of table 8 indicate that, compared with regular full-time workers, individuals in nonstandard work arrangements were significantly less likely to be covered by health insurance from any source, even when controlling for other factors. The bracketed number below each coefficient estimate is the percentage point change in the probability of being covered by health insurance if an individual has the specified characteristic or is in a particular arrangement. Comparisons of the percentage point change estimates from the probit models with the proportions in table 7 indicate that the industry, occupation, and personal characteristics of agency temporaries, on-call workers, and regular part-time workers do help to explain why workers in these arrangements were less likely to be covered. Even controlling for other factors, however, agency temporaries were 38.0 percentage points less likely to have health insurance coverage than were regular full-time workers, while on-call workers were 16.5 percentage points less likely, and regular part-time workers were 8.7 percentage points less likely.

Perhaps even more interesting, the estimated percentage point differences in health insurance coverage between regular full-time workers and regular self-employed workers, independent contractors, direct-hire temporaries, and contract company workers from the probit models were larger than the simple proportions indicated, generally by 2 to 3 percentage points. This could suggest that these workers are less risk-averse with regard to health care expenses than comparable regular full-time workers or, for those who were not self-employed, that they were less able to obtain health insurance from their employers. The probit estimates of the probability of being offered health insurance by their employers, presented later, help to shed light on the latter hypothesis for direct-hire temporaries and contract company employees.

The third and fourth columns of table 8 contain estimates of the probability of workers being offered health insurance by their employer when controlling for various demographic and job characteristics but not for wages. These estimates indicate that agency temporaries, on-call workers, direct-hire temporaries, contract company workers, and regular part-time workers were significantly less likely to be offered health insurance by their employers, even when controlling for other factors. Further, the estimated percentage point differences between regular full-time workers and direct-hire temporaries, contract company workers, and agency temporaries are larger in the probit models than in the proportions shown in table 7. This implies that neither the observed characteristics of the workers nor their industries and occupations can account for their lower offer rates.

On the other hand, the estimated percentage point differences from the probit models for on-call and regular part-time workers were smaller than the differences in the proportions. This suggests that in these instances the smaller likelihood of being offered health insurance is not simply due to the arrangements. Nevertheless, in 1997, even controlling for other factors, on-call workers were 54 percentage points less likely to be offered health insurance than were regular full-time workers, while regular part-time workers were 41 percentage points less likely.

The lower probability of agency temporaries, on-call workers, direct-hire temporaries, contract company workers, and regular part-time workers being offered health insurance suggests that employers may be using these arrangements to reduce costs. Of course, some workers could be trading off health insurance for higher wages, in which case there may be no cost savings to employers. To test this hypothesis, hourly earnings were included as a control variable. The coefficient estimates in the last two columns in table 8 indicate that, in both 1995 and 1997, having a higher wage significantly increased the probability of being offered health insurance. Furthermore, while the percentage point differences between regular full-time workers and those in the other arrangements in the probability of being offered health insurance decreased slightly when hourly earnings were controlled for, the differences remained large and of roughly the same magnitude as when earnings were not included. Consequently, there is relatively little evidence that individuals in nonstandard arrangements are trading off health insurance for higher wages. Instead, the evidence suggests that low-wage jobs tend to have low benefits.

Preference for a Different Type of Arrangement

The final measure of economic well-being we consider is workers' satisfaction with their current situation or, alternatively, their desire to be in a different type of arrangement. Using information from both the supplements and the basic CPS, we constructed a measure of the desire of individuals who were not in regular full-time jobs (with the exception of contract company workers) to be in a different type of arrangement. The constructed categories (based on questions tailored according to the arrangement) were (1) satisfied with work arrangement (would not prefer to be in another arrangement), (2) dissatisfied with arrangement (would prefer to be in another arrangement), or (3) it depends.[22]

The results in table 9 indicate that the degree of satisfaction varies considerably across arrangements. In 1997, fully 69.9% of agency temporaries, 52.7% of on-call workers, and 51.5% of direct-hire temporaries indicated that they were dissatisfied with their arrangement. In contrast, fewer than 10% of independent contractors or the regular self-employed said that they would prefer to be a wage and salary worker. Regular part-time workers were in between the two extremes, with approximately 21% indicating that they would prefer to work full time. Perhaps consistent with an expansionary period, the level of satisfaction generally rose between 1995 and 1997 for those arrangements that were comparable.[23] However, this increase was statistically significant only for agency temporaries and on-call workers.

To examine whether certain types of workers were more satisfied with their arrangements, we turn again to multivariate analysis. Table 10 shows, for each arrangement separately, the results of probit models in which the independent variable is equal to 1 if an individual indicates dissatisfaction with the arrangement and 0 otherwise. The models also include controls for age, gender, race, ethnicity, educational attainment, marital status, school enrollment, region, population density, and poverty area. Because we do not have complete preference data for direct-hire temporaries in 1995, only the results for 1997 are presented.[24]

TABLE 9

Workers by Employment Arrangement and Preference for Current Arrangement,
February 1995 and February 1997

Preference	Agency temporaries	On-call workers	Direct-hire temporaries	Independent contractors	Regular self-employed	Regular part-time
1995						
Dissatisfied	76.22	61.13	48.37	10.59	7.30	21.90
Satisfied	19.32	33.91	33.68	81.90	86.32	67.96
It depends	3.03	3.05	3.85	4.90	4.29	—
Hours full time	—	—	—	—	—	5.91
Data not available	1.43	1.91	14.09	2.61	2.10	4.23
1997						
Dissatisfied	69.91	52.73	51.47	9.98	6.33	21.24
Satisfied	26.12	38.18	41.03	83.11	87.54	67.86
It depends	1.65	5.63	5.49	4.53	3.78	—
Hours full time	—	—	—	—	—	6.89
Data not available	2.32	3.46	2.01	2.39	2.35	4.00

Note: All numbers are percentages. Dash indicates not applicable.

Table 10
Probit Estimates of the Probability of Being Dissatisfied with Current Employment Arrangement, February 1997[1]

Characteristic	Agency temporaries	On-call workers	Direct-hire temporaries	Independent contractors	Regular self-employed	Regular part-time
Age	-0.021***	-0.023***	-0.018***	-0.0057**	-0.0053	-0.023***
	[-0.006]	[-0.009]	[-0.007]	[-0.0009]	[-0.0006]	[-0.006]
Female	-0.231	-0.106	-0.082	-0.017	0.128	-0.188***
	[-0.067]	[-0.042]	[-0.033]	[-0.003]	[0.014]	[-0.050]
Black	0.258	0.186	0.254*	0.323**	0.029	0.442***
	[0.072]	[0.073]	[0.100]	[0.064]	[0.003]	[0.131]
Other	-0.0017	0.674**	0.121	-0.224	0.368**	0.120
	[-0.0005]	[0.245]	[0.048]	[-0.032]	[0.052]	[0.032]
Hispanic	0.114	0.047	0.224	0.121	0.586***	0.450***
	[0.032]	[0.019]	[0.089]	[0.021]	[0.096]	[0.134]
Less than high school diploma	0.087	-0.038	-0.003	-0.390***	-0.077	-0.050
	[0.025]	[0.015]	[-0.001]	[0.079]	[-0.008]	[-0.013]
Some college, no degree	0.133	0.065	0.108	0.089	-0.281***	-0.071***
	[0.038]	[0.026]	[0.043]	[0.015]	[-0.028]	[-0.018]
Bachelor's degree	-0.245	0.106	0.019	-0.155	-0.531***	-0.409***
	[-0.077]	[0.042]	[0.008]	[-0.024]	[-0.045]	[-0.089]
Advanced degree	-0.163	0.046	0.023	-0.196	-0.484***	-0.105
	[-0.051]	[0.018]	[0.009]	[-0.030]	[-0.040]	[-0.025]
Married	-0.331*	-0.044	-0.024	-0.121*	-0.180*	-0.400***
	[-0.093]	[-0.017]	[-0.009]	[-0.021]	[-0.021]	[-0.100]
Enrolled	-0.855**	-0.722***	-1.278***	-0.123	0.572	-1.663***
	[-0.307]	[-0.276]	[-0.464]	[-0.019]	[0.096]	[-0.307]

South	-0.508°°	-0.270°	0.012	-0.102	-0.097	-0.091
	[-0.159]	[-0.108]	[0.005]	[-0.016]	[-0.010]	[-0.023]
Midwest	-0.283	-0.125	0.059	-0.160	-0.072	-0.072
	[-0.087]	[-0.050]	[0.023]	[-0.025]	[-0.008]	[-0.018]
West	-0.275	0.140	-0.022	-0.113	-0.073	0.154°°
	[-0.085]	[0.056]	[-0.009]	[-0.018]	[-0.008]	[0.041]
Central city	0.231	-0.230	0.085	0.156°°	-0.100	0.100°°
	[0.067]	[-0.092]	[0.034]	[0.027]	[-0.010]	[0.026]
Rural	0.282	0.119	-0.185	-0.087	0.104	0.210°°°
	[0.075]	[0.047]	[-0.074]	[-0.014]	[0.012]	[0.057]
Poverty	-0.282	0.128	0.265°°	0.129	0.114	0.154°°
	[-0.088]	[0.051]	[0.105]	[0.023]	[0.013]	[0.041]

† All models also include an intercept. Excluded categories include white, high school graduate, suburb, and Northeast. All estimates were calculated using supplement weights. Standard errors for the coefficient estimates were calculated using pseudo-cluster and strata codes to account for the complex sample design of the CPS. The bracketed terms are the derivatives of the probability of being dissatisfied with the current employment arrangement with respect to a change in the explanatory variable, evaluated at the mean of the explanatory variable.

° significance of the coefficient estimate at the .10 level
°° significance of the coefficient estimate at the .05 level
°°° significance of the coefficient estimate at the .01 level

One almost universal result is that being a year older significantly decreases the probability of workers being dissatisfied with their particular arrangement (except self-employment). This effect of age on satisfaction, and the decreasing probability by age of being in nonstandard arrangements, may reflect the fact that older individuals are further along in their careers and thus are more likely to have deliberately chosen their work arrangement.

Also apparently reflecting individuals' choices, workers appear to use nonstandard arrangements while in school to balance paid work with their studies. According to the probit estimates, part-time workers and agency temporaries who were in school were 30.7 percentage points less likely to say they were dissatisfied than other agency temporaries. Similarly, students were 27.6 percentage points less likely to be dissatisfied with working on call and 46.4 percentage points less likely to be dissatisfied with working as a direct-hire temporary than were those in these arrangements who were not enrolled in school.

Being married also significantly increased the probability of preferring several of the work arrangements. For instance, compared with their unmarried counterparts, married part-time workers were 10.0 percentage points less likely to be dissatisfied, and independent contractors and the self-employed were 2.1 points less likely, confirming the notion that these arrangements may help some workers accommodate family commitments.[25]

The effect of other demographic characteristics on satisfaction, however, suggests that even in arrangements where most workers are highly satisfied there are subgroups that have accepted that type of nonstandard employment involuntarily. For instance, the simple proportions show that 21.1% of blacks were dissatisfied with being independent contractors in 1997, compared with just under 10% of all independent contractors. Marginal probabilities derived from the probit estimates indicate a smaller differential, but being black still increased the probability of dissatisfaction with independent contracting by 6.4 percentage points. Other nonwhites were 5.2 percentage points more likely than whites to say that they were dissatisfied with being in regular self-employment when other factors were controlled for. Similarly, Hispanics were 9.6 percentage points more likely than non-Hispanics to indicate dissatisfaction with being in regular self-employment and 13.4 percentage points more likely to be dissatisfied with being regular part-time workers.

In summary, there is considerable variation in the level of satisfaction across the work arrangements. At one end of the spectrum, the regular self-employed and independent contractors seem quite satisfied with their arrangements. At the other end, most agency temporaries would rather be in a permanent position or one not intermediated by an agency. However, even in arrangements with high levels of dissatisfaction, there are sizable numbers who prefer that type of work. School enrollment and marriage increase the probability of being satisfied for agency temporaries, on-call workers, direct-hire temporaries, and regular part-time workers, suggesting that these arrangements may help some individuals balance paid work with other activities. On the other side, within the arrangements with high levels of satisfaction, there were groups of workers who expressed lower levels of satisfaction. Blacks, other nonwhites, and Hispanics were less likely to be satisfied with independent contracting and self-employment, suggesting that these minorities may be more likely to enter into such work because of a lack of alternatives.

Conclusion

The goal of this chapter was to examine the incidence and composition of nonstandard employment, as well as the economic consequences for workers in these arrangements. Our estimates show that agency temporaries, on-call workers, direct-hire temporaries, contract company workers, and independent contractors together constituted 12.5% of the employed in both February 1995 and February 1997. If regular self-employed and regular part-time workers are included, the proportion of workers who were not in regular full-time positions was 32.2% in 1995 and 31.3% in 1997.

The characteristics of workers in these arrangements vary considerably, however, as do the types of jobs they perform. Measures of job quality such as earnings and satisfaction also differ greatly. In short, our findings show that there is virtually nothing that conceptually or empirically ties together agency temporaries, on-call workers, direct-hire temporaries, contract company workers, independent contractors, regular self-employed workers, and regular part-time workers, except that they are not in regular full-time jobs.[26] For these reasons, we believe that combining all of these workers into a single category would be arbitrary and misleading and that all jobs in nonstandard arrangements cannot be automatically classified as "bad jobs."

Notes

[1] Examples of researchers who considered these arrangements to be "bad jobs" include Appelbaum (1989), Belous (1989), Callaghan and Hartmann (1991), Jorgensen (1999), Kalleberg et al. (1997), Parker (1994), and Rogers (1995).

[2] For detailed information on the concepts and methods behind the Current Population Survey, see the Explanatory Note in any 1997 issue of *Employment and Earnings*.

[3] The supplement was repeated again in February 1999; results are available from Bureau of Labor Statistics (BLS).

[4] A 1989 BLS Industry Wage Survey indicated that permanent full-time staff constituted 3.2% of employment in the help supply services industry.

[5] For a detailed explanation of the questions in the Contingent and Alternative Work Arrangement supplements, see Polivka (1996a).

[6] Throughout this paper, all estimates were calculated using supplement weights. Standard errors also were estimated using supplement weights, as well as pseudo-cluster and strata codes, in order to generate estimates that account for the complex survey design of the CPS. We would like to thank Carol Gunlick of the Census Bureau for constructing these codes. In general, in this text we discuss only differences that were statistically significant.

[7] For instance, Christensen (1988) states, "Contingent work is an umbrella term used to describe changes in employer-employee relations. It typically covers a variety of forms including part-time, temporary, self-employed, independent contracting, and occasionally home based arrangements." Christensen and Murphree (1988) write, "Workers are being hired on a part-time, temporary contractual, or leased basis. Collectively, this trend has been referred to as the 'contingent workforce.'" Dillon (1988) states, "Contingent workers include in their ranks part-time workers, temporary workers, self-employed, contract workers, at home workers, and leased employees." Christopherson (1988) states, "In addition to growth in the part-time workforce, other forms of contingent work have emerged, including a large temporary industry workforce." See also Belous (1989), Blank (1998), and Kalleberg et al. (1997).

[8] BLS has constructed three measures of contingent work using data from the February CPS supplements. BLS defines a contingent worker as an individual who does not have an explicit or implicit contract for long-term employment. The BLS measures rely on workers' current job tenure, expected tenure, and their perception that their job was temporary or would not last as long as they desired for an economic reason. For a further explanation of BLS's measures of contingent work, see Polivka (1996a).

[9] Persons of Hispanic origin, which is an ethnicity rather than a race, are included in the white, black, and other nonwhite population groups.

[10] Given that the primary interest is in descriptive statistics, as opposed to a dynamic choice model of employment, probit models were used instead of a multinomial logit or a multinomial probit.

[11] For independent continuous variables, these derivatives provide an estimate of the effect of a one-unit change. For independent categorical variables, such as gender,

the derivatives provide an estimate of the percentage point change if an individual has the specified characteristic. The derivatives are computed as $\hat{\beta}\phi(\bar{X}\,\hat{\beta})$, where $\hat{\beta}$ is the vector of estimated parameters of the probit model, $\bar{X}$ is the vector of the means of the explanatory variables, and ϕ is the standard normal probability density function. For example, in table 3a-1, the bracketed term below the coefficient estimate for school enrollment indicates that students were 6.7 percentage points more likely to be on-call workers than were regular full-time workers.

[12] Occupation and industry were not included in the probit analysis, as they are not considered characteristics of the individual, but rather the result of individuals' employment choices.

[13] Weekly earnings data for regular full-time and regular part-time workers were collected in the basic CPS from the one quarter of the sample that was in the outgoing rotations, while for other workers, they were collected in the supplement. The questions were identical in the basic CPS and the supplement. Supplement weights (which account for nonresponse to the supplement) were used in all of the analyses; however, they were adjusted for regular full-time and regular part-time workers to account for the fact that their earnings information was collected only for a portion of the sample. Hourly wages were constructed from weekly earnings using the methodology outlined in Polivka (1998), were restricted to those between $2.00 and $150.00 an hour, and were converted to real earnings using the February 1997 Consumer Price Index for All Urban Consumers (CPI-U) as a deflator.

[14] The level, rather than the log of real hourly earnings, was used as the dependent variable due to the right skewness of the earnings distribution (greater frequency of higher earnings) of the regular self-employed and independent contractors.

[15] For a construction of tenure, see Houseman and Polivka (1999). The OLS earnings regression was estimated using weights that accounted for nonresponse to both the earnings and tenure questions.

[16] Refining estimates of the effects of the various arrangements on earnings to control for individuals' propensity to select an arrangement will be an area of future research by the authors.

[17] Ferber and Waldfogel (this volume) discuss the impact of some types of nonstandard work on other benefits.

[18] Individuals were classified as having health insurance if they answered affirmatively to the question, "Do you have health insurance from any source?" Individuals were classified as being covered by employer-provided health insurance if they received health insurance from their employer or if they could have participated in employer-provided health insurance, even if they opted out of receiving coverage.

[19] Given that the regular self-employed are excluded from the estimation, a dummy variable for this group is not included in the offer probit model. A dummy variable for independent contractors is included for those classified as wage and salary workers. However, the parameter estimates for this variable are not reported due to the restricted nature of this subgroup of independent contractors.

[20] These proportions were all significantly lower than the proportion for regular full-time workers at standard statistical levels.

[21] A comparison of changes in the offer rates among the various types of arrangements between 1995 and 1997 suggests that the provision of health insurance by employers who hire workers directly is declining but that provision by employment intermediaries is increasing. For instance, the offer rates for agency temporaries and contract companies increased 4.3 and 7.1 percentage points, respectively, between 1995 and 1997, while the offer rates for part-time workers and direct-hire temporaries declined 1.5 and 1.7 percentage points, respectively. However, none of the changes from 1995 to 1997 in the differences in the offer rates between directly hired workers and those with intermediate arrangements were statistically significant at standard levels.

[22] These categories were constructed from questions that were tailored to the worker's arrangement. Regular full-time workers were not asked whether they would like to work in a different type of arrangement.

[23] In 1997, the satisfaction measure covered all direct-hire temporaries. However, in 1995, some direct hires—namely, potentially contingent workers who expected to be employed longer than a year—were not asked whether they preferred a nontemporary job. Thus, the 1995 and 1997 estimates for direct-hire temporaries were not strictly comparable. Information on contract company workers' preference for their arrangement was not collected.

[24] Estimates for February 1995 are available from the authors upon request.

[25] In general, the effect of marriage on the probability of being dissatisfied with an arrangement did not differ significantly by gender, with the exception of part-time workers. Coefficient estimates from a probit model that included an interaction term for married women indicated that they were significantly less likely to be dissatisfied with working part time, while marriage was estimated to have no statistically significant effect on the probability of men being dissatisfied with working part time.

[26] Workers in these arrangements do tend to have lower levels of health insurance coverage, but high-wage self-employed workers' not purchasing health insurance is quite different from low-wage agency temporaries' not being offered health insurance by their employer.

References

Appelbaum, Eileen. 1989. "The Growth in the U.S. Contingent Labor Force." In Robert Drago and Richard Perlman, eds., *Microeconomic Issues in Labour Economics*. New York: Harvester Wheatsheaf.

Belous, Richard S. 1989. *The Contingent Economy: The Growth of the Temporary, Part-Time and Subcontracted Workforce*. NPA Report 239. Washington, DC: National Planning Association.

Blank, Rebecca M. 1998. "Contingent Work in a Changing Labor Market." In Richard B. Freeman and Peter Gottschalk, eds., *Generating Jobs: How to Increase Demand for Less-Skilled Workers*. New York: Russell Sage.

Brophy, B. 1987. "The 'Just in Time' Worker." *U.S. News and World Report*, Vol. 103, no. 21, pp. 45-46.

Callaghan, Polly, and Heidi Hartmann. 1991. *Contingent Work: A Chart Book on Part-Time and Temporary Employment.* Washington, DC: Economic Policy Institute.

Carnevale, A. P. 1994. "The Growing Contingent Workforce: Flexibility at the Price of Fairness." Labor and Human Resources Conference, testimony before U.S. Senate Subcommittee on Labor.

Castro, Janice. 1993. "Disposable Workers." *Time,* Vol. 140, no. 1, pp. 43-47.

Christensen, Kathleen. 1988a. "Rising Use of Part-Time and Temporary Workers: Who Benefits and Who Loses." Testimony before the Committee on Government Operations, U.S. House of Representatives. Washington, DC: U.S. Government Printing Office.

Christensen, Kathleen. 1988b. "Women's Labor Force Attachment: Rise of Contingent Work." In *Flexible Workstyles: A Look at Contingent Labor.* Washington, DC: U.S. Department of Labor Women's Bureau.

Christensen, Kathleen, and Mary Murphree. 1988. "Introduction." In *Flexible Workstyles: A Look at Contingent Labor.* Washington, DC: U.S. Department of Labor Women's Bureau.

Christopherson, Susan. 1988. "Production Organization and Worktime: The Emergence of a Contingent Labor Market." In *Flexible Workstyles: A Look at Contingent Labor.* Washington, DC: U.S. Department of Labor Women's Bureau.

Cohany, Sharon R. 1998. "Workers in Alternative Employment Arrangements: A Second Look." *Monthly Labor Review,* Vol. 121 (November), pp. 3-21.

Dillon, Rodger. 1988. "The Changing Labor Market—Contingent Workers." Testimony before the Committee on Government Operations, U.S. House of Representatives. Washington, DC: U.S. Government Printing Office.

Freedman, Audrey. 1985. *The New Look in Wage Policy and Employee Relations.* Conference Board Report No. 865. New York: Conference Board.

Hipple, Steven. 1998. "Contingent Work: Results from the Second Survey." *Monthly Labor Review,* Vol. 121 (November), pp. 22-35.

Houseman, Susan N., and Anne E. Polivka. 1999. "The Implications of Flexible Staffing Arrangements for Job Stability." Upjohn Institute Staff Working Paper 99-56; BLS Working Paper 317. Kalamazoo, MI: W. E. Upjohn Institute for Employment Research and Washington, DC: Bureau of Labor Statistics.

Jorgensen, Helene J. 1999. *When Good Jobs Go Bad.* Washington, DC: 2030 Center.

Kalleberg, Arne L., Edith Rasell, Naomi Cassirer, Barbara F. Reskin, Ken Hudson, David Webster, Eileen Appelbaum, and Roberta M. Spalter-Roth. 1997. *Nonstandard Work, Substandard Jobs: Flexible Work Arrangements in the U.S.* Washington, DC: Economic Policy Institute.

Parker, R. E. 1994. *Flesh Peddlers and Warm Bodies: The Temporary Help Industry and Its Workers.* New Brunswick, NJ: Rutgers University Press.

Polivka, Anne E. 1996a. "Contingent and Alternative Work Arrangements, Defined." *Monthly Labor Review,* Vol. 119 (October), pp. 3–9.

Polivka, Anne E. 1996b. "Into Contingent and Alternative Employment: By Choice?" *Monthly Labor Review,* Vol. 119 (October), pp. 55–74.

Polivka, Anne E. 1998. "Using Earnings Data from the Current Population Survey after the Redesign." BLS Working Paper No. 306. Washington, DC: Bureau of Labor Statistics.

Rogers, Jackie K. 1995. "Just a Temp: Experience and Structure of Alienation in Temporary Clerical Employment." *Work & Occupation,* Vol. 22, pp. 137–166.

Schellenbarger, S. 1995. "When Workers' Lives are Contingent on Employers' Whims." *Wall Street Journal,* February 1, p. 4.

U.S. Senate Committee on Labor Resources, 103 Congress. 1993. "Toward a Disposable Workforce: The Increasing Use of 'Contingent Labor.'" Washington, DC: Government Printing Office.

Chapter 3

Limits to Market-Mediated Employment: From Deconstruction to Reconstruction of Internal Labor Markets

Philip Moss, Harold Salzman, and Chris Tilly
University of Massachusetts at Lowell

Is the internal labor market dead? For much of this century, a substantial portion of workers in the United States benefited from internal labor markets (ILMs), featuring guarantees (usually implicit) of long-term employment, as well as access to tenure-linked pay increases and job ladders (Gordon, Edwards, and Reich 1982; Osterman 1988). However, the last two decades have seen considerable evidence of a widespread deconstruction of ILMs in larger firms in the United States (Cappelli 1995; Tilly 1997). Downsizing, outsourcing, job-hopping, and expanded use of contingent labor are the most visible evidence of the unmaking of implicit long-term employment guarantees and career paths within a single enterprise.

Many have argued that the deconstruction of ILMs has resulted in a drop in employment security for most workers (International Labour Organization 1997, p. 94). Instead of offering long-term attachment to a single employer, the "new social contract" is said to place responsibility for designing a career in the hands of the worker, with the employer responsible for alerting the worker to new skill needs—a transformation widely noted in the popular business literature (Mandel 1996; Pasternack and Viscio 1998).

The question of whether the deconstruction of ILMs is reversible and the nature of the new job structures have extremely important implications. In this paper, we are particularly concerned about the decline in within-firm job security and mobility for low-skill workers who face difficulty securing employment in the first place (Holzer 1996; Moss and Tilly 2000). There is evidence that reduced job security and the shift of job mobility from within a company to between companies tend to reduce wage growth for all but the most-skilled workers (Rose

1995; Tilly 1997). Indeed, some analysts (Moss forthcoming; Howell 1997) have linked the collapse of wage levels for low-skill workers in part to the diminished role of ILMs; the growing wage gap between black and white workers with limited experience may also result in part from these changes (Moss and Tilly 1991), because lower-skilled workers have traditionally learned most skills on the job.

Moreover, to the extent that sustained competitive advantage flows in part from the organizational integration of employees, as some have argued (Lazonick and O'Sullivan forthcoming; Jones 1997), "deintegration" may undermine businesses' competitive advantages as well. After all, it has long been argued that ILMs were devised in the first place to solve a variety of performance difficulties, including the principal-agent problem for workers and firms' difficulty in reaping returns from investments in training (Doeringer and Piore 1987, new introduction; Williamson 1985).

Most empirical research on the subject is based, explicitly or implicitly, on the assumption that the decline in the use of long-term employment relations and internal job ladders is a permanent one. (Cappelli et al. [1997] provide a recent, comprehensive review; see also Noyelle [1987] for an important early statement of the argument and Heckscher, this volume.) We contest this assumption of permanence on both theoretical and empirical grounds. Theoretically, we hold, with Tilly and Tilly (1997), that workers' desire for job security and employers' need for a predictable source of adequately skilled workers create strong, continuing pressures to rebuild something akin to ILMs. Further, in our view, restructuring is a protracted process of experimentation, blundering, and learning for most firms, so that attempts to declare the process complete may be premature (Ortmann and Salzman 1998; Tilly and Tilly 1997). Firms grope among alternative strategies, sometimes imitating leading firms (Scott 1987; DiMaggio and Powell 1991), sometimes adopting consultant-driven fads (Eccles, Nohria, and Berkley 1992), and sometimes shifting objectives.

As for empirical evidence, despite case studies suggesting the devolution of ILMs, some aggregate indicators of the vigor of ILMs have changed relatively little (Bernhardt and Marcotte, this volume). The differential in tenure between large and small firms, which one would expect to narrow over time if ILMs have significantly declined, shows no change between the 1980s and 1990s (Allen, Clark, and Schieber 1998). Estimates of the firm-specific components of wages, one way of assessing the extent to which ILMs shelter wages, also show essentially no change

over the last couple of decades (Groshen and Levine 1998). One interpretation of this apparent contradiction between case study and aggregate
data is compositional: the case studies represent changes that characterize
only a small and perhaps atypical subset of firms. But these disparate
findings are also consistent with a world in which firms intermittently tear
down and rebuild ILMs, averaging out to little change in the aggregate.
Smith (forthcoming) reports case study results with a similar flavor: managers at a high-technology manufacturer that uses a large number of temporary employees have found ways to integrate these temporary workers
as quasi-permanent workers. Indeed, even the business press has suggested that, in the words of a *Wall Street Journal* headline, "Hiring a Full
Staff May Be the Next Fad for Management" (Lancaster 1998).

We examined several large corporations that have undergone restructuring and reduced long-term employment at various skill levels. The
financial services and high-technology electronics manufacturing companies under study downsized, outsourced, and increased the size of their
contingent workforces. However, particularly when restructuring jobs at
the higher end of the low-skill spectrum, they found that there were negative effects on quality and innovative capacity. In response, some of
them have partially reconstructed ILMs in a variety of ad hoc ways,
which typically do *not* include reestablishment of previously existing
ILMs. These reactions are far from constituting a countertrend but certainly represent a deviation from the unidirectional dismantling of ILMs
described in much of the literature.

Methods and Data

We conducted case studies of large businesses in insurance and in
high-technology electronics manufacturing during 1996–98. Both industries historically offered jobs at a wide range of skill levels and built
ILMs offering job security as well as wage and/or functional mobility
within the firm. Both industries have experienced product market turbulence, and businesses in each industry have undertaken a variety of
forms of organizational restructuring.

We selected four leading firms in each sector for case studies and
used these cases to generate hypotheses, not to draw general conclusions.
Since these are large, trend-setting businesses in their respective markets, their experiences are likely to be widely noted—and either emu-
lated or avoided—by other companies. In this paper, we focus primarily
on two firms in each industry, which we call Electronicus and Monarch
(electronics) and Steadfast and InsurAll (insurance). We omit many

identifying details to maintain confidentiality for these companies. The two electronics companies are multiplant divisions of larger corporations, subject to guidelines from their corporate parents but enjoying substantial autonomy. In the case of the insurance companies, we studied each corporation as a whole.

In each firm, we spoke with human resource and operations managers, professionals, and frontline workers between 1996 and 1998. Where outsourcing was an issue, we also interviewed purchasing and sourcing managers, and owners or managers of a small number of supplier firms. At the four companies on which we focus in this paper, we conducted a total of 126 interviews, many with multiple respondents, somewhat unevenly distributed across the companies. For three of the four companies (all except Electronicus), we carried out multiple interviews up to two years apart, allowing us to follow changes as they took place.

Our interviews examined the motivation for and nature of corporate restructuring. We asked about a wide range of changes—in organizational form, in job structure, in the "value chain" through practices such as outsourcing—to the extent that they changed job quality, skill levels, or skill-development mechanisms. We attempted to learn how actions, reactions, and adjustments of businesses evolved after the initial decision to restructure. The managers we spoke to were most concerned about how all of these changes affected firm performance and whether they constituted successful competitive strategies.

The processes involved in corporate organizational restructuring are legion. Seven major ones—which often coexist and to some extent overlap—directly affect ILMs for lower-skill jobs:

1. Outsourcing
2. Shifting of some functions to remote sites
3. Expansion of contingent work
4. Abrogation of implicit lifetime employment guarantees (e.g., via downsizing)
5. Broadening of jobs so that more mobility takes place *within* jobs
6. Flattening of the organization (by removing or shrinking levels of supervisory staff)
7. "Rung removal"—filling higher-level jobs by external hires rather than internal promotions

In addition, restructuring possibilities include a variety of organizational changes that do not bear as directly on ILMs: the adoption of high-performance work practices; mergers, acquisitions, or shedding of divisions to focus on perceived "core competencies"; the adoption of two-tier wage and benefit schemes; and so on. Finally, many restructuring actions do not involve revision of organizational form per se: for example, automation, deskilling and upskilling, speedup, changes in product mix, and outright relocation of an entire company.

We saw a wide variety of types of restructuring in our case studies, but in this paper we focus on types 1 through 5, because they are the changes in work organization about which we learned the most. We view these changes as "intermediate" processes (figure 1). They are spurred by a variety of drivers and in turn generate a variety of outcomes. We are particularly concerned about job quality outcomes: pay level, permanence, skill requirements, and opportunities to gain new skills and to advance. Firm managers, on the other hand, are particularly interested in performance outcomes, including changes in productivity, quality, labor turnover, and innovative capacity (encompassing both process and product innovation).

In principle, restructuring ILMs could follow a variety of trajectories over time. To provide a clearer picture of the possible dynamic paths, we plot over time a variable such as real wage or probability of promotion for a given job category (figure 2). Among the possible patterns are

- A flat line, indicating no change in pay or opportunities for advancement.
- A capital gamma (Γ), showing that job quality rises and stays high. The business press has typically described "employability" and the "new social contract" in this way, arguing that they widen opportunities for workers rather than constricting them.
- An L, denoting that pay or advancement possibilities fall and remain low. The scholarly literature tends to emphasize this outcome.
- A reverse J, with job quality declining, then rising, but never reaching its former level.
- A U, in which job quality initially declines, then rebounds to its former level.

Though far from exhausting all possibilities, this set of diagrams suggests some of the variation one might expect to encounter.

Findings

In the companies studied, recent corporate restructuring involved three analytically distinct waves of changes in corporate organization and strategy. While these waves overlapped, with firms sometimes pursuing

FIGURE 1
Drivers of Corporate Restructuring, Restructuring Processes, and Outcomes

Drivers of restructuring →
- Competitive pressure
- Stockholder pressure
- Emulation of others
- Consultant advice

Restructuring processes →
- *Organizational—affecting ILMs*
  - *Outsourcing*
  - *Geographic deintegration*
  - Etc.
- Other organizational
  - High-performance practices
  - Etc.
- Other

Outcomes
- *Job quality*
  - *Pay level*
  - *Job security*
- *Skills required*
  - *Opportunities for skill acquisition*
  - *Opportunities for promotion*
- Firm performance
  - Unit labor costs/productivity
  - Quality
  - Turnover
  - Innovative capacity

Note: Items in *italics* denote a particular focus of the proposed study.

FIGURE 2

Some Possible Dynamic Paths for Job Quality Following Deintegration

X-axis: Time

Y-axis: Some measure of job quality or the strength of internal labor markets

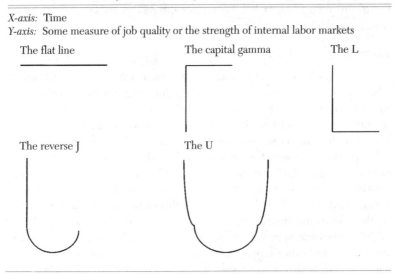

two different, and potentially conflicting, objectives at the same time, we find it useful to separate these waves analytically and to identify the process as dynamic and ongoing. This shows the need to be cautious about concluding that current restructuring will lead to a new stable state. (Carré [1993] has reported similar findings in her case study of contingent work in the French financial services industry.)

The first wave of corporate restructuring involves achieving organizational focus, primarily through shedding less-central business lines and in some cases purchasing more closely related ones. This ranges from the breakup of diversified conglomerates to narrowing the variety of products sold by a firm (e.g., reducing the number of lines in a multiline insurance company). The second wave involves improving operational efficiency through downsizing, delayering, outsourcing, and changing jobs in ways such as "broadbanding" (increasing the range of tasks within a job) and increasing workloads but generally without significant changes in the nature of the job activities. Second-wave changes thus typically involve the deconstruction of ILMs—decreasing long-term employment and within-firm mobility.

The third wave of restructuring, for innovation and growth, is only in its early stages in the companies we observed. The forms are still quite varied, and a dominant form is apparently not yet established. We do, however, postulate that the dynamic in this wave is and will continue to be toward rebuilding ILMs. Given our interest in ILMs, we zero in on waves 2 and 3 in this paper.

Electronics Case Studies

Our two electronics firms are electronic instrument manufacturers, whose products are low volume and engineering intensive and involve rapid innovation. Despite this high-tech profile, many instrument production processes involve low-end jobs—stuffing circuit boards, assembling cabinets and boxes—in addition to high-end jobs requiring technical expertise. Through the postwar period, these instrument producers developed into highly vertically integrated firms. Nearly all parts production—even basic fabrication such as screw production—was done in house until the mid- to late 1980s. Traditionally, outsourcing was done in the electronic instruments area only for a few specialty parts for which an outside supplier offered unique expertise. Increasingly, however, these and other large producers are subcontracting or outsourcing the low-end, high-volume work, leaving them to focus instead on new product development and niche markets for state-of-the-art equipment.

Monarch Products. Monarch Products, a large, high-technology manufacturer, dramatically expanded its use of outsourcing beginning in the late 1980s as one of a set of wave 2 changes. After deciding to restructure, Monarch outsourced 12,000 parts over 18 months. This was justified primarily in terms of cost reductions, though managers also spoke of reaping the advantages of specialization.

In the 1990s, however, Monarch began to encounter the limitations of outsourcing as its strategy changed in two ways. Whereas earlier this firm had purchased primarily commodity components, it now began to purchase more complex subsystems involving assembly work. This was a response to the frustrations of working with the suppliers of 12,000 parts. Rather than providing suppliers with a full specification for such subsystems, Monarch increasingly furnished only functional specifications that required the suppliers to solve problems and even to participate in the innovation process. Outsourcing thus changed to subsystem assembly, engineering, and even innovation. Despite this expansion of supplier responsibilities, Monarch demanded that suppliers meet cost constraints. One result, we were told by Monarch managers, was a dramatic increase in problems, including late delivery (or even failure to deliver), serious quality flaws, cost overruns, and loss of key engineering capabilities within Monarch.

Consider, for example, the case of Monarch supplier Angstrom Tools, a precision machine shop that for years simply supplied component parts. In the early 1990s, Monarch approached Angstrom about producing a high-value-added subsystem requiring assembly, integration of electronic and electrical components, and testing—in addition to Angstrom's customary machining work. Angstrom took the plunge. Monarch then accounted for about 30% of Angstrom's total revenue, and Angstrom became the sole supplier to Monarch for a critical subsystem.

Angstrom, however, was not able to deliver the product at the time promised, at the price quoted, or at a sufficient level of quality. Unit costs for the product ran nearly 30% above the original estimate, largely due to added engineering costs. Monarch agreed to pay some of the additional costs, but the supplier still had to bear a significant portion, seriously straining its finances and raising the specter of bankruptcy.

With hindsight, Angstrom's failure was not surprising. As a machine shop focusing on components, the supplier had a moderately skilled labor force and little management infrastructure. Its low cost was largely the result of low wages and low overhead, which also meant it lacked the skilled workforce needed for a highly engineered product that had to be manufactured to exacting specifications. Probably more important, Angstrom lacked systems to ensure quality, to manage complicated financial arrangements and contracts (e.g., with an expanded group of subsuppliers), and to track its own costs in a more complicated subsystem assembly. As one of Monarch's managers exclaimed, "These systems require *real* engineering, *real* processes, *real* production capabilities— these job shops just don't have that capacity!" Another added, "There's a reason why these small shops have remained small for years—they just don't have the management, resources, and whatever to do a complicated product." Trying to develop these systems and capabilities naturally increased the supplier's costs, making it impossible to deliver the expected cost reductions. In addition, Angstrom's problems producing and delivering the product increased Monarch's monitoring, engineering, and warranty repair costs of the final installed product.

Setbacks like those experienced with Angstrom were repeated with many other suppliers. Monarch responded to these problems in a variety of ways. In the short run, it adopted ad hoc solutions, such as sending a group of engineers to "camp out" at a supplier's plant and solve design problems or deploying added production staff to test or rework components. Over the long run, Monarch managers acknowledged that small, low-cost suppliers lacked the capacity for these more complex and innovative tasks and therefore moved on to wave 3 actions. They once again insourced some components, helped small suppliers to vertically integrate and thus become larger, and increasingly shifted to larger suppliers—including some diversified companies comparable in size to Monarch itself. Commented one purchasing manager, "I went from looking for a $2 million [per year in sales] company to produce subassemblies to $5 million, $10 million, $15 million—now I think it takes more like a $50 million company."

Corollary to these shifts in the locus of production were shifts in the degree to which fabrication and assembly work took place within ILMs. The initial outsourcing relocated work from Monarch's well-developed ILMs to predominantly small firms with few layers of management and sharply limited chances for advancement. Insourcing, vertical integration of suppliers, and gravitation toward larger suppliers all represent a move of these activities back to more developed ILMs.

Another initiative at Monarch was downsizing. This occurred most sharply in the late 1980s, as part of the process of outsourcing and organizational change. Monarch and its corporate parent reduced layers of management, creating a flat management structure relative to many other firms of similar size. Workloads increased as the ranks thinned and total work volume grew. These changes were part of a culture change that called for every person to "push," to do more with less. The people we interviewed, those who survived and thrived, generally agreed that there was a genuine effort to be a responsive, nonbureaucratic organization that pushed people to take chances and "go beyond their comfort zone" and supported them when they did. But downsizing and "pushing" did not receive a uniformly positive evaluation. A number of managers commented that these changes had led to a punishing pace, with people overloaded beyond their capacity. "We're always running in the red on the tach[ometer]" was one manager's summary of the situation. A new senior manager from another industry said that he had never experienced anything like the pace at Monarch. It was true, he said, that Monarch moved quickly without a lot of constraining bureaucracy, but "when does anyone get a chance to think? When does anyone here have the time to figure out what to do before they act?" Similarly, another manager suggested that Monarch's standard operating procedure amounted to "ready, fire, aim."

Unlike Monarch's course correction on outsourcing, there is little sign of a third-wave adjustment to downsizing and speedup. At one point in the mid-1990s, top corporate-level executives did instruct managers to ease up somewhat and to let people catch their breath. But this directive had little effect amid a blizzard of demands for higher productivity and lower costs.

Electronicus, Inc. Electronicus, rather than outsourcing *products,* outsourced *workers,* dramatically increasing its use of contingent labor. In the late 1980s, facing declining profits, Electronicus's corporate parent launched a restructuring plan that eliminated several layers of management, imposed cost controls, and focused on improving its engineering process. Contrary to many companies, the corporation developed an "alternative downsizing" strategy involving voluntary relocation, a worker loan program (loan of displaced workers to other divisions on a temporary basis), and early retirement. Two years later, in the face of continued profit problems, Electronicus's corporate parent engaged in a broader restructuring effort. It decided to reduce or close some of the plants doing fabrication, consolidate other plants (reducing manufacturing plants from 12 to just 5), and change organizational structure. It separated product groups and operational areas into autonomous profit-and-loss centers and made these smaller units accountable for performance and costs.

During this restructuring, Electronicus's parent started developing a "buffer" workforce of temporary employees that could be easily adjusted to protect the employment security of the core workforce. The stated goals included both short-term cost control and avoidance of the massive layoffs that occurred during the recession of the early 1980s. Initially, the company declared that its aim was to maintain a contingent workforce of about 10% of the total. While the rationale for most companies was to cut costs by not paying benefits, Electronicus and its parent were among the few to pay contingent workers a premium in lieu of benefits. After six experimental programs, they implemented the "buffer-force" policy corporation-wide in the early 1990s. Employment of temporary workers, at its height, grew to about 13% of the parent corporation's workforce.

In line with this policy, Electronicus began to hire 25% of production workers (10% of its total workforce) through temporary agencies. The main agency maintained a hiring office on site. Like the surge of outsourcing at Monarch, the sizable expansion of the contingent workforce at Electronicus precipitated a number of problems. Historically, this firm has relied on long-term employment guarantees and opportunities for promotion to motivate workers. However, official company policy is to lay off temporary workers after two years and to treat them as outsiders in bidding for promotions. Additionally, benefits available to permanent employees, most notably profit sharing, are not available to temporary workers. During a plant visit, a quarterly profit announcement over the public address system was met by spontaneous cheers and then sudden and awkward silence as workers realized that a quarter of their "associates" and "teammates" had much less to cheer about. This, one manager observed, was symbolic of problems in using a large temporary workforce.

Some managers think that Electronicus's dual labor force creates tensions among workers, impedes the integration of temporary workers into the work process, and reduces the level of commitment of a large part of the workforce. "It may not be such a good idea to have contract [temporary] employees," commented one human resource (HR) manager. "You want to have people you can count on." She contrasted the use of temporary workers in the company's main productive activities with more "contained" contracting for photocopying, the mailroom, and janitorial work, which she said "works quite well."

In practice, many Electronicus managers have acted to subvert the official policy with respect to temporary workers. They lay temporaries off for the required three months after two years but then rehire them, essentially turning them into long-term employees with periodic unpaid leaves. ("This is not what we planned when we set up our contract workforce!" an HR manager exclaimed.) They do their best to fill a permanent opening by hiring a temporary who has been doing a job for two years rather than hiring the permanent employee who is nominally entitled to the job. Given the perceived problems and frontline managers' reactions, a top Electronicus HR official told us, "We need to take another look at using so many temporary workers. Twenty-five percent is too much." Whereas Electronicus's push toward a temporary workforce shifted substantial amounts of work out of the ILM, both the unplanned long-term integration of temporary workers and the company's determination to reexamine the policy of widespread use of temporaries mark a return toward ILMs.

Insurance Case Studies

Like electronics manufacturing, financial services—and insurance companies in particular—offer rich opportunities for studying the evolution of ILMs. First, insurance companies historically have had highly developed ILMs. Until recently, middle management (and even CEOs in some cases) moved up from entry-level clerical and service areas. Second, the industry has undergone tremendous restructuring over the last 20 years, spurred by financial deregulation, technological change, and financial and marketing innovation (Salzman and Buchau 1997). The planned merger of Citicorp with Travelers Group marks only one recent example.

Third, one important dimension of this change has been the reshaping of the job structure, typically in ways that reduce the scope and role of ILMs (Tilly 1996). Many financial service companies have been spinning off back-office and customer service functions into remote sites—for example, call centers used for billing, sales, or service. As in the case of call centers in telecommunications services (Batt and Keefe 1998), such dispersion isolates functions that were once part of broad jobs geographically and organizationally connected to large bureaucracies (Herzenberg, Alic, and Wial 1998). Reflecting the growth of call-center and back-office jobs, over the 1980s and 1990s financial institutions saw the number of bill and account collectors, new accounts clerks, credit authorizers, and clerical supervisors grow at a pace that far outstripped overall employment expansion in the industry (by a factor of 11 in the case of collectors; U.S. Bureau of Labor Statistics 1998). These growing positions require social skills, unlike occupations such as record processing, which are diminishing in relative importance. Customer service skills, even among low-level financial services employees, appear to be a critical building block of competitive advantage in financial services (Frei, Harker, and Hunter 1995), so to the extent that mobility opportunities are needed to attract, retain, and provide incentives for such frontline workers, dismantling ILMs may have negative effects on firm performance. Job structure modifications have also had consequences for the workforce at the industry level, including a dramatic widening of wage disparities (Brown and Campbell 1998).

Steadfast Insurance. When we visited Steadfast Insurance, the company was just initiating wave 3 restructuring, while nearing completion of its first and second restructuring efforts. Wave 1, the process of identifying and concentrating on core businesses, had occurred over five years. The multiline business was disaggregated into separate small or strategic business units (SBUs) in order to "expose" each SBU's profits and losses. Analysis of each of these business units and its market then led to selling some of them. The intent was to make each SBU a "business within a business."

The wave 2 push toward greater cost effectiveness and operational efficiency had also been proceeding for several years before our first visit and was projected to continue for several more. This effort involved cost cutting, some outsourcing, downsizing, delayering, and broadbanding of jobs for the remaining employees. The attempt at cost reduction and greater efficiency was spurred in part by a consultant's study that found Steadfast's cost structure to be much higher than that of the industry leader. Closing this "cost gap" became the central theme shaping restructuring efforts, primarily by job cutting and workload increases, though some technology initiatives were also pursued.

Employee morale, not surprisingly, tumbled during this period. By the time of our interviews, it was clear that the gap had not been eliminated and that the two waves of downsizing that had already occurred would be followed by at least one more, adding to the climate of uncertainty. Additionally, the workforce reduction ran the risk of losing key people with skills and organizational knowledge crucial to the success of the campaign. The climate of downsizing encouraged people with the most marketable skills to leave. Because Steadfast's organizational structure had been built around individual products, certain employees had very deep knowledge about particular products, and this knowledge had never been codified. Therefore, there was great concern about losing such people.

It is not surprising that key organizational knowledge of individual employees had never been documented. Steadfast had been noteworthy for lifetime employment, often referred to as the "Mother Steadfast" culture. While the firm was criticized as sedate, this culture clearly provided benefits in maintaining important organizational knowledge but also made it difficult for the organization to downsize while focusing the remaining employees on a new culture of cost consciousness and innovative selling.

A crisis of sorts was reached around the time we began our study of this firm. Steadfast had made some progress in reducing its workforce and its costs and had begun to assess how it was going to develop a strategy for increasing its share of the financial services market. Then, because of external pressures, management sent down an edict to cut costs another 10%. A line manager commented, "But we realized we couldn't cut staffing any more. We had to reorganize work to work smarter instead." Although the 10% cut was implemented, it represented a turning point. Many in the company realized that achieving the transformation into a broader financial services company required changes in job structure at all levels as well as organizational changes. As a result, Steadfast is integrating products into a more unified offering and integrating strategic business units that have been separate.

To strengthen the new organizational structure, the company made significant changes in its job structure. Over the past two years, Steadfast has created jobs that encompass several previously separate functional areas. This eliminated the former finely graded hierarchy based on narrow job descriptions. Instead, there are broader categories such as "customer associate," which encompasses the responsibilities of six former discrete jobs. The company went from 7,000 separate job descriptions and classifications to only 2,000. Advancement now involves increased mastery of "competencies" rather than specific task skills. This has resulted in greater skill demands at the entry level and larger skill "distance" between jobs but also greater skill development, responsibilities, and wage progression within each broad functional job category.

Combining cutbacks (wave 1 restructuring) with reorganization (wave 2) has at times created problems. Our interviewees mentioned the difficulty in getting personnel to think positively about the job redesign effort while there was so much flux and uncertainty about the security of their jobs. As a consequence of layoffs, the remaining workforce was being asked to assume many of the responsibilities of the personnel that had been eliminated. This both reduced morale and impeded the implementation of training and support programs that would facilitate the development of the new job redesign efforts.

In a separate initiative, in 1997 Steadfast created a call center geographically removed from the home office, in an area we call MetroWest. There were several reasons for this, beyond the simple need for more call-center capacity. One was to provide backup to the home office call center in the event of a sustained power outage, as had occurred during a recent winter ice storm. A second was to allow easier coverage of longer hours of operation by taking advantage of the difference in time zones. MetroWest also offered the opportunity to break out of what was seen as the tradition-bound culture at the home office, try some new techniques of organization and management, and serve customers who needed a broader range of information and more technical assistance.

Given the distance between MetroWest and the home office, Steadfast did not plan to offer substantial promotion opportunities to the MetroWest workforce. Unexpectedly, however, the combination of worker involvement and the relative abundance of college-educated talent in MetroWest resulted in many highly qualified employees. Also, the growth that came with staffing a new and developing organization provided opportunity for fairly rapid advancement for some early hires. These circumstances led to a relatively strong talent pool of entry-level workers whom the managers were interested in retaining beyond the expected tenure for a customer service representative. One HR manager at the home office opined that the call centers should be particularly good places from which to draw candidates for management because success in the call center required good customer and teamwork skills and developed good knowledge of the company and its products. The geographic isolation of MetroWest, where the most talented customer service representatives were employed, prevented upward movement into lower-management jobs in the company. In response, the MetroWest management team began to create "team champion" and "team leader" positions, providing some upward mobility to the more capable customer service representatives in the hope of keeping them. They were rebuilding the ILM that geographic deintegration had dismantled, albeit in a very limited way.

Thus, Steadfast shifted from dismantling to reconfiguring and even reconstructing ILMs. After repeated rounds of downsizing, managers decided to "reorganize work to work smarter," fashioning a new ILM structure. Establishing a distant call center initially created jobs isolated from job ladders, but managers found ways to reinvent upward mobility for customer service representatives at the remote site.

InsurAll. Another insurance company, InsurAll, also initially undertook wave 1 (focusing on core businesses) and wave 2 (operational efficiency), restructuring in ways similar to Steadfast. InsurAll historically had a less-integrated structure. Each insurance unit had a president, with profit-and-loss responsibilities. When the industry became more competitive in the late 1980s, InsurAll evaluated the financial strengths of each line and sold units that did not meet profit goals or fit with its core business strategy. This process led to internal restructuring, downsizing, and layoffs. InsurAll also introduced some new technology and decentralized to each business unit various functions, such as information services and the human resource function.

In the early 1990s, InsurAll decided to move one of the business lines out of the home office building in a major metropolitan downtown area. InsurAll solicited bids from cities for tax breaks and training incentives in addition to evaluating each city's workforce and business climate. A southern city submitted the winning bid.

The move was considered a success, and a year later some administration and back-office functions moved. The company's goal was to obtain lower labor costs but also to eliminate an existing workforce that they didn't want to retrain—with selective offers of relocation to incumbents viewed as trainable. Using a discriminating hiring process based on careful documentation of job requirements, along with intensive training, InsurAll was successful in building a more productive back-office workforce.

At the time of our first interview, about a year after this second step, there was a high level of excitement about the success of the first two moves and discussion of moving many—perhaps even all—functions out of their current home office location, starting by moving several hundred jobs to two midwestern and southern states. The jobs in question were high-level clerical, technical/clerical, and mid- to low-level professional jobs.

But when we returned to the company 18 months and then 24 months later, InsurAll managers told a different story. The company had not moved any more jobs out; in fact, they had moved some *back* from remote sites in order to regain advantages of proximity and organizational integration. In contrast with earlier enthusiasm, managers saw the relocation efforts as only moderately successful or, perhaps more accurately, as successful for some functions but not a strategy that could be expanded.

Managers' strategies for altering job structures also evolved during this time. As in most insurance companies, advancement in InsurAll was traditionally through internal career ladders, starting at or near the bottom and "growing up in the company." Additional training and education were not required. But in the 1990s, one HR manager explained, "The term 'ladder' is archaic in financial services," since one doesn't advance "in lockstep" to a specified position. Under the new regimen, people have to expand their job skills and responsibility and "are more *personally* valuable to the extent that they [see] things in a way that others don't."

Much like Steadfast, InsurAll collapsed jobs into several broad categories. They identified a set of "competencies" needed in multiple jobs. For instance, the same principles underlie communication skills for dealing with external customers and for internal communications, though the specifics differ. Compensation has changed as well; it now includes base pay, performance bonuses awarded each year, and pay raises driven by increases in skill level. In contrast with old rules that specified automatic pay increases and added performance increments to pay for a given job at a given skill level, base pay now increases only if an employee demonstrates mastery of new skills, which eventually will lead to a new job.

Under the new system, supervisors are evaluated in part on the extent to which their employees attain new skills. Although this approach is too new for us to be able to assess its impact, its logic and incentives place increased pressure on both workers and supervisors to engage in constant skill development and to seek mobility. Indeed, one goal is to impel people to continually move to new jobs, even if they only make moves that would have formerly been considered lateral.

In short, InsurAll also has progressed from weakening ILMs to rebuilding them. Seized initially by enthusiasm for relocating functions to far-flung sites, managers soon recognized that they had underestimated the advantages of co-location. They halted the creation of remote facilities and even pulled some activities back into the home office. The company ended the traditional system of internal advancement but replaced it with a new system likewise focused on internal mobility.

Another Look at the Consequences of Restructuring

Each type of corporate restructuring we examined had consequences both for ILMs and for firm performance. In this section, we offer a summary balance sheet, drawing on case materials beyond those we have already highlighted. *Downsizing,* first of all, undermined job security. At both Monarch and Steadfast, workers and managers also reported that downsizing has significant and long-lasting impact on worker morale. Many managers said that they now viewed downsizing, at least as carried out, as mistaken because of the costs to morale, workforce commitment, and productivity. In fact, HR managers said their major problem in the mid-1990s was rebuilding the trust and commitment that downsizing had weakened.

These morale problems outlasted the downsizing itself. In one firm, for example, ongoing "involuntary turnover," namely, those employees who left under pressure, was only 3% to 4% per year in the late 1990s. However, about 60% of the workforce indicated in response to a survey that they strongly believed that they were not secure in their job. Thus, ongoing fear of job loss was far greater than warranted by the actual threat. None of the firms saw repeated downsizing as a viable ongoing strategy for improving performance, nor did the managers think that there was a need for ongoing workforce turnover.

Outsourcing took place at three levels. The first involved infrastructure services, such as security and custodial services. This entailed little change in skill requirements or opportunities for mobility, since these were generally low-skill jobs with limited job ladders. However, reductions in pay, benefits, and job security were common.

At the second level, companies subcontracted operational areas such as part fabrication and data processing, targeting lower costs. Outsourcing for the most basic commodity parts and services was widespread across all firms, with some firms (including Monarch) going as far as to eliminate entire production areas. Such outsourcing usually, though not always, results in lower-paying jobs with fewer benefits, less job security, and less unionization. This is particularly true when cost savings come from subcontracting to firms such as Angstrom that pay lower wages and have less management infrastructure. At the same time, in some cases the shift did increase access to jobs by lower-skilled workers and opportunities for informal skill development. Also, the picture with respect to stability of employment was mixed. Without unions, suppliers offer less employment protection, but those suppliers with more diversified product markets than their customers may be less susceptible to market-specific cycles.

Some cost-driven outsourcing reaped savings by shifting activities to specialized firms able to reap economies of scale and better machine utilization. For example, the electronics companies outsourced printed circuit boards to large, specialized suppliers with highly developed infrastructures and ILMs. In these cases, the suppliers offered lower pay than the purchasing companies, but there was no appreciable change in other aspects of job quality and perhaps greater stability because the board suppliers had a more diversified market.

Finally, we observed a third level of outsourcing for product innovation, primarily tapping engineering talent outside the core firm. There were no appreciable negative effects on job quality. In many instances, in fact, job quality appeared to improve, with the outside firm paying engineers more and, probably due to its smaller size, offering a more flexible environment. There was less opportunity for those with high-level managerial aspirations.

Various companies used *contingent workers* differently, for varying strategic goals. We have highlighted the case of Electronicus, where temporary workers were an important part of a strategy to *preserve* job quality for the permanent workforce. This firm tried to treat its temporary workers relatively well in terms of pay and some (albeit not officially sanctioned) opportunity for longer-term employment. On the other hand, several electronics supplier companies explicitly used the temporary workforce as a way to reduce costs and as a screening device. One core company subsidiary maintained a temporary workforce in part because the nonemployee status of these workers artificially reduced the denominator of the company's sales-to-employee ratio, thus improving its image in the eyes of its investors. Although temporary workers were paid less at this company, managers did not believe that this reduced costs much, if at all, because of the increased administrative and turnover costs and reduced productivity. At Steadfast, one unit supervisor used temporary status as an implied (or sometimes explicit) threat to motivate performance; but this tactic was deemed ineffective or even harmful by a subsequent supervisor who, with one stroke, made all the workers permanent.

Managers generally voiced negative opinions about the results of using temporary workers, including lower productivity, higher turnover, and lower morale. Temporary positions were not always worse in terms of pay but uniformly lacked job security, opportunities for skill development, and mobility. Most managers agreed that these workers were useful for conducting narrowly defined tasks but not for contributing to the broader organizational performance that firms in the third wave were trying to improve. These employees were used as a "disposable workforce" and reciprocated in attitude and behavior. One insurance manager commented that temporary workers would go across the street for 10 cents an hour more, whereas their permanent workers would stay because of the long-term opportunities at the firm. At an electronics production facility, contingent workers had (unplanned) annual turnover approaching 50%, compared with under 10% for the rest of the company's workforce. Further, even in basic production areas, sense of purpose and *esprit de corps* was hampered when there were workforce divisions. Moreover, since temporary workers were cut off from ongoing training and education within the firm, their presence shrank the pool of internal candidates for advancement.

Given all of these negatives, many of the managers we spoke to were seeking ways to contain the use of a temporary workforce: by limiting its size, by specifying a limited period of time after which such workers become eligible for permanent employment, or both. Thus, to the extent that these firms are representative, the evidence suggests that use of temporaries has limits, that some retrenchment is likely, and that their use is not likely to expand in its present forms.

The companies also used *geographic deintegration* in a variety of ways. Manufacturers often deintegrate in search of lower costs, to enter new markets abroad, or to create a hedge against economic changes in particular countries (e.g., currency fluctuations). Monarch developed geographic dispersion to a far greater extent than other instrument companies.

In fact, all the others were very concerned about the problems such a policy might create, and some (e.g., Electronicus) consolidated most facilities in one geographical area. InsurAll disintegrated to cut costs, whereas Steadfast did so in pursuit of more varied objectives.

Geographic deintegration affects job quality primarily by reducing the vertical and horizontal moves available to workers, especially in small or homogeneous remote units. Removing the lower occupational rungs from the core offices of a firm also limits entry opportunities for people with few skills. This marks a significant shift for the insurance industry, which traditionally provided mobility for the less skilled—at least in certain jobs such as sales and customer service—both because advancement was possible on the basis of job performance and on-the-job learning and because the firms often provided assistance in obtaining further education. On the other hand, dispersion generally improves employment opportunities in the communities where the new spin-offs are located.

Analogous to the problems created by the use of contingent workers, geographic deintegration had drawbacks when it affected *core* workers. The issues of co-location of productive activities, extensively studied in various manufacturing activities, pertain to service work as well. Units that can benefit from interaction with other units are likely to suffer from geographic isolation. However, managers view many jobs, such as outbound calling (e.g., for solicitations), as providing little organizational learning benefit and thus not subject to this constraint.

Some of the other firms also engaged in *job broadening*. In addition to Steadfast and InsurAll, two of the electronics companies introduced new production methods that entailed expansion of skills and broader job responsibilities. The resulting redesign of jobs into broad functional categories and elimination of a finely graded hierarchy present new opportunities as well as new barriers: both the skill barriers to entry and the gaps between job functions are greater (and may require outside education or training to traverse), but skill development, responsibilities, and wage progression are also much greater within each broad functional area. In large firms, low-level jobs may hold the possibility of relatively higher levels of skill and wage development than in the past but fewer opportunities for internal progression to middle-level jobs without external education and training.

Wave 3 efforts to broaden jobs tend to generate new demands for training, but businesses typically had greatly reduced their training capacity during wave 2 by shrinking and decentralizing human resource functions. Most managers we spoke to seemed determined to limit added training to managerial levels during wave 3. Despite headlines about labor shortages, they planned to hire more-educated workers or to make employees responsible for their own education and training rather than to provide additional training to frontline workers (Moss, Salzman, and Tilly 1998). It remains to be seen whether this approach will succeed in meeting the skill needs of these businesses.

In table 1, we summarize the predominant outcomes of each type of restructuring of jobs. Actual outcomes varied, depending on the type of jobs affected and the specific restructuring strategy.

Alternatives to Wave 1 and Wave 2 Restructuring

We can also learn something by comparing firms that adopted a particular restructuring strategy with those that did not. Here we briefly refer to our other cases, as well as the ones discussed already. For example, Monarch aggressively pursued outsourcing, but Electronicus and two European companies, Precision and MeasureAll, did so far less. Precision and MeasureAll, as well as their suppliers, were constrained by European labor laws, so outsourcing often did not alter pay or benefits, and in at least one case, workers were directly transferred to the supplier. These two companies and Electronicus emphasized innovation, control over the production process, and informally acquired design and production knowledge as competitive advantages, whereas Monarch placed greater emphasis on systems integration and strong distribution and service networks, although relying on innovation as well. Particularly striking was the contrast with MeasureAll. Monarch outsourced circuit board production relatively early in its move to externalize production. Its managers argued that driving down board costs depends on constantly investing in new equipment, which Monarch's volume of board use could not justify. MeasureAll reported similar issues of economies of scale in board production but, rather than outsourcing boards, began marketing them to other firms, scaling up their board shop into a profit center. They did this with other components as well, so that of their 25 "suppliers" of subsystems, 20 were manufacturing centers *within* MeasureAll or its parent company.

In the insurance sector, the most striking contrast was between mutual companies (owned by their policyholders) and companies owned by stockholders. Steadfast and InsurAll, stock companies directly exposed to investor pressure, avidly engaged in wave 2–style restructuring and then showed signs of swinging toward wave 3. The two mutual companies, in

TABLE 1
Summary of the Impact of Restructuring on Jobs

	Access/entry (e.g., education/ skill requirements)	Skill requirements (to perform the job/ of the job tasks)	Pay	Mobility/skill development	Security/ tenure
Outsourcing	Decrease	No change or decrease	Decrease	Increase	Decrease
Contingent work	Decrease	Decrease or no change	Decrease	Decrease	Decrease
Geographical deintegration	No change	No change	Decrease or no change	Decrease	No change
Job broadening	Increase	Increase	No change or increase	Increase	No change or increase

contrast, were buffered from the stock market and approached restructuring in a much more deliberate manner. Though managers in these companies also described strategies of change, we did not see much of the turbulence of wave 2 downsizing and deintegration nor the improvisation of wave 3 reconstruction of ILMs. Of course, these companies are also cut off from a key source of capital. As a result, quite a few mutuals, including the two in our study, have recently converted or announced plans to convert to stock ownership or some sort of mutual-equity combination.

One final contrast represents a small but noteworthy divergence in strategies. Recall that Electronicus managers, while bemoaning the effects of an expanded temporary workforce, thought that contracting out of peripheral functions such as security and photocopying worked well. Interestingly, Steadfast considered contracting out their home office cafeteria in similar fashion but then decided instead to try to build it into a profit center—and succeeded in doing so, while also increasing quality. It is now considering providing cafeteria services to other companies in the region. Apparently, even activities quite remote from a company's central business can become "core competencies."

In summary, each company that restructured did so in response to a set of perceived imperatives. But other businesses, even within the same industry, reacted to the same imperatives in very different ways and remained strong competitors. Clearly, businesses have some degree of latitude as to whether to engage in a particular type of restructuring.

Conclusion

The four companies we profiled in detail in this paper followed somewhat similar restructuring trajectories. All four, in hot pursuit of wave 2 goals of cost reduction and operational efficiency, radically restructured in ways that weakened or dismantled ILMs. However, they discovered significant disadvantages to their strategies, especially as they expanded to encompass more complex and innovative activities and more technical functions. All four, therefore, advanced in various ways to wave 3, reconfiguring and rebuilding ILMs rather than continuing to tear them down. This looks to us more like the groping of firms dealing with bounded rationality than the smooth adjustments expected of rational optimizers.

The moves to rebuild ILMs are, so far, limited in scope and scale. For the most part, the managers we spoke to are content that restructuring succeeded when applied to the most routine functions: outsourcing commodity parts, hiring contract labor for such tasks as security or mailroom work, or establishing remote sites for low-level call-center and back-office tasks. They are attempting to strengthen ILMs in areas of work where commitment, communication, and the ability to innovate are most critical. Moreover, these companies are not restoring ILMs to their former state. With the limited exception of some companies' bringing back activities that had been outsourced or turned over to remote facilities, they are constructing or supporting new and different mechanisms for internal mobility and job security, including, in the case of Monarch, some that are actually located in supplier firms. In the early phases of wave 3, corporations were reducing or modifying their reliance on outsourcing, contingent work, and geographic deintegration, all of which had predominately negative impacts on ILMs and job quality. They were also carrying out more job broadening (which has a much more positive mix of impacts). In terms of the possible trajectories sketched in figure 2, these cases come closest to the reverse J: extensive deconstruction of ILMs followed by their partial reconstruction.

While we cannot conclude that the future for low-skill workers is any more promising than the present, there is ample evidence that the story is not over and that reports of the death of ILMs are greatly exaggerated. Will the third wave prove a will-o'-the-wisp, a temporary adjustment to cyclical labor shortages? Or will it instead herald a growing realization that attachment based on long-term employment and internal employment opportunities is critical for the performance of low-skill as well as high-skill jobs? The complex corporate trajectories of the recent past suggest that the future path of ILMs warrants careful scrutiny.

Acknowledgments

This research was supported by generous funding from the General Electric Fund and the Alfred P. Sloan Foundation. Research assistance was provided by Radha Roy Biswas, Katrina Buchau, and Michael Handel. An earlier version was presented at the National Bureau of Economic Research Summer Institute, July 1998.

References

Allen, Steven G., Robert L. Clark, and Sylvester J. Schieber. 1998. "Has Job Security Vanished in Large Corporations?" Paper presented at the National Bureau of Economic Research Summer Workshop, Cambridge, MA, July 27–31.

Batt, Rosemary, and Jeffrey Keefe. 1998. "Human Resource and Employment Practices in Telecommunications Services, 1980–1998." Report to the New American Realities Committee, National Planning Association, Washington, DC, April.

Brown, Claire, and Benjamin Campbell. 1998. "Changes in Wage Inequality by Industry, 1979–95." Presentation at the Sloan Foundation Industry Studies Meeting, Berkeley, CA, April 2–4.

Cappelli, Peter. 1995. "Rethinking Employment." *British Journal of Industrial Relations*, Vol. 33, no. 4, pp. 563–602.

Cappelli, Peter, Laurie Bassi, Harry Katz, David Knoke, Paul Osterman, and Michael Useem. 1997. *Change at Work*. New York: Oxford University Press.

Carré, Françoise. 1993. "Temporary, Short-Term, and Part-Time Employment in French Banks and Insurance Companies during the 1980s: An Institutionalist Approach." Ph.D. Diss., Department of Urban Studies and Planning, Massachusetts Institute of Technology.

DiMaggio, Paul, and Walter Powell. 1991. "Introduction." In Walter Powell and Paul DiMaggio, eds., *The New Institutionalism in Organizational Analysis*. Chicago: University of Chicago Press, pp. 1–38.

Doeringer, Peter, and Michael Piore. 1987. *Internal Labor Markets and Manpower Analysis*, 2nd ed. Armonk, NY: M. E. Sharpe.

Eccles, Robert G., Nitin Nohria, and James D. Berkley. 1992. *Beyond the Hype*. Boston: Harvard Business School Press.

Frei, Frances X., Patrick T. Harker, and Larry W. Hunter. 1995. "Performance in Consumer Financial Services Organizations: Framework and Results from the Pilot Study." Working Paper 95-03. Philadelphia: Wharton Financial Institutions Center, University of Pennsylvania.

Gordon, David M., Richard Edwards, and Michael Reich. 1982. *Segmented Work, Divided Workers: The Historical Transformations of Labor in the United States*. New York: Cambridge University Press.

Groshen, Erica L., and David I. Levine. 1998. "The Rise and Decline (?) of U.S. Internal Labor Markets." Research Paper No. 9819. New York: Federal Reserve Bank of New York.

Herzenberg, Steven, John A. Alic, and Howard Wial. 1998. *New Rules for a New Economy: Employment and Opportunity in Postindustrial America*. Ithaca, NY: Cornell University Press.

Holzer, Harry. 1996. *What Employers Want*. New York: Russell Sage Foundation.

Howell, David. 1997. "Institutional Failure and the American Worker: The Collapse of Low-Skill Wages." Working Paper. Annandale-on-Hudson, NY: Jerome Levy Economics Institute, Bard College.

International Labour Organization. 1997. *World Labour Report: Industrial Relations, Democracy and Social Stability, 1997–1998*. Geneva: International Labour Office.

Jones, B. 1997. *Forcing the Factory of the Future: Cybernation and Societal Institutions*. Cambridge: Cambridge University Press.

Lancaster, Hal. 1998. "Managing Your Career: Hiring a Full Staff May Be the Next Fad in Management." *Wall Street Journal*, April 28, p. B1.

Lazonick, William, and Mary O'Sullivan. Forthcoming. "Corporate Governance and Corporate Employment: Is Prosperity Sustainable in the United States?" In William Lazonick and Mary O'Sullivan, eds., *Corporate Governance and Sustainable Prosperity*. New York: Macmillan.

Mandel, Michael J. 1996. *The High-Risk Society: Peril and Promise in the New Economy*. New York: Times Business.

Moss, Philip. Forthcoming. "Earnings Inequality and the Quality of Jobs." In William Lazonick and Mary O'Sullivan, eds., *Corporate Governance and Sustainable Prosperity*. New York: Macmillan.

Moss, Philip, Harold Salzman, and Chris Tilly. 1998. *Policy Implications of Corporate Restructuring and the Transformation of Internal Labor Markets*. Lowell: Center for Industrial Competitiveness, University of Massachusetts at Lowell.

Moss, Philip, and Chris Tilly. 1991. *Why Black Men Are Doing Worse in the Labor Market: A Review of Supplyside and Demandside Explanations*. Working Paper. New York: Social Science Research Council Committee on the Urban Underclass.

Moss, Philip, and Chris Tilly. 2000. *Stories Employers Tell: Race, Skill, and Hiring in America*. New York: Russell Sage Foundation.

Noyelle, Thierry. 1987. *Beyond Industrial Dualism*. Boulder, CO: Westview Press.

Ortmann, Günther, and Harold Salzman. 1998. *Changing Corporate Structures in the Global Economy: Maximizing, Satisficing, and Viability*. Working Paper. Hamburg: University of Hamburg.

Osterman, Paul. 1988. *Employment Futures: Reorganization, Dislocation, and Public Policy*. New York: Oxford University Press.

Pasternack, Bruce A., and Albert J. Viscio. 1998. *The Centerless Corporation: A New Model for Transforming Your Organization for Growth and Prosperity*. New York: Simon and Schuster.

Rose, Stephen J. 1995. *Declining Job Security and the Professionalization of Opportunity*. Research Report 95-04. Washington, DC: National Commission on Employment Policy.

Salzman, Harold, and Katrina Buchau. 1997. "An Overview of the U.S. Insurance Industry." Unpublished paper, Jobs for the Future, Boston.

Scott, W. Richard. 1987. "The Adolescence of Institutional Theory." *Administrative Science Quarterly*, Vol. 32, pp. 493–511.

Smith, Vicki. Forthcoming. "Teamwork vs. Tempwork: Managers and the Dualism of Workplace Restructuring." In Karen Campbell, Daniel Cornfield, and Holly McCannon, eds., *Working in Restructured Workplaces: New Directions for the Sociology of Work*. Newbury Park, CA: Sage.

Tilly, Chris. 1996. *Half a Job: Bad and Good Part-Time Jobs in a Changing Labor Market*. Philadelphia: Temple University Press.

Tilly, Chris. 1997. "Arresting the Decline of Good Jobs in the U.S.A.?" *Industrial Relations Journal*, Vol. 28, no. 4, pp. 269–274.

Tilly, Chris, and Charles Tilly. 1997. *Work under Capitalism*. Denver: Westview Press.

U.S. Bureau of Labor Statistics. 1998. Statistics from industry-occupation employment matrix for 1983–1995. Unpublished data provided by BLS staff.

Williamson, Oliver. 1985. *The Economic Institutions of Capitalism*. New York: Free Press.

CHAPTER 4

The Evolution of the Demand for Temporary Help Supply Employment in the United States

MARCELLO ESTEVÃO
International Monetary Fund

SAUL LACH
*The Hebrew University of Jerusalem and
National Bureau of Economic Research*

Introduction

In the last 10 years or so, employment in the temporary help supply (THS) industry has more than tripled in the United States. The increased use of individuals hired from THS firms is evident in the payroll data published by the Bureau of Labor Statistics (BLS). Although employment in the THS industry represented only about 2% of total nonfarm employment in 1997, it accounted for 10% of the net increase between 1991 and 1997. Since 1972, employment in the THS industry has risen at an annual rate of more than 11%, while total nonfarm employment expanded only 2% per year (figure 1).

In addition, the variability and cyclical sensitivity of THS jobs have been extraordinarily high (Golden 1996). If we wish to understand the reasons for the timing and magnitude of the changes in employment in the THS industry, we need to know more about the changing demand for this type of nonstandard worker. Knowledge of precisely where THS employees actually work is a first step toward this goal. Furthermore, this information is essential to assess the impact of the rapid growth in the THS industry on the performance of the sectors that hire such workers (Segal and Sullivan 1995; Estevão and Lach 1999).

There is, however, very scant direct evidence concerning the industry of assignment of THS workers. Because the BLS classifies employees by the industry of the employing firm rather than by the industry

FIGURE 1

Employment

Log scale

← ▬ Temporary Help Supply (NATSS)
← --- Help Supply Services (SIC 7363 - CES)
······ Nonfarm employment (BLS) →

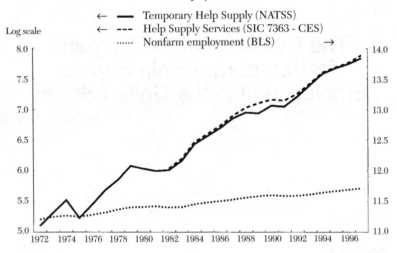

Share of THS (NATSS) in nonfarm employment

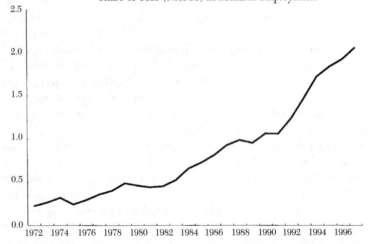

where they are actually working, THS workers are not included in the regularly reported measures of employment in those industries. This chapter aims to remedy this problem by combining different sources of information about the THS industry to generate estimates of the flow of these workers going to major U.S. industries from 1977 to 1997.

In the next section, we define the measurement problem in more detail and discuss the different data sources that can be used to analyze the recent developments in the THS industry. In the third section, we provide estimates for the proportion of THS employees working in each major sector of the U.S. economy. These estimates are based on the analysis of input-output tables published by the Bureau of Economic Analysis (BEA) for 1977, 1982, 1987, and 1992, and on the Contingent Worker Supplement to the Current Population Survey (CPS) of February 1995 and February 1997. These two supplements constitute the only direct evidence of where THS employees actually work. The fourth section decomposes the recent increase in THS employment into the contribution of two different sources of growth: changes in the size and changes in the THS-intensity of eight major sectors of the U.S. economy. Conclusions are presented in the final section.

The Measurement Problem and Data Sources

The inherent measurement difficulty stems from the fact that BLS establishment surveys classify THS agency workers as employed in SIC (Standard Industrial Classification) 7363 (Help Supply Services) rather than including them in the measured employment of the industries actually using their labor. This occurs because THS workers are not on the payroll of the *using* firm.

Let $y_t = 1$ denote the event that an individual is a THS worker in period t. The time subscript is hereafter omitted for notational convenience. The parameters of interest are the probability that an individual working in industry i (e.g., manufacturing or services) is a THS, denoted by $\theta_i\ P(y = 1|i)$, and the probability that a THS employee works in industry i is denoted by $\alpha_i = P(i|y = 1)$.

The two parameters are related as shown below:

$$(1) \qquad \theta_i \equiv P(y=1|i) = P(i\,|\,y=1)\frac{P(y=1)}{P(i)} = \alpha_i\,\frac{P(y=1)}{P(i)}$$

This expression for θ_i means, for example, that if a THS worker has a 30% chance of working in manufacturing ($\alpha_i = 0.30$), then the number of

THS workers employed in manufacturing relative to total employment is 0.30 times $P(y = 1)$, which, given that the THS industry constituted about 2% of the workforce in 1997, equals 0.006. Using 0.15 as the value for $P(i)$, the proportion of THS workers relative to manufacturing employment, θ_i would be 4%.

In order to estimate θ_i, we need to estimate $P(y = 1)$, $P(i)$, and the assignment probability $\alpha_i = P(i|y = 1)$. The first two probabilities are readily estimated from available data by the observed proportions of THS and industry i workers in every year. The last probability, however, is problematic because there is no systematic information about the distribution of THS workers by the industry where they work (the "industry of use"). Nevertheless, under certain assumptions, estimates of the assignment probability can be extracted from selected data sources for particular years.

Note that the number of workers in industry i—the denominator in the estimate of θ_i—should be the *true* number of workers, that is the reported number plus the THS employees working in the industry. Under these conditions, the probability of finding a THS worker in industry i is estimated by

$$(2) \qquad \hat{\theta}_i = \hat{P}(y = 1 \mid i) = \frac{\overbrace{\hat{P}(i \mid y = 1)N_{y=1}}^{N_{y=1,i}}}{N_{y=0,i} + \underbrace{\hat{P}(i \mid y = 1)N_{y=1}}_{N_{y=1,i}}}$$

where $\hat{P}(i|y = 1)$ is some estimate of the assignment probability, and $N_{y=1}$ and $N_{y=0,i}$ are the observed number of THS and industry i workers, respectively. The numerator in equation (2) is the number of THS workers in industry i, while the denominator is the total number of workers in industry i including THS workers.

Several data sets provide both direct and indirect information that can be used to calculate the conditional probabilities in equation (2). Table 1 summarizes these data sources.

The Current Employment Survey (CES) of the BLS is an establishment-based survey providing information on the number of workers on the payroll of firms belonging to SIC 7363—Help Supply Services. This is a slightly broader category than purely THS firms but nonetheless almost identical to data collected by the National Association of Temporary and Staffing Services (NATSS) on THS firms (upper chart of figure 2).[1]

TABLE 1
Data Sources for Temporary Help Supply Employment and Hours

	Level of aggregation	Periods covered	Frequency of data	Information about workers' characteristics	Information about industry of use
National Association of Temporary Staffing Services (NATSS)	Employment in THS firms (NATSS uses the BLS-CES series for before 1987)	1972-97	Quarterly	Aggregate proportions by major occupations	No
Current Employment Survey (CES)[a]	Employment in THS firms (SIC 7362) during 1972-82; employment and hours in SIC 7363 (THS firms plus residual category) from 1982 onward	1972-97	Monthly	No	No
Current Population Survey (CPS)[a] March tapes	Employment and hours in SIC 736	1972-97	Annual	Yes	No
Contingent Worker Supplement[a] February tapes	Employment and hours in THS firms	1995 and 1997	Two data points	Yes	Yes
Input-output tables[b]	Flow of output from SIC 736 to other industries	1977, 1982, 1987, 1992	Every 5 years	No	Estimated

Sources: [a] Bureau of Labor Statistics
[b] Bureau of Economic Analysis

FIGURE 2

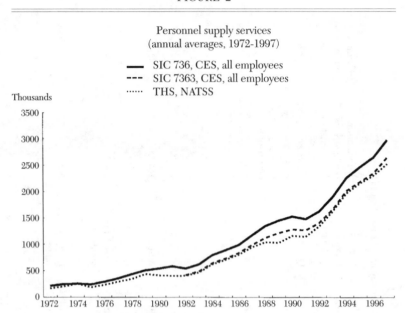

Personnel supply services
(annual averages, 1972-1997)

— SIC 736, CES, all employees
--- SIC 7363, CES, all employees
..... THS, NATSS

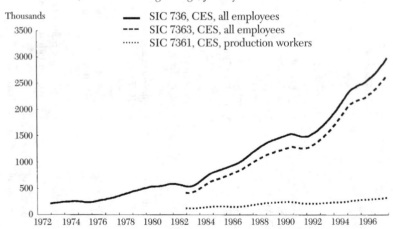

Personnel supply services
(12 month moving average, January 1972-December 1997)

— SIC 736, CES, all employees
--- SIC 7363, CES, all employees
..... SIC 7361, CES, production workers

In other words, the residual category that explains the difference between the NATSS and the CES series for THS employment is of trivial size. The number of THS workers appearing in equation (2), $N_{y=1}$, is from the NATSS. The number of industry workers appearing in equation (2), $N_{y=0,i}$, is from the CES.

The Current Population Survey (CPS) is a household-based survey providing information on households' and individuals' characteristics. It assigns each worker to the industry where he or she is employed, broadly equivalent to a three-digit SIC industry. Therefore, individuals are not identified as employed in the THS industry as such but in the three-digit industry (SIC 736) that contains THS, that is, the personal supply services (PSS) industry. However, the share of THS firms in total PSS employment was about 90% in 1997, and, as shown in the lower chart of figure 2, changes over time in manufacturers' use of PSS workers mainly reflect changes in the use of THS workers. Unfortunately, the regular CPS does not include a question about the industry to which PSS employees are assigned.[2]

The Contingent Worker Supplements to the CPS of February 1995 and February 1997 are other sources of data on the THS industry. In these supplements, respondents were asked directly if they were paid by a THS agency. Furthermore, the supplements recorded the respondents' industry of assignment. Thus, these surveys constitute the only *direct* evidence of the distribution of THS workers by industry of use.

Finally, under certain assumptions, input-output tables from the BEA provide estimates of the distribution of PSS workers among different industries. The commodities-use tables measure the dollar amount of output from one sector that is used as input to another sector. These transactions are registered at approximately a three-digit level of aggregation; therefore, input-output tables do not provide information on THS firms but on PSS firms (SIC 736). When wages of PSS workers and fees paid to THS firms are largely independent of their industry of assignment, the proportion of the PSS industry's output that goes to industry i (the input-output coefficient) is equivalent to the proportion of PSS hours used by industry i.

Formally, the nominal output in the PSS sector can be written as $Y = w_m H_m N_m + w_r H_r N_r$, where the subscript indicates the industry of assignment (m = industry under study and r = remaining industries), w is the hourly wage plus hourly overhead fees (including the profit per hour of the THS agency), H is the average hours of work, and N is the number of workers assigned to industry m or r. If w_m is approximately equal to

w_r, then the proportion of PSS output going to industry m (the input-output coefficient) is approximately equal to the share of total hours of PSS work going to industry m. In addition, if H_m is approximately equal to H_r, then the input-output coefficient is also a reasonable approximation for the share of employment directed to industry m. Unfortunately, we do not have information on the time-series behavior of these series. Therefore, estimates of the assignment probabilities using input-output coefficients should be viewed as rough approximations. In any case, input-output tables with the relevant information on the PSS industry are available for 1977, 1982, 1987, and 1992.

The Sectoral Evolution of THS Employment

Under the assumptions discussed earlier, input-output coefficients can be used as estimates of the assignment probability, α_i, for 1977, 1982, 1987, and 1992. Direct estimates of α_i can also be obtained for 1995 and 1997 using the Contingent Worker Supplement to the February CPS for each of these years.

In principle, these sources of data provide information at the three-digit level of aggregation. Because the statistical noise and potential biases of the estimators decrease with the level of aggregation, we conduct our analysis at the level of eight major industries: (1) construction; (2) manufacturing; (3) transportation, communication, and utilities (TCU); (4) retail and wholesale trade; (5) finance, insurance, and real estate (FIRE); (6) services; (7) public sector; and (8) other industries (mining, agriculture, forestry, and fisheries). Figure 3 reports the assignment probabilities.

A few points are worth mentioning here. During 1982–1987, the service and public sectors accounted for the lion's share of THS workers. After the 1982 peak of 40%, the proportion of THS workers employed in the public sector (includes federal, state, and local administration and public enterprises) declined dramatically—to almost zero in 1997. In contrast, the share in manufacturing increased no less dramatically—it tripled between 1987 and 1997—and accounted for about 30% of the THS workers at the end of this period. The demand for THS workers from the service sector also increased substantially. Together, manufacturing and services firms accounted for about 75% of all THS employees in 1997.

The radical changes in the assignment distribution of THS workers must have been accompanied by changes in the characteristics of THS workers. In particular, the shift from the public sector to manufacturing suggests that there must also have been a shift in the direction of more male, blue-collar workers in the 1990s, presuming that public-sector

FIGURE 3
Assignment probabilities (%)

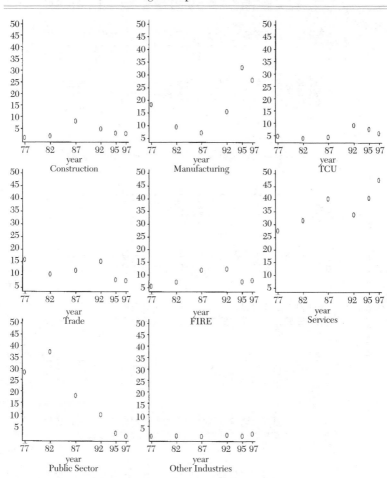

employers were primarily hiring female and/or clerical and service workers.

Using data from the March CPS files, table 2 displays the changes in the average characteristics of individuals working in personnel supply services. While blue-collar workers constituted 14% of the workforce hired by PSS firms in 1977 and only 6% in 1985, they accounted for about 25% by the mid-1990s. The particularly rapid increase in the proportion of blue-collar workers in the 1990s is consistent with the evidence from the

TABLE 2

Distribution of Characteristics among Personnel Supply Services Workers (%)

Year	Male	White	Average age	Usual number of hours per week	Part-time	High school graduate	Some college	College graduate	Pink collar[a]	Blue collar[b]	White collar[c]
1977	34.46	94.97	33.91	32.51	46.75	38.81	28.83	18.83	31.06	14.37	36.10
1978	29.02	79.35	34.12	32.81	46.82	34.23	28.43	19.05	39.83	6.68	29.95
1979	25.26	89.05	38.12	32.06	41.47	35.50	25.49	23.51	33.99	9.56	30.19
1980	30.49	83.93	34.34	34.17	36.80	42.74	23.51	19.19	38.80	14.38	25.56
1981	28.46	87.90	32.97	33.73	43.30	30.02	27.30	32.85	45.41	9.88	29.80
1982	32.35	80.74	33.97	33.52	42.42	32.23	35.79	22.40	43.97	8.39	27.83
1983	28.74	80.42	34.65	34.06	41.72	31.34	29.70	25.06	33.67	8.91	33.91
1984	22.42	79.42	36.89	32.89	46.41	38.99	27.66	22.71	30.32	8.52	36.30
1985	17.03	81.08	37.27	33.80	44.37	33.49	29.91	24.94	31.49	5.97	35.11
1986	26.38	81.14	35.87	33.86	41.02	31.86	30.22	27.43	31.09	10.28	27.83
1987	31.96	76.27	37.13	34.33	41.03	31.14	33.79	21.92	27.12	14.83	36.36
1988	25.40	75.76	36.00	33.31	42.08	32.49	31.49	23.11	27.61	11.40	32.57
1989	25.42	73.91	35.71	33.25	44.40	33.38	31.70	22.54	33.02	9.89	27.18
1990	26.47	76.65	34.88	33.46	42.20	31.98	36.20	21.71	32.63	12.43	26.77
1991	33.55	76.54	35.52	34.10	40.94	34.17	31.58	26.42	30.07	16.91	28.48
1992	31.00	77.84	34.92	33.40	43.10	37.01	29.68	21.62	29.39	18.73	25.90
1993	37.77	75.80	36.23	33.60	39.15	35.93	28.12	24.35	25.73	20.82	31.70
1994	37.66	82.04	34.64	34.08	40.56	31.03	36.30	21.74	37.35	20.31	23.63
1995	44.09	77.13	35.76	35.07	38.56	39.38	31.69	20.64	33.06	25.05	22.29
1996	42.24	72.45	35.04	34.69	39.79	27.61	39.83	23.55	37.46	27.12	22.70
1997	37.35	76.95	36.19	35.04	37.40	33.85	28.54	22.95	35.25	24.33	26.59
1977-87	27.87	83.12	35.39	33.43	42.92	34.58	29.15	23.44	35.16	10.16	31.72
1987-97	34.10	76.51	35.49	34.00	40.82	33.68	32.51	22.86	32.16	18.70	26.78
1992-97	38.35	77.04	35.47	34.31	39.76	34.14	32.36	22.48	33.04	22.73	25.47

[a] Mainly clerical workers.
[b] Includes craftsmen, operatives, and nonfarm laborers.
[c] Nonfarm managers and administrators, and professional and technical workers.

input-output tables and the Contingent Worker Supplements, pointing to a surge in the demand for THS employment from manufacturing firms. Most of this increase was matched by reductions in the proportion of white-collar workers, while the proportion of clerical workers (pink-collars) only edged down.[3]

Table 2 presents additional evidence suggesting structural changes in the demand for THS workers. The average proportion of male workers in the PSS industry in 1992–1997 was more than 10 percentage points higher than in 1977–1987. The share of PSS employees working part time (less than 35 hours of work per week) declined, although it remained well above the average for the whole labor force. The increase in the proportion of male workers, the reduction in the proportion of employees working part time, and the slight rise in their usual weekly hours of work are also consistent with larger flows of THS employees to manufacturing firms.[4] As an aside, the average PSS worker seems to have acquired only a bit more education over time: The proportion of individuals with at least some college increased from 52.5% between 1977 and 1987 to about 55% between 1992 and 1997, while the proportion of PSS workers without a high school diploma declined somewhat.

Composition Effects or Structural Changes?

As shown in figure 1, the proportion of THS workers in total nonfarm employment increased from 1% in 1990 to about 2% in 1997. According to NATSS, in 1990 the THS industry comprised about 1.2 million workers; in 1997 it reached more than 2.5 million workers.

The aggregate data, however, mask distinct sectoral trends. Our estimates of θ for different industries over time [per equation (2)] are shown in figure 4.

We used payroll employment data from the CES to compute $N_{y=0,i}$ for seven of our eight industry groups. Data from the monthly Employment Situation BLS release for farms, fisheries, and forestry were combined with payroll data from the CES for mining to form the "other industries" category. In addition, for the sake of presentation, we used a linear interpolation of the assignment probabilities shown in figure 3 to estimate the missing observations when computing θ_i.[5]

What stands out is the rapid and sharp increase in manufacturing use of THS workers, from 1% of the sector's workforce in 1992 to about 4% in 1997, about the same level of THS intensity as in service industries. Finance, insurance, and real estate (FIRE) and transportation, communications, and utilities (TCU) have also shown significantly larger THS

FIGURE 4

Proportion (%) of THS in each sector's employment

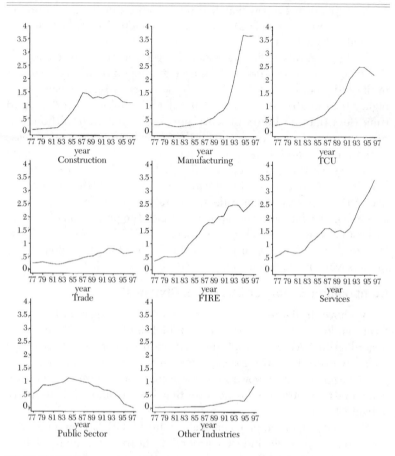

intensity in the 1990s. But—in contrast to manufacturing—services, FIRE, and TCU arrived at this level of THS intensity through steady growth since the early 1980s. The proportion of THS workers in construction increased substantially between 1982 and 1987 but has remained roughly constant since then.

Within manufacturing, THS intensity increased a bit more in durable goods industries than in others (figure 5). In addition, the increase was somewhat more noticeable in high-tech industries—here defined as office and computing equipment (SIC 357) and electrical machinery,

FIGURE 5

Proportion (%) of THS employment in manufacturing industries

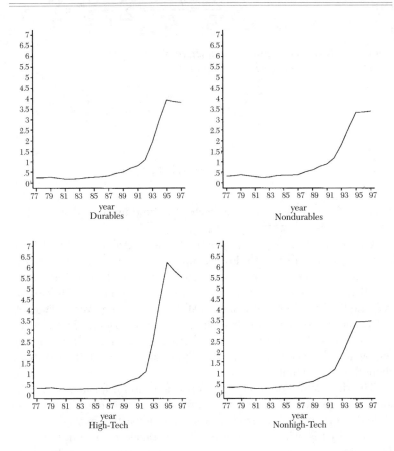

Durables

Nondurables

High-Tech

Nonhigh-Tech

related equipment, and supplies, excluding household appliances (SIC 36 excluding SIC 363).[6]

The proportion of the THS industry in total civilian employment, $\theta_t = T_t / E_t$, where T is the number of THS workers and E is total nonfarm employment, is equal to a weighted average of the θ_{it}'s in different industries, with weights given by the employment share of each industry. Thus, the changes over time in the aggregate proportion θ_t depend on changes in the proportion of THS workers used by each industry, θ_{it}, and on the size of the various industries. More precisely,

(3)
$$\theta_t = \frac{T_t}{E_t} = \frac{\sum_{i=1}^{I} T_{it}}{E_t} = \sum_{i=1}^{I} \frac{E_{it}}{E_t} \frac{T_{it}}{E_{it}} = \sum_{i=1}^{I} s_{it} \theta_{it}$$

where $s_{it} = E_{it}/E_t$ is the employment share of industry i.

The change in θ over τ years is therefore

$$\Delta \theta_t = \theta_t - \theta_{t-\tau} = \sum_{i=1}^{I} (s_{it} - s_{it-\tau}) \bar{\theta}_{it} + \sum_{i=1}^{I} (\theta_{it} - \theta_{it-\tau}) \bar{s}_{it}$$

(4)

$$= \sum_{i=1}^{I} \Delta s_{it} \bar{\theta}_{it} + \sum_{i=1}^{I} \Delta \theta_{it} \bar{s}_{it}$$

where a bar over the variable indicates the time mean of that variable, for example, $\bar{s}_{it} = \frac{s_{it} + s_{it-\tau}}{2}$.

Equation (4) can be used to compute the contribution of individual sectors to aggregate growth. For example, the employment share of the manufacturing sector declined from 25% in 1977 to 15% in 1997. Thus $\bar{s}_{it} = 0.20$ and $\Delta s_{it} = -0.10$. However, the proportion of THS workers increased from 0.00001 to almost 0.04 during the same years. Thus, $\bar{\theta}_{it} \cong 0.02$ and $\Delta \theta_{it} \cong 0.04$. Putting all this information together, we calculate that the contribution of the manufacturing sector to the change in aggregate θ between 1977 and 1997 is $-0.10 \times 0.02 + 0.04 \times 0.20$, or about 0.5–0.6 percentage points.

The decomposition in equation (4) is also useful for identifying the sources of growth. At one extreme, growth in the aggregate proportion of THS workers can occur even when no industry increased its THS intensity, that is, when $\Delta \theta_{it} = 0$ for all i, as a consequence of the more THS-intensive industries increasing their size over time. In this case, aggregate growth is due to a purely *compositional component*.

On the other hand, all industries may be growing at the same pace, $\Delta s_{it} = 0$ for all i, so that changes in the aggregate θ are directly related to changes in industry-specific θ_{it}'s, their THS intensity, indicating changes in the hiring pattern within individual industries. This is the *within component* of aggregate growth.

Table 3 shows the contribution of the compositional and the within components to the growth in the ratio of THS workers to total civilian employment. The data clearly show that most of the growth in this ratio can be

TABLE 3

Growth Decomposition of the Ratio of THS to Total Civilian Employment
(%)

	Compositional component	Within component	Total change
1977-82	.008	.087	.095
	(8.5)	(91.5)	
1982-87	.023	.441	.464
	(5.0)	(95.0)	
1987-92	.019	.284	.303
	(6.2)	(93.8)	
1992-97	.029	.777	.805
	(3.6)	(96.4)	
1977-97	.046	1.622	1.668
	(2.8)	(97.2)	
1977-87	.042	.517	.559
	(7.5)	(92.5)	
1987-97	.054	1.055	1.109
	(4.8)	(95.2)	

Note: Contribution to total change in parentheses.

attributed to increases in the latter. In fact, in the most recent period, between 1992 and 1997, this component accounted for more than 96% of the increase in the proportion of THS workers among all civilian employees.

Table 4 presents a breakdown of the two components by different sectors. As the third row shows, the public sector was the only one making a negative contribution to the growth of aggregate θ. More than 90% of its negative contribution came from a change in hiring behavior (the within component) and not from the observed relative shrinking of public-sector employment (the compositional effect). The service sector accounted for about half of the increase in THS use in the United States since 1977 (0.86 of a percentage point of the 1.67 percentage point increase in the aggregate θ), while manufacturing accounted for about a third of the increase (0.50 of a percentage point).

Virtually all of the contribution from manufacturing between 1987 and 1997 originated from the within component, suggesting a dramatic structural change in manufacturers' hiring behavior during this period. This structural change is all the more remarkable because it coincided with a significant decline in the share of manufacturing employment and, therefore, a negative contribution of this sector to the compositional component.[7]

Within manufacturing, as shown in table 5, the change in THS intensity in durable goods industries (the within component shown in the

TABLE 4
Growth Decomposition of the Ratio of THS to Total Civilian Employment by Industry
(percentage points)

	Mfg.	Services	Public	Construct.	Trade	FIRE	TCU	Other	Total change
1977-97									
Comp.	-.150	.198	-.006	.000	.005	.008	-.004	-.007	.046
Within	.648	.660	-.089	.048	.092	.127	.104	.033	1.622
Total	.499	.858	-.095	.048	.097	.135	.100	.026	1.668
1977-87									
Comp.	-.015	.051	-.011	.002	.005	.011	-.002	-.001	.042
Within	.015	.216	.075	.065	.045	.077	.023	.002	.517
Total	.000	.267	.064	.068	.050	.088	.021	.002	.559
1987-97									
Comp.	-.055	.130	-.004	-.003	-.002	-.011	.001	-.003	.054
Within	.553	.461	-.156	-.016	.049	.059	.078	.027	1.055
Total	.498	.592	-.160	-.019	.047	.048	.079	.024	1.109

TABLE 5
Growth Decomposition of the Ratio of Manufacturing THS to Total Manufacturing Employment
(percentage points)

	Durables	Nondurables	Total change	High-Tech	Low-Tech	Total change
1977-1997						
Between	.006	-.005	.000	.051	-.033	.018
Within	2.105	1.272	3.378	.523	2.837	3.360
Total	2.111	1.267	3.378	.574	2.804	3.378
1977-1987						
Between	.000	.000	.000	.005	-.006	-.002
Within	.048	.026	.074	.001	.074	.076
Total	.048	.026	.074	.006	.068	.074
1987-1997						
Between	.007	-.007	.001	-.008	.005	-.003
Within	2.056	1.247	3.303	.576	2.731	3.306
Total	2.063	1.241	3.304	.568	2.736	3.304

Note: High-tech industries defined as office and computing equipment (SIC 357) and electrical machinery, related equipment, and supplies, excluding household appliances (SIC 36 excluding SIC 363).

second row) accounts for about 62% of the 3.4 percentage point increase during 1977–1997. Compositional effects are insignificant. High-tech industries explain about 17% of the total variation in manufacturing THS intensity, even though they constitute only 10% of manufacturing employment.

Using the estimates of industry-specific THS employment and shares, we adjust the observed employment levels in each industry upward. Figure 6 plots the evolution of annual employment levels from 1977 to 1997 after taking into account the employment of THS workers.[8] As noted earlier, while employment other than THS has been going up in most industries, it declined in manufacturing, so that at the end of 1997 manufacturing employment remained significantly below the peak reached in 1989. However, after correcting for THS hires (the dots in figure 6), manufacturing employment in 1997 was only slightly lower than the level observed in 1989.

Conclusion

This chapter focuses on estimating the distribution of THS workers across eight major sectors of the U.S. economy using input-output data and information from the 1995 and 1997 Contingent Worker Supplement to the CPS. In 1997, about 75% of all THS employees worked in manufacturing or service-sector firms, compared with 40% in 1982. This reallocation of THS workers occurred at the expense of the public sector. It was accompanied by changing characteristics of the THS employees in the direction of significantly more males and blue-collar workers who are, on average, a bit more educated now than they had been in the 1980s.

Our results show that the recent large increase in the proportion of THS workers in the economy is due to a change in the hiring behavior of firms in the private sector rather than to a reallocation of workers from the less to the more THS-intensive industries. This suggests that the reasons for the dramatic growth in THS employment should be traced to the forces underlying changes in firms' hiring patterns.

Many reasons to explain the rapid spread of THS arrangements have been advanced elsewhere in this volume and in the literature. These include the potential for employers to implement a lower wage rate and a two-tier wage structure by contracting with intermediaries that pay less for similar work, to realize scale economies due to specialization in the provision of specific tasks, to increase productivity given that THS employees may be better screened or trained than temporary workers hired directly by the firm (Autor 1998; Polivka 1996), and to facilitate more rapid

FIGURE 6

Reported and Adjusted Payroll Employment (thousands), 1977–1997
— Reported   o Adjusted

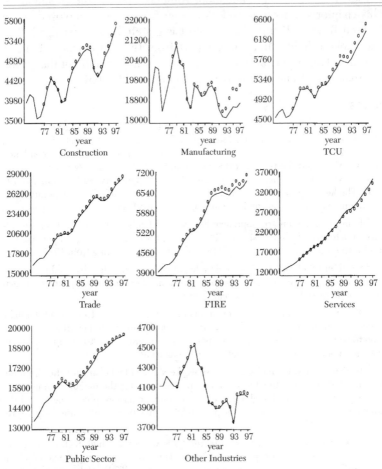

changes in firms' levels of employment in response to temporary or unpredictable changes in demand (Abraham and Taylor 1996; Golden 1996).

The estimates of temporary employment by sector discussed in this chapter should provide guidance for future research aimed at testing some of these potential explanations. In particular, researchers must account for the observed differences in the timing of the changes in firms' hiring behavior in the manufacturing and service-sector industries.

Acknowledgments

We would like to thank Carol Corrado, Ellen Dykes, Marianne A. Ferber, Lonnie Golden, and Beth Anne Wilson for their comments. This chapter was written while Marcello Estevão was employed at the Federal Reserve Board; their support is gratefully acknowledged. Saul Lach acknowledges financial support from the Employment Policies Institute. This paper presents the authors' own view and not that of the International Monetary Fund or any members of its staff.

Notes

[1] Prior to the 1987 revision of the Standard Industrial Classification (SIC) scheme, THS firms were classified as SIC 7362 and were part of SIC 736, which also included Employment Agencies (7361) and a residual category. The 1987 revision combined the THS firms and the residual category (excluding facilities and continuing maintenance services) into a single category named "Help Supply Services," classified as SIC 7363. The help supply industry employment includes the staff of the temporary agencies themselves, as well as employee-leasing agency workers.

[2] Using a nonparametric approach, Estevão and Lach (1999) use workers' individual characteristics from the March CPS tapes to provide a tight range of possible values for the probability of finding a THS worker in manufacturing from 1972 to 1997.

[3] Segal and Sullivan (1995) had already pointed out that the observed rise in the proportion of blue-collar workers among THS employees in the early 1990s was evidence of increased demand from manufacturers.

[4] The proportion of male workers in manufacturing (67% in 1997) is substantially larger than in the rest of the economy (48% in 1997). Also, manufacturing employees tend to work longer hours: 41.5 hours per week on average in 1997, as opposed to an average of 36.8 hours per week outside manufacturing.

[5] In Estevão and Lach (1999), we use workers' individual characteristics from the March CPS tapes to estimate assignment probabilities for the manufacturing sector in the missing years. Although those estimates provide a more precise picture of the annual variations in the assignment probabilities, they do not affect the longer-term trends discussed here.

[6] Given the breakdown provided by the CPS, we defined high-tech industries as the lowest aggregate that captures developments in office and computing equipment (SIC 357), semiconductors and related products (SIC 3674), and communications equipment (SIC 366).

[7] The combination of the two effects suggests that manufacturers may have substituted temporary workers hired from THS firms for directly hired temporary workers.

[8] To add up regular and THS employees, we must assume that THS workers are full-time equivalents and are not merely replacing temporary absent regular employees. The general perception is that THS workers are regarded as fully substitutable for regular employees.

References

Abraham, Katherine G., and Susan K. Taylor. 1996. "Firms' Use of Outside Contractors: Theory and Evidence." *Journal of Labor Economics*, Vol. 14, no. 3, pp. 394–424.

Autor, David. 1998. "Why Do Temporary Help Firms Provide Free General Skills Training?" Unpublished paper, JFK School of Government, Harvard University.

Estevão, Marcello, and Saul Lach. 1999. *Measuring Temporary Labor Outsourcing in U.S. Manufacturing*. NBER Working Paper No. 7421. Cambridge, MA: National Bureau of Economic Research.

Golden, Lonnie. 1996. "The Expansion of Temporary Help Employment in the U.S., 1982–1992: A Test of Alternative Economic Explanations." *Applied Economics*, Vol. 28, pp. 1127–1141.

Polivka, Anne E. 1996. "Are Temporary Help Agency Workers Substitutes for Direct Hire Temps? Searching for an Alternative Explanation of Growth in the Temporary Help Industry." Unpublished paper, Bureau of Labor Statistics.

Segal, Lewis M., and Daniel G. Sullivan. 1995. "The Temporary Labor Force." *Economic Perspectives*, Vol. 19, pp. 2–19.

Segal, Lewis M., and Daniel G. Sullivan. 1997. "The Growth of Temporary Services Work." *Journal of Economic Perspectives*, Vol. 11, no. 2 (Spring), pp. 117–136.

Chapter 5

Organization Size and Flexible Staffing Arrangements in the United States

Arne L. Kalleberg and Jeremy Reynolds
University of North Carolina at Chapel Hill

Introduction

Organizational studies are useful for addressing debates about the nature and growth of nonstandard or flexible staffing arrangements. We use the term *flexible staffing arrangements* to refer to the use of employment intermediaries, such as temporary help agencies and contract companies, as well as part-time, on-call, and other temporary nonstandard workers that an organization may hire directly. (Figure 1 describes these flexible staffing arrangements.) It is important to examine employers' motivations for using flexible staffing arrangements, since it has been argued that their growth is due more to employers' demands for such kinds of work than to the needs and desires of employees (see for instance Golden and Appelbaum 1992). Moreover, hiring employees from intermediaries such as contract companies or temporary help agencies creates interorganizational relationships that need to be better understood.

Despite their potential importance, studies of how and why diverse organizations use flexible staffing arrangements are relatively scarce. Research on nontraditional work arrangements (such as the studies represented in this volume) tends to focus on individuals or industries. Studies that do examine organizations are often restricted to a few selected establishments or firms or to large organizations. Table 1 summarizes the relatively few surveys of flexible staffing arrangements in the United States that study both small and large organizations.[1]

In this chapter, we argue that examining the use of flexible staffing arrangements in organizations of different sizes helps us to better understand employers' motivations for using them. We maintain that an organization's number of employees is both a proxy for other size-linked organizational features (such as degree of organizational slack, bureaucratization,

145

FIGURE 1

Flexible Staffing Arrangements

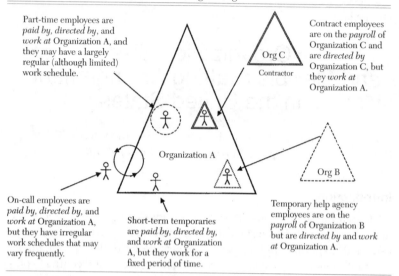

Part-time employees are *paid by, directed by*, and *work at* Organization A, and they may have a largely regular (although limited) work schedule.

Contract employees are on the *payroll* of Organization C and are *directed by* Organization C, but they *work at* Organization A.

Organization A

Org C

Contractor

Org B

On-call employees are *paid by, directed by*, and *work at* Organization A, but they have irregular work schedules that may vary frequently.

Short-term temporaries are *paid by, directed by*, and *work at* Organization A, but they work for a fixed period of time.

Temporary help agency employees are on the *payroll* of Organization B but are *directed by* and *work at* Organization A.

or unionization) and an independent source of variability in organizations' use of flexible staffing arrangements. We first describe our survey of flexible staffing arrangements among U.S. establishments. Then we present data from this survey that show to what extent the use of such arrangements differs among small and large organizations. Finally, we discuss some of the reasons organizations of different sizes vary in their use of flexible staffing arrangements.

The Second National Organizations Survey (NOS-II)

The NOS-II survey[2] studied flexible staffing arrangements used by organizations with different numbers of employees. This variability with regard to number of employees makes it possible for us to examine the use of flexible staffing arrangements by small as well as big organizations. Table 2 compares the distribution of establishments in the NOS-II sample by size (defined here as the sum of full-time and part-time employees[3] within the establishment) to the overall size distribution (defined in the same way) in the United States in 1995.

The NOS-II sample was drawn from a list of U.S. establishments provided by Dun and Bradstreet (D & B) Information Services that was stratified by number of employees. Stratifying by establishment size is needed because the overwhelming majority of work organizations in the

TABLE 1

Studies of Flexible Staffing Arrangements in Small and Large U.S. Organizations

Source	Date of survey	Data/sample	Types of flexible staffing arrangements studied
Mangum, Mayall, Nelson (1985)	1981	882 firms of all sizes in 6 industries	Temporary help agencies, on-call and short-term hires
Davis-Blake and Uzzi (1993)	1980, 1982	2,752 establishments of all sizes, sampled from 28 SMSAs by U.S. Department of Labor	Temporary jobs, independent contractors
Harrison and Kelley (1993)	1986-87	1,015 plants in 21 U.S. metalworking industries, size-stratified random sample	Subcontractors (outsourcing)
Kalleberg and Schmidt (1996)	1991	724 U.S. establishments of all sizes	Temporary, subcontracting, part-time
Houseman (1997)	1996	550 U.S. establishments with 5 or more employees	Temporary help agencies, on-call and short-term hires, independent contractors, part-time

United States are small: over half (54.7%) have between 0 and 4 employees (see the U.S. percentage column denoted by *b* in table 2). Small establishments are likely to have relatively similar human resource practices with regard to their use of flexible staffing arrangements. To ensure that the sample contained many mid-sized and large organizations (which are more likely to have diverse employment relations), we sampled establishments with probability proportional to their size (see Kalleberg, Knoke, and Marsden 1995). The resulting sample of establishments in the NOS-II survey is thus reasonably representative of the percentage of people employed by establishments of various sizes in the United States (see last column of table 2) and is useful for examining how flexible staffing arrangements vary accordingly among different-sized organizations.

TABLE 2

Number and Percentage of Establishments by Size, NOS-II Survey and United States

Size (FT + PT emp.)	NOS-II		U.S.[a]		
	n^b	$\%^b$	n^b	$\%^b$	$\%^c$
0-4	106	10.7	3,615,128	54.7	6.2
5-9	72	7.3	1,299,747	19.7	8.6
10-19	89	9.0	817,905	12.4	11.0
20-49	152	15.3	544,197	8.2	16.4
50-99	103	10.4	185,305	2.8	12.7
100-249	126	12.7	107,370	1.6	16.0
250-499	85	8.6	27,206	0.4	9.3
500-999	72	7.3	10,335	0.2	7.0
1,000+	186	18.8	6,027	0.1	12.9
Total	991	100.0	6,613,218	100.0	100.1

[a] *Source: County Business Patterns*, 1995
[b] Numbers and percentages of establishments in each size category
[c] Percentage of people employed in each size category

Organizational Size and Flexible Staffing Arrangements: Past Research

Previous studies of the relationship between organization size and flexible staffing arrangements have focused on various types of nonstandard work (e.g., temporary help agencies: Mangum, Mayall, and Nelson 1985; contractors: Abraham and Taylor 1996). They have often yielded inconsistent findings about organizations' use of these arrangements, especially their use of workers from temporary and contract companies.

Temporary Workers

The evidence regarding whether larger establishments are more likely to use temporary employees is conflicting. Davis-Blake and Uzzi (1993) hypothesize that there should be a negative association between the size of the establishment and its use of temporaries. In part, they argue that this is because large establishments are more bureaucratic and seek stable and committed employees; thus, larger establishments are less likely to prefer temporary workers, who are seen as being unstable and transient. In addition, they suggest that larger organizations tend to have greater slack and hence have more available employees who can be reassigned to meet temporary needs in case of increased demand.[4] Larger organizations also have more job titles to which they can reassign employees in case of decreased demand. Consistent with their hypotheses, Davis-Blake and Uzzi (1993) found that size (measured by the number of employees) was negatively related to whether the organization used temporary workers at all, as well as to the proportion of temporaries within the organization.[5]

By contrast, Mangum et al. (1985) found that the use of temporary help agency, on-call, and limited-duration hires was positively associated with firm size. They argued that large firms had more rationalized hiring systems and were thus better able to identify when and where temporary workers could be used efficiently. Larger organizations may also have a harder time discharging standard workers and adjusting their hiring practices to changing conditions. Mangum et al. (1985) found that firms that used only "permanent" workers to cover their temporary work needs were likely to be small and to have less costly benefit structures.

Moreover, Görg, Killen, and Ruane's (1998) analysis of Irish manufacturing firms found that large firms use nonstandard employment arrangements (part-time, temporary, and short-term contract) more often than small firms. They reasoned that large firms are more likely to have built up an efficient core group of permanent, regular employees and are able to absorb nonstandard employees more easily. However, they also found that small firms use a larger proportion of nonstandard employees if they use them at all. Michon and Ramaux (1993) also found support for both of these hypotheses in France.

Houseman (1997) found that larger establishments in the United States were more likely to use agency temporaries, on-call workers, and short-term hires (i.e., higher incidence of use), even when controlling for industry, occupation, percentage unionized, fringe benefits, and the area unemployment rate. On the other hand, she found that size was unrelated to the percentage of temporary help agency workers and short-term hires in the establishment's labor force (i.e., intensity of use), once these other variables were controlled. Kalleberg and Schmidt (1996) also found that larger establishments in the United States are more likely to use temporary help agencies, though they found that small establishments had the highest proportion of temporary employees.

Finally, Lautsch (1995) observed that establishments with 500–999 employees used relatively more temporary help agency employees in "core" occupations than did establishments with 50–99 employees (the omitted category) but not more direct hire temporaries. She found no other differences among size categories.[6]

Contractors

In contrast to their results for temporaries, Davis-Blake and Uzzi's (1993) analysis showed that establishments with a larger number of employees were more likely to use independent contractors. They explained this as also being due partly to the impact of bureaucratization: since independent contractors control their own work, they constitute a source of stability and do not disrupt routine organizational practices. Beyond that, they suggested that large organizations need more specialized skills and services on a short-term basis because they produce a wider range of products or services.

Uzzi and Barsness (1998) also found that the number of full-time employees was positively related to the use of fixed-term contractors (persons hired to work on site for a preset, limited time who have administrative control over their work assignments). They offer four explanations for this relationship: (1) larger organizations have a larger and more diverse pool of jobs that can be filled by nonstandard workers; (2) larger organizations are better able to achieve economies of scale and thus have lower marginal costs of training and managing nonstandard workers; (3) bigger organizations produce a larger range of products or services and are thus more likely to require access to expertise that might not be cost efficient to develop in house (see also Harrison and Kelley 1993); and (4) bigger organizations offer better opportunities for permanent employment and so may be more likely to attract nonstandard workers.

Penn (1992) also found that firm size had a positive effect on use of independent contractors. So too did Harrison and Kelley (1993), who found that the larger the parent company, the more likely some portion of machining production operations is to be subcontracted out. They reasoned that maintaining subcontracting relationships with outside firms is likely to be an important objective of larger companies, in order to give them an external buffer capacity for expansion if there were to be unexpected surges in demand. Kalleberg and Schmidt (1996) also found that larger establishments are more likely to use subcontractors. Similarly, Houseman (1997) found that larger establishments in the United States were more likely to use contract workers, even after controlling for industry, occupation, unionization, fringe benefits, and the area unemployment rate.

On the other hand, Abraham and Taylor (1996) found that larger organizations are less likely to contract out work. They explained this by arguing that small or medium-sized organizations may not find it cost effective to do a certain function in house (though the establishments in their survey were not that small, with minimum sizes ranging from 20 to 100 employees). They discovered that smaller establishments are more likely to contract out machine maintenance, engineering, drafting, accounting, and computer services (but not janitorial services). This is consistent with their argument that there are important economies of scale associated with these functions since it does not pay for small organizations to do them. Harrison and Kelley (1993) also found that the probability of contracting out functions was greater in production processes within plants with a smaller number of machining employees. They explained this by arguing that the smaller the operation, the more likely it is that the plant has a capacity or specialty constraint and thus needs to depend more on subcontractors to meet its requirements. Finally, Russell and Hanneman (1997) found that firm size was negatively related to the use of independent contractors in Russia.

Measuring Flexible Staffing Arrangements (FSAs): New Evidence

The NOS-II survey asked managers about the establishment's use of nonstandard workers, such as part-time, direct-hire temporary, and on-call workers. Organizations' use of temporary help agencies and contract companies was assessed indirectly from a series of questions about the characteristics of the employment arrangements associated with different activities. The appendix provides details on our operationalization of these flexible staffing arrangements.

Organizational Size and FSAs

Table 3 presents two kinds of measures of the use of flexible staffing arrangements by establishments of different sizes.[5, 7] First, we provide estimates of the incidence of use: whether or not establishments in each

TABLE 3

Use of Flexible Staffing Arrangements by Establishment Size, NOS-II Survey

	Direct hires						Employment intermediaries							
	Part-time		On-call		Temporaries		Temporary help agency				Contract company			
							On site		Off site		On site		Subcontract	
Size (FTE)	%	Mean % in estab.	%	Mean % in estab.	%	Mean % in estab.	%	Mean prop. in estab.	%	Mean prop. in estab.	%	Mean prop. in estab.	%	Mean prop. in estab.
0-4	44	53	17	60	15	45	10	0.23	20	0.24	9	0.26	36	0.34
5-9	64	40	19	15	26	36	12	0.36	10	0.18	8	0.19	48	0.26
10-19	73	34	14	7	23	20	19	0.20	22	0.22	10	0.20	35	0.24
20-49	68	28	22	25	25	16	15	0.20	16	0.23	15	0.19	26	0.25
50-99	82	26	18	4	22	15	20	0.22	13	0.18	20	0.24	24	0.17
100-249	80	18	22	6	28	12	24	0.19	15	0.17	25	0.16	19	0.19
250-499	75	19	31	4	49	6	38	0.19	13	0.17	26	0.16	27	0.16
500-999	91	17	29	6	49	8	51	0.25	9	0.14	33	0.21	18	0.16
1,000+	82	15	41	4	43	7	42	0.26	6	0.15	32	0.20	15	0.15
All establishments	73	25	25	14	30	14	25	0.23	13	0.20	20	0.20	26	0.23
Correlation with log FTE	.258**	-.174**	.180**	-.091**	.219**	-.101**	.275**	.226**	-.114**	-.134**	.208**	.151**	-.197**	-.268**
Independent	70	26	23	14	30	16	21	0.23	15	0.21	18	0.19	27	0.24
Part of larger org	78	23	30	13	29	11	34	0.24	10	0.17	24	0.21	22	0.20
Correlation with "Larger org"	.082*	-.013	.069*	.012	-.006	-.050	.140**	.113**	-.073*	-.080*	.067	.066*	-.055	-.082*

* $p < .05$; ** $p < .01$

size category use each flexible staffing arrangement (e.g., 44% of establishments with four or fewer FTE employees use part-timers). Second, we present estimates of the intensity or extensiveness with which the flexible staffing arrangement is used. We report the mean percentage of the establishment's workforce constituted by part-timers, on-call workers, and direct-hire temporaries (e.g., direct-hire temporaries constitute, on average, 45% of the workforce in establishments with four or fewer FTE employees that use such temporaries at all). We use the proportion of functional activities for which the establishment uses each type of intermediary as our measure of the intensity of use of employment intermediaries.[8] In addition, we provide correlations between the establishment's size (measured both by the log of its FTE employees and by whether it is part of a larger firm) and both the incidence and intensity of its use of the flexible staffing arrangement.

These data show that organizations with more employees are more likely to have part-time employees. However, smaller establishments are more likely to have a higher proportion of part-time employees (see also Montgomery 1988). By contrast, Houseman's (1997) survey of U.S. establishments found that establishment size was unrelated to the organization's use of part-time workers and positively related to the proportion of part-time workers in its workforce.

Establishment size was also correlated positively with the use of on-call workers. The largest organizations in the NOS-II (250+ and especially 1,000+) were most likely to employ on-call workers. The proportion of on-call workers within the establishment, however, was negatively correlated with number of employees. Large establishments were also more likely to use direct-hire temporaries, though these temporaries again constituted a bigger proportion of the workforce in small establishments.

Organization size was related in more complex ways to the use of on-site versus off-site employees from temporary help agencies and contract companies. An establishment's size is positively related to both the incidence and intensity of use of on-site employees from temporary help agencies. On the other hand, both the incidence and extensiveness of use of off-site employees from temporary help agencies are negatively and significantly related to establishment size.

We observe a similar pattern for contract company workers. Larger establishments are more likely to employ the services of contract companies in which workers work on site, while small establishments are more likely to use subcontractors, who do the work off site. These patterns are similar for both the incidence and extensiveness of use of contract companies.

Moreover, establishments that are part of a larger firm are more likely than independent firms to use part-timers, on-call workers, and on-site employees of temporary help agencies but are less likely to use off-site temporary help agency employees. They are also slightly more likely to use on-site contract companies more intensively, while independent firms are slightly more likely to use off-site contract companies (i.e., subcontractors) more intensively.

Taken as a whole, these results suggest that large establishments are more likely than small establishments to use part-time, on-call, and short-term temporary employees. Large establishments are also more apt to utilize some kinds of temporary help agencies and contract companies. However, small employers also use flexible staffing arrangements to a substantial degree and may use some types—such as off-site temporary help agency employees and subcontractors—more frequently and extensively than large organizations. Moreover, when they use such workers at all, a bigger proportion of the workforce of small organizations than of large organizations appears to consist of part-timers, on-call workers, and direct-hire temporaries.

Why Small and Large Organizations Use Flexible Staffing Arrangements

One way to ascertain why organizations of different sizes differ in their use of flexible staffing arrangements is by asking managers directly about their reasons for using them. Managers were asked to evaluate the relative importance of four common reasons for the use of flexible staffing arrangements: (1) meeting fluctuations in the organization's demand for workers; (2) lowering costs (fringe benefit costs and costs associated with administrative tasks); (3) providing unique or special skills that the establishment cannot or chooses not to have in house; and (4) screening potential employees. Table 4 presents the answers they provided concerning their use of temporary help agency and contract company workers.[9]

Dealing with fluctuations in demand appears to motivate both small and large organizations to use temporary help agencies and contract companies. Thus, there appears to be no overall difference among organizations of different sizes in the importance placed on this concern.

There is also relatively little overall difference between large and small organizations in the extent to which they use temporary help agencies and contract companies to lower fringe benefit costs. However, managers of organizations with 10–49 employees are less likely to place high importance on this than are managers in smaller or larger establishments.

TABLE 4

Reasons for Using Temporary Help Agencies and Contract Companies, NOS-II Survey

"How important are the following reasons for using workers from outside your organization?"
1 = Not at all important; 2 = Slightly important; 3 = Moderately important; 4 = Very important

Reason	Mean scores by establishment size (FTE)										r with log FTE
	0-4	5-9	10-19	20-49	50-99	100-249	250-499	500-999	1,000+	Total	
The **demand** for work varies	3.1	2.9	2.5	2.5	2.7	2.6	2.5	3.0	2.7	2.7	-0.055
Lowers costs by avoiding fringe benefits	2.2	2.4	1.8	1.9	2.1	2.2	2.2	2.4	2.3	2.2	0.065
Simplifies **administrative** tasks	2.7	2.3	2.2	2.4	2.2	2.1	2.3	2.5	2.2	2.3	-0.080°°
They provide **special skills**	3.0	2.6	3.1	3.0	2.9	2.8	2.6	2.4	2.7	2.8	-0.104°
See performance before hiring	2.0	2.2	1.6	2.0	2.0	2.2	2.4	2.3	2.1	2.1	0.085°°

° $p < .05$; °° $p < .10$

The frequency with which the other reasons are mentioned, however, differs by size. Small establishments are more likely than large
ones to use temporary help agencies and contract companies to obtain
workers with special skills. This is consistent with the "economies of
scale" argument suggested by Abraham and Taylor (1996). Managers of
small establishments are also more apt to say that they use temporary
help agencies and contract companies because they simplify administrative tasks. This consideration is likely to be especially important to small
establishments, since they are less likely to have staff members who can
be assigned such responsibilities. Generally, larger companies more
often have workers with specialized skills in house. On the other hand,
large establishments may be slightly more likely than small ones to use
intermediaries in order to better screen prospective employees before
hiring them permanently. Mangum et al. (1985) suggest that this is
because the costs of monitoring and firing employees are greater in
larger firms.[10]

Multivariate Analyses

Another way of assessing why large and small organizations differ in
their use of flexible staffing arrangements is by estimating multivariate
models that include variables representing hypothesized reasons for
their use. To the extent that these additional explanatory variables
decrease or eliminate the significance of the size coefficients, these
additional variables can be said to help account for the size difference in
the flexible staffing arrangement.

Table 5 presents estimates of the "direct" or net effects of size, controlling for a set of explanatory variables.[11] We also include a measure of
whether the establishment was part of a larger firm in our models but
do not report results, since very little difference is revealed in the use of
flexible staffing arrangements between establishments that are independent firms and those that are part of a larger firm.

The explanatory variables included in the regressions are indicators
of labor demand (seasonal variations, cyclical variations, and the manager's perception of the extent to which the organization is committed to
avoiding layoffs); whether the organization has a human resources strategy that emphasizes a core–periphery distinction; costs of labor (level of
fringe benefits and extent of unionization); degree of foreign competition (which we use as an indicator of pressure on the organization to
minimize costs); the relative importance to the organization's competitive strategy of maintaining quality versus lowering costs; degree of

TABLE 5

Effects of Establishment Size on Flexible Staffing Arrangements,
NOS-II Survey

	Net size effects	ln(FTE)
	β	SE
Direct hires		
Part-time	0.467°	0.102
Percentage part-time	-1.654°°	0.742
On-call	0.092	0.093
Percentage on-call	-3.136°	0.864
Temp (direct hire)	0.247°	0.081
Percentage temp (direct hire)	-0.369	0.394
Employment intermediaries		
THA (on site)	0.516°	0.103
Proportion THA (on site)	0.017°	0.003
THA (off site)	-0.098	0.114
Proportion THA (off site)	-0.004	0.003
Contractor (on site)	0.225°°	0.099
Proportion contractor (on site)	0.005	0.003
Subcontractor	-0.172°°°	0.091
Proportion subcontractor	-0.010°	0.004

Equations include measures of industry seasonality, industry cyclicality, organizational commitment to avoiding layoffs, distinction between permanent and nonpermanent employees, fringe benefits, amount of foreign competition, difficulty keeping employee skills up to date, perceived labor shortage, establishment growth, unionization, government regulation, boundarylessness, nonprofit status, emphasis on quality, bureaucratization, firm internal labor markets, ownership by a larger organization, percentage of full-time workers who are female, establishment age, and dummy variables representing two-digit SIC industry codes.
° $p < .01$; °° $p < .05$; °°° $p < .10$

bureaucratization; extent of firm internal labor markets; need for labor (perceived labor shortage, degree to which the establishment has grown in the past two years, and the extent to which the organization's employees have difficulty in keeping up with new technology); the extent to which the organization is connected to suppliers and customers; whether the establishment is a profit-seeking or a nonprofit organization; the presence of government reporting requirements; the gender composition of the establishment's full-time workforce; the establishment's age; and a set of dummy variables representing the establishment's industry. All these variables are described in appendix table 1. A number of them are significantly related to the organization's use of flexible staffing arrangements. For example, industry seasonal variations are associated with more extensive use of part-timers and direct-hire temporaries, industry cycles are associated with more extensive use of on-call employees, and organizations committed to avoiding layoffs are more likely to use both on- and off-site temporary help agency employees. Results for these explanatory variables are discussed in Kalleberg, Reynolds, and Marsden (1999).

The coefficients in table 5 indicate that small and large establishments differ in their use of many of the flexible staffing arrangements, even after controlling for the additional explanatory variables previously described. For instance, large establishments are more likely to use part-timers and direct-hire temporaries at all, while small establishments are more likely to use a higher proportion of part-time and on-call workers. Establishment size does not affect the likelihood of using on-call workers or the proportion of workers who are likely to be direct-hire temporaries.

Moreover, large establishments are more likely to use on-site temporary help agency employees and contractors and to use on-site temporaries for a larger proportion of their functional activities (there is no size difference in the proportion of activities for which on-site contractors are used). Small establishments are slightly more apt to use off-site subcontractors and to use them for a greater number of activities. However, the correlation between size and the use of off-site temporary help agency employees that we observed in table 3 appears to be accounted for by the other explanatory variables in our model, since there is no net size difference in the use of off-site temporary help agencies in table 5.

Conclusions

Small as well as large organizations use flexible staffing arrangements. Restricting studies of flexible staffing arrangements to large organizations thus neglects to consider the workplaces in which many people work, as well as the greatest number of establishments in the economy. The analysis has shown that while small establishments are more likely to use off-site employment intermediaries (though size was significantly and negatively related only to off-site subcontractors in the multivariate analysis), large establishments are more likely to use on-site intermediaries. Moreover, among those that use flexible staffing arrangements, smaller employers tend to use subcontractors relatively more extensively.

They are also more likely than large organizations to use employment intermediaries to obtain special skills and to lower administrative costs. However, large establishments appear to use employment intermediaries more often than small ones to screen potential employees.

The multivariate results indicate that large and small establishments use different flexible staffing arrangements and that those differences cannot always be explained away by correlates such as variability in demand, labor costs, degree of bureaucratization, the need for skills, organization's human resource strategy, workforce composition, unionization, and industry differences. Organizational size thus appears to have a distinct impact on employers' use of a number of flexible staffing arrangements that cannot be attributed to characteristic differences in industry, unionization, or a number of other variables that are often thought to account for the prevalence of nonstandard work. Some of the net effects of organizational size may represent the consequences of the sheer number of employees. Simmel (1950, pt. 2, chs. 1 and 2) offers a theoretical basis for the argument that the number of individuals in a group affects its social characteristics. For example, organizations with a greater number of standard employees may be more able to absorb additional nonstandard workers and still maintain stability and continuity. In other cases, size may be a proxy for a variety of organizational characteristics that we have not measured, such as other human resource practices or forms of structure associated with size (e.g., Kalleberg and Van Buren 1996).

Improving our understanding of the organizational sources of variation among employers in the use of flexible staffing arrangements remains an important goal for research. The nature and types of employment arrangements that emerge in the 21st century will depend in part on the complex trends in the size of organizations (see Acs and Audretsch 1993). For example, if larger organizations continue to downsize and adopt lean staffing practices, opportunities for career advancement within organizations may decline and be replaced by employment in smaller establishments that are linked by subcontracting relations and greater possibilities for interorganizational mobility (see, e.g., Kiechel 1993). To reach a better understanding of how and why U.S. organizations use flexible staffing arrangements, it is necessary to examine these networks among organizations more closely.

Acknowledgments

We thank Susan Houseman and the editors for helpful comments on earlier versions of this paper. This research was supported by National Science Foundation grant SBR-9507964 to Kalleberg.

Appendix: Measuring Flexible Staffing Arrangements in the NOS-II Survey

The following questions were used in the NOS-II interview to measure flexible staffing arrangements.

Regular part-time workers: "In total, how many part-time employees were on the payroll of [organization] as of June 1, 1996? By 'part-time' we mean less than 35 hours per week."

Direct-hire temporary workers: (If one or more full-time employees): "Were any of these full-time employees temporary workers?" (If one or more part-time employees): "Were any of these part-time employees temporary workers?"

On-call workers: "Are there any on-call workers at [organization]? On-call workers are temporary employees of [organization] or [larger organization] who don't have regularly scheduled work but are only called to work as needed, for example, substitute teachers."

Temporary help agency workers and contractors: "We'd like to know about who does various activities at [organization]. For each of the following activities, please tell me whether it is done by [organization]'s employees, by employees of [larger organization], or by someone else:"

[The functional activity areas are core product or service; secretarial, clerical, or other office work; computer information systems; accounting or payroll; research and development of new products and services; marketing or sales work; security services; janitorial services; repairs or service of machinery.]

If the respondent said that someone does the functional activity for [organization] and that it is done by someone other than employees of [organization] or [larger organization], then the respondent was asked whether the work is directed by someone at [organization] or by someone at the other organization and whether the work is done at [organization] or someplace else. The employment intermediaries were coded in the following way:

> *On-site temporary help agency:* Work is done in at least one of the functional activity areas, is directed by someone at [organization], and is done at [organization].

> *Off-site temporary help agency:* Work is done in at least one of the functional activity areas, is directed by someone at [organization], and is done someplace other than at [organization].

> *On-site contractor:* Work is done in at least one of the functional activity areas, is directed by someone other than [organization], and is done at [organization].

> *Subcontractor:* Work is done in at least one of the functional activity areas, is directed by someone other than [organization], and is done someplace other than at [organization].

APPENDIX TABLE 1
Definitions of Additional Explanatory Variables

Variable name	Variable definition
Industry seasonality	Measure of industry seasonality created using BLS nonfarm employment data from 1974 to 1994. The number is calculated by regressing the logarithm of monthly employment in the establishment's four-digit SIC code industry on month dummy variables and then finding the standard deviation of the set of 12 dummy variables. (Where the four-digit information was not available, we used three-digit or two-digit information.)
Industry cyclicality	Measure of industry cyclicality created using BLS nonfarm employment data from 1974 to 1994. The number is calculated by regressing the logarithm of the change in monthly employment in the establishment's four-digit SIC code industry on the logarithm of the change in monthly nonfarm employment plus month dummy variables. The measure is the coefficient of the logarithm of the change in monthly nonfarm employment. (Where the four-digit information was not available, we used three-digit or two-digit information.)
Organizational commitment to avoiding layoffs	Has your organization made any explicit or implicit commitment to its employees to avoid layoffs, except in extreme circumstances? (0 = no; 1 = yes)
Distinction between permanent and nonpermanent employees	Your human resource management strategy divides the workforce into permanent and nonpermanent employees. (1 = strongly disagree; 4 = strongly agree)
Fringe benefits	Sum of benefits provided by organization to its employees (pension, health insurance, payment of all medical/hospital benefits, payment of medical/hospital benefits more than 18 months into retirement)
Amount of foreign competition	How much competition would you say there is in your main market or service area from foreign organizations . . . none, very little, a moderate amount, or a great deal? (1 = none; 4 = a great deal)
Difficulty keeping employee skills up to date	Your employees have difficulty keeping their skills up to date. (1 = strongly disagree; 4 = strongly agree)

APPENDIX TABLE 1 (*Continued*)
Definitions of Additional Explanatory Variables

Variable name	Variable definition
Perceived labor shortage	Composite measure of labor shortage, based on four items: the manager's overall evaluation of how "difficult it is to find highly skilled workers" and the perceived difficulty of hiring workers with the necessary skills for the core, clerical, and managerial occupations
Establishment growth	Net increase in number of jobs in past two years
Unionization	Are any of your employees represented by a union or unions? (0 = no; 1 = yes)
Government regulation	Is [organization] required to report the sex, race, and age composition of its employees to any government agency? (0 = no; 1 = yes)
Boundarylessness	Measures the boundarylessness of an establishment: the extent to which the establishment's customers participate in the design, production, or service decisions and in the work, and how closely the establishment works with suppliers (High scores indicate more boundarylessness.)
Nonprofit status	Is this a NON-profit (= 1) or a FOR-profit (= 0) organization?
Emphasis on quality	Organization competes best by holding down costs versus organization; competes best by offering high-quality products or services (0 = costs; 1 = quality)
Bureaucratization	Measure of formalization and the number of levels between the frontline supervisor and the top official
Firm internal labor markets	Weighted average of FILM scales (based on promotion opportunities within the organization for that occupation) for the core, clerical, and managerial occupations
Ownership by a larger organization	Is [organization] in any way part of a larger organization, or is it completely independent? (0 = independent; 1 = part of larger organization)
Percentage of full-time workers who are female	In total, how many full-time employees were on the payroll of [organization] at [address] as of June 1, 1996? By "full-time" we mean 35 or more hours per week. Of these, about how many were women?
Establishment age	Age of establishment

Notes

[1] Not included in table 1 are the surveys that focused on relatively large organizations or only those above a certain size (such as 50 employees).

[2] The Second National Organizations Survey (NOS-II) was a telephone survey of 1,002 establishments carried out in 1996 by interviewers from the Center for Survey Research at the University of Minnesota. It was sponsored by the National Science Foundation (NSF) and was designed to provide social scientists with data on flexible staffing arrangements, training, and related topics for a representative sample of U.S. organizations (see Kalleberg, Knoke, and Marsden 1995). The NOS-II is the second such omnibus national survey of organizations in the United States sponsored by NSF; the first is summarized in Kalleberg, Knoke, Marsden, and Spaeth (1996).

[3] An organization's size can also be measured in terms of other dimensions, such as its profitability, market share, or assets.

[4] Larger organizations may also be more likely to have alternative flexible scheduling arrangements (e.g., flextime) that should reduce their need to hire temps (Christensen 1989).

[5] There are two distinct ways to measure the prevalence of organizations' use of temporaries and other flexible staffing arrangements: (1) the percentage of establishments using any temporary or flexible staff at all (the incidence of use) and (2) temporaries or flexible staff as a percentage of establishments' workforces (the intensity or extensiveness of use). We utilize both measures in our subsequent analysis.

[6] This partly reinforces Gordon and Thal-Larsen's (1969) earlier finding that use of temporary workers did not vary with firm size.

[7] In tables 3 to 5, we measured establishment size as the number of full-time equivalent (FTE) employees, which we approximated as the number of full-time workers plus 1/2 the number of part-time workers. We also measured size by whether or not the establishment is part of a larger firm.

[8] For example, the .25 figure for the use of on-site temporaries by establishments with 500–999 employees indicates that establishments of this size that use any on-site temporaries at all do so in an average of .25 of their functional areas. Thus, if they have four functional areas, they use intermediaries in one area; if they have eight areas, they use them in two areas, and so on.

[9] Unfortunately, the NOS-II survey does not permit us to distinguish between reasons why managers use temporary help agencies rather than contract companies.

[10] Wage expenses are also greater in larger firms (Brown, Hamilton, and Medoff 1990; Kalleberg and Van Buren 1996).

[11] We estimate logistic regressions predicting the presence or absence of a particular flexible staffing arrangement. We estimate OLS regressions for the proportions of part-time, on-call, or temporary workers in the establishment's total staff and for the proportions of functional areas in which employment intermediaries are used.

References

Abraham, Katharine G., and Susan K. Taylor. 1996. "Firms' Use of Outside Contractors: Theory and Evidence." *Journal of Labor Economics,* Vol. 14, no. 3, pp. 394–424.

Acs, Zoltan J., and David B. Audretsch. 1993. "Has the Role of Small Firms Changed in the United States?" In Zoltan J. Acs and David B. Audretsch, eds., *Small Firms and Entrepreneurship: An East-West Perspective.* Cambridge: Cambridge University Press, pp. 55–77.

Brown, Charles, James Hamilton, and James Medoff. 1990. *Employers Large and Small.* Cambridge, MA: Harvard University Press.

Christensen, Kathleen. 1989. *Flexible Staffing and Scheduling in U.S. Corporations.* Conference Board Bulletin No. 240. New York: Conference Board.

Davis-Blake, Alison, and Brian Uzzi. 1993. "Determinants of Employment Externalization: A Study of Temporary Workers and Independent Contractors." *Administrative Science Quarterly,* Vol. 38, pp. 195–223.

Golden, Lonnie, and Eileen Appelbaum. 1992. "What Is Driving the Boom in Temporary Employment?" *American Journal of Economics and Sociology,* Vol. 51, pp. 473–492.

Gordon, Margaret S., and Margaret Thal-Larsen. 1969. *Employer Policies in a Changing Labor Market.* Berkeley: Institute of Industrial Relations, University of California.

Görg, Holger, Lynn Killen, and Frances Ruane. 1998. "Nonstandard Employment in Irish Manufacturing: Do Firm Characteristics Matter?" *Labour,* Vol. 12, no. 4, pp. 675–699.

Harrison, Bennett, and Maryellen R. Kelley. 1993. "Outsourcing and the Search for 'Flexibility.'" *Work, Employment and Society,* Vol. 7, no. 2, pp. 213–235.

Houseman, Susan N. 1997. "Temporary, Part-Time, and Contract Employment in the United States: New Evidence from an Employer Survey." Unpublished paper, W. E. Upjohn Institute for Employment Research.

Kalleberg, Arne L., David Knoke, and Peter V. Marsden. 1995. "Interorganizational Networks and the Changing Employment Contract." *Connections,* Vol. 18, no. 2, pp. 32–49.

Kalleberg, Arne L., David Knoke, Peter V. Marsden, and Joe L. Spaeth. 1996. *Organizations in America: Analyzing Their Structures and Human Resource Practices.* Thousand Oaks, CA: Sage.

Kalleberg, Arne L., Jeremy Reynolds, and Peter V. Marsden. 1999. "Externalizing Employment: Flexible Staffing Arrangements in U.S. Organizations." Unpublished paper, Department of Sociology, University of North Carolina at Chapel Hill.

Kalleberg, Arne L., and Kathryn Schmidt. 1996. "Contingent Employment in Organizations: Part-Time, Temporary, and Subcontracting Relations." In Arne L. Kalleberg, David Knoke, Peter V. Marsden, and Joe L. Spaeth, *Organizations in America: Analyzing Their Structures and Human Resource Practices.* Thousand Oaks, CA: Sage, pp. 253–275.

Kalleberg, Arne L., and Mark E. Van Buren. 1996. "Is Bigger Better? Explaining the Relationship between Organization Size and Job Rewards." *American Sociological Review,* Vol. 61, pp. 47–66.

Kiechel, Walter, III. 1993. "How We Will Work in the Year 2000." *Fortune,* May 17, pp. 38–52.

Lautsch, Brenda A. 1995. "Institutionalizing Uncertainty: Growth in Contingent Employment and Change in Internal Labor Markets." Unpublished paper, Industrial Relations Section, Sloan School of Management, MIT, Cambridge, MA.

Mangum, Garth, Donald Mayall, and Kristin Nelson. 1985. "The Temporary Help Industry: A Response to the Dual Internal Labor Market." *Industrial and Labor Relations Review,* Vol. 38, no. 4, pp. 599–611.

Michon, F., and C. Ramaux. 1993. "Temporary Employment in France: A Decade Statement." *Labour,* Vol. 7, pp. 93–116.

Montgomery, Mark. 1988. "On the Determinants of Employer Demand for Part-Time Workers." *Review of Economics and Statistics,* Vol. 70, pp. 112–117.

Penn, Roger. 1992. "Flexibility in Britain during the 1980s: Recent Empirical Evidence." In G. Nigel Gilbert, Roger Burrows, and Anna Pollert, eds., *Fordism and Flexibility: Divisions and Change.* New York: St. Martin's Press, pp. 66–88.

Russell, Raymond, and Robert Hanneman. 1997. "The Use of Part-Time Employees and Independent Contractors by Small Enterprises in Russia." Paper presented at Annual Meetings of the American Sociological Association, Toronto, Canada.

Simmel, Georg. 1950. *The Sociology of Georg Simmel.* Translated and edited by K. Wolff. New York: Free Press.

Uzzi, Brian, and Zoe Barsness. 1998. "Contingent Employment in British Establishments: Organizational Determinants of the Use of Fixed-Term Hires and Part-Time Workers." *Social Forces,* Vol. 76, no. 3, pp. 967–1007.

CHAPTER 6

Nonstandard and Contingent Employment: Contrasts by Job Type, Industry, and Occupation

DALE BELMAN
Michigan State University

LONNIE GOLDEN
Penn State University, Delaware County

The nature of nonstandard work arrangements in the United States is analyzed here through the lens of their industrial and occupational characteristics and the consequences they have for workers in the various types of jobs. The dispersion by industry and occupation and the differentials in compensation by nonstandard job type allow one to infer the probable causes underlying the prevalence of such jobs. Generally, the evidence suggests that nonstandard jobs have characteristics that are different from those of jobs in the "standard" job sector. However, all nonstandard jobs should not really be conceived as being "secondary," as distinct from "primary" jobs. Instead, the characteristics of such jobs tend to mirror the heterogeneity and segmentation that are evident among standard jobs as well. Consequently, there is a primary-secondary bifurcation within the nonstandard job sector itself. While all nonstandard employment, except for some part-time jobs, is almost by definition insecure, only some workers in certain types of such jobs, and particularly in certain occupations and industries, are penalized further by receipt of lower compensation than otherwise comparable workers. In trying to explain this, many researchers have focused more on supply-side factors, such as the human capital of workers, as well as their gender, race, and age. This focus conflicts with the popular view that growth of nonstandard work is being driven largely by demand-side forces, that shifting external economic conditions and internal reorganization strategies of firms are prompting them to adopt more nonstandard jobs. Although employer actions differ somewhat by sector, we conclude that this view is essentially realistic. Our evidence suggests that reducing labor costs is indeed likely to be the primary motivating factor, despite employer claims to the contrary in surveys.

The main source of data for this research is the U.S. Bureau of Labor Statistics' (BLS) Contingent and Alternative Work Survey (CWS), a supplement to the bureau's Current Population Survey (CPS) conducted in February 1997. One advantage of these data over those collected previously is that most workers identify the industry where they were employed in the prior week rather than merely their formal employer (e.g., the temporary help service agency). It is this information that makes the focus of this paper on the distribution of contingent and nonstandard jobs by detailed industry and occupational classification possible. These data enable us to determine separately the number of workers in nonstandard and contingent jobs. The employment arrangements of nonstandard workers (NSW) and contingent workers (CW) differ from regular jobs with a single employer and explicit or implicit contracts for long-term employment. Not surprisingly, the two categories overlap. Most nonstandard jobs are also more likely to be contingent: 57% of temporary agency workers and 27% of on-call or day laborers fall into this category. At the same time, this is true of only 17% of contract firm workers and 4% of independent workers. A considerably greater percentage is contingent, however, if one applies the original BLS definition of contingent work, which includes not only work that respondents know is not permanent but also work that involves irregular hours and lack of access to benefit coverage (see Polivka and Nardone 1989).

After a review of the relevant literature regarding the sectoral distribution of various nonstandard and contingent jobs and the forces that underlie the creation of all such jobs, this paper mainly considers four issues:

1. Whether the distribution of employment of NSWs across industries and occupations mirrors that of standard employees. Differences presumably reflect the varied opportunities and returns to nonstandard work arrangements (NSWAs) by sector.
2. Whether the definition of contingency adopted in the CWS, based exclusively on workers' perceived limited job duration, understates the extent to which work has for many become more contingent in the sense that it provides less income security. This involves returning to the notion of contingency that includes irregular work hours and lack of access to benefits.

3. Whether and to what extent the CWs, as now defined by BLS, receive higher wages relative to otherwise comparable workers, as conventional wage theory would suggest, or alternatively a wage penalty, whether this varies in different occupational and industrial sectors, and whether the CWs are payroll employees as opposed to self-employed.
4. Whether and to what extent the various categories of NSWs receive wage rates and employee benefit coverage similar to what otherwise comparable standard workers earn.

To answer the last two questions, we apply a model that controls for workers' demographic and human capital characteristics and focuses on their specific occupation, industry, and job status.

The Presence and Use of Contingent and Nonstandard Jobs

Both cross-sectional and time-series research suggest that nonstandard jobs are becoming more common. BLS collects data on employment in the temporary help supply (THS) sector in its monthly survey of establishments. BLS shows that this type of employment tripled in the 1980s and rose by an additional two thirds between 1990 and 1999. One-time surveys offer snapshots of the magnitude and scope of nonstandard work, whether they are "yellow pages surveys," which collect data on establishments' use of various types of workers, or "white pages surveys," which collect data on employees. The former includes a Bureau of National Affairs survey (BNA 1988) that found that 84% of companies used agency temporaries, 59% used direct-hire temporaries, and 57% used contractors. Among manufacturing enterprises, 88% used agency hires, and 54% used direct-hire temps, while outside contractors were used by 63%, as compared with 47% by those who were not in manufacturing. Similarly, an Upjohn Institute for Employment Research survey of private-sector employers in 1997 found that 78% of firms used at least one type of what they termed a "flexible staffing arrangement." As many as 46% used temporary agency workers, 44% used independent contractors, 38% used short-term direct hires, and 27% used on-call workers (Houseman and Erickcek 1997).

These surveys have some limitations. Apart from the fact that they do not provide longitudinal data, they tend not to distinguish between firms that occasionally hire NSWs to cover for ill or vacationing employees and others that have integrated large numbers of NSWs into their labor force. Nor do these data show the detailed industries and occupations where THS workers and other NSWs are assigned to work. Nonetheless, they do provide upper-bound estimates of the general prevalence of such employees and lend credence to the view that more firms were using nonstandard and temporary workers in the 1980s and 1990s than in earlier years.

One-time surveys of the distribution of contingent employment by occupational category provide a perspective on the relative importance of various types of nonstandard employment. The BLS industry-occupational matrix (part of its employment projections program) indicates that of the 1.65 million workers employed in the help supply industry in 1992, fully 42% were in administrative support (clerical) and 24% in industrial occupations but only 6% in managerial and professional occupations. Among detailed occupations, the largest single category by far was helpers, movers, and materials movers; followed by general office clerks, word processors, secretaries, and records processing clerks; then by other clerical; and finally by health care occupations (Thomson 1995). A 1995 Conference Board survey found that three in four firms used temporary workers in clerical positions (Filipczak 1995). Findings from a 1995 survey of large firms similarly showed that the vast majority of direct-hire and agency temporary jobs were in clerical/administrative support occupations, although they are found among production/laborer and professional/technical jobs as well (Christensen 1998).

Consistent with these findings, 37% of firms in a 1997 survey identified clerical work, 33% blue-collar work, and 16% service work as the dominant occupation of their contingent workers (Osterman 1999). Finally, a series of surveys by the National Association of Temporary and Staffing Services (NATSS), conducted quarterly since 1991, shows that the proportion of temporary workers who are clerical workers has fallen from 47.6% of industry jobs in 1991 to 38.7% in 1996 and that their proportion of positions in health care occupations declined from 8.4% to 5.7%. On the other hand, the proportion of temporary jobs in industrial occupations rose from 27.4% to 31.8% and in professional jobs from 2.4% to 6.3%, but the proportion of temporary agency positions in these occupations rose only very slightly from 13% to 14% over the same period. Thus, we expect to find that clerical occupations, as well as perhaps several other occupations, enhance the likelihood that a given worker is either a temporary or contingent worker.

The use of various nonstandard jobs among seven major industries in the late 1990s is evident in a survey of employers by the Upjohn Institute (Houseman and Erickcek 1997). The percentage of establishments using THS workers ranged from 37% in trade to 72% in manufacturing. On the other hand, direct-hire temps among nonagricultural industries was lowest in manufacturing (23%) and highest in services (42%). On-call labor was used in service industries at over double the rate in other industries. Contract workers were used least in agriculture and trade, by only half the percentage of establishments that used them in other industries.[1] In sum, employers in all major industries used nonstandard workers, but the type of nonstandard job upon which employers rely the most varies considerably. Thus, we expect to find that being employed in certain industries enhances the likelihood that a worker is a nonstandard or contingent worker.

Economic Models of Contingent Labor: Labor Supply, Labor Demand, and Segmentation

A wide range of theories has been offered to explain the purpose, presence, and distribution of contingent and nonstandard jobs. Some portray them as innovative "market-mediated" forms of employment that enhance the flexibility of both firms and the labor market. In stark contrast, others view them as a new way of degrading labor to one more standardized and replaceable commodity, with all the negative connotations for workers this implies.[2] Few claim that workers choose impermanent employment as a utility maximizing strategy per se. However, differences between well-established, secure workers and marginal workers in their evaluation of the probability of losing their jobs could create a gap between the wages of these two groups, because the latter may fear that higher wages would further increase the chances that they will lose their jobs (Prachowny 1997).[3]

Although neoclassical economists generally assume that differences in wages will arise to compensate for the insecurity of contingent work, as they would for other adverse working conditions, alternative models of the labor market, such as the "job attributes" view, suggest that various forms of higher compensation, including wages, are likely to be complements to, rather than substitutes for, security and other attractive features of jobs. In addition, some workers might select contingent employment, even when otherwise comparable potentially permanent opportunities are available, despite the unattractive conditions. Young people and other new labor force entrants may want to expand their range of work experience by rotating through a variety of positions and accumulate more diverse forms of human capital than they would in just one firm, job, occupation, or industry. In addition, workers who are planning a temporary spell in the labor force may want to avoid making the implied commitment inherent in taking a regular position. Finally, contingent employment will be attractive to individuals who have competing demands on their time, such as family responsibilities or schooling, as long as it provides them the opportunity to refuse work without rebuke.

Microeconomic models of the creation of nonstandard jobs more often emphasize the role of employer demand and assume that firms' creation of such jobs reflects optimizing behavior. Further, these models often assume that efficiency wage setting for employees in the primary labor market, above the competitive market level, together with the threat of job loss if they are caught shirking, will greatly reduce the need for the costly direct monitoring of workers. In contrast, jobs in the secondary sector are assumed to have low monitoring costs, so there is little reason for firms to pay more than the competitive wage to elicit work effort. Further, when the demand for a firm's product is variable and unpredictable, employees in the primary sector, highly trained and expensive to replace, nonetheless will be retained during downturns, but those in the secondary market will be viewed as expendable (Bulow and Summers 1986; Rebitzer and Taylor 1991; Saint-Paul 1991; Foote 1998).[4] Therefore, the size of the workforce in the secondary sector generally varies directly with fluctuations in demand (Houseman and Erickcek 1997).

There are other possible reasons for hiring nonstandard workers. It is widely believed that organizations adopt flexible work practices, including the creation of contingent jobs, when they have to compete in the global market (Osterman 1999; Roberts and Hyatt 1998).[5] However, one additional reason may be an uncertain availability of standard workers (Abraham 1990; Abraham and Taylor 1996). Hiring more staff through agencies not only is more likely to ensure a steady supply of temporary workers but these workers have often received additional training from the agency (Milner and Pinker 1997) and may be screened as potential candidates for regular jobs. The construction, information technology, and skilled nursing sectors have been particularly likely to adopt these strategies. Firms in other sectors have made greater use of internal pools of temporary workers, particularly when a good deal of firm-specific knowledge is required, as is the case, for instance, in the postal service and in the fast-food industry. Finally, laws designed to protect only standard workers, which have somewhat eroded the employment-at-will system (Grunewald 1995; Gonos 1997; Belman and Belzer 1998; Lester 1998; Walwei 1998), may also have caused employers to expand their hiring through temporary agencies—in particular for clerical, assembly, laborer, and other jobs where potential turnover costs are relatively low—in order to reduce their exposure to various legal risks and costs (Autor 2000).[6]

Savings on employee benefit expenses associated with standard employees are often considered to be a primary reason that employers create temporary and other nonstandard jobs (Mangum, Mayall, and Nelson 1985; Montgomery 1988; Tilly 1991; Golden 1996; Nollen 1996; Richman 1999). Fully 38% of firms with temp workers, 59% with short-term hires, and 73% with on-call workers report lower wages and benefit expenses with such staffing. Surprisingly, however, less than 12% of the same employers using temporary agency workers and under 10% of those using short-term and on-call staff report that cost savings are one of the reasons for hiring them (Houseman and Erickcek 1997). In a separate survey of establishments, "cutting direct labor costs" and "reducing health care costs" fall in the bottom half of a list of perceived benefits associated with temporary work arrangements. At the same time, employers indicated that they were not concerned about such arrangements being costly (Christensen 1998). Thus, labor cost savings are likely to be a stronger motivator for creating nonstandard jobs than employers care to admit to survey takers.

A firm's greater use of flexible employment arrangements is also attributable to its adopting an explicit strategy of becoming the lowest-cost producer in their market (Gramm and Schnell 1997). The absence of unions plays a role in making such strategies possible, for unions often use collective bargaining agreements to limit employers' ability to substitute contingent or other lower-cost workers for their core labor force. In addition, unions may try to include flexible workers under the contract and thus extend at least some benefits to them, thus reducing the cost advantage to the employer (Gramm and Schnell 1997; Houseman and Erickcek 1997). The effect of these union practices appears to have outweighed the cost incentives unionization may create for employers to increase use of contingent employment because of the union wage premium, the work rules incorporated in collective bargaining agreements, and the additional resources required to maintain amicable relations between unions and management.

Much of the research of trends at the aggregate level has centered on whether outcomes in the nonstandard labor market reflect the dominance of supply or demand forces. Empirical models of growth in THS sector employment suggest that demand-side variables hold sway. Demand-side variables include the extent of international competition, level of nonwage labor costs for regular employees such as employee benefits, costs of hiring and replacement, level of unionization, and volatility of demand (Golden and Appelbaum 1992; Laird and Williams 1996).[7] Although, on the labor-supply side, the increased presence of married women in the labor force also has contributed to its growth, it is clear that the characteristics of employers, including the industry in which they are situated, are the predominant determinant of the extent to which nonstandard jobs are being created.

Estimates of the Use of Contingent and Nonstandard Workers by Industry and Occupation

We now examine the role of industry and occupation in determining the use of contingent and nonstandard work arrangements. The foundation for this analysis is the CWS. The BLS constructs three progressively broader classifications of contingent workers. The first, referred to here as CW1, includes wage and salary workers who had less than one year's tenure with their current employer at the time of the survey and expected their job to last no more than a year. CW2 adds in self-employed and independent contract workers in the same situation. CW3 expands the definition further by including wage and salary workers who have more than one year's job tenure or who expect their job to end but not necessarily within the next year, although the self-employed and independent contractors are included only if their expected tenure is no more than one year. All those who were identified as working in contingent jobs were asked in what industry they were employed the longest time in that job. The responses were reported as three-digit Standard Industrial Classification (SIC) industries, then aggregated into 52 detailed and 23 major SIC industries.[8]

Using the broadest of the BLS's definitions, 4.3% of workers were classified as CW3 in 1999, showing a slight decline from 4.5% in 1997 and 4.9% in 1995, but well within the sampling error (U.S. Dept. of Labor 1999).[9] Since 1995, the proportion of employment that is contingent did increase in services; agriculture; finance, insurance, and real estate (FIRE); and trade, but this was balanced by declines in construction and manufacturing (Hipple 1998), industries that have traditionally been the most cyclically sensitive. These developments suggest that the share of temporary jobs may shrink as an economic expansion matures, initially because many of them are transformed into permanent positions and eventually because firms begin to eliminate such jobs first before laying off members of their regular staff at the onset of a recession (Golden 1996). Among occupations, the proportion of contingent employees rose from the mid- to late 1990s in three classifications: professional specialty, technicians, and related support; administrative support; and farming, forestry, and fishing workers. These were, however, offset by slight declines in managerial, craft, operator, and service occupations.

The CWS also provides estimates of the proportion of NSWs, those who are employed as independent contractors or on-call workers (including day labor) or are hired through either THS firms or contract firms. According to the BLS estimate, they constituted 9.3% of total employment in 1999 and 9.9% in 1997. However, this might have been as high as 13% if short-term direct hires and contract workers who have more than one customer had been included (Carré and Joshi 1998; Houseman and Polivka 1998; Kalleberg et al. 1997). Adding in part-time employees raises the proportion of nonstandard workers considerably, to 29.4%. While there were slight shifts across major industries, the percentage of workers in alternative arrangements remained virtually unchanged between 1995 and 1999, except that the proportion of independent contract workers dipped after 1997. Over this period of cyclical expansion, the proportion of employment that is nonstandard grew in the service and trade industries, while declining in the cyclically sensitive industries of construction and manufacturing, as well as in public administration.[10]

By job type, the share of workers provided by contract firms has grown most in manufacturing, FIRE, and public administration. The proportion of independent contractors has risen in services and wholesale/retail trade, while it has declined in other industries. The percentage of on-call workers rose in services and also increased in construction and public administration until 1997 but then declined by 1999. The percentage of temporary agency employees has risen in FIRE and slightly in wholesale/retail trade and mining. Meanwhile, the proportion of temporary workers in manufacturing declined somewhat. Thus, the distribution of nonstandard positions among industries does not necessarily remain stable through time and over the business cycle.

Table 1a shows the distribution of CWs by detailed industry in 1997, using the broadest definition CW3, and table 1b shows the distribution of NSWs. CWs can be found in virtually every sector, but their distribution across sectors is far from uniform. The five industries that have the largest proportion of CWs, household services, educational services, business services, construction, and national and internal security, account for over half of contingent employment. Private household services together with social and business services account for the greatest share of the self-employed and of independent contractors as well.

TABLE 1a
Contingent Work by Industry[a]

Rank	Detailed industry	% CW3	SIC #	Self-employed or independent contractor		Hours vary		No health insurance		
				Detailed industry (top 12)	%	Detailed industry	%	Detailed industry	%	% among CW3
1	Private household service	15.7	37	Private household service	4.0	Agriculture, other	27.3	Private household service	54.4	58.5
2	Educational services	11.4	44	Social services	3.0	Agricultural services	21.83	Other metals	42.1	100
3	Business services	10	38	Business services	2.0	Private household service	21.2	Eating/drinking retail	41.9	39.8
4	Construction	7.2	4	Construction	1.0	Forestry/fisheries	18.4	Agricultural services	40.2	65.3
5	National security/internal	6.95	50	Furniture	1.0	Tobacco	17.5	Apparel	33.1	59.4
6	Entertainment/recreation	6.85	41	Machinery, electric	1.0	Auto/repair	13.6	Construction	30.9	43.8
7	Forestry/fisheries	6.85	47	Other transport. equipment	1.0	Construction	13.6	Auto/repair	29.5	54.2
8	Petroleum/coal	6.43	26	Professional/photo/watches	1.0	Personal services	13.5	Personal services	26.7	35.4
9	Other public admin.	6.39	51	Misc. manufacturing	1.0	Entertainment/recreation	12.7	Lumber	26.6	89.6
10	Social services	6.21	45	Chemicals	1.0	Transportation	12.4	Agriculture, other	26.0	48.1
11	Personal services	5.72	40	Rubber/plastic	1.0	Other professional services	10.6	Misc. manufacturing	22.8	45.9
12	Agriculture, other	5.69	2	Personal services	1.0	Eating/drinking	10.6	Business services	22.6	42.9
13	Apparel	4.61	22			Toys/sporting	10.6	Toys/sporting	21.8	0
14	Agricultural services	4.39	1			Lumber	9.86	Tobacco	21.3	100
15	Admin. of human resources	4.37	49			Textiles	9.79	Entertainment/recreation	20.6	35.1
16	Tobacco	4.09	20			Mining	9.61	Forestry/fisheries	20.5	54.3

Insurance/real estate	9.08	Other retail trade	19.4	38.4
Other retail trade	8.8	Furniture	19.2	0
Business services	8.68	Social services	18.9	26.1
Health services	7.17	Textiles	17.5	71.7
Aircraft	7.15	Transportation	14.9	35.4
Food	6.85	Leather	14.8	100
Printing/publishing	6.49	Printing/publishing	14.0	27
Hospitals	6.35	Health services	13.8	33.1
Wholesale trade	6.35	Insurance/real estate	12.1	25.6
Misc. manufacturing	6.33	Wholesale trade	12.0	43.6
Paper	6.18	Food	10.5	32
Social services	6.14	Stone/glass	10.5	83.1
Educational services	6	Fabricated metals	10.3	64
Primary metals	5.59	Other professional services	10.0	25.5
Petroleum/coal	5.59	Rubber/plastic	9.2	46
Chemicals	5.43	Mining	7.9	24.9
Stone/glass	5.07	Communication	7.9	10.8
Rubber/plastic	4.74	Machinery, electric	7.4	12.8
Communication	4.65	Machinery nonelectrical	7.3	41.1
Leather	4.58	Educational services	6.2	16.9
Utilities	4.56	Motor vehicles	6.1	32.8
Fabricated metals	4.5	Professional/photo/watches	5.8	25.8
Banking/finance	4.25	Hospitals	5.0	12.7
Machinery, nonelectrical	4.19	Banking/finance	5.0	21.1

17	Mining	3.96	3
18	Hospitals	3.78	42
19	Other professional services	3.6	46
20	Eating/drinking retail	3.26	33
21	Professional/photo/watches	3.01	16
22	Other transport equipment	2.81	15
23	Communication	2.77	30
24	Transportation	2.74	29
25	Machinery, nonelectric	2.54	11
26	Machinery, electric	2.53	12
27	Chemicals	2.49	25
28	Food	2.45	19
29	Auto/repair	2.44	39
30	Health services	2.37	43
31	Leather	2.36	28
32	Other retail trade	2.26	34
33	Motor vehicles	2.22	13
34	Banking/finance	2.2	35
35	Misc. manufacturing	2.2	18
36	Textiles	2.2	21
37	Wholesale trade	2.06	32
38	Insurance/real estate	2.03	36
39	Aircraft	1.95	14
40	Utilities	1.86	31

TABLE 1a (*Continued*)
Contingent Work by Industry

Rank	Self-employed or independent contractor[a] Detailed industry (top 12)	% CW3	SIC #	Hours vary Detailed industry	%	No health insurance Detailed industry	%	% among CW3
41	Lumber	1.75	5	Justice/public order/safety	3.78	Aircraft	4.6	27
42	Fabricated metals	1.61	9	Machinery, electric	3.71	Paper	4.0	53.7
43	Toys/sporting	1.5	17	Apparel	3.58	Primary metals	3.8	0
44	Justice/public order/safety	1.47	48	National security/internal	3.41	Chemicals	3.6	35.9
45	Printing/publishing	1.46	24	Furniture	3.37	Other public admin.	3.6	18.5
46	Paper	1.28	23	Other transport. equipment	2.97	Armed forces	3.6	18.5
47	Rubber/plastic	0.98	27	Motor vehicles	2.88	Admin. of human resources	3.4	14.9
48	Furniture	0.73	6	Other public admin.	2.68	Petroleum/coal	3.0	46.4
49	Stone/glass	0.62	7	Armed forces	2.68	National security/internal	2.8	10.5
50	Primary metals	0.52	8	Admin. of human resources	2.21	Utilities	2.6	17.1
51	Other metals	0	10	No response	2.21	Justice/public order/safety	2.4	7.11
52			52	Professional/photo/watches	1.40	Other transport. equipment	2.2	34.6
				Other metals	0			
	Mean	3.66		Mean	8.07	Mean	38.6	
	Standard deviation	2.9		Standard deviation	5.46	Standard deviation	25.3	
						Median	35.2	

[a] Computed by subtracting CW1 from CW2.

TABLE 1b

Nonstandard Work as Percentage of Total Industry Employment

% Sum, 4 NS	Detailed industry	SIC #	% Temp	% Ind. contract	% Contract firm	% On-call/ day	% Self-employed	% Usual hours > 45	Employment as % labor force, ranked
35.85	Agricultural services		0.9	30.3	0.0	4.6	51.4 Agricultural services	33.8 Machinery, nonelectrical	11.4 Eating/drinking
33.03	Business services	38	11.3	13.7	6.3	1.8	30.2 Business services	33.4 Motor vehicles	8.0 Health services
30.38	Construction		0.3	22.5	2.1	5.6	28.6 Other professional services	31.5 Agricultural, other	6.3 Mining
27.69	Private household service	37	1.1	17.5	0.0	9.1	23.6 Mining	30.5 Wholesale trade	5.1 Wholesale trade
18.11	Other professional services	46	0.9	15.4	0.9	0.9	22.1 Auto/repair	29.2 Mining	4.9 Hospitals
18.06	Forestry/fisheries	47	0.0	18.1	0.0	0.0	20.7 Social services	29.0 Other professional services	4.9 Private household service
16.82	Auto/repair	39	0.3	14.2	0.8	1.6	18.8 Educational services	28.8 Chemicals	4.6 Social services
15.07	Insurance/real estate	36	0.7	13.4	0.4	0.6	16.5 Banking/finance	28.3 Petroleum/coal	4.4 Leather
14.26	Entertainment/ recreation	41	0.5	10.7	0.0	3.1	16.3 Private household service	27.9 Primary metals	3.9 Entertainment/ recreation
14.08	Agricultural, other	40	0.0	9.4	0.2	4.5	13.6 Personal services	27.1 Auto/repair	3.8 Utilities
13.50	Personal services		0.1	11.3	0.1	2.1	11.5 Eating/drinking	26.8 Forestry/fisheries	3.4 Banking/finance
10.76	Transportation	29	0.6	6.9	0.9	2.4	11.4 Utilities	26.5 Aircraft	2.7 Other retail trade
8.64	Social services	45	0.4	6.5	0.8	0.9	11.0 Construction	25.1 Transportation	2.6 Auto/repair
8.47	Health services	43	0.9	4.9	0.8	1.9	10.5 Toys/sporting	24.9 Professional/photo/ watches	2.5 Educational services
8.11	Misc. manufacturing	18	0.6	7.2	0.0	0.3	10.2 Hospitals	24.8 Fabricated metals	2.0 Other metals
7.89	Lumber		0.5	7.3	0.1	0.0	9.7 Professional/photo/ watches	24.7 Food	1.8 Business services

TABLE 1b (Continued)

Nonstandard Work as Percentage of Total Industry Employment

% Sum, 4 NS	Detailed industry	SIC #	% Temp	% Ind. contract	% Contract firm	% On-call/day	% Self-employed	% Usual hours > 45	Employment as % labor force, ranked
7.83	Printing/publishing	24	0.8	5.4	0.1	1.5	9.2 Leather	24.7 Machinery, electric	1.8 Personal services
7.75	Wholesale trade	32	0.5	6.1	0.3	0.8	8.2 Paper	23.9 Paper	1.7 Forestry/fisheries
7.32	Mining		1.3	2.5	2.2	1.3	6.2 Lumber	23.6 Stone/glass	1.5 Agricultural services
6.28	Other retail trade	34	0.0	5.0	0.1	1.2	6.0 Wholesale trade	23.3 Communication	1.5 Machinery, nonelectrical
5.27	Stone/glass		0.0	4.3	0.0	1.0	4.7 Other retail trade	22.5 Banking/finance	1.5 Armed forces
4.86	Furniture		0.3	3.8	0.0	0.8	4.4 Agricultural, other	22.4 Lumber	1.4 National security/internal
4.53	Educational services	44	0.1	0.9	0.2	3.3	4.2 Textiles	22.1 Printing/publishing	1.4 Paper
4.44	Banking/finance	35	0.9	3.0	0.2	0.3	3.9 Furniture	22.0 Misc. manufacturing	1.3 Misc. manufacturing
4.32	Apparel	22	1.0	2.8	0.0	0.6	3.9 Other transport. equipment	21.2 Business services	1.2 Transportation
4.18	Communication	30	1.1	2.2	0.3	0.5	3.9 Primary metals	21.2 Other transport. equipment	1.1 Communication
4.13	Eating/drinking	33	0.1	2.1	0.2	1.7	3.3 Transportation	20.6 Justice/public safety	1.1 Primary metals
4.09	Tobacco	20	0.0	0.0	0.0	4.1	2.8 Other metals	19.9 Insurance/real estate	1.0 Printing/publishing
3.89	Fabricated metals		1.7	2.2	0.0	0.0	2.6 Misc. manufacturing	19.6 Furniture	1.0 Machinery, electric
3.81	Machinery, electric	12	1.6	1.2	0.4	0.5	2.1 Petroleum/coal	19.5 Rubber/plastic	0.7 Petroleum/coal
3.79	Utilities	31	0.6	0.2	1.0	2.0	1.5 Machinery, nonelectrical	19.4 Construction	0.7 Textiles

3.74	Hospitals	42	0.3	0.4	0.2	2.7	1.3 Tobacco	19.4 Toys/sporting	0.7 Insurance/real estate
3.71	Machinery, nonelectrical	11	1.6	1.3	0.7	0.1	1.3 Health services	18.6 Other retail trade	0.7 Construction
3.41	Petroleum/coal	26	1.9	1.2	0.0	0.2	1.1 Apparel	17.3 Agricultural services	0.7 Justice/public order/safety
3.38	Aircraft	14	2.5	0.0	0.9	0.0	1.0 Machinery, electric	17.2 Entertainment/ recreation	0.6 Other transport. equipment
3.26	Textiles	21	0.7	1.2	0.0	1.3	0.9 Communication	17.0 Educational services	0.6 Lumber
3.23	Justice/public order/safety	48	0.0	0.2	0.6	2.4	0.9 Aircraft	16.4 Utilities	0.6 Stone/glass
3.21	Professional/photo/ watches	16	1.6	0.7	0.3	0.6	0.7 Chemicals	15.7 Textiles	0.5 Tobacco
3.15	Toys/sporting	17	0.0	3.2	0.0	0.0	0.7 Insurance/real estate	14.6 Personal services	0.5 Admin. of human resources
3.10	Rubber/plastic	27	1.4	0.7	0.0	1.0	0.6 Rubber/plastic	14.2 Social services	0.5 Agricultural, other
2.74	Motor vehicles	13	1.9	0.0	0.6	0.2	0.6 Printing/ publishing	14.1 Apparel	0.5 Apparel
2.43	Chemicals	25	1.8	0.3	0.2	0.0	0.3 Entertainment/ recreation	13.8 Eating/drinking	0.5 Furniture
2.37	Food	10	0.3	0.4	0.2	1.5	0.3 Stone/glass	12.8 Health services	0.4 Aircraft
2.35	Paper	23	1.7	0.0	0.0	0.7	0.0 Fabricated metals	11.5 National security/internal	0.4 Toys/sporting
2.14	Other transportation equipment	15	0.2	0.1	1.8	0.0	0.0 Motor vehicles	11.2 Private household service	0.4 Motor vehicles
2.07	National security/internal	50	0.0	0.0	1.0	1.0	0.0 Food	10.2 Leather	0.1 Professional/ photo/watches
1.62	Other public administration	51	0.0	0.5	0.2	1.0	0.0 Forestry/fisheries	9.7 Hospitals	0.1 Chemicals

TABLE 1b (*Continued*)

Nonstandard Work as Percentage of Total Industry Employment

% Sum, 4 NS	Detailed industry	SIC #	% Temp contract	% Ind. contract	% Contract firm	% On-call/ day	% Self-employed	% Usual hours > 45	Employment as % labor force, ranked
1.62	Armed forces	52	0.0	0.5	0.2	1.0	0.0 Justice/public order/safety	9.6 Other public admin.	0.1 Rubber/plastic
0.30	Primary metals	10	0.3	0.0	0.0	0.0	0.0 Admin. of human resources	5.0 Tobacco	0.1 Other professional services
0.00	Other metals	28	0.0	0.0	0.0	0.0	0.0 National security/internal	5.0 Admin. of human resources	0.1 Food
0.00	Leather		0.0	0.0	0.0	0.0	0.0 Other public administration	0.0 Other metals	0.0 Other public admin.
0.00	Admin. of human resources	49	0.0	0.0	0.0	0.0	0.0 Armed forces	NA Armed forces	0.0 Fabricated metals
7.79	Average		0.87	5.04	0.49	1.39	0.07	20.2	
4.16	Median		0.50	2.21	0.17	0.95	0.04	21.2	
8.41	Std. dev.		1.61	6.68	0.97	1.71	0.10	7.6	
1.08	Std. dev./average		1.85	1.33	1.99	1.23	1.37	0.4	

Not too surprisingly, the greatest concentration of nonstandard workers—temporary agency employees, independent contractors, contract firm workers, and on-call or day laborers—is found in many of the same sectors where workers are contingent. In order, agricultural industries, business services, construction, private household services, other professional services, forestry and fishing, auto and repair services, personal services, and transportation all have nonstandard arrangements among more than 10% of their industry's workforce. Temporary jobs are most prevalent in business services[11] and also constitute a disproportionately high share in the aircraft, motor vehicle, petroleum/coal, and chemicals industries. Independent contractors are most prevalent in agricultural services, construction, forestry and fishing, and private household services. Contract firm employees appear disproportionately in business services, mining, construction, and transportation equipment manufacturing. On-call or day labor is widely dispersed but highest in private household services, construction, agriculture, tobacco, and entertainment and recreation.

Occupational Distribution of Contingent Work, Including Work-Hour Patterns and Benefit Coverage

Table 2 displays the levels of contingent work by occupation. Contingent jobs are the most common among college and university teachers and constitute more than 10% of natural scientists, as well as construction, private household service, sales, and forestry occupations. On the other hand, contingent jobs are rare in the managerial occupations but abundant in the professional specialties.

One aspect of "contingent" work is that, even when the employment relationship is not expected to be completely severed, employees are often expected to work irregular or unpredictable hours and days. One response option to the question in the CPS asking a worker's "usual hours" of work per week is that "hours vary" and are so irregular that the worker is unable to specify a regular workweek. By industry, irregular workweeks are most common in agricultural production and in private household services, followed by tobacco manufacturing, repair services, and construction. By occupation, computer operator, farm/forestry, construction trade, vehicle operator, personal service, and sales workers are most apt to have a usually variable workweek. In 1997, only 6.3% of regular full-time workers and 10.7% of part-time workers reported that their usual hours varied, but 20.7% of nonstandard workers did.[12] This proportion is as high as 54% for day laborers, 30% for on-call

TABLE 2

Contingent Work by Detailed Occupation Classification

Rank	% in CW3		% Self-emp. and in indep. contract jobs		% Whose hours vary	
	%	Occupation	%	(#SOC) Occupation	%	Occupation
1	28.38	Teachers, college/university	3.70	(#27) Private household service	81.8	Computer equipment operators
2	14.70	Construction labor	3.54	(#32) Personal service	30.0	Farm operators
3	14.47	Private household service	2.98	(#40) Construction labor	22.3	Forestry
4	11.63	Natural scientists	1.74	(#15) Other technicians	19.0	Construction trades
5	11.15	Sales-related	1.31	(#37) Fabricators	18.6	Personal service
6	10.84	Forestry	1.22	(#23) Secretaries/typists	17.1	Sales reps, finance, and business service
7	9.95	Personal service	1.08	(#43) Farm operators	15.2	Farm workers
8	8.67	Farm workers	1.03	(#34) Construction trades	14.9	Motor vehicle operators
9	8.23	Other handlers and laborers	1.02	(#42) Other handlers and laborers	13.8	Other technicians
10	7.53	Construction trades	0.96	(#14) Engineering, science technicians	11.8	Food service
11	7.44	Health diagnosing	0.88	(#44) Farm workers	11.5	Other transportation
12	6.98	Other administrative support	0.80	(#38) Motor vehicles	10.6	Sales workers, retail and personal services
13	6.41	Engineering, science technicians	0.76	(#45) Forestry	9.8	Health service
14	6.35	Other technicians	0.65	(#12) Other professional	8.8	Freight handlers
15	6.21	Teachers, except college/university	0.62	(#11) Lawyers and judges	8.6	Construction labor
16	5.79	Secretaries/typists	0.56	(#18) Sales reps, commodities, except retail	8.2	Other handlers and laborers
17	5.26	Other professional	0.51	(#17) Sales reps, finance, business service	8.2	Other administrative support
18	4.95	Public administration	0.51	(#16) Sales supervisors and proprietors	8.0	Lawyers and judges
19	4.93	Fabricators	0.51	(#31) Cleaning and building service	7.9	Health technicians
20	4.84	Computer equipment operators	0.47	(#5) Mathematical scientists	7.7	Cleaning and building service
21	4.51	Freight handlers	0.46	(#6) Natural scientists	6.8	Health diagnosing
22	4.20	Health service	0.41	(#8) Health assessment and treating	5.9	Machine operators, tenders, except precision
23	4.20	Mail and message distributing	0.41	(#30) Health service	5.8	Mechanics and repairers
24	3.73	Food service	0.40	(#9) Teachers, college and university	5.6	Fabricators

25	3.68	Engineers	0.40	(#41) Freight handlers	5.4	Other precision production
26	3.41	Supervisors, administrative support	0.38	(#24) Financial records, processing	4.9	Financial records, processing
27	3.27	Financial records, processing	0.34	(#3) Management related	4.9	Sales reps, commodities, except retail
28	3.21	Other transportation	0.33	(#19) Sales, retail and personal services	4.6	Mail and message distributing
29	3.10	Motor vehicles	0.32	(#36) Machine operators and tenders	4.2	Engineers
30	3.10	Management related	0.32	(#26) Other administrative support	4.2	Managers
31	2.99	Sales, retail and personal services	0.30	(#4) Engineers	4.2	Engineering and science technicians
32	2.96	Lawyers and judges	0.27	(#2) Managers	4.0	Natural scientists
33	2.93	Cleaning and building service	0.27	(#10) Teachers, except college and university	4.0	Sales supervisors and proprietors
34	2.92	Mathematical scientists	0.23	(#25) Mail and message distributing	3.1	Protective service
35	2.66	Protective service	0.20	(#33) Mechanics and repairers	2.9	Sales related
36	2.55	Machine operators and tenders	0.18	(#39) Other transportation	2.8	Other professional
37	2.33	Sales reps, finance, business service	0.15	(#35) Other precision production	2.6	Supervisors - administrative support
38	2.24	Other precision production	0.13	(#13) Health technicians	2.0	Mgmt Related
39	2.22	Health assessment and treating	0.07	(#29) Food service	1.7	Teachers, except college and university
40	2.04	Health technicians	0.00	(#1) Public administration	1.6	Mathematical scientists
41	1.80	Mechanics and repairers	0.00	(#7) Health diagnosing	1.6	Health assessment and treating
42	1.80	Managers	0.00	(#20) Sales-related	0.9	Secretaries, stenographers, and typists
43	1.22	Farm operators	0.00	(#21) Supervisors, administrative	0.0	Public admin
44	1.04	Sales reps, commodities, except retail	0.00	(#22) Computer equipment operators	NA	Teachers, college and university
45	0.90	Sales supervisors and proprietors	0.00	(#28) Protective service	NA	Private household service
46	0.00	Armed forces, unemployed	0.00	(#46) Armed forces, unemployed	NA	Armed forces, unemployed
	0.00	No response				
Mean	5.52		0.66		9.7	
S.D.	4.89		0.84		57.9	

workers, and 22% for independent contractors. While standard workers may be compensated for such irregularity in hours by receiving more discretion over the timing of their working hours (Golden 2000) or higher wages (Walwei 1998), this is much less likely to be the case for most nonstandard workers.

Table 3a shows that adding in those workers with irregular hours increases the figure for CW3 in 1997 from 4.4% to 10.7% of the workforce (without double counting). Adding those who lack access to health insurance from any source brings the figure up to 24.4%, and including those lacking employer-sponsored pension plans raises it further to 42% of the workforce. Focusing on nonstandard workers, we combine those employed through temporary firms and on-call and day laborers into a single category (NS1) and those employed as independent contractors and through contracting firms into a second category (NS2). Over 61% for the higher-skill NS2 and 77% of the lower-skill NS1 subset of workers fall into this very broad category of contingent workers.

TABLE 3a-1

Broader Definitions of Contingent Work

	Limited duration job (BLS)	Variable work hours	No health coverage	No pension coverage
% of employed labor in "contingent" work, 1997[a]	4.47	10.7	24.4	42.3

[a] Note that while these figures represent the union of these conditions they do not double-count individuals with these characteristics.

TABLE 3a-2

Broader Contingent Status among Nonstandard Worker (NS) Groups

	NS1 (Temp/on-call day labor)	NS2 (Independent contractor/ contract firm)
	77.6	61.7
Sample size (n)[a]	1,327	3,907

[a] The number of standard workers in the sample, by contract, is 46,571.

Table 3b shows correlation coefficients based on all 52 detailed industries that enable us to examine whether the presence of nonstandard job types, contingent (CW3) jobs, and variable hours are means of

TABLE 3b-1

Correlations among Types of Labor Flexibility within Major Industry Groups

	% CW3	% Temps	% Indep. contractors	% Contract firm	% On-call/ day labor	% Hours vary	% No health insurance
Correlation coefficients							
% CW3		0.239	0.412	0.288	0.652		
Hours vary	0.430	-0.066	0.707	-0.008	0.678		
%, Usual hours per week							
> 45	-0.207	0.219	0.081	0.136	-0.246	0.073	
< 40	0.451	0.056	0.626	0.050	0.522	0.764	0.333

TABLE 3b-2

Correlations by Occupation with Hours Vary

% CW3	% (CW2 - CW1)
0.091	0.199

achieving labor flexibility that are associated with one another. The correlations show that industrial sectors with more CWs also tend to have more independent contractors and on-call or day laborers. In addition, independent contractors, on-call and day laborers, and, to an extent, CWs generally are used by employers in conjunction with variable weekly hours and with employees working at least 45 hours a week.[13] Interestingly, industries with more long-hours employees are somewhat less apt to also hire on-call or day laborers or to use CWs but more likely to hire temps. Industries utilizing jobs featuring workweeks that are either variable or less than 40 hours tend to employ more CWs as well.

Multivariate Analysis with Industry and Occupation Effects

If the labor market resembled the competitive model of neoclassical economic theory, with worker mobility, adequate information, and flexible wages, workers' earnings would reflect their innate and acquired human capital, at least in the long run, independent of their occupation or the industry in which they were employed. If, however, industry and occupation exert an independent influence on workers' terms of employment or if workers' job type affects their compensation when industry and occupation are controlled for, that calls into question the relevance of the neoclassical theory to real-world labor markets.

Table 4 shows the probability that a worker's job is contingent according to CW3, the broadest BLS definition. The model is first estimated with only the conventional human capital variables, consisting of a worker's demographic characteristics. The dependent variable is dichotomous (1, 0), indicating the contingent or "noncontingent" employment status of the worker. This provides the baseline for comparison to the same model with major and detailed industry and occupational classifications added. The results show whether workers' characteristics significantly influence the probability that they are in a contingent job. They also show whether and to what extent the job sector in which they are employed exerts any additional influence, as indicated by the significance and size of the reduction of the coefficients of the various characteristics. These calculations also enable us to determine whether any particular major and detailed industries and occupations increase the probability that a worker has a contingent job, as the frequency distributions in tables 1 and 2 lead us to expect.

The coefficient estimates may be interpreted as the effects of the explanatory variables evaluated at their means on the probability of being a contingent worker. Column 1 contains the baseline estimates of

TABLE 4

Probability of Being a Contingent Worker (CW3): Effects of Industry and Occupation

Dependent variable: CW3	No controls		With controls for major industry		With controls for detailed industry	
	Derivative of probit	z-statistic	Derivative of probit	z-statistic	Derivative of probit	z-statistic
Personal characteristics						
Female	0.0080	4.66	0.0039	2.18	0.0041	2.30
Age	-0.0053	-15.46	-0.0047	-15.14	-0.0044	-14.39
Age^2	0.0001	13.69	0.0000	13.46	0.0000	12.91
Married	-0.0131	-6.70	-0.0109	-6.31	-0.0100	-6.02
Black	0.0060	1.81	0.0024	0.83	0.0017	0.62
Other	0.0212	5.04	0.0207	5.40	0.0184	5.04
Hispanic	0.0110	3.20	0.0069	2.31	0.0057	1.99
Education level						
Ed2 (some high school)	-0.0085	-1.88	-0.0038	-0.93	-0.0033	-0.83
Ed3 (high school degree)	-0.0099	-2.44	-0.0068	-1.87	-0.0064	-1.83
Ed4 (some college)	0.0027	0.62	0.0039	0.98	0.0035	0.90
Ed5 (associate's degree)	-0.0062	-1.30	-0.0026	-0.58	-0.0018	-0.42
Ed6 (college graduate)	0.0039	0.86	0.0031	0.71	0.0033	0.79
Ed7 (postgraduate)	0.0204	3.68	0.0083	1.62	-0.0007	-0.15
Region						
NE	-0.0102	-4.33	-0.0072	-3.42	-0.0064	-3.17
Midwest	-0.0137	-6.10	-0.0104	-5.18	-0.0099	-5.15
South	-0.0130	-5.94	-0.0102	-5.25	-0.0094	-5.01
Metro	-0.0001	-0.03	0.0015	0.74	0.0000	-0.01
City 1 mil	-0.0038	-1.91	-0.0015	-0.87	-0.0013	-0.75
Major industry						
Agriculture			0.0080	0.86		
Mining			0.0351	2.56		
Construction			0.0834	12.26		

TABLE 4 (Continued)

Probability of Being a Contingent Worker (CW3): Effects of Industry and Occupation

Dependent variable: CW3	No controls		With controls for major industry		With controls for detailed industry	
	Derivative of probit	z-statistic	Derivative of probit	z-statistic	Derivative of probit	z-statistic
Manufacturing, durable goods			0.0017	0.39		
Manufacturing, nondurable goods			0.0051	1.03		
Transportation			0.0112	1.98		
Communication			0.0190	2.01		
Public utilities			0.0149	1.48		
Wholesale trade			0.0042	0.74		
Finance, insurance, and real estate			0.0053	1.13		
Private households service			0.3299	6.83		
Business, auto and repair services			0.0795	13.53		
Personal services (except private household)			0.0453	6.64		
Entertainment and recreation			0.0450	5.63		
Hospitals			0.0223	3.76		
Medical			0.0042	0.83		
Educational services			0.1168	18.27		
Social service			0.0551	7.62		
Other professional service			0.0263	4.64		
Forestry/fishing			0.0492	1.90		
Public administration			0.0510	7.72		
Major occupations						
Managerial			-0.0207	-8.23		
Professional			-0.0091	-3.34		
Technicians			-0.0052	-1.21		
Sales			-0.0153	-5.02		
Private household service			-0.0274	-2.99		

Protective service	-0.0244	-5.30
Other service	-0.0076	-2.71
Craft	-0.0090	-2.79
Operators	-0.0025	-0.58
Transportation operatives	-0.0077	-1.77
Laborers	0.0122	2.59
Farming	0.0100	1.12
Detailed industry		
Agricultural services	0.0019	0.17
Agricultural, other	0.0276	2.01
Mining	0.0185	1.44
Construction	0.0369	4.14
Lumber	-0.0163	-1.56
Furniture	-0.0208	-1.74
Stone/glass	-0.0195	-1.46
Primary metals	-0.0185	-1.42
Fabricated metals	-0.0100	-1.07
Machinery, nonelectrical	-0.0028	-0.35
Machinery, electrical	-0.0029	-0.34
Motor vehicles	0.0014	0.13
Aircraft	0.0016	0.10
Other transport. equipment	0.0072	0.50
Professional/photo/watches	-0.0044	-0.37
Toys/sporting goods	-0.0184	-0.90
Misc. manufacturing	-0.0101	-0.77
Food	-0.0029	-0.33
Tobacco	0.0222	0.50
Textiles	-0.0095	-0.72
Apparel	0.0186	1.49
Paper	-0.0144	-1.08
Printing/publishing	-0.0098	-1.17
Chemicals	0.0034	0.33
Petroleum/coal	0.0534	1.89
Rubber/plastic	-0.0127	-1.12

TABLE 4 (Continued)
Probability of Being a Contingent Worker (CW3): Effects of Industry and Occupation

Dependent variable: CW3	No controls		With controls for major industry		With controls for detailed industry	
	Derivative of probit	z-statistic	Derivative of probit	z-statistic	Derivative of probit	z-statistic
Leather					-0.0133	-0.60
Transportation					0.0022	0.33
Communication					0.0117	1.18
Utilities					0.0012	0.13
Wholesale trade					-0.0007	-0.11
Other retail trade					-0.0053	-0.98
Banking/finance					-0.0021	-0.30
Insurance/real estate					-0.0002	-0.03
Private household services					0.2666	5.78
Business services					0.0887	8.74
Auto/repair services					0.0053	0.60
Personal services					0.0269	3.35
Entertainment/recreation					0.0320	3.56
Hospitals					0.0144	1.84
Health services					-0.0043	-0.67
Educational services					0.0911	9.67
Social services					0.0308	3.60
Other professional services					0.0147	2.05
Forestry/fisheries					-0.0037	-0.19
Justice/public order/safety					-0.0020	-0.22
Admin. of human resources					0.0248	2.02
National security/internal					0.0560	3.57
Other public administration					0.0498	4.59

the size and significance of the effects of personal characteristics, some of them often thought to be associated with labor suppliers' preference for short-duration jobs.[14] For example, being female and being single raises the likelihood of having a contingent job by about 18%. The relationship to education is more complex since people who have some high school education (Ed2) or have graduated high school (Ed3) are less likely to be contingent workers than either those with the least or the most education (Ed7). Being employed in the public sector, particularly at the state level, reduces the significance of the effect of gender and race, suggesting that the demand side is playing a role in determining their effect on the likelihood of being contingent.

The addition of all the major industry and major occupational variables, other than the benchmark industry and occupation, tends to alter the earlier estimates slightly. So does the inclusion of 50 detailed industry and 44 occupation controls (which exclude both the benchmark industry and the armed forces industry and occupation), suggesting that the sector of employment exerts an independent, albeit small effect. While these effects appear to be orthogonal to that of workers' characteristics, there are exceptions. The effect of being female is halved after controlling for industry, occupation, or being a public-sector employee. This shows that women's concentration in industries and occupations where there are more contingent jobs is important. Similarly, the demand side accounts for at least part of the differences in the representation among contingent workers of various racial/ethnic groups and of individuals with different amounts of education.

There are seven major industries that exhibit higher probabilities of having contingent workers than the benchmark industry (retail trade), to which we compare all others. Table 4 also shows that a total of 13 detailed industries have a significantly higher probability of contingency than retail trade other than eating and drinking establishments, the reference industry. These are, in descending order, private household, educational services, business and repair services, national and internal security, petroleum/coal (the lone manufacturing industry), other public administration, construction, entertainment and recreation services, social services, agricultural (other), personal (excluding private household) services, other professional services, and hospitals (weakly). The only manufacturing industry that raises the likelihood of being in contingent employment even slightly is petroleum/coal.

None of 13 major occupations except for laborers exhibits a significantly higher probability of having contingent workers than clerical workers, the occupation to which all others are compared. In fact, the likelihood is smaller in all but technicians, machine and transport operatives, and farm laborers. On the other hand, among detailed occupations (not reported in the table), eight have higher probabilities, most notably forestry and fishing, college teachers, and construction laborers. Fifteen have lower probabilities, for the most part service occupations requiring low levels of skill.

Effect on Earnings and Benefits of Contingent and Nonstandard Jobs by Industry and Occupation

How does employment as a contingent or nonstandard employee affect a worker's earnings and benefits coverage—specifically, employer-provided health insurance and pension plans? Does this penalty, or premium, vary by type of contingent and nonstandard employment? Do dissimilarities in compensation reflect differences in the distribution of contingent and nonstandard employment by industry and occupation? Finally, do contingent and nonstandard employees share in industry and occupational "rents" earned by comparable noncontingent and standard employees? We address these issues with a series of models for earnings and benefits, beginning with an investigation of the effects of contingency as defined by the BLS. We estimate a conventionally specified human capital equation incorporating indicators for the three forms of contingent status for earnings, pension coverage, and health insurance (model 1). In model 2, we control for part-time employment to determine whether the effects of contingency are distinct from those of part-time employment. Model 3 adds controls for major industry and occupation to distinguish the consequences of contingency from those of the distribution of contingent workers across industries and occupations. Model 4 tests whether contingent workers earn industry and occupational rents and whether their rents are similar to those found for noncontingent employees, with the addition of interactions between contingent worker status and indicators of major industry and occupation. Finally, parallel analyses of earnings, pensions, and health insurance are performed for nonstandard employment.[15]

Estimates for contingent work are found in panel A of table 5, using the categories CW1, CW2, and CW3; estimates for nonstandard employment are in panel B. To simplify the interpretation of the coefficients and standard errors, we have redefined the contingent worker classification so that the categories do not overlap. The variable CW1 includes only those workers who have been with their current employer for less than a

TABLE 5

The Effect of Contingent and Nonstandard Employment on Worker Earnings and Benefit Coverage

	ln(Hourly earnings)			Pension coverage			Health insurance From employer			Health insurance From any source		
	Model 1	Add part-time Model 2	Add ind & occ Model 3	Model 1	Add part-time Model 2	Add ind & occ Model 3	Model 1	Add part-time Model 2	Add ind & occ Model 3	Model 1	Add part-time Model 2	Add ind & occ Model 3
A. Contingent workers												
CW1	-0.130	-0.109	-0.117	-0.459	-0.440	-0.428	-0.497	-0.467	-0.454	-0.294	-0.242	-0.231
	(-5.93)	(-4.99)	(-5.486)	(-21.86)	(-19.60)	(-18.61)	(-25.73)	(-22.53)	(-21.02)	(-20.70)	(-17.54)	(-16.83)
CW2	-0.027	-0.010	0.020	-0.449	-0.433	-0.401	-0.546	-0.538	-0.523	-0.003	0.032	0.035
	(-0.64)	(-0.23)	(0.492)	(-11.37)	(-10.34)	(-8.84)	(12.65)	(-12.00)	(-11.06)	(-0.14)	(1.63)	(1.85)
CW3	-0.100	-0.080	-0.089	-0.293	-0.239	-0.249	-0.304	-0.230	-0.233	-0.261	-0.205	-0.202
	(-4.679)	(-3.756)	(-4.285)	(-16.87)	(-12.79)	(-13.23)	(17.94)	(-12.57)	(12.44)	(-19.08)	(-15.40)	(-15.20)
Part-time		-0.118	-0.052		-0.381	-0.347		-0.487	-0.454		-0.248	-0.223
		(-10.23)	(-4.285)		(-51.86)	(-44.20)		(-69.41)	(60.9)		(-53.55)	(-47.65)
B. Nonstandard work arrangements												
Temp	-0.12	-0.13	-0.12	-0.49	-0.50	-0.48	0.55	-0.56	-0.56	-0.19	-0.21	-0.21
	(-4.763)	(-5.038)	(-4.64)	(-15.58)	(-15.66)	(-14.45)	(-19.72)	(-20.44)	(-20.11)	(-9.38)	(-10.18)	(-9.76)
Independent	0.06	0.10	0.11	-0.42	-0.38	-0.41	-0.45	-0.41	-0.38	-0.30	-0.23	-0.21
	(1.95)	(3.42)	(3.95)	(-14.94)	(-13.04)	(-11.82)	(-17.29)	(-14.70)	(-12.78)	(-13.05)	(-10.08)	(-9.21)
Contract firm	0.08	0.08	0.05	-0.18	-0.17	-0.13	-0.16	-0.15	-0.12	-0.13	-0.12	-0.11
	(2.55)	(2.73)	(1.66)	(-5.55)	(-5.20)	(-3.78)	(-5.33)	(-4.93)	(-3.84)	(-4.96)	(-4.73)	(-4.34)
On-call/ day labor	-0.03	0.03	0.00	-0.36	-0.28	-0.28	-0.42	-0.33	-0.32	-0.23	-0.12	-0.12
	(-1.627)	(1.43)	(-0.166)	(-17.95)	(-12.72)	(-9.41)	(-22.02)	(-15.50)	(-14.79)	(-14.69)	(-7.79)	(-7.69)
Part-time		-0.23	-0.15		-0.39	-0.36		-0.49	-0.46		-0.36	-0.33
		(-19.192)	(-12.51)		(-49.95)	(-42.15)		(-68.98)	(-60.39)		(-60.58)	(-53.90)

year and expect to remain with that employer for less than a year. CW2 includes only those workers who identify themselves as self-employed or independent contractors, and CW3, only those who consider their jobs to be contingent but have either worked for their current employer for more than a year *or* expect to remain with their current employer for more than a year. Reclassification allows coefficient and t-statistics to be used directly rather than having to be summed and otherwise recalculated, as would have been the case using the BLS definitions directly.

Turning first to the effect of contingency on earnings without controlling for part-time employment, industry, or occupation (model 1), the estimated coefficients for CW1 and CW3 are similar in magnitude and sign and distinctly different from that for self-employed and independent contract workers (CW2). CW3 workers earn almost 10% less than comparable noncontingent workers. Those who have been with and expect to be with their employer for less than a year (CW1) suffer a slightly larger earnings penalty, earning more than 12% less than otherwise comparable noncontingent employees. In contrast, the self-employed and independent contractors do not suffer a statistically significant earnings disadvantage relative to the otherwise similar workers whose jobs are not contingent.

Adding a control for part-time work in model 2 affects the estimated effects of contingency only modestly. Point estimates for CW1 and CW3 decline to 10% and 8%, respectively, but neither is significantly different from the model 1 estimates. The effect of self-employment and independent contracting remains nonsignificant. The effect of part-time work, which reduces earnings by 11%, is distinct from that associated with contingency. Thus, CW1 and CW3 workers who also work part time would earn 18% to 21% less than full-time noncontingent employees. This double penalty affects the 44% of the contingent workforce who are also part-time employees (U.S. Dept. of Labor 1999).

The reduced earnings of CW1 and CW3 employees are not the result of a disproportionate concentration of contingent jobs in low-wage industries or occupations. Addition of controls for industry and occupation in model 3 results in only a modest increase in the magnitude of coefficients relative to model 2. In contrast, addition of these controls reduces the estimated effect of part-time employment by half, from 11% to 5%. This suggests that part-time employment is concentrated in low-wage industries and occupations.

Next, we consider whether the earnings of contingent employees include industry and occupation rents similar to those earned by noncontingent employees. Model 4 drops the three contingent worker indicator variables and substitutes interactions of contingent worker status and the worker's major industry and occupation.[16] The coefficients on the industry and occupation variables that are not interacted with contingent worker status measure the effect of such factors on all employees. The coefficients on the industry and occupation variables interacted with contingent worker status capture differences in the rents realized by contingent employees. Given the similarity of the effects of CW1 and CW3 status in models 1 through 3, we combine these in forming the interactions but include a separate set of industry and occupational interactions for self-employment and independent contractor status (CW2).

The model 4 coefficient estimates in table 6 have the expected sign and size regarding the effects of age, educational level, gender, and race control variables. As found in other research, there is considerable variation in industry-specific earnings, with employees in all industries other than private household services and social services earning more than those in retail trade. The ranking of occupations is also conventional, with managerial, professional, and technical workers earning more than those in other occupations.[17] Earnings of contingent workers (CW1 and CW3) in the professional and sales occupations, however, are lower than those for their noncontingent counterparts.

Many contingent employees realize smaller industry rents than noncontingent employees, as indicated by the significance of an F-test for the entire set of industry coefficients. The difference ranges from 2% for communications workers to 25% for miners. In contrast, contingent workers in the construction industry earn 25% more than noncontingent employees. This may be explained by the unique pay structure in that industry, which pays a premium to workers in building construction, who frequently move between jobs while enduring some unemployment in the interim periods, relative to maintenance employees in the sector, who are better assured of year-round employment.

The pattern of occupational and industry earnings is quite different for the self-employed and contractors. Although the wage differences between their occupations are generally small, those in managerial and professional positions receive large wage premiums, over 76% and 200%, respectively. These large differentials suggest that self-employed and independent contract workers in these two occupations have highly valued skills. Among the industry effects, all but those for medical services, construction, and manufacturing are negative (most significantly so), with reductions as large as 72% in educational services and 35% in the construction industry. These industry effects may partially offset the

TABLE 6

The Effect of Contingent Worker Status on Earnings with Interactions for Industry, Occupation, and Alternative Definitions of Contingent Work

Log (hourly earnings)	Coefficient	t	Contingent by status			
			CW1 or CW3		CW2	
			Coefficient	t	Coefficient	t
Female	-0.147	-13.945				
Age	0.029	14.611				
Age^2	-0.000	-11.897				
Ed2	0.113	4.179				
Ed3	0.196	8.553				
Ed4	0.264	11.006				
Ed5	0.277	10.257				
Ed6	0.379	14.963				
Ed7	0.523	18.385				
Married	0.067	6.728				
Black	-0.088	-5.119				
Other	-0.049	-2.343				
Hispanic	0.018	0.000				
NE	0.019	1.449				
Midwest	-0.021	-1.706				
South	-0.033	-2.754				
Metro	0.067	5.635				
City 1 mil	0.010	0.000				
Part-time	-0.043	-3.596				
Federal	0.061	1.887				
State	-0.005	-0.186				
Local	0.020	0.838				
Occupational effects						
Managerial	1.530	30.877	-0.030	-0.372	0.568	2.221
Professional	1.594	31.703	-0.116	-1.671	0.931	3.214
Technicians	1.495	27.120	0.072	0.712	0.354	1.159

Sales	1.391	28.756	-0.164	-2.414	-0.161	-0.873
Clerical	1.273	25.614	0.064	0.947	0.285	1.068
Private household service	1.339	5.164	-1.176	-3.276	-0.389	-0.630
Protective service	1.207	19.660	-0.002	-0.011	(dropped)	
Other service	1.146	23.613	0.052	0.810	0.427	1.449
Craft	1.376	27.429	0.011	0.129	0.318	1.104
Operators	1.220	23.275	0.076	0.765	0.272	0.972
Transportation operatives	1.271	23.873	-0.043	-0.403	-0.322	-0.965
Laborers	1.166	22.482	-0.062	-0.743	0.411	1.416
Farming, forestry/fishing	1.174	17.674	-0.034	-0.231	0.333	0.645
Industry effects						
Agriculture	0.187	3.782	-0.035	-0.221	-0.482	-0.937
Mining	0.465	7.854	-0.289	-1.431	-0.095	-0.140
Construction	0.302	12.480	0.225	2.582	-0.438	-1.513
Durable goods	0.238	10.260	-0.122	-1.241	-0.238	-0.833
Nondurable goods	0.174	6.850	-0.137	-1.349	-0.283	-0.713
Transportation	0.271	9.657	-0.022	-0.186	-0.482	-1.469
Communication	0.282	6.188	0.037	0.221	-0.453	-0.710
Utilities and sanitary services	0.357	7.266	0.051	0.257	-0.170	-0.338
Wholesale trade	0.190	7.073	-0.044	-0.332	1.561	5.074
Retail trade	—	—	—	—	—	—
Finance, insurance, and real estate	0.274	12.103	-0.200	-2.017	0.202	0.699
Private household services	-0.245	-0.980	0.984	2.940	0.813	1.448
Business and repair services	0.145	6.753	-0.130	-1.723	-0.364	-1.424
Personal service, except private household	0.073	2.534	-0.166	-1.689	-0.496	-1.400
Entertainment and recreation	0.156	3.996	-0.142	-1.310	-1.262	-2.523
Hospitals	0.170	5.694	-0.189	-1.900	0.466	0.910
Medical service	0.137	5.341	-0.096	-0.917	-0.641	-1.702
Educational services	0.056	1.933	-0.196	-2.834	-1.018	-2.727
Social service	-0.135	-4.266	0.097	0.843	-0.571	-1.865
Other professional services	0.148	5.944	-0.114	-1.216	-0.705	-2.270
Forestry/fishing	0.412	3.691	-0.540	-1.609	(dropped)	
Public administration	0.257	7.350	-0.200	-2.241	(dropped)	

large positive effects of professional and managerial self-employment. For example, a doctor who worked in his or her own office would get a positive occupational effect of 93% and a negative industry effect of 64% for a net increase of about 30%. Similarly, working in the professional services occupation yields a net occupation and industry effect of 25%. In construction, the negative effect of self-employment is at least partly offset by the premium for the occupation, for a net loss of 11% compared with noncontingent employees in other crafts.

We next analyze the effect of contingency on pension and health benefit coverage using counterparts of earnings models 1, 2 and 3, as shown in the remaining columns of panel A in table 5. As coverage is a discrete outcome, the models are estimated by probit. We report the derivatives of these functions, evaluated at the mean value of the characteristics, with respect to both contingent and part-time job status variables. Being a contingent worker substantially reduces the likelihood that a worker has pension coverage from his or her current employer. Model 1, which includes the contingent worker variables but does not control for part-time status, industry, or occupation, indicates that CW1 workers are 46% less likely than are noncontingent employees to participate in an employer-provided pension plan. In contrast to their advantage in earnings, the self-employed and independent contractors suffer a 45% reduction in the likelihood of pension coverage, even larger than the 29% for other contingent employees. Addition of a control for part-time employment moderates the loss of coverage of CW3 workers, to 24%, but does not otherwise alter the results. Part-time employees are 38% less likely to receive pensions than full-time employees. Addition of industry and occupation controls moderates the negative effect of self-employment on participation in pensions, from 43% to 40%. Sector of employment does not substantially affect the likelihood of pension coverage for other contingent employees.

Turning to medical insurance, contingent employees again are less likely than standard employees to receive employer-sponsored coverage. Those who are CW1 are 50% less likely, the self-employed and contractors are 55% less likely, and those who are CW3 are 30% less likely to have such insurance. As with pension coverage, control for part-time employment reduces the medical coverage disadvantage of CW3 employees somewhat, from 30% to 23% (the difference between part-time and full-time employees is almost 50%), but does not affect other estimates. The last three columns of table 5 show estimates of the effect of contingency on coverage by medical insurance from any source. Here,

addition of industry and occupation controls has little effect on the likelihood of coverage for contingent employees because a substantial number of such workers receive medical insurance through sources other
than their employer. Model 1 estimates indicate that employees in CW1
and CW3 are between 26% and 30% less likely than noncontingent
employees to be covered by medical insurance, although those in
CW2—the self-employed and contractors—are just as likely as standard
employees to have medical coverage. A small share of this disadvantage,
as with pensions and earnings, is attributable to part-time employment.
Such employees are almost 25% less likely to have medical coverage
from any source. The addition of controls for industry and occupation in
model 3 has little effect on the estimates.

Thus, the size and direction of the effect of contingent job status
depend on whether the contingent worker is an employee or is self-
employed, and the effect varies by type of benefit. While the self-
employed are only disadvantaged with regard to pension coverage, other
contingent workers, specifically in the categories CW1 and CW3, have
substantially lower earnings as well as lower pension and medical coverage. Therefore, contingent workers tend to be less expensive for employers than comparable noncontingent employees (net of fees paid to a
THS or leasing agency). The lack of health insurance from their employers is a serious problem and would be more serious had not some contingent employees obtained coverage from other sources.

How does employment in a nonstandard, as opposed to contingent,
position affect earnings and benefit coverage? We follow a parallel strategy of estimating progressively more complete models but substitute
temporary workers, independent contractors, those employed through
contracting firms, and on-call or day laborers for the contingent employee classifications. The model 1 earnings equation (first columns of
panel B, table 5) indicates that independent contractors and those working through contracting firms earn between 6.2% and 8.3% more than
comparable standard employees, while day laborers earn about the same
as standard employees, and employees who obtain work through temporary help firms earn 11% less. Controlling for part-time employment further increases the earnings advantage of independent contractors to 11%
but does not alter the other estimates. Part-time employment reduces
earnings by 21%, twice that estimated in the contingent worker equations. Addition of the part-time variable had a larger effect on the coefficients of contingent workers than on those of nonstandard workers, suggesting that there is less overlap between part-time and nonstandard

workers than between part-time and contingent workers. Addition of industry and occupation controls reduces the effect of employment through a contracting firm to a nonsignificant 5% and reduces the effect of part-time employment to −14%. This suggests that part-time employment is concentrated in low-wage industries and occupations.

Table 7 provides estimates of the earnings effect of nonstandard employment by industry and occupation. To reduce the complexity of the estimates, we combine those employed through temporary firms and on-call or day laborers into one category (NS1) and those employed as independent contractors and through contracting firms into a second (NS2). The industry and occupational rents received by most NS1 workers do not differ from those earned by standard employees. Occupational returns are generally not significant, but managerial employees suffer a 16% earnings penalty. The effects of industry are also small, and among those that are significant, equal numbers are positive and negative. On-call and day workers in construction and hospitals earn 33% and 20% more, respectively, than their standard counterparts but earn 21% and 20% less, respectively, in nondurable goods manufacturing and educational services.

The pattern for independent contractors and contract firm employees parallels that of the self-employed in table 5. Their earnings are mainly dependent on their occupation, while industry plays a relatively more modest role for them than for standard employees. All of the 21 industry coefficients are negative, 7 significantly so. The negative industry differentials are concentrated in goods-producing sectors, ranging from 12% in construction to 38% in communications, but are also substantial in wholesale trade, social service, and educational services. Nonstandard workers of all types are less likely than standard workers to be covered by retirement and medical plans provided by employers, but the extent of the disadvantage varies substantially between different types of nonstandard employment arrangements. At one extreme, workers who are employed by temporary agencies are half as likely to have a pension plan and less than half as likely to be covered by employer-provided medical insurance than comparable standard employees. At the other extreme, employees who work for contracting firms are only 18% to 13% less likely to have pension coverage and 16% to 12% less likely to have health plans. As estimates in the first column of table 5 show, part-time employment has an effect distinct from that of nonstandard work arrangements. Part-time workers are between 39% and 36% less likely than full-time employees to participate in pension plans and are almost 50% less likely to be covered by employer-provided medical insurance.

TABLE 7

The Effect of Nonstandard Employment on Earnings with Interactions for Industry, Occupation and Contingent Work Status

| | | | Nonstandard | | | |
| | | | Temporary firm & day laborer | | Self-employed | |
Log (hourly earnings)	Coefficient	t	Coefficient	t	Coefficient	t
Female	-0.140	-13.724				
Age	0.029	14.801				
Age^2	-0.000	-12.019				
Ed2	0.103	4.027				
Ed3	0.186	8.523				
Ed4	0.252	11.027				
Ed5	0.267	10.313				
Ed6	0.365	15.090				
Ed7	0.504	18.387				
Married	0.066	6.858				
Black	-0.080	-4.870				
Other	-0.061	-3.024				
Hispanic	0.017	0.000				
NE	0.018	1.413				
Midwest	-0.018	-1.488				
South	-0.032	-2.673				
Metro	0.071	6.112				
City 1 mil	0.010	0.000				
Federal	0.077	2.410				
State	-0.015	-0.565				
Local	0.055	2.375				
Part-time	-0.068	-5.907				

TABLE 7 (Continued)
The Effect of Nonstandard Employment on Earnings with Interactions for Industry, Occupation and Contingent Work Status

| | | | Nonstandard | | | |
| | | | Temporary firm & day laborer | | Self-employed | |
Log (hourly earnings)	Coefficient	t	Coefficient	t	Coefficient	t
Occupational effects						
Managerial	1.553	32.517	-0.170	-1.633	0.206	3.928
Professional	1.600	33.110	0.028	0.311	0.158	2.663
Technicians	1.504	28.301	0.080	0.707	0.476	4.517
Sales	1.357	29.345	-0.099	-1.083	0.333	7.925
Clerical	1.298	27.304	-0.050	-0.593	0.337	4.834
Private household service	0.419	1.944	0.738	2.068	-0.631	-0.964
Protective service	1.292	21.279	-0.056	-0.374	-0.173	-1.519
Other service	1.182	25.589	-0.004	-0.054	0.132	1.981
Craft	1.404	28.878	-0.117	-1.181	0.198	3.327
Operators	1.217	24.088	0.043	0.407	0.518	5.268
Transportation operatives	1.269	24.289	-0.010	-0.098	0.273	3.169
Laborers	1.171	23.532	-0.002	-0.018	0.291	2.764
Farming, forestry/fishing	1.198	17.824	-0.018	-0.088	0.203	1.723
Industry effects						
Agriculture	0.156	2.942	0.115	0.565	-0.087	-0.757
Mining	0.475	7.729	-0.249	-1.244	-0.238	-1.405
Construction	0.272	9.948	0.286	2.776	-0.131	-2.149
Durable goods	0.255	11.024	-0.168	-1.498	-0.262	-3.329
Nondurable goods	0.203	7.998	-0.243	-2.227	-0.412	-4.332
Transportation	0.251	8.602	0.042	0.367	-0.149	-1.760
Communication	0.278	6.149	-0.139	-0.722	0.006	0.035

Utilities and sanitary services	0.390	8.035	-0.031	-0.186	-0.472	-1.978
Wholesale trade	0.226	8.191	0.071	0.475	-0.310	-4.116
Retail trade	—	—	—	—	—	—
Finance, insurance, and real estate	0.246	10.091	-0.209	-1.577	-0.094	-1.660
Private household services	0.628	3.108	-0.716	-2.194	0.825	1.279
Business and repair services	0.116	4.748	-0.022	-0.267	-0.080	-1.375
Personal service, except private household	0.047	1.577	-0.123	-0.817	-0.069	-0.868
Entertainment and recreation	0.091	2.262	-0.032	-0.215	0.028	0.306
Hospitals	0.141	4.870	0.182	1.608	-0.100	-0.582
Medical service	0.113	4.354	-0.062	-0.584	0.086	1.058
Educational services	0.007	0.277	-0.221	-2.347	-0.148	-1.344
Social service	-0.117	-3.693	-0.054	-0.341	-0.217	-2.337
Other professional services	0.118	4.366	-0.007	-0.052	-0.063	-0.979
Forestry/fishing	0.264	2.267	(dropped)		0.232	0.871
Public administration	0.210	6.237	-0.068	-0.482	0.010	0.060

In sum, industry and occupational affiliation as well as part-time status have distinct effects on earnings and particularly large effects on benefit coverage, depending on the type of employment arrangement and the benefit under consideration. Industry and occupation have little effect on benefit coverage for temporary workers or on pension coverage for independent contractors but reduce the disadvantage in health insurance coverage for independent contractors and the disadvantage in both health and pension coverage for employees of contract firms and on-call or day laborers. At least part of the disadvantage in benefit coverage suffered by nonstandard employees is thus a result of employment as part-time workers and in industries that are less likely to provide pensions and health insurance to standard workers.

Less than half of workers employed through temporary agencies receive health insurance through their employer, and a similar though less dramatic lack of coverage is found for independent contractors and day laborers. A smaller proportion of all such workers report that they do not have any health insurance from any source, but on the other hand, few contract employees have health insurance other than from their employers. Inclusion of controls for part-time employment reduces the size of the estimated negative effect of nonstandard work arrangements on having any health insurance coverage, perhaps because more people working part time are covered by their parents' or spouse's policy, but industry and occupational affiliation have no meaningful effect.

Summary and Conclusions

Total compensation for both nonstandard and contingent workers varies substantially across different types of employment arrangements. The self-employed, independent contractors, and contract employees generally fare better than other categories of nonstandard workers with respect to both earnings and benefits, while workers who have limited-term wage and salary jobs or work for temporary help agencies or as on-call or day laborers are at a substantial disadvantage. All contingent and nonstandard employment arrangements, however, provide lower levels of health and pension benefits.[18]

We also find substantial differences in the compensation of nonstandard and contingent workers by occupation and industry. The self-employed, independent contractors, and contract workers tend to earn premiums relative to standard workers in their occupation, while other types of contingent and nonstandard employees tend to receive earnings penalties. This points to the conclusion that the prevalence and growth of contingent and nonstandard employment in certain sectors is due at least in part to the labor cost advantages derived by employers who use such arrangements. These advantages are typically larger for lower-skilled than more higher-skilled contingent and nonstandard labor. Thus, we find that a form of segmentation exists among both nonstandard and contingent workers not unlike that found for the workforce as a whole.

Notes

[1] See also Abraham and Taylor (1996) for differences by industry in firms' contracting out for business support services.

[2] Regarding the former see, for instance, Abraham (1990), Lenz (1996), Barkhume (1994), and Katz and Krueger (1999), and for the latter, see Gottfried (1992), Parker (1994), Gonos (1997), and Lester (1998). Lester's (1998) framework contrasts the neoclassical "strong segmentationalist" and new Keynesian economic paradigms regarding explanations of the growth in contingent work.

[3] Another reason for taking a nonstandard job is that underemployment serves as a second-best alternative, superior to unemployment (Farber 1997; Bernasek and Kinnear 1999).

[4] One weakness in applying the otherwise insightful Bulow and Summers (1986) schema to explain contingent work is that it implies higher rates of unemployment in primary labor markets, while secondary labor markets would presumably "clear." In reality, temporary workers' rate of unemployment is almost three times that of non–temporary agency workers (Segal and Sullivan 1997).

[5] There is a great deal of evidence that both trends in temporary employment and their causes are quite similar in the European Union (EU). The reason for using temporary workers mentioned most often by EU employers who are cited in the literature is to adjust staffing to business needs; the second reason is to cover for absences due to maternity and sick leaves and to staff limited-time projects (IRS Employment Trends 1994).

The percentage of production workers with temporary contracts ranged from 2.4% in Belgium to over 29% in Spain. The percentages of professional workers in the same two countries were 5.8% and 18.7%, respectively (DeGrip, Hoevenberg, and Willems 1997; Bentoilla and Dolado 1994).

[6] For the role played by internal factors, such as work reorganization strategies, in increasing contingent and nonstandard jobs, see Appelbaum (1992), Davis-Blake and Uzzi (1993), Kalleberg (1995), and Christensen (1998).

[7] Abraham and Taylor (1996) find that similar factors are responsible for the degree to which certain jobs and tasks are outsourced by firms rather than undertaken with in-house employees.

[8] Multiple jobholders were asked to identify the industry of employment for their primary and their secondary jobs.

[9] Perhaps more problematic is the large proportion of workers who were unable to answer the question of whether they were contingent. If those who were unable to

classify themselves were all classified as contingent workers, the proportion in the labor force that is contingent would approach 10%.

[10] However, 13% of THS workers did not identify the industry to which they were assigned (Cohany 1998).

[11] This concentration may, however, partly reflect that respondents may report the temporary agencies themselves, which are classified as in business services, as their industry of employment.

[12] Also see Jorgensen (1998).

[13] This is largely consistent with the portrait of temporary help industry workers drawn from the March 1993 CPS outgoing rotation files. They are more likely to be underemployed, largely because they face both shorter and more variable hours of work per week and experience higher ratios of involuntary to voluntary part-time employment than other workers (Segal and Sullivan 1995, 1997; Fallick 1998).

[14] The human capital coefficients may, however, still absorb some of the industry and occupation effects because of an endogeneity problem. For example, employers may hire more women since women may be relatively more willing to work in contingent positions in certain sectors or jobs.

[15] Wiens-Tuers (1998) uses the 1995 CWS to create a slightly different taxonomy of categories of nonstandard workers. Whether the worker is a homeowner is also used as an outcome measure and dependent variable, in addition to being a CW3 or receiving health insurance.

[16] In addition, the constant is dropped from the equation and a full set of occupational indicators is used, resulting in a separate intercept for each occupation. The industry indicators, both those that are simply entered in the equation and those interacted with contingent worker status, omit retail trade, which provides the base against which other industry effects are measured.

[17] We do not discuss private household service occupations or employment in the private household industry because the two groups substantially overlap and the industry and occupation effects are large but substantially offsetting.

[18] Workers in contingent jobs get less health and pension benefit coverage in part because of certain firm characteristics ("Company Size" 1995), even in those establishments using high-performance work systems, although under such systems they do receive greater access to childcare benefits (Lautsch 2000).

References

Abraham, Katherine G. 1990. "Restructuring the Employment Relationship: The Growth of Market-Mediated Work Arrangements." In Katherine Abraham and Robert B. McKersie, eds., *New Developments in the Labor Market: Toward a New Institutional Paradigm*, Cambridge, MA, and London: MIT Press, pp. 85–119.

Abraham, Katherine G., and Susan Taylor. 1996. "Firms' Use of Outside Contractors: Theory and Evidence." *Journal of Labor Economics*, Vol. 14, no. 3 (July), pp. 394–424.

Appelbaum, Eileen. 1992. "Structural Change and the Growth of Part-Time and Temporary Employment." In Virginia duRivage, ed., *New Policies for the Contingent Workforce*, Armonk, NY: M. E. Sharpe, pp. 1–22.

Autor, David. 2000. *Outsourcing at Will: Unjust Dismissal Doctrine and the Growth of Temporary Help Employment*. NBER Working Paper No. 7557, February. Cambridge, MA: National Bureau of Economic Research.

Barkhume, Anthony. 1994. "A Labor Market Intermediation Perspective on Employment in the Temporary Help Industry." Unpublished paper, Bureau of Labor Statistics, January.

Belman, Dale, and Michael Belzer. 1998. "The Regulation of Labor Markets: Balancing the Benefits and Costs of Competition." In Bruce Kaufman, ed., *Government Regulation of the Employment Relationship*, Industrial Relations Research Association Series, Champaign, IL: Industrial Relations Research Association, pp. 178–219.

Bentoilla, S., and J. Dolado. 1994. "Labor Flexibility and Wages: Lessons from Spain." *Economic Policy*, Vol. 9, no. 18, pp. 53–99.

Bernasek, Alexandra, and Doug Kinnear. 1999. "Workers' Willingness to Accept Contingent Employment." *Journal of Economic Issues*, Vol. 33, no. 2 (June), pp. 461–469.

Bulow, Jeremy, and Lawrence Summers. 1986. "A Theory of Dual Labor Markets with Application to Industrial Policy, Discrimination and Keynesian Unemployment." *Journal of Labor Economics*, Vol. 4, no. 3, pp. 376–414.

Bureau of National Affairs (BNA). 1988. "Special Personnel Policies Forum Report: Part-Time and Other Alternative Staffing Practices." *Bulletin to Management*, Vol. 39, no. 25, part II (June 23).

Carré, Françoise, and Pamela Joshi. 1998. *Temporary and Contracted Work: Policy Issues and Innovative Responses*. Working Paper No. WP02, June. Cambridge, MA: Task Force on Reconstructing America's Labor Market Institutions, Radcliffe Public Policy Institute.

Christensen, Kathleen. 1998. "Countervailing Human Resource Trends in Family-Sensitive Firms." In K. Barker and K. Christensen, eds., *Contingent Work: American Employment Relations in Transition*, Ithaca, NY: Cornell University Press, pp. 103–125.

Cohany, Sharon. 1998. "Workers in Alternative Employment Arrangements: A Second Look." *Monthly Labor Review*, Vol. 121, no. 11 (November), pp. 3–21.

"Company Size, Unionization Are Best Predictors of Work/Family Benefits, Research Says." 1995. *Employee Benefit Plan Review*, Vol. 50, no. 3 (September), p. 36.

Davis-Blake, Allison, and Brian Uzzi. 1993. "Determinants of Employment Externalization: A Study of Temporary Workers and Independent Contractors." *Administrative Science Quarterly*, Vol. 38, no. 2 (June), pp. 195–223.

DeGrip, A., J. Hoevenberg, and E. Willems. 1997. "Atypical Employment in the European Union." *International Labor Review*, Vol. 136, no. 1 (Spring), pp. 49–71.

Fallick, Bruce C. 1998. *Part-Time Work and Industry Growth*. Finance and Economics Discussion Series, 1998-16. Washington, DC: Federal Reserve Board.

Farber, Henry. 1997. *Alternative Employment Arrangements as a Response to Job Loss*. Working Paper No. 391, October. Princeton, NJ: Princeton University, Industrial Relations Section.

Filipczak, B. 1995. "Contingent Worker Numbers Will Grow." *Training*, Vol. 32, no. 11 (November), p. 12.

Foote, Chris. 1998. "Review of *Dual Labor Markets: A Macroeconomic Perspective*" [by G. Saint-Paul, Cambridge, MA, and London: MIT Press, 1996]. *Journal of Economic Literature*, Vol. 36, no. 3, pp. 1519–1521.

Golden, Lonnie. 1996. "The Expansion of Temporary Help Employment in the US, 1982–1992: A Test of Alternative Economic Explanations." *Applied Economics*, Vol. 28, no. 9 (September), pp. 1127–1141.

Golden, Lonnie. 2000. "Better Timing? Work Schedule Flexibility and Policy Directions." In Lonnie Golden and Deborah Figart, eds., *Working Time: International Trends, Theory and Policy*, London and New York: Routledge, pp. 212–231.

Golden, Lonnie, and Eileen Appelbaum. 1992. "What Was Driving the 1982–1988 Boom in Temporary Help Employment: Preferences of Workers or the Decisions and Power of Employers?" *American Journal of Economics and Sociology*, Vol. 51, no. 4 (October), pp. 473–492.

Gonos, George. 1997. "The Contest over 'Employer' Status in the Post-War United States: The Case of Temporary Help Firms." *Law and Society Review*, Vol. 31, no. 1, pp. 81–110.

Gottfried, Heidi. 1992. "In the Margins: Flexibility as a Mode of Regulation in the Temporary Help Service Industry." *Work, Employment and Society*, Vol. 6, no. 3 (September), pp. 443–460.

Gramm, Cynthia, and John Schnell. 1997. "The Use of Flexible Employment Arrangements in Core Production Jobs." Unpublished paper, College of Administrative Science, University of Alabama in Hunstville, December.

Grunewald, Mark H. 1995. "Introduction: Symposium on the Regulatory Future of Contingent Employment." *Washington and Lee Law Review*, Vol. 52, no. 3, pp. 725–730.

Hipple, Steven. 1998. "Contingent Work: Results from the Second Survey." *Monthly Labor Review*, Vol. 121, no. 11 (November), pp. 22–35.

Houseman, Susan, and George Erickcek. 1997. "A Report on Temporary, Part-Time and Contract Employment in the United States: A Report on the W. E. Upjohn Institute's Employer Survey on Flexible Staffing Policies." Unpublished paper, W. E. Upjohn Institute for Employment Research, Kalamazoo, MI, June.

Houseman, Susan, and Anne Polivka. 1998. "The Implications of Flexible Staffing Arrangements for Job Security." Paper prepared for Russell Sage Foundation Conference on Changes in Job Stability and Job Security, December, presented at the Midwest Economics Association, Nashville, TN.

IRS Employment Trends. 1994. "Diversity and Change—Survey of Nonstandard Working." *Industrial Relations Review and Report*, Vol. 570 (October), pp. 7–18.

Jorgensen, Helene. 1998. "Odd Jobs: Does Nonstandard Work Increase Flexibility in Hours?" Unpublished paper, AFL-CIO Department of Public Policy, December.

Kalleberg, Arne. 1995. "Part-Time Work and Workers in the U.S.: Correlates and Policy Issues." *Washington and Lee Law Review*, Vol. 52, no. 3, pp. 771–798.

Kalleberg, Arne L., Edith Rasell, Ken Hudson, David Webster, Barbara F. Reskin, Naomi Cassirer, and Eileen Appelbaum. 1997. *Nonstandard Work, Substandard Jobs: Flexible Work Arrangements in the U.S.* Economic Policy Institute Report, September. Washington, DC: Economic Policy Institute.

Katz, Lawrence, and Alan Krueger. 1999. "The High-Pressure US Labor Market of the 1990s." *Brookings Papers on Economic Activity*, no. 1, pp. 1–89.

Laird, Karylee, and Nicholas Williams. 1996. "Employment Growth in the Temporary Help Industry." *Journal of Labor Research*, Vol. 17, no. 4, pp. 663–681.

Lautsch, Brenda. 2000. "Benefits for All? Outcomes for Contingent Workers in High Performance Work Systems." Unpublished paper, Simon Fraser University.

Lenz, Edward. 1996. "Flexible Employment: Positive Work Strategies for the 21st Century." *Journal of Labor Research*, Vol. 17, no. 4, pp. 555–566.

Lester, Gillian. 1998. "Careers and Contingency." *Stanford Law Review*, Vol. 52, no. 1 (November), pp. 73–145.

Mangum, Garth, Donald Mayall, and Kristen Nelson. 1985. "The Temporary Help Industry: A Response to the Dual Internal Labor Market." *Industrial and Labor Relations Review*, Vol. 38, no. 4 (July), pp. 599–612.

Milner, Joseph, and Edieal Pinker. 1997. *Optimal Staffing Strategies: Use of Temporary Workers, Contract Workers and Internal Pools of Contingent Labor.* CIS 97-07 Working Paper. Rochester, NY: W. E. Simon Graduate School of Business Administration, University of Rochester, December.

Montgomery, Mark. 1988. "Determinants of Employer Demand for Part-Time Workers." *Review of Economics and Statistics*, Vol. 70, no. 1 (February), pp. 112–117.

Nollen, Stanley. 1996. "Negative Aspects of Temporary Employment." *Journal of Labor Research*, Vol. 17, no. 4 (Fall), pp. 567–582.

Osterman, Paul. 1999. *Securing Prosperity: The American Labor Market: How It Has Changed and What to Do about It.* Princeton, NJ: Princeton University Press.

Parker, Robert E. 1994. "Why Temporary Workers Have Become a Permanent Fixture." *Business and Society Review*, Vol. 91 (Fall), pp. 36–42.

Polivka, Anne, and Thomas Nardone. 1989. "On the Definition of 'Contingent Work.'" *Monthly Labor Review*, Vol. 112, no. 12, pp. 9–16.

Prachowny, Martin F. J. 1997. *Working in the Macroeconomy: A Study of the U.S. Labor Market.* Studies in the Modern World Economy, Vol. 8. London and New York: Routledge.

Rebitzer, James, and Lowell Taylor. 1991. "A Model of Dual Labor Markets When Product Demand Is Uncertain." *Quarterly Journal of Economics*, Vol. 106, no. 4 (November), pp. 1373–1383.

Richman, D. 1999. "Microsoft Raises Standard for Temp Workers' Benefits." *Seattle Post-Intelligencer Reporter,* April 3, p. A1.

Roberts, Karen, and Doug Hyatt. 1998. "Free Trade, Global Markets and Alternative Work Arrangements: Canada versus the U.S." Unpublished paper, Michigan State University, February.

Saint-Paul, Gilles. 1991. "Dynamic Labor Demand with Dual Labor Markets." *Economics Letters,* Vol. 36, pp. 219–222.

Segal, Lewis, and Daniel Sullivan. 1995. "The Temporary Labor Force." *Economic Perspective (Federal Reserve Bank of Chicago)*, Vol. 19, no. 2 (March/April), pp. 2–19.

Segal, Lewis, and Daniel Sullivan. 1997. "The Growth of Temporary Services Work." *Journal of Economic Perspectives*, Vol. 11, no. 2 (Spring), pp. 117–136.

Thomson, Allison. 1995. "The Contingent Work Force." *Occupational Outlook Quarterly*, Vol. 39, no. 1 (Spring), pp. 45–48.

Tilly, Chris. 1991. "Reasons for the Continued Growth of Part-Time Employment." *Monthly Labor Review,* Vol. 114, no. 3 (March), pp. 10–18.

U.S. Department of Labor, Bureau of Labor Statistics. 1999. *Contingent and Alternative Employment Arrangements in February 1999.* Washington, DC: U.S. Bureau of Labor Statistics, December 21.

Walwei, Ulrich. 1998. "Flexibility of Employment Relationships: Possibilities and Limits." In Thomas Donley and Margaret Oppenheimer, eds., *International Review of Public Policy,* Vol. 10, pp. 35–50.

Wiens-Tuers, Barbara. 1998. "The Relationship of Race and Outcomes of Non-Standard Labor." *Journal of Economic Issues,* Vol. 32, no. 2 (June), pp. 575–585.

CHAPTER 7

The Effects of Part-Time
and Self-Employment on Wages
and Benefits: Differences
by Race/Ethnicity and Gender

MARIANNE A. FERBER
University of Illinois, Urbana-Champaign

JANE WALDFOGEL
Columbia University School of Social Work

Introduction

An extensive literature has accumulated in recent years concerning the extent to which nonstandard jobs tend to be good, bad, or indifferent for employers, employees, and the economy as a whole. The conclusions reached by different authors range from enthusiastic to dire. For instance, Lenz (1996, p. 3) claims that such "work arrangements not only offer business a way to more effectively manage their workforces, but also afford employees flexibility, independence, supplemental income, skills training, 'safety net' protection while between permanent jobs, and . . . an opportunity to find permanent work." In contrast, Kalleberg et al. (1997), focusing on the outcomes for workers, conclude that "nonstandard jobs pay less than regular full-time jobs to workers with similar characteristics, are less likely to provide health insurance or a pension, and are more likely to be of limited duration." They further note that these negative outcomes are no less serious because they are to some extent explained by the fact that workers in nonstandard jobs are more likely than "regular full-time" workers to be employed in low-quality jobs.

Most of the researchers have tended to lean toward the latter view (e.g., Cohany 1996; Levitan and Conway 1992), in part because there is evidence that a substantial proportion of nonstandard workers would prefer standard employment (e.g., Carré 1992; Tilly 1991), but most also recognize that not all nonstandard jobs are alike and that therefore broad generalizations are, for the most part, unwarranted. Thus, Blank (1990), for example, says that the answer to the question of whether part-time jobs are bad jobs is "it depends." Similarly, Tilly (1992) writes about "the two faces of part-time work." In addition, Houseman and Polivka (1999) report that "workers in flexible staffing arrangements have less stability than those in regular full-time arrangements in the sense that they are more likely to switch employers, become unemployed, or voluntarily drop out of the labor force within a year" but that this is not true of independent contractors. Our detailed investigation of two types of nonstandard jobs confirms how diverse the outcomes are among nonstandard workers.

In our earlier work (Ferber and Waldfogel 1998), we examined the long-term effects of nonstandard employment,[1] focusing specifically on part-time, temporary, and self-employment. Our results confirmed that both men and women in nonstandard employment tend to have different earnings and benefits than those in standard work, even when other characteristics are controlled for, and further showed that, in spite of the tendency for employment type to persist over time, nontraditional employment has long- as well as short-run effects on earnings and benefits. In addition, we examined all these relationships separately for men and women and found that they were not the same.

We now extend this work in two directions. Because other researchers have generally examined "very limited and poorly defined fringe benefits" (Blank 1990, p. 148) and because in our prior work we examined only two types of benefits (health insurance and retirement benefits), in this paper we also investigate the effects of nonstandard employment on several of the other most important employee benefits: sick leave and maternity or paternity leave. And, having found in the preceding study that there are substantial differences in effects by gender, we now investigate possible differences by race and ethnicity as well.

Learning more about the impact of nonstandard work on various employee benefits is important because they constitute an increasingly large and crucial portion of the total compensation package that workers receive. Although there is a large literature on the determinants of benefits (see, for instance, Belous 1989; Carré 1992; Levitan and Conway 1992; Snider 1995), they have been less frequently studied than wages, and the relationship between earnings and benefits is not clear. Standard economic theory, which says that some wages are higher than others at least in part because of "compensating differentials" that make up for disadvantages associated with particular jobs, suggests that fewer benefits should be associated with higher wages.[2] In fact, however, numerous studies show that earnings and benefits are positively correlated (see, for instance, Blank 1990; Kalleberg et al. 1997; Tilly 1992).

Among benefits, health insurance and retirement benefits have been studied most often. Expanding the analysis to include leave coverage is particularly interesting in light of recent policy changes, such as the passage of the Family and Medical Leave Act (FMLA) in 1993, which mandates that employers provide parental leave, as well as leave for one's own or a family member's illness, to qualified employees; however, employees must have worked a requisite number of hours in the past year to qualify. As a result, family leave coverage continues to be much higher among full-time employees than among part-time employees (Waldfogel 1999).

Recent welfare reforms, both at the state and federal level, have also increased interest in the topic of employee benefits, because health insurance and sick leave are likely to be particularly important in enabling women with young children to make a successful transition from welfare to work. Since a disproportionately large share of the women leaving welfare for work will be African American or Hispanic, understanding the effect of nonstandard employment on benefits for these groups is particularly important. More generally, discovering whether there are differences in the effects of various types of nonstandard work on members of particular racial/ethnic groups and, if so, what they are, is useful because in the absence of such evidence, there may be a tendency to assume that whatever relationships have been found to hold for whites are the same for minorities. Or it may be assumed that they are necessarily worse for blacks and Hispanics, without knowing whether or to what extent this is the case. Either way, there is no accurate estimate of the potential costs and benefits of nonstandard work for minorities as compared with whites.

This work, in common with our prior research (Ferber and Waldfogel 1998), focuses on the long-term effects of workers' current job decisions. It thus makes an important distinction between the short- and long-run effects of nonstandard employment. Analyzing the long-run effects provides useful information for worker decision making, even among those workers who tend to discount the future, if nonstandard employment results in major gains or severe penalties in workers' earnings or benefits.

Data and Methodology

Our data come from the National Longitudinal Survey of Youth (NLSY), which follows a nationally representative sample of young men and women who were ages 28 to 36 by 1993. We use the work history data in the NLSY to track respondents' employment histories from 1979 in 1993 to determine whether they are currently employed part time or are self-employed, and whether they have been in such jobs in the past. To be able to do an in-depth investigation, we narrowed our focus in this paper to two kinds of nonstandard employment, part-time work (PT) and self-employment (SE), the only categories for which adequate data are available.[3] The two categories examined are, however, of great interest, part-time workers because they constitute by far the largest category of nonstandard workers, and the self-employed because the effect of being in this classification is so markedly different for men and women.

A person's current job is coded as PT, SE, or neither PT nor SE. Individuals are coded as currently PT if their main job in 1993 was less than 35 hours per week. They are coded as currently SE if they report being self-employed in their main job in 1993. These two categories are not mutually exclusive: a worker may be both PT and SE. Any respondent whose current job is neither PT nor SE is coded as not currently PT or SE.[4]

We exploit the historical information in the NLSY to also identify those who have been in part-time jobs or self-employed in the past, even if they are not working part time or self-employed currently. Taking 1993 as the "current" year, information from the 1979 to 1993 surveys (including retrospective information on the period 1975–1978 contained in the 1979 survey) is used to track each individual's labor market experience, beginning with the year s/he turned 18 (or the year s/he left high school, if before age 18, but in no case earlier than age 16) and continuing to the present (1993). We define a respondent as previously PT if s/he worked part time in the past but is not doing so currently. We define a respondent as previously SE if s/he was self-employed in the past but is not currently. Again, these categories are not mutually exclusive: a worker may have been previously PT and previously SE. We code a respondent as never PT or SE if s/he never worked part time and was never self-employed in the past and is not working part time or self-employed currently.

We further take advantage of the work history data in the NLSY to compute actual work experience (in years) for each respondent. In addition, we use the detailed demographic data in the NLSY to define variables for the respondents' age, educational level, marital status, and number of children, as well as race/ethnicity and sex. Our three racial/ethnic groups are non-Hispanic whites, non-Hispanic African Americans, and Hispanics.

Multivariate analysis is used to investigate the effects of current and previous part-time or self-employment on current earnings and benefits. In both cases, we estimate ordinary least-squares (OLS) models that include controls for age, work experience, level of education, marital status, number of children, race, and ethnicity for women and men. Our measure of earnings is the log of hourly wages. We use four measures of benefits, drawing upon the NLSY questions about whether the respondent's employer provided health insurance, retirement benefits, sick leave, and maternity or paternity leave.[5]

To determine whether the effects of nonstandard employment differ by race and ethnicity, as well as sex, we estimate models for women and men where the controls for part-time and self-employed are interacted with dummy variables for African American and Hispanic. These models allow us to see whether any effects of part-time or self-employment are different for these groups, in addition to the average effects of part-time or self-employment, which are common across all three racial/ethnic groups.

Overview of Part-Time and Self-Employment among White, Black, and Hispanic Women and Men

Some indication that there can be substantial differences among the three racial/ethnic groups is seen in table 1, which shows the proportion of employed men and women of each group who are part-time or self-employed. The data confirm the well-known fact that women are disproportionately represented among part-time workers and men among the self-employed. They also show that white women are most likely to work part time, 19.6%, followed by 14.3% of Hispanics, and only 10.4% of African Americans, while the opposite is true for men, where the figures are 3.6%, 3.8%, and 4.1%, respectively. In contrast, both white men and women are more highly represented among the self-employed, 10.3% and 7.3%, respectively, followed by 8.8% and 5.4% of Hispanics, with African Americans the least likely to be self-employed, at 5.8% and 2.0%. A small share of workers (less than 1% of men and 1% to 2% of women) are both part-time and self-employed. We shall return to some of the implications of these findings later.

TABLE 1

Share of Young Women and Men Who Were Part-Time (PT)
or Self-Employed (SE) in 1993, by Race and Ethnicity

	Not PT or SE	PT	SE	Both PT and SE
Women				
White	75.36%	19.58%	7.33%	2.27%
African American	88.32	10.41	2.03	0.76
Hispanic	82.41	14.26	5.37	2.04
Men				
White	86.73%	3.59%	10.34%	0.66%
African American	90.49	4.14	5.82	0.45
Hispanic	88.33	3.79	8.83	0.95

Notes: Tabulated from the NLSY. Rows sum to more than 100% because some workers are both part-time and self-employed.

Earnings and Benefits of Current and Prior Part-Time or Self-Employed Workers

Table 2 displays mean current wages and benefits for women and men in the NLSY, by current employment status. The top panel of the table shows that among young women, those who work part time or are self-employed have lower wages than those who do not work in such jobs. Those working part time, and especially those who are self-employed, are less likely to have benefits. The patterns for men are similar, except that those who are self-employed earn higher wages, on average, than part-time workers or those who are neither part-time or self-employed. Perhaps surprisingly, with the exception of the self-employed, men tend to have somewhat lower levels of benefit coverage than do women working in comparable types of jobs, although, as would be expected, their wages tend to be higher, except for those working part time.

Individuals who are currently not working part time or self-employed may of course have had periods of part-time or self-employment in the past, and such employment may be associated with lower levels of current wages and benefits. This may be the case because they obtained less training and less valuable experience,[6] because there was some negative self-selection into those types of jobs, or because employers think that may have been the case. Table 3 explores this possibility by showing mean current wages and benefits for five groups of workers: those who have never worked part time or been self-employed, those who worked part time previously (but are not working part time currently), those

TABLE 2

Mean Wages and Benefits for Young Women and Men in 1993,
by Current Employment Status

	Not PT or SE	Part-time	Self-employed
Women			
Log wage	6.85	6.71	6.71
Health insurance	85.13 %	39.30%	3.29%
Retirement benefits	71.67%	33.43%	2.63%
Sick leave	75.24%	36.88%	5.30%
Maternity/paternity leave	84.13%	50.91%	5.92%
Men			
Log wage	7.00	6.71	7.14
Health insurance	80.11%	27.17%	12.20%
Retirement benefits	62.35%	20.88%	6.44%
Sick leave	61.13%	20.88%	8.25%
Maternity/paternity leave	54.42%	23.08%	5.76%

Note: Tabulated from the NLSY.

who were self-employed previously (but are not self-employed currently), those who are working part time currently, and those who are self-employed currently.

The data show that, as before, men earn more in all categories except for those currently working part time but receive fewer benefits. We can also see that benefits are highest for those who have never worked part time or been self-employed, somewhat lower for those who previously worked part time or were self-employed, and considerably lower for those who work part time or are self-employed currently. The wage patterns are less clear-cut, which may reflect differences between groups, for instance in educational level.[7] The analysis that follows controls for such factors.

Effects of Current and Prior Part-Time or Self-Employment by Race/Ethnicity

Table 4 displays coefficients (and standard errors) from models that estimate the effects of current part-time or self-employment on current wages and benefits of women and men, controlling for race and ethnicity, as well as age, years of work experience, level of education, marital status, and number of children. In the log wage models, the coefficients can be interpreted roughly as percentage effects; for instance, a coefficient of

TABLE 3

Mean Current Wages and Benefits for Young Women and Men, by Current and Previous Employment Status

	Never PT or SE	Previously PT	Previously SE	Currently PT	Currently SE
Women					
Log wage	6.83	6.86	6.68	6.71	6.71
Health insurance	89.54%	79.38%	62.64%	39.30%	3.29%
Retirement benefits	73.61%	67.84%	49.08%	33.43%	2.63%
Sick leave	75.31%	71.83%	59.30%	36.88%	5.30%
Maternity/paternity leave	86.38%	79.43%	68.80%	50.91%	5.92%
Men					
Log wage	7.00	7.02	6.92	6.71	7.14
Health insurance	84.09%	73.20%	63.37%	27.17%	12.20%
Retirement benefits	64.77%	57.87%	44.75%	20.88%	6.44%
Sick leave	59.95%	58.90%	48.44%	20.88%	8.25%
Maternity/paternity leave	56.51%	49.55%	41.48%	23.08%	5.76%

Notes: Tabulated from the NLSY. Previously PT is defined as part-time prior to 1993 but not in 1993, previously SE is defined as self-employed prior to 1993 but not in 1993, currently PT is defined as working part time in 1993, and currently SE is defined as self-employed in 1993.

TABLE 4

Effects of Current Part-Time and Self-Employment or Current Wages and Benefits

	Log wage	Health insurance	Retirement benefits	Sick leave	Maternity/ paternity leave
Women					
Part-time	-.0469**	-.3130**	-.2446**	-.2514**	-.1936**
	(.0223)	(.0211)	(.0254)	(.0254)	(.0221)
Self-employed	-.0952**	-.6750**	-.5645**	-.5856**	-.6885**
	(.0352)	(.0301)	(.0360)	(.0355)	(.0310)
Black	-.0593**	.0445**	.0823**	.0389*	.0444**
	(.0200)	(.0170)	(.0205)	(.0206)	(.0176)
Hispanic	.0488**	.0010	.0051	.0757**	-.0219
	(.0217)	(.0189)	(.0226)	(.0227)	(.0195)
Adjusted R-squared	.3132	.3151	.2249	.2202	.2544
N	2,870	2,684	2,659	2,528	2,650
Men					
Part-time	-.1616**	-.3109**	-.2102**	-.2145**	-.1510**
	(.0410)	(.0404)	(.0479)	(.0483)	(.0505)
Self-employed	.1310**	-.6534**	-.5375**	-.4985**	-.4680**
	(.0273)	(.0232)	(.0274)	(.0279)	(.0290)
Black	-.1253**	.0138	.0433*	.1080**	.0783**
	(.0196)	(.0169)	(.0199)	(.0204)	(.0214)
Hispanic	-.0627**	-.0178	-.0074	.0833**	.0605
	(.0211)	(.0181)	(.0214)	(.0221)	(.0229)
Adjusted R-squared	.2676	.2740	.1905	.1839	.1165
N	3,337	3,271	3,254	3,087	3,135

Note: Coefficients (and standard errors in parentheses) from ordinary least-squares (OLS) models. All models also include controls for age, years of actual work experience, high school only, some college, college or more, married, previously married, and number of children. Sample sizes vary because of missing data for some benefit variables.
* statistically significant at $p < .10$
** statistically significant at $p < .05$

.10 means that a one-unit increase in that variable would increase log wages by about 10%. In the benefits models, the coefficients can also be interpreted as percentage effects (because these are linear probability models); therefore, a coefficient of .10 indicates that a one-unit increase in that variable would raise the probability of having coverage by about 10%.

Looking first at the results of the log wage model, shown in column 1, part-time employment has a negative effect on wages for both women and men. Working part time reduces women's wages by 5% and men's by 16%. Self-employment, on the other hand, is associated with lower wages for women but higher wages for men.[8] Race and ethnicity also have significant effects. Black women and men as well as Hispanic men have lower wages than non-Hispanic whites, while Hispanic women have higher wages than non-Hispanic white women.

The coefficient estimates in columns 2 through 5 suggest that part-time employment and self-employment significantly reduce the likelihood of receiving benefit coverage for both men and women. The reductions range from 15% to 31% for part-time workers, with the largest reduction in the case of health insurance coverage, and from 47% to 69% for the self-employed. Race and ethnicity also have some significant albeit far smaller effects. African American women are significantly more likely to have each of the four types of benefits, and the same is true for three of the four types of benefits for African American men.[9] Both Hispanic women and men are significantly more likely to have sick leave coverage.

The evidence in table 4 cannot, however, tell us whether the effects of nonstandard employment differ for whites, African Americans, and Hispanics. To address this question, we reran our models with interaction terms in addition to the controls included in the original models.[10] The results of these interaction models are shown in table 5. The coefficient on each nonstandard work variable—PT or SE—shows the main effect of that type of nonstandard employment that is common across whites, African Americans, and Hispanics. The coefficient on each interaction term—PT°Black, PT°Hispanic, SE°Black, or SE°Hispanic—indicates the additional effect of that type of nonstandard employment for African Americans or Hispanics. Looking at these, we find only a few significant interactions between nonstandard employment and race/ethnicity. In fact, of the 40 interactions displayed in this table (4 per model times 5 models for women and men each), only 6 are statistically significant. Among women, Hispanics who currently work part time have significantly higher wages than other part-time workers, but they are also

TABLE 5
Effects of Current Part-Time or Self-Employment on Current Wages and Benefits, with PT and SE Employment Interacted with Black and Hispanic

	Log wage	Health insurance	Retirement benefits	Sick leave	Maternity/paternity leave
Women					
Part-time	-.0662°°	-.3463°°	-.2614°°	-.2325°°	-.2054°°
	(.0277)	(.0263)	(.0318)	(.0315)	(.0276)
Part-time°Black	-.0149	.0769	.0337	.0189	.0046
	(.0571)	(.0523)	(.0630)	(.0637)	(.0547)
Part-time°Hispanic	.1219°°	.1113°	.0616	-.1524°°	.0711
	(.0596)	(.0595)	(.0713)	(.0727)	(.0625)
Self-employed	-.1256°°	-.6780°°	-.5738°°	-.5781°°	-.6868°°
	(.0417)	(.0352)	(.0421)	(.0413)	(.0363)
SE°Black	.0356	-.0289	-.0256	-.0667	-.0426
	(.1160)	(.0995)	(.1189)	(.1165)	(.1025)
SE°Hispanic	.1320	.0346	.0704	.0053	.0112
	(.0920)	(.0816)	(.0976)	(.0970)	(.0841)
Black	-.0625°°	.0357°°	.0780°°	.0405°	.0441°°
	(.0213)	(.0180)	(.0217)	(.0218)	(.0187)
Hispanic	.0222	-.0139	-.0059	.0916°°	-.0300
	(.0239)	(.0203)	(.0244)	(.0244)	(.0210)
Adjusted R-squared	.3141	.3124	.2243	.2206	.2357
N	2,870	2,684	2,659	2,528	2,650
Men					
Part-time	-.2434°°	-.3776°°	-.2536°°	-.2625°°	-.1588°°
	(.0568)	(.0536)	(.0639)	(.0638)	(.0667)

TABLE 5 (Continued)

Effects of Current Part-Time or Self-Employment on Current Wages and Benefits, with PT and SE Employment Interacted with Black and Hispanic

	Log wage	Health insurance	Retirement benefits	Sick leave	Maternity/ paternity leave
Part-time°Black	.1233	.0870	.0083	.0593	-.0684
	(.0940)	(.0981)	(.1160)	(.1184)	(.1220)
Part-time°Hispanic	.2333°°	.2362°°	.2084°	.1877	.1412
	(.1092)	(.1060)	(.1254)	(.1260)	(.1348)
Self-employed	.1136°°	-.6492°°	-.5559°°	-.4573°°	-.4476°°
	(.0345)	(.0293)	(.0346)	(.0352)	(.0366)
SE°Black	.0672	-.0161	.0835	-.0952	-.0289
	(.0725)	(.0618)	(.0729)	(.0737)	(.0770)
SE°Hispanic	.0220	-.0138	.0093	-.1307°	-.0852
	(.0716)	(.0611)	(.0721)	(.0733)	(.0761)
Black	-.1347°°	.0123	.0375°	.1137°	.0830°°
	(.0205)	(.0175)	(.0207)	(.0214)	(.0223)
Hispanic	-.0733°°	-.0233	-.0142	.0904°°	.0649
	(.0224)	(.0191)	(.0226)	(.0234)	(.0242)
Adjusted R-squared	.2618	.2743	.1906	.1844	.1162
N	3,337	3,271	3,254	3,087	3,135

Note: Coefficients (and standard errors in parentheses) from ordinary least-squares (OLS) models. All models also include controls for age, years of actual work experience, high school only, some college, college or more, married, previously married, and number of children. Sample sizes vary because of missing data for some benefit variables.
° statistically significant at $p < .10$
°° statistically significant at $p < .05$

less likely to have sick leave coverage. Among men, Hispanics who work part time not only have significantly higher wages than other part-time workers but are more likely to have health insurance and retirement benefits; at the same time, we also find that Hispanics who are self-employed are somewhat less likely to have sick leave coverage than other self-employed workers. The remainder of the interactions are not significantly different from zero, suggesting that the penalties for part-time or self-employment are roughly the same regardless of a worker's race or ethnicity.

As we noted earlier, some of those not currently working part time or self-employed may have worked part time or been self-employed in the past, and this may have long-run effects on current wages and benefits, even if the workers are no longer working part time and are no longer self-employed. The models shown in table 6 address this question by adding controls for previous part-time and self-employment. As suggested by the patterns in the raw data presented in table 3, the results in table 6 show that there are penalties for prior part-time and self-employment, although they are not as large as those for current part-time or self-employment. Those who previously worked part time or were self-employed have wages that are 6% to 8% lower than those who never worked part time or were self-employed, and they are also up to 18% less likely to have benefits. These results confirm that there are lasting effects of these two types of nonstandard employment on wages and benefits, even for those who leave such employment, return to full-time work, and are no longer self-employed. It is less clear exactly why that is the case. It may be that part-time workers accumulate less human capital because they accumulate less experience and generally receive less on-the-job training and that the experience of the self-employed is less valuable to them as employees. It is also possible, however, that employers discount the experience and the potential value of those who have been nonstandard workers because they look askance at their experience, whether or not this is justified. Our study does not enable us to determine to what extent each of these explanations plays a part.

Last, we address the question of whether these effects of previous part-time and self-employment differ by race/ethnicity. The results in table 7 suggest that on the whole they do not. Among men, there are no significant interactions between part-time or self-employment and race/ethnicity. Among women, there are significant interactions in only 4 out of 20 cases: in the models for health insurance and for sick leave, the effect of previous part-time employment is more positive for African

TABLE 6

Effects of Past Part-Time or Self-Employment on Current Wages and Benefits

	Log wage	Health insurance	Retirement benefits	Sick leave	Maternity/ paternity leave
Women					
Previously part-time	-.0398**	-.0751**	-.0460**	-.0360*	-.0372**
	(.0190)	(.0159)	(.0191)	(.0193)	(.0165)
Previously self-employed	-.0790**	-.1304**	-.1354**	-.0682**	-.0848**
	(.0261)	(.0230)	(.0277)	(.0280)	(.0241)
Currently part-time	-.0724**	-.3623**	-.2742**	-.2748**	-.2177**
	(.0258)	(.0235)	(.0284)	(.0286)	(.0247)
Currently self-employed	-.1066**	-.6927**	-.5837**	-.5951**	-.7003**
	(.0354)	(.0300)	(.0361)	(.0357)	(.0312)
Black	-.0709**	.0262	.0653**	.0288	.0335*
	(.0202)	(.0170)	(.0206)	(.0208)	(.0177)
Hispanic	.0432**	-.0084	-.0036	.0709**	-.0271
	(.0217)	(.0187)	(.0225)	(.0227)	(.0195)
Adjusted R-squared	.3162	.3261	.2334	.2227	.2590
N	2,870	2,684	2,659	2,528	2,650
Men					
Previously part-time	-.0796**	-.0517**	-.0279*	-.0069	-.0388**
	(.0166)	(.0140)	(.0166)	(.0173)	(.0180)
Previously self-employed	-.0636**	-.1653**	-.1834**	-.1171**	-.1275**
	(.0215)	(.0183)	(.0217)	(.0227)	(.0234)
Currently part-time	-.1948**	-.3158**	-.2003**	-.2041**	-.1539**
	(.0418)	(.0405)	(.0482)	(.0490)	(.0512)
Currently self-employed	.1205**	-.6835**	-.5716**	-.5204**	-.4915**
	(.0275)	(.0232)	(.0274)	(.0281)	(.0291)

Black	-.1242°°	.0067	.0334°	.1006°°	.0728°°
	(.0196)	(.0167)	(.0198)	(.0205)	(.0214)
Hispanic	-.0612°°	-.0207	-.0115	.0803°°	.0584°°
	(.0210)	(.0178)	(.0212)	(.0221)	(.0228)
Adjusted R-squared	.2749	.2961	.2092	.1906	.1264
N	3,337	3,271	3,254	3,087	3,135

Note: Coefficients (and standard errors in parentheses) from ordinary least-squares (OLS) models. All models also include controls for age, years of actual work experience, high school only, some college, college or more, married, previously married, and number of children. Sample sizes vary because of missing data for some benefit variables.

° statistically significant at $p < .10$
°° statistically significant at $p < .05$

TABLE 7

Effects of Past Part-Time or Self-Employment on Current Wages and Benefits, with Past PT or SE Employment Interacted with Black and Hispanic

	Log wage	Health insurance	Retirement benefits	Sick leave	Maternity/paternity leave
Women					
Previously part-time	-.0527*	-.1043**	-.0572**	-.0608**	-.0315
	(.0271)	(.0226)	(.0273)	(.0274)	(.0236)
Prev. PT*Black	.0398	.0588*	.0433	.0853**	.0127
	(.0425)	(.0354)	(.0427)	(.0431)	(.0369)
Prev. PT*Hispanic	-.0051	.0518	-.0127	.0007	-.0452
	(.0493)	(.0411)	(.0496)	(.0498)	(.0429)
Previously self-employed	-.1071**	-.0941**	-.1328**	-.0130	-.0710**
	(.0318)	(.0282)	(.0341)	(.0341)	(.0298)
Prev. SE*Black	.0506	-.0739	.0571	-.0652	.0258
	(.0745)	(.0637)	(.0766)	(.0793)	(.0669)
Prev. SE*Hispanic	.0998	-.1360**	-.0635	-.2235**	-.0934
	(.0676)	(.0602)	(.0729)	(.0721)	(.0627)
Black	-.1060**	-.0151	.0298	-.0169	.0251
	(.0358)	(.0298)	(.0360)	(.0363)	(.0311)
Hispanic	.0069	-.0450	-.0024	.1082**	.0028
	(.0406)	(.0338)	(.0408)	(.0409)	(.0353)
Adjusted R-squared	.3171	.3278	.2325	.2262	.2586
N	2,870	2,684	2,659	2,528	2,650
Men					
Previously part-time	-.0755**	-.0535**	-.0433*	-.0226	-.0395
	(.0224)	(.0189)	(.0224)	(.0233)	(.0243)

Prev. PT°Black	.0165	.0076	.0252	.0460	.0114
	(.0377)	(.0319)	(.0378)	(.0393)	(.0409)
Prev. PT°Hispanic	-.0487	-.0030	.0341	.0197	-.0086
	(.0421)	(.0355)	(.0423)	(.0441)	(.0455)
Previously self-employed	-.0597°°	-.1612°°	-.1931°°	-.1069°°	-.0993°°
	(.0281)	(.0238)	(.0282)	(.0295)	(.0305)
Prev. SE°Black	-.0356	.0369	.0358	.0038	-.0534
	(.0523)	(.0450)	(.0534)	(.0560)	(.0574)
Prev. SE°Hispanic	.0169	-.0726	.0007	-.0636	-.0895
	(.0570)	(.0487)	(.0577)	(.0602)	(.0621)
Black	-.1384°°	-.0048	.0083	.0824°°	.0795°°
	(.0287)	(.0242)	(.0288)	(.0299)	(.0312)
Hispanic	-.0503	-.0136	-.0365	.0878°°	.0820°°
	(.0314)	(.0265)	(.0316)	(.0331)	(.0339)
Adjusted R-squared	.2753	.2966	.2089	.1908	.1258
N	3,337	3,271	3,254	3,087	3,135

Note: Coefficients (and standard errors in parentheses) from ordinary least-squares (OLS) models. All models also include controls for age, years of actual work experience, high school only, some college, college or more, married, previously married, and number of children. Sample sizes vary because of missing data for some benefit variables.

° statistically significant at $p < .10$

°° statistically significant at $p < .05$

Americans than for non-Hispanic whites, while the effect of previous self-employment is more negative for Hispanics than for non-Hispanic whites. But overall, the results suggest that the penalties for previous part-time or self-employment are not very different across racial and ethnic groups.

Discussion and Conclusions

Because the results of this research concerning the effects of current and previous part-time and self-employment on wages of women and men essentially confirm our earlier findings, we focus here on the questions we had not previously investigated: how these effects differ by race and ethnicity and what the effects are on specific benefits. In both instances, while some of the facts uncovered are consistent with what would be expected, others are rather surprising. For example, in the raw data shown in tables 2 and 3, as would be anticipated, men who are neither part-time nor self-employed earn more than women, as do men who are self-employed, while the mean earnings of men and women part-time workers are the same.[11] Similarly, our findings that both female and male part-time and self-employed workers are considerably less likely to receive benefits are not new (e.g., Abraham 1990; Blank 1990) and may to some extent reflect the self-selection of lower-skilled workers in such jobs (Blank 1990). At the same time, the discovery that women who work part time also receive more of all four types of benefits than men who work part time, while self-employed men, whose earnings are higher than those of men who are not part-time or self-employed, receive more of all these benefits except maternity/paternity leave, lends support to the "job attributes" model. According to this model, favorable or inferior terms of employment are correlated, as opposed to the "compensating differentials" hypothesis. Interestingly, however, we find that among workers who were previously part-time but are now working full time, men earn more than women. As for benefits, the outcomes are very clear: they are highest for both men and women who have never worked part time or been self-employed, somewhat lower for those who did so previously, and much lower for those who do so now. Therefore, the main penalty for nonstandard employment is in reduced benefits coverage.

Adding race/ethnicity provides additional useful information. As seen in table 4, being black has a significant negative effect on wages for both men and women; being Hispanic, however, has a significant negative effect only for men, while the opposite is true for women. In contrast, we also find that the coefficients on all the benefits for blacks are positive and furthermore are significant in all instances except for health insurance for men. These results do tend to support the "compensating differentials" hypothesis, but it may also be the case that black women, who can least afford to give up benefits, are less likely than white women to work part time or to choose to become self-employed unless they receive benefits (this latter interpretation is consistent with the fact that black women are more likely to work in large firms that offer such benefits). The findings for Hispanics are less striking; both men and women are significantly more likely to receive sick leave, but while the signs in all instances except health insurance for men are positive, none of these are significant. Finally, when we introduced interactions with race/ethnicity to examine whether the effects of part-time and self-employment are significantly different for the three groups, the results, shown in table 5 and discussed in greater detail earlier, can best be summarized by saying that race/ethnicity makes surprisingly little difference. In fact none of the effects are significant for blacks. Nor did we find many differences in the long-run effects of part-time and self-employment between whites, blacks, and Hispanics.

Overall, this study does not change our earlier conclusion that both part-time and self-employment tend to have negative effects on wages and benefits in the long run as well as the short run for both women and men, with the one exception that current self-employment is associated with higher wages for men. At the same time, our results also show that the effects are not the same on all types of benefits. With regard to race/ethnic differences, we found few differences in the effects of part-time and self-employment for blacks, Hispanics, and whites, but we discovered that the differences do not always favor whites. Additional investigations that consider other types of nonstandard employment and that examine older workers may well add further valuable insights. The focus here on a sample of younger workers may have led to results that underestimate the long-run effects of nonstandard employment for workers' future success in the labor market.

Acknowledgments

We are grateful to Wen-Jui Han and Andrew Lenney for help with the data used in this project. Jane Waldfogel also gratefully acknowledges funding support from the National Institute of Child Health and Development.

Notes

[1] There is, as yet, no generally accepted terminology. Various authors have used other terms, such as *nontraditional* or *contingent*. Nor do all researchers include all the same categories. In this paper, we use the term *nonstandard*, in conformity with the introduction to this volume.

[2] Interestingly, a number of other countries specifically require that part-time workers be compensated for the lack of benefits (Duffy and Pupo 1992), but this is not the case in the United States.

[3] While temporary workers are included in Ferber and Waldfogel (1998), unfortunately they could not be included in this study because the NLSY does not enable us to identify those who are currently in a temporary job, only those whose job ended already because it was temporary.

[4] Regrettably, we have no information about other categories of nonstandard workers, such as temporary and on-call workers, so they may be included in our category of not PT or SE workers as long as they are employed full time and are not self-employed.

[5] The health insurance question in the NLSY is "Does/did your employer make available to you medical, surgical, or hospital insurance that covers injuries or major illnesses off the job?" The retirement benefits question is "Does/did your employer make available to you a retirement plan other than Social Security?" The sick leave question asks the number of sick days to which the employee is entitled each year; if the number is greater than zero, we code the person as having sick leave coverage. The maternity/paternity leave question is "Does/did your employer make available to you maternity/paternity leave that will allow you to go back to your old job or one that pays the same as your old one?"

[6] Frazis, Gittleman, Horrigan, and Joyce (1998) found that employers tend to provide more training to employees with whom they expect to have a long-term relationship.

[7] Such differences may exist in part because young people often work part time while they go to college.

[8] In results not shown, when we include an interaction term for being both part-time and self-employed, we find that the coefficient is positive for both men and women. However, we do not place much weight on this result, given the small numbers in this category (22 men and 52 women).

[9] These results are consistent with prior research on family leave coverage (reported in Commission on Family and Medical Leave 1996), which found that African Americans were more likely to be covered, in large part because they were more likely to work in large firms.

[10] We also estimated separate models for African Americans, Hispanics, and whites, and the results (not shown) do not differ from those reported here. We prefer the interaction approach because it allows us to see easily whether the effects of nonstandard employment are significantly different for the different groups.

[11] This is consistent with earlier evidence (Ferber and Waldfogel 1998) that working part time voluntarily has a positive effect on women's hourly earnings but a particularly large negative effect on men's earnings. This difference may occur because

such men are penalized for violating a social norm of what is expected of them. Another contributing factor could be that married women may tend to prefer working shorter hours in response to an increase in their wage rates (see Nakamura, Nakamura, and Cullen 1979).

References

Abraham, Katherine G. 1990. "Restructuring the Employment Relationship: The Growth of Market-Mediated Arrangements." In Katherine Abraham and Robert McKersie, eds., *New Developments in the Labor Market. Toward a New Institutional Paradigm,* Cambridge, MA: MIT Press, pp. 85–119.

Belous, Richard S. 1989. "How Human Resource Systems Adjust to the Shift Toward Contingent Workers." *Monthly Labor Review,* Vol. 112, no. 3 (March), pp. 7–12.

Blank, Rebecca M. 1990. "Are Part-Time Jobs Bad Jobs?" In Gary Burtless, ed., *A Future of Lousy Jobs?* Washington, DC: Brookings Institution, pp. 123–155.

Carré, Françoise. 1992. "Temporary Employment in the Eighties." In Virginia L. duRivage, ed., *New Policies for the Part-Time and Contingent Workforce,* Armonk, NY: Economic Policy Institute, M. E. Sharp, pp. 45–87.

Cohany, Sharon R. 1996. "Workers in Alternative Employment Arrangements." *Monthly Labor Review,* Vol. 119, no. 10 (October), pp. 31–45.

Commission on Family and Medical Leave. 1996. *A Workable Balance: Report to Congress on Family and Medical Leave Policies.* Washington, DC: U.S. Department of Labor, Women's Bureau.

Duffy, Ann, and Norene Pupo. 1992. *Part-Time Paradox: Connecting Gender, Work, and Family.* Toronto: McClelland and Stewart.

Ferber, Marianne A., and Jane Waldfogel. 1998. "The Long-Term Consequences of Non-Standard Work." *Monthly Labor Review,* Vol. 121, no. 5 (May), pp. 3–12.

Frazis, Harley, Maury Gittleman, Michael Horrigan, and Mary Joyce. 1998. "Results from the Survey of Employer Provided Training." *Monthly Labor Review,* Vol. 121, no. 6 (June), pp. 3–13.

Houseman, Susan N., and Anne E. Polivka. 1999. *The Implications of Flexible Staffing Arrangements for Job Stability.* Upjohn Institute Staff Working Paper 99-56. Kalamazoo, MI: W. E. Upjohn Institute for Employment Research.

Kalleberg, Arne L., Edith Rasell, Ken Hudson, David Webster, Barbara F. Reskin, Naomi Cassirer, and Eileen Appelbaum. 1997. *Nonstandard Work, Substandard Jobs: Flexible Work Arrangements in the U.S.* Washington, DC: Economic Policy Institute.

Lenz, Edward A. 1996. "Flexible Employment: Positive Work Strategies for the 21st Century." *Journal of Labor Research,* Vol. 17, no. 4 (Fall), pp. 555–566.

Levitan, Sar A., and Elizabeth A. Conway. 1992. "Part-Timers: Living on Half-Rations." In Barbara Warme, Katherine P. Lundy, and Larry A. Lundy, eds., *Working Part-Time: Risks and Opportunities,* New York: Praeger, pp. 45–60.

Nakamura, Alice O., Masao Nakamura, and David Cullen. 1979. "Job Opportunities, the Offered Wage, and the Labor Supply of Married Women." *American Economic Review,* Vol. 69, no. 5 (December), pp. 788–805.

Snider, Sarah. 1995. "Characteristics of the Part-Time Work Force and Part-Time Employee Participation in Health and Pension Benefits." *Journal of Labor Research,* Vol. 16, no. 3 (Summer), pp. 239–248.

Tilly, Chris. 1991. "Reasons for the Continuing Growth of Part-Time Employment."
    Monthly Labor Review, Vol. 114, no. 3 (March), pp. 10–18.
Tilly, Chris. 1992. "Two Faces of Part-Time Work: Good and Bad Part-Time Jobs." In
    Barbara Warme, Katherine P. Lundy, and Larry A. Lundy, eds., *Working Part-
    Time: Risks and Opportunities,* New York: Praeger, 1992.
Waldfogel, Jane. 1999. "Family Leave Coverage in the 1990s." *Monthly Labor
    Review,* Vol. 122, no. 10 (October), pp. 13–21.

CHAPTER 8

The Bottom-Line Impact of Nonstandard Jobs on Companies' Profitability and Productivity

SHULAMIT KAHN
Boston University School of Management

The increasing use of temporary and other nonstandard work arrangements (NSWAs) may be attributable either to supply-side factors (increasing supply of individuals desiring such jobs) or to demand factors (factors leading companies to want more nonstandard employees). The limited empirical evidence more strongly supports the dominance of demand-side factors. Golden (1996) finds that employer-related influences, including the variation of output demand from trend, the relative magnitude of nonwage labor costs, and intensified competition, all have important effects on temporary help employment, while demographic variables have much smaller effects. Laird and Williams (1996) find that two demand factors, increasing aggregate output and heightened foreign competition, encouraged firms to hire temporary workers. Segal and Sullivan (1997) argue that supply factors, particularly female labor force growth, are unlikely to have been a major factor in the growth of temporaries.

Given the primacy of demand-side factors, the relation between a company's use of NSWAs and its financial performance is key to understanding NSWA trends and impacts. However, there is very little research on the impact of NSWAs on financial performance measures such as profitability or productivity. The only direct study of a link between profitability and usage of temporary workers ("temps") is Kahn, Foulkes, and Heisler (forthcoming), which approaches this issue in two ways, both using microdata from individual companies. There we first correlate survey data on companies' changes in temp usage over the past five years with three alternative measures of their financial performance: earnings per share (EPS), operating margin (OPM), and share prices. We find that changes in share prices and changes in EPS are positively correlated with the proportion of temps. A second part of the paper looks at the change in share prices and changes in EPS of two companies that made sudden, radical shifts toward an intensive use of temporaries. These two companies, and six control companies that had not made any radical changes, were all from the same region (the South) and the same industry (fibers/textiles). The analysis reveals that financial performance *fell* drastically in one company immediately after the change and had no impact on the other company. Together, these findings concerning a possible correlation between profits and temp use are quite mixed.

Other studies indirectly suggest by inference the profitability of increasing temp use. Surveys of companies show the variety of reasons why increasing (or decreasing) their use of temporaries may enhance profits (Abraham 1988; Houseman 1996). Abraham links use of temps with perceived variability in demand, while Houseman links it with industry seasonality and covariance with the business cycle. Golden (1996), by matching the use of temporary help agency employment to demand factors, implicitly argues that the use of temps is profitable in periods when there is more variability of demand, foreign competition, and/or expensive benefits. Segal and Sullivan (1997) document the advantages that temps bring to companies, particularly in terms of flexibility and a two-tier compensation system. This chapter extends this literature. It focuses on the demand-side of NSWAs, and specifically temp growth, by asking human resource (HR) executives about the role of temporary workers and whether and how their use may increase companies' profitability and/or productivity. The interviews are supplemented with an empirical analysis of the relationship at the industry level between NSWA use and firm performance variables.

Economists generally assume that decision makers in companies choose profit-maximizing strategies. Thus, if they choose to use temporary workers, they must expect that use to be profitable. By the same logic, they must think it unprofitable to use temporary workers in jobs filled by regular employees. Therefore, it might be suggested that if we study the correlation between temp use and profitability measures, we may find no correlation because all companies choose the most profitable course when filling each position.

Even if this were the case, however, examining statistical correlations remains legitimate if we depart from an equilibrium model that assumes companies instantaneously choose the most profitable HR policies. I have observed substantial evidence of nonequilibrium behavior at semiannual meetings of Boston University's Human Resource Policy Institute (HRPI), where HR vice presidents discuss current challenges and their potential solutions. The HR VPs do not demonstrate the kind of confidence that neoclassical economists place in them. They are not sure that they are making the most profitable choices. Instead, they are always seeking more profitable approaches by learning from their own experience and that of others in the HRPI and elsewhere. Over the decade, these meetings have provided a portrayal of the diffusion process of HR innovations. Successful new HR policies (e.g., outsourcing HR functions) are those that become widely diffused, while less successful ones are adopted only by a handful of firms. However, it takes years even for successful new HR policies to be adopted by a majority of HRPI corporations. Thus, if extensive use of temps were profitable for most companies, the slow diffusion would nevertheless allow researchers to capture a positive causal correlation between the use of temps and profitability.[1]

Analysis of interviews with executives does not suffer from the same inherent problems as examining statistical correlations, since interviews are by nature impressionistic. In the interviews reported here, HR executives indeed considered the impact of temp use on their own company's profitability. The HR executives were asked to recall their reasoning behind decisions to increase (or decrease, in some cases) temp use and to compare the present with past periods or with a hypothetical counterfactual case. Thus, in the analysis of interviews, I presume neither optimizing behavior nor its absence but instead rely on HR executives' impressions of the profitability of extensive use of temps in their companies. Of course, impressionistic interviews have their own weaknesses insofar as individuals may not recall accurately or may not be aware of all factors leading to decisions.

The next section presents the results of in-depth interviews with HR executives. The section after that uses industry-level data to explore correlations between the use of NSWAs and measures of both productivity and profitability.

Interviews with HR Executives of Fortune 500 Companies on the Profitability of NSWAs

Background

The qualitative information we were able to obtain from the interviews with Fortune 500 companies' senior human resource executives during the spring of 1996 and early 1999 is useful for gaining greater understanding concerning the use of NSWAs. In the interviews, the executives were asked about their company's use of temporary employees and independent contractors working on site. The responses to both surveys detail how HR executives view NSWAs, while a comparison of responses to the two surveys gives a sense of changes over this three-year period.

The 35 interviews conducted in 1996 were with executives of a random sample of Fortune 500 companies, intended to be representative of large establishments. Respondents typically were HR vice presidents (ranging from assistant to senior levels) or held another executive HR position such as corporate personnel manager or staffing manager.[2] The executives interviewed in 1999 worked for 15 companies selected from corporate members of Boston University's HRPI. Once again, the respondents were HR vice presidents of Fortune 500 companies. In both years, interviews were limited to executives who were familiar with the basis for their company's NSWA policy decisions, whether or not they themselves had actively participated in the decision making. In some cases, additional interviews were obtained in the same company from lower-level executives directly in charge of administering temporary employees.

Because the 1999 interviews were drawn from the HRPI membership, they are not a random sample of large companies. Therefore, although the corporate members of HRPI interviewed were not chosen on the basis of their policies toward NSWAs, but rather on their availability during the interview period, there is a potential bias. HRPI membership implies that company leadership places a relatively high value on the function of HR, so that these companies may have more innovative HR practices than is the norm.

Corporate Decision-Making Processes Concerning NSWA Use

One way to ascertain whether the use of NSWAs increases profitability is simply to ask officers of companies whether it does. A deeper understanding of their yes/no responses can come from learning about the reasoning behind companies' hiring decisions and from their policies affecting NSWA use. With this in mind, our focus in the interviews was on eliciting information about the decision-making process through questions such as, "Who makes decisions about whether to hire more NSWAs? What recent decisions have been made to change NSWA use? What factors did you/they take into account when this decision was made?"

We found that by 1999 the human resource executives—with one exception—had consciously evaluated expanding the use of NSWAs at some point(s) in time in recent years.[3] Based on this evaluation, they made decisions ranging from vastly increasing their NSWA use to eliminating all NSWA use. Moreover, many were *continuously* revising their policy as their company's or business units' situation changed.

In their evaluation, executives typically compared relative costs of NSWAs versus regular employees on the one hand and relative productivity on the other. Some had done a quantitative analysis of relative productivity, while others had not, for two very different kinds of reasons. A fair number of HR executives dismissed the need to calculate the impact of NSWAs on productivity and profitability. In the words of one executive, "You know, it's not rocket science," that is, the advisability of hiring nonstandard workers in any specific case was so easy to judge that no explicit calculations were required. Other executives, however, reported that they found the analysis impossible because of the difficulty in attributing productivity to individuals. The HR VP in one manufacturing firm, for instance, highlighted the hopelessness of attempting this calculation in a multitask and multiperson assembly-line process.

The 1996 interviews had a different flavor than did the 1999 ones. In the earlier period, the executives demonstrated less sophistication in their choices involving NSWAs. This may to some extent have been due to the difference between the two samples. I had, however, spoken to executives of some of the same HRPI companies included in the 1999 sample as an exploratory exercise in 1996. Similar increasing sophistication was evident within these individual companies.

These findings suggest that in 1999 HR executives were more likely to consider NSWA use as a strategy for particular situations beyond merely hiring temps to replace employees who were temporarily absent. They were more likely to have analyzed the profitability and productivity aspects of NSWAs and to have modified their use of them accordingly; they had developed policies that gave managers what they thought were appropriate incentives to use—or not to use—NSWAs.[4]

It was generally hard to elicit information about which specific individual(s) made any decision regarding NSWA use. This may have been due to the complicated nature of decision making in a large company, general reticence to talk about internal power bases, or more specifically the HR executives' reluctance to admit that they themselves did not make a key HR decision.

The interviews identified two kinds of corporate cultures about decision making on temp issues. In the first, the direct supervisors and/or the area or line managers make the microdecisions about whether to hire an individual temp. In these kinds of companies, central management influences NSWA use only through the corporate policies they set, which affect their agents, the line managers. In the second kind, central management is more heavily involved in decisions about whether to adopt, abolish, increase, or decrease NSWA use in specific categories of jobs within specific business units. In these companies, the line managers typically worked along with central management agents—represented by HR or other senior executives—in analyzing the advisability of each option. The final decision was, however, made by the senior executive.

Factors Affecting the Choice of NSWA Intensity

What kinds of factors do companies consider when choosing a specific level of NSWA usage? Previous surveys have asked companies to identify or categorize the general reasons for increased or decreased use of NSWAs (e.g., Abraham 1990; Houseman 1996; Kahn, Foulkes, and Heisler forthcoming). Here I move beyond categorization and investigate the executives' reasoning in more depth.

Productivity. Officers of several companies shared information on the outcomes of explicit calculations comparing the productivity of nonstandard and regular employees. In one major department-store chain, customer service and satisfaction increased sharply with the salesperson's seniority. In contrast to standard employees, temps generally considered themselves as "hired guns" and did not treat customers as well, even when they had the same technical expertise. These facts led the company to hire everyone (even during the peak holiday season) as regular employees, able to stay indefinitely as long as they received satisfactory performance ratings.

A second company analyzed productivity of telephone customer service representatives by monitoring the number of customers served and listening to a sample of phone conversations. ("Your call may be monitored for quality-assurance purposes.") They found that temps' performance was identical to that of regular employees on both quantity and quality measures. As a result, the company has been increasingly staffing these jobs with temps, particularly when there is an unusually large volume of calls due to specific promotional initiatives.

A third company had analyzed the productivity of temps and standard employees in manufacturing. It found that the manufacturing process itself drove productivity and that the process progressed equally smoothly in either case. The company also analyzed the probability of "catastrophic mistakes" and found that temps were no more likely to make them. The general conclusion of the VP of that company was that "in manufacturing, (employee) commitment is not important."

The productivity comparisons between temps and regular employees differed in each of these three case studies. However, the three cases are similar in that executives in each firm carefully analyzed the productivity comparisons and made decisions on temp use based on this analysis.

Direct Costs. The company officers to whom I spoke had all done calculations at some point about the direct costs of hiring a temp for a job compared with the cost of hiring a regular employee, and most had revisited this question over the years as well. In these calculations, they compared the sum of wages plus benefits of regular employees with the sum of wages plus agency markups plus any benefits received by temps. Temporary agency employees typically receive few if any benefits from their host company because the agency is expected to provide them. One executive also mentioned the often high cost of overtime pay for temps.

Whether the total cost of a temp was less than that of a regular employee differed in 1996 and 1999. In 1996, the majority concluded that it was slightly lower for temps, but in 1999, while a couple of companies still found the cost lower, the majority believed that temps cost at least as much as regular employees. Several HR executives specifically noted that this differential had changed and attributed the higher cost of temps to increasingly tight labor markets.

One company had just reevaluated its temp policy and was about to change its policies to discourage extensive use of temps. Their finance officers had decided that temps were too expensive, based on the fact that the 25% markup over salary for regular employees for benefits was substantially smaller than the 32% markup of temporary agencies. They concluded (and the CEO concurred) that they should adopt policies that would radically cut back the use of long-term temps.

When answering the questions about direct costs, some of the respondents with lower direct costs also explicitly discussed balancing costs versus other factors. "I wonder if the lower costs justify some of the additional risks," one said. Another noted, "There is a belief that temps are cheaper but that doesn't include the time in training." Finally, an executive in the department store (discussed earlier) that had decided against temp use said that he does not know whether compensation was higher or lower but strongly feels that "it is not the defining issue. The defining issue is commitment."

"We Don't Staff to Peak." The first response of executives who use NSWAs extensively is that they do it to have adequate staff during periods of high demand without the expenses of extra personnel during slower periods. The statement "We don't staff to peak," a buzz-phrase in the business lexicon, was repeated by many executives. There are different reasons for periods of high labor demand in different industries. In many cases the peak is seasonal. For banks and accounting firms, high demand coincides with IRS quarterly and annual deadlines. For others, it is the result of holiday sales or the agricultural cycle.

Many companies also hire NSWAs for temporary, one-time projects, such as opening new stores, setting up new systems, or supporting a specific promotional offer. Often they do so because they need skills that they do not have in house and do not require on a regular basis. A major reason given in 1999 for vastly expanded use of NSWAs in information technology was the Y2K problem. In all these cases, the companies believe that they can improve their bottom line by paying for employees only when the employees are actually needed.

For some companies, the variability is over longer product cycles. For instance, one company producing computer components hired a large number of temporary employees because it had a new product for which there was exceptionally large demand. This allowed the company to avoid layoffs of regular workers in the face of large variations in demand and extreme uncertainty. As a result, regular employees felt more secure in their jobs, and the managers believed that the temporaries had been placed in other companies.

These examples suggest that the strategic usefulness of NSWAs to companies and to the economy is far greater than the observed proportion of *temporary employees* suggests. Availability of temps improves profitability because they can be hired *only* when circumstances call for them. Having this option increases the value of companies, whether or not they are presently exercising it.

Which Jobs Can Be Filled by Temps? In their decisions about the level of temp use, managers were extremely aware of the kinds of jobs where temps were useful and the kinds of jobs where this was not the case. For instance, one manager noted, "Temps can describe the products we sell and take orders, but we would never hire a temp to handle customers unsatisfied with the service." Managers also knew that when company-specific knowledge and experience were needed for the job, temps were inappropriate. Alternatively, when only a modest amount of firm-specific experience was necessary, companies made sure that the temps were sufficiently versed in the institutional knowledge, including acquaintance with the firms' computer systems, by using the same temps repeatedly. This was done by using in-house temp rosters or by forming partnerships with one or a few temp agencies.

Further, there was another class of jobs for which companies tended not to hire temps: those where employees had access to confidential or proprietary information. For instance, fearing corporate espionage, one pharmaceutical company had a policy of not hiring temps for clinical studies of drugs. At the same time, companies that hired temps in sensitive jobs tried to minimize the security risks by requiring background checks.

Facilitating Recruiting and Discharging. In addition to the reasons already discussed, some companies hire temps on a regular basis as a way to identify employees suitable to hire for permanent jobs. In both the 1996 and 1999 interviews, many managers reported increases in "temp-to-perm" transitions. This trend was encouraged by a number of innovations in temporary agency contracting, such as partnerships between a company and a temporary agency in which the company agrees to obtain temps exclusively from a single agency in exchange for zero or low penalties for hiring the temps into permanent positions.

Temp-to-perms are mainly used when it is difficult to gauge applicants' suitability for a position, such as unskilled blue-collar jobs where work habits are of prime importance. Even for other jobs, however, many companies find it advantageous to "try before you buy." A probationary period as a temp allows companies to avoid the legal and financial costs of discharge and to reduce the distress to both the HR manager and the new employee. Moreover, in a tight labor market such as that of the late 1990s, the personnel networks developed by temporary agencies are also an excellent resource for identifying new employees, so that temporary agencies were sometimes asked to recruit *regular* employees for companies as well.

Corporate Policy Decisions Affecting Temps

Head-Count Restrictions. The corporate policy with the most significant impact on temp use is head-count restriction, a common mechanism used by central management to control costs and keep major decisions in their own hands, while allowing line managers some flexibility in hiring. Head count has the advantage of being easily measurable and not affected by conditions beyond the line manager's control, such as fluctuating market wage rates or material prices.

The use of temps, however, throws a wrench into the efficacy of head-count restrictions when temps are not included in these restrictions. Thus, as a result of such head-count restrictions, line managers are encouraged to hire temps for jobs that would otherwise be more profitably staffed by permanent employees, and the head-count limitation loses its value as a control mechanism. In the earlier survey, managers of a slight majority (54%) of companies thought that avoiding head-count restrictions (presumably of permanent employees) was a factor in their use of temps. For instance, in one company, a hiring freeze—an extreme head-count restriction—had led line managers to hire temps when they needed extra people. The HR executive of another company told how line managers had to "play games with head count when, head-count considerations aside, regular hiring would have made much more sense."

By 1999, many companies had modified their head-count restrictions to close this loophole. Some combined temps with regular employees into a single full-time equivalent (FTE) head-count measure. Others imposed separate restrictions for temps and regular employees, with differing levels of flexibility, depending on which kinds of employment they wanted to encourage. In the words of one executive with more stringent restrictions on permanent employees, they "keep the [company's] future long-run commitment to new regular employees low" in light of existing uncertainty. Nonetheless, at least two companies still had standard head-count restrictions in 1999. In one of these, central management achieved most of its control through strict budgets so that the head-count restriction was practically irrelevant, but in the other company, an executive acknowledged the suboptimality of this policy.

Length-of-Stay Restrictions. A second corporate policy that influences use of temps is limitations on the minimum and maximum length of time a temp can stay. Whenever a temp is hired, the company incurs one-time costs due to the need for administrative attention and on-the-job training before the temp reaches adequate productivity. Therefore, companies find it profitable to hire temps for at least a minimum length of time. Typically, the line managers themselves avoid hiring temps for short stays for budgetary reasons. However, in one case, this was reinforced by a company-wide policy of a minimum term of two weeks.

Many more companies impose maximum-stay requirements for temps, beyond which the supervisor must either hire them for a regular position or let them go. More rarely, this maximum is applied to the position itself and not just the specific person occupying it. The most widely mentioned reasons for maximum stays are the IRS regulations that require an employer to pay FICA taxes on all its employees. A still-developing body of legal cases and government regulations defines who is employed or "co-employed" by the host company for IRS purposes, but a length of stay of no more than 90 days is the single most important criterion. This distinction is crucial because employees and co-employees, but not temps, are protected by a variety of labor laws and their wages are subject to tax withholding.

Officers of large companies, while aware of co-employment laws, run the gamut in the measures they take to avoid lawsuits or IRS penalties. Some have tried to limit the length of stay for temps so that their companies will not be considered co-employers; others have not. A manager in one company explained long temp stays and other practices that skirt the definition of co-employment as follows, "We consider it a business risk we are taking. We worry, but we've decided to ignore it. If you paid attention, you'd never hire temps." Some believe that they are legally covered by obtaining their temps through a third-party temporary agency. Finally, some companies chose a hybrid approach, such as giving benefits to temps who had worked more than 1,000 hours.[5]

However, IRS regulations and legal considerations are not the only reasons that companies impose maximum restrictions. When analysis indicates that net profits per hour from temps are lower than from regular employees, companies themselves are more likely to adopt lower maximums than required by the IRS 90-day guideline.

Partnerships with Agencies. Central management helps to encourage NSWA use when it streamlines the process of hiring temps. By 1999, executives at companies that used temps reported that they had extensively overhauled this process. Record keeping and billing had been computerized and centralized, and partnerships had been created with chosen temporary agencies, which increasingly involved a temporary-company representative housed within the corporation whose job was to quickly respond to line managers' needs. These partnerships also allowed companies to bargain for the small or zero penalties for hiring temps for permanent positions.

Analysis of NSWA Use, Productivity, Profitability, and Variability Using Industry-Level Data

Complementing the qualitative interviews, this section investigates whether industry-level data provide any evidence of an impact of NSWAs on productivity and profitability. These data are also used to investigate the link between variability of a firm's value and the use of NSWAs.

Data Sources

The statistical association among productivity, profitability, and the extent of use of NSWAs is analyzed by combining Bureau of Economic Analysis (BEA) industry-specific data with data provided by the Bureau of Labor Statistics' (BLS) Contingent Worker Supplements to the February 1995 and February 1997 Current Population Survey (CPS). All workers in the private sector were allocated to 40 industries for the analysis of *productivity*, although because of problems of data availability, the analysis of *profitability* is limited to 39 industries, and the analysis of *industry variability* to only 36 industries.[6] Two-digit Standard Industrial Classifications (SICs) are used but with some modifications. First, extremely small two-digit industries are merged with other related industries. For instance, "leather" is merged with "apparel." Second, because NSWAs are common in service industries, two more specifically defined three-digit industries, legal services and membership services, are separated out from "other professional services." Data availability did not allow breakdowns of other two-digit service industries.

Both profitability and productivity measures are derived from the BEA's establishment-based industry data used to create the National Income and Products Accounts (NIPA). Profit rates are corporate before-tax profits as a proportion of industry value added (or "gross product"). BEA data were not adequate to calculate an industry-specific return on equity, which might have been preferable as a profit measure.

The analysis uses two different measures of productivity. The first is based entirely on NIPA data. It is calculated by dividing the value added of each industry by the total number of full-time equivalent employees (FTEs) in each industry. NIPA calculates FTEs by combining information on number of employees and average hours per employee. This method might result in systematic underestimation of employment, since establishments were not given explicit instructions to include non-standard workers hired through outside intermediaries, and hence also to an upward bias in productivity when NSWAs are used at establishments but not counted in FTE data (see Estevão and Lach, this volume). The second method uses industry employment and hours from the CPS survey of individuals to calculate FTEs. Here, industry employment is calculated to include people temporarily contracted by that industry from temporary agencies or contract companies. This method also has a drawback. Ideally, the output (the numerator) and FTE employment (the denominator) would be taken from the same sample. When the two measures are taken from different samples, the true ratio is likely to be measured quite inaccurately.[7]

In addition to linking NSWA use to profitability and productivity, I explore the relationship between the variability across time and NSWA use. I use a measure developed by Lambson and Jensen (1998), which calculates variability of publicly traded firms as the spread between the maximum and minimum inflation-adjusted market value of the firm between 1973 and 1992, inclusive.[8] The firm-level data are then averaged over the industry. Since firms' values are believed to reflect expected future profits, these values are also a measure of market expectations about each company, which tend to be highly correlated with the permanent components of present profits.[9]

Measures of NSWA

Three distinct measures of NSWAs are employed in the analysis here:

NSWA#1: People employed by temporary agencies, people employed by contract companies, on-call employees, and all additional workers who do not fall into one of these categories but expect their jobs to last for less than a year for nonpersonal reasons.[10] This differs from the BLS definition of contingent workers because it includes people employed by contract companies but excludes independent contractors working on site.

NSWA#2: Independent contractors as a separate category of workers with potentially different effects on profitability or productivity.

NSWA#3: NSWA#1 plus NSWA#2.

The proportion of the workforce in each category is given in table 1.

Limitations of Analysis

Unfortunately, even in surveys as large as the CPS, the proportion in NSWAs at the detailed industry level may not be fully reliable. Of the 51,489 people who worked in identifiable industries in the February 1997 CPS, 5,592 (10.9%) were either temporary employees, contract workers, and/or independent contractors (see table 1). This translates into an average of only 140 per two-digit industry, not a large number of individuals on which to base estimates of the entire industry's nonstandard employment. Moreover, more than 50% of these are independent

TABLE 1
NSWA Observations in February 1995 and February 1997 CPS

	1995 Number of observations		1997 Number of observations	
Total employed	58,366		51,489	
Average employed per industry*	1,459		1,287	
	Number	% of employed	Number	% of employed
Number of NSWA				
On-call workers	909	1.6	811	1.6
Employed by temporary agency	460	0.8	466	0.9
Contract company	241	0.4	267	0.5
Additional people who say that their job will continue < 1 year for nonpersonal reasons	1,147	2.0	905	1.8
Total in one or more of above NSWA categories (NSWA#1)**	2,733	4.7	2,429	4.7
Independent contractors (NSWA#2)	3,642	6.2	3,193	6.2
Total in one or more of above NSWA categories (NSWA#3)	6,326	10.8	5,592	10.9
Average per 2-digit industry in one or more of above NSWA categories*	158		140	

* 40 two-digit private-sector industries. The industry classifications used in this paper merge a few of the smallest two-digit industries with related industries (e.g., leather is merged with apparel). Two three-digit service industries, legal services and membership services, are divided from other services because the data allow this additional specificity and because service industries tend to have larger per-centages of NSWAs.

** Numbers do not add up because of individuals in multiple categories. There are 24 people in 1995 and 20 in 1997 who consider themselves simultaneously on-call workers and workers employed by contract companies. There are 49 independent contractors in 1995 and 30 in 1997 who believe that their jobs will continue for less than a year.

contractors, who are separated from the other NSWAs for much of the following analysis because of potentially different effects on profitability. Thus, measuring the impact of NSWA use on companies' profitability may be confounded by small-sample measurement error. Further compounding small-sample problems, some of the analysis uses first differences, which typically have even greater measurement error.

Another potential source of measurement bias concerns identifying the industry that utilizes temporary agency and contract workers. The Contingent Worker Supplements ask two follow-up questions that allow this identification to be made directly: "Earlier you told me you worked for [X company]. Is this the place where your temporary help agency assigned you to work or is this a temporary help agency?" and "What is the name of the company where you were working?" Assignment of temporary agency or contract workers to industries utilizing them was based on these follow-up questions, but the questions were not answered by 48% of those employed by temporary agencies or contract companies. When no industry was identified in the follow-up questions, the industry classification was assigned based on the original CPS industry question, and 16% of people employed by temporary agencies are still identified as being in business services (which includes the personnel supply service industry, SIC 731). To ensure that misclassification into business services is not skewing results, key analyses that follow are repeated excluding business services. Also, some of the analysis excludes the private household industry, since the informal nature of the majority of jobs in this industry raised doubt about the accuracy of data collected on it and since some data are not even available for it.

Given these limitations and caveats regarding the sample size and aggregation of data, the results are likely to be biased toward zero. Consequently, any significant result would be noteworthy in light of this bias. At the same time, when significant relations are found, they must be interpreted with caution, since causality may run in both directions. NSWA use might affect profitability as discussed in the first section, but profitability might in turn affect NSWA use as well. In case of the latter direction of causality, the sign of the relationship is uncertain. For instance, profitability would increase NSWAs if the high profitability is accompanied by rapid growth in demand for output, inducing firms to hire temps because they are unable to find regular employees to staff newly created positions. Conversely, profitability would decrease NSWAs to the extent that profitable firms are more able to afford regular employees, while financially struggling companies "downsize" their regular employees and hire nonstandard ones instead. Finally, a significant relationship may be evidence of correlation but not causality. Heterogeneous industries differ on other dimensions that may simultaneously affect both firm performance and NSWA adoption.

The analysis investigates the timing of the various developments to better disentangle the causality. If profits in a given year are more strongly correlated with prior use of NSWAs than with contemporaneous or subsequent use of NSWAs, this suggests that causality runs from use of NSWA to profitability.[11] In addition, the analysis is repeated for first differences, since these changes are less dominated by heterogeneous industry characteristics.

Finally, an increase in the extent to which firms use nonstandard workers such as temps is often embedded in larger strategic HR changes. For instance, a new CEO or a reorganization may lead to increased use of temps, new employee stock option programs and bonuses, and new performance appraisal and feedback methods. When this is the case, the analysis in essence identifies the impact of an entire HR strategy package rather than the impact of a single policy.

Estimation Results

Productivity. It may be easier to discern an effect of human resource policies on productivity than on profitability since the latter is strongly affected by capital-related factors as well as arbitrary accounting decisions. Table 2 presents bivariate correlations between productivity and NSWAs, while table 3 presents regression results of productivity variables.[12] In these tables, PROD#1 refers to productivity based on BEA employment numbers, while PROD#2 refers to productivity based on CPS employment.

Concentrating initially on productivity levels rather than first differences, there are conflicting results. Subsequent productivity shows no significant relationship with NSWA#1, but the *log* of subsequent productivity is strongly negatively related with the same variable. Using PROD#1, the relationship is much weaker when the two questionable industries are excluded ($t = .94$) but is significant using PROD#2 even when these are excluded.

Different patterns are seen with first differences. Earlier, I argued that the relationship between *changes* in NSWAs and productivity is less likely to be overpowered by industry heterogeneity. On the other hand, since the CPS sample is not the same each year, random changes in the sample may be large enough to swamp any systematic relationships.

TABLE 2

Productivity and NSWAs: Bivariate Correlation Coefficients

	Productivity using BEA employment (PROD#1)					
	1997	ln 1997	ln 1997[a]	1995	Δ 1995-97	Δln 1995-97
Levels in 1995						
NSWA#1	-.203	-.406°	-.157	-.201	-.096	-.174
	(.209)	(.009)	(.346)	(.213)	(.556)	(.283)
NSWA#2	-.162	-.254	-.137	-.140	-.191	-.195
	(.317)	(.114)	(.412)	(.388)	(.239)	(.228)
NSWA#3	-.201	-.346°	-.167	-.182	-.191	-.222
	(.213)	(.029)	(.317)	(.262)	(.238)	(.168)
Changes between 1995 and 1997						
NSWA#1	.342°	.323°	.341°	.375°	-.033	-.020
	(.031)	(.042)	(.036)	(.017)	(.842)	(.902)
NSWA#2	.039	.234	.055	.023	.109	.179
	(.809)	(.146)	(.744)	(.890)	(.505)	(.268)
NSWA#3	.217	.328°	.259	.226	.043	.109
	(.179)	(.039)	(.116)	(.161)	(.794)	(.503)

TABLE 2 (*Continued*)

Productivity and NSWAs: Bivariate Correlation Coefficients

| | Productivity using CPS employment (PROD#2) | | | | | |
	1997	ln 1997	ln 1997[a]	1995	Δ 1995-97	Δln 1995-97
Levels in 1995						
NSWA#1	-.235	-.429°	-.371°	-.224	-.153	-.176
	(.144)	(.006)	(.022)	(.154)	(.345)	(.276)
NSWA#2	-.126	-.164	-.099	-.094	-.203	-.200
	(.437)	(.311)	(.555)	(.565)	(.210)	(.216)
NSWA#3	-.182	-.284°	-.188	-.152	-.219	-.226
	(.260)	(.076)	(.258)	(.350)	(.175)	(.160)
Changes between 1995 and 1997						
NSWA#1	.431°	.413°	.405°	.415°	.263	.178
	(.005)	(.008)	(.012)	(.008)	(.102)	(.273)
NSWA#2	-.009	.136	.011	-.023	.060	.129
	(.958)	(.402)	(.946)	(.889)	(.713)	(.428)
NSWA#3	.236	.327°	.268	.216	.191	.199
	(.143)	(.040)	(.104)	(.180)	(.237)	(.218)

Note: Refer to text for definitions. *p* values in parentheses.
° Correlations with *p* values greater than or equal to .10.
[a] Excludes household services and business services.

TABLE 3
Regression Results: Productivity and NSWAs
(standard errors in parentheses)

	Productivity 1997	ln 1997 Productivity	Δ 1995-97	1997	ln 1997	1995	Average	Δ 1995-97	Δln 1995-97
		PROD#1 (using BEA employment)			*Productivity excluding 2 industries**				
1995 NSWA#1	-321.1 (328.2)	-8.011* (3.520)		-204.7 (543.6)	-4.978 (5.804)				
1995 NSWA#2	-80.04 (130.0)	-1.139 (1.394)		-79.2 (134.4)	-1.049 (1.457)				
1997 NSWA#1	-84.28 (324.3)								
1997 NSWA#2	-117.4 (131.0)								
1995 NSWA#3	-146.2 (115.5)								
Δ1995-97 NSWA#1	1812.7* (810.5)	20.39* (9.09)	-23.84 (145.7)	1870.6* (829.5)		1890.8* (758.2)	1880.7* (790.9)	-20.22 (153.1)	-.071* (1.456)
Δ1995-97 NSWA#2	230.6 (613.1)	11.56* (6.86)	72.18 (110.2)	-179.5 (700.9)		-238.8 (640.6)	-209.1 (668.3)	59.23 (129.4)	1.097 (1.231)
constant	95.22* (16.54) 87.26* (17.21) 90.73* (14.70) 76.61* (8.70)	4.536* (.177) 4.133* (.098)	3.816* (1.564)	90.64* (23.68) 79.10* (10.3)	-4.418* (.252)	75.19* (8.11)	77.14* (8.47)	-3.905* (1.639)	.035* (.016)
Adj. R²	.00 .03 .02 .07	.14 .12	.00	-.04 .08	-.02	.11	.10	-.05	-.03

TABLE 3 (*Continued*)

Regression Results: Productivity and NSWAs
(standard errors in parentheses)

	Productivity 1997	ln 1997 Productivity	Δ 1995-97	PROD#2 (using CPS employment)	Productivity excluding 2 industries[°°]				
				1997	ln 1997	1995	Average	Δ 1995-97	Δln 1995-97
1995 NSWA#1	-322.2 (251.8)	-9.565° (3.577)		-387.9 (417.0)	-13.41° (5.824)				
1995 NSWA#2	-30.19 (99.70)	-0.170 (1.417)		-38.07 (104.7)	-.521 (1.462)				
1997 NSWA#1	-74.41 (250.8)								
1997 NSWA#2	-72.69 (101.3)								
1995 NSWA#3	-102.1 (89.25)								
Δ1995-97 NSWA#1	1746.6° (600.2)	26.01° (9.115)	217.4° (129.1)	1734.1° (619.0)		1492.3° (569.3)	1613.2° (590.0)	241.8 (133.6)	2.410 (1.848)
Δ1995-97 NSWA#2	-45.08 (454.0)	7.420 (6.894)	-45.86 (97.68)	-248.4 (523.0)		-272.6 (481.0)	-260.5 (499.3)	241.7 (112.8)	1.139 (1.561)
constant	79.62° (12.69) 71.60° (13.30) 73.96° (11.36) 64.01° (6.44)	11.28° (0.180) 10.87° (0.098)	-3.774 (1.385)	82.24° (18.17) 65.47° (6.625)	11.44° (.254)	61.44° (6.09)	63.46° (6.32)	4.03 (1.43)	.051° (.020)
Adj. R^2	.01 -.03 .01 .14	.14 .15	.02	-.02 .15	.09	.13	.14	.03	.51

Refer to text for definitions.

°Coefficients with *p* values greater than or equal to .10.

°°Excludes household services and business services.

There is a strong positive relation between changes in NSWA#1 1995–1997 and the *levels* of productivity, whether in log or linear form, apparent both in the bivariate statistics of table 2 and the multiple regressions of table 3. The same magnitude and significance levels are obtained for subsequent (1997), prior (1995), or average productivity (1995, 1996, and 1997). A similarly positive relationship is found between changes of both NSWA#1 *and* PROD#2. For PROD#1, the log version is significant but not the level version.

These findings indicate significant but puzzling relationships between productivity and NSWAs that do not conform to a single story of causality. While the log results find that industries with high NSWAs are *less* productive, the first-difference results suggest that increasing NSWA use is correlated with both *high* and increasing productivity. These two sets of results can be simultaneously true only if the traditional uses of NSWA are quite different from the new uses of NSWAs that have swelled their number in the 1990s. For instance, it may be that the traditional replacement uses of NSWA tended to occur in relatively inefficient (low productivity) industries, perhaps because low-productivity industries tended to have high absenteeism or because financially struggling companies tended to hire NSWA employees. New NSWAs seem to be quite different. They are associated with both growing and high productivity. However, the similar results for both subsequent and prior productivity do not allow us to ascertain whether higher productivity leads to increased NSWA use or vice versa. Finally, in contrast to other NSWAs, independent contracting is not correlated with productivity in any specification.

Profitability. The analysis of profitability[13] presented in tables 4 and 5 provides no evidence that companies improve subsequent profitability by using more temps and other NSWAs. In fact, profitability was unrelated to companies' subsequent, contemporaneous, or prior use or to first differences of NSWA#1. This is in marked contrast to productivity.

Although company profitability data are highly variable due to lumpy capital expenditures and arbitrary accounting decisions, the industry-level analysis could be expected to average out much of this noise. Moreover, the analysis showed significant relationships between industry profitability and other variables besides NSWAs. This suggests that the absence of a statistically significant relationship between NSWAs and profits may not be due merely to a lack of statistical power.

While NSWAs except independent contracting are not related to profit rates, the use of independent contractors (NSWA#2) is significantly

TABLE 4

Profitability and NSWAs: Bivariate Correlation Coefficients
(p values in parentheses)

	Profit rate 1997	Profit rate excluding 2 industries[**]	ln Profit rate 1997	Profit rate 1995	Change 1995-97 Profit rate
Levels in 1995					
NSWA#1	-.033	-.003	-.178	-.059	.074
	(.840)	(.988)	(.298)	(.719)	(.657)
NSWA#2	-.3108[*]	-.296[*]	-.241	-.323[*]	.114
	(.056)	(.072)	(.157)	(.045)	(.491)
NSWA#3	-.2938[*]	-.278[*]	-.266	-.313[*]	.124
	(.070)	(.092)	(.117)	(.052)	(.450)
Changes 1995-1997					
NSWA#1	.090	.016	.113	-.086	.012
	(.585)	(.927)	(.513)	(.604)	(.942)
NSWA#2	.186	.032	.181	.153	.034
	(.257)	(.850)	(.290)	(.352)	(.836)
NSWA#3	.050	.053	.189	.024	.052
	(.761)	(.759)	(.271)	(.882)	(.775)

[*] Correlations with p values greater than or equal to .10.
[**] Excludes household services and business services. Analysis of profit rates excludes household services because data are unavailable.

negatively correlated with profit rates in both the bivariate and the multiple regression analysis,[14] although the low R^2 statistics indicate that they explain very little of the variation in profit rates. When the log of the profit rate is used, the significance of the negative relationship between independent contracting and subsequent profitability falls to marginal levels.[15] The timing of the relationships sheds little light on the nature of causality between independent contractors and profitability. The results are similar for prior, contemporaneous, or subsequent productivity. However, we see no similar relationship between the 1995–1997 *change* in independent contracting and either the 1995–1997 change in profit rates or the prior (1995) level of independent contracting.

There are two possible interpretations for levels but not first differences of independent contracting having a significant relationship with profitability. The first and most likely is simply the general tendency for greater relative measurement errors in first differences than in levels. Indeed, adjusted R^2 is lower in specifications with first differences. The

TABLE 5

Regression Results: Profitability and NSWAs
(standard errors in parentheses)

	Profit rate 1997					Profit rate 1995		Average profit rate	1995-97 Δ profit rate	ln 1997 profit rate
1995 NSWA#1	-.222 (.738)	.045 (.717)						-.073 (.795)		-8.097 (10.36)
1995 NSWA#3		-.384° (.189)								
1995 NSWA#2			-.381° (.184)					-.437° (.204)		-3.403 (2.684)
1997 NSWA#1				-.228 (.689)		-.354 (.761)				
1997 NSWA#2					-.343° (.185)		-.406° (.205)			
Avg. 95-97 NSWA#1								-.083 (.741)		
Avg. 95-97 NSWA#2								-.393° (.187)		
1995-97 ΔNSWA#1						-.387 (1.257)			.030 (.581)	
1995-97 ΔNSWA#2							1.074 (1.058)		.115 (.489)	
% VA growth 1995-1997	.145 (.127)	.168 (.120)	.165 (.121)	.167 (.122)	.127 (.127)	.190 (.135)	.189 (.135)	.163 (.123)	-.020 (.059)	1.285 (1.701)
constant	.092° (.033)	.118° (.023)	.104° (.032)	.113° (.032)	.086° (.016)	.119° (.036)	.110° (.035)	.110° (.033)	.003° (.008)	-2.194° (.469)
Adj. R^2	-.02	.08	.07	.05	-.01	.07	.08	.07	-.08	.005

Refer to text for definitions.

° Coefficients with p values greater than or equal to .10.

second possibility is that there has been a historically negative relationship between independent contracting and profits that is now weakening. This latter interpretation is buttressed by the drop—albeit insignificant—in the magnitude of the regression coefficient on contemporaneous independent contracting from 1995 to 1997 in table 5.

To summarize, no relationship is uncovered between NSWA#1 and profitability. There is, however, a tendency for less-profitable industries to use more independent contracting, although this relation may be declining since it was not observed in first-difference data.

Variability. Companies with high variability in market value would be expected to use NSWAs more than more-stable companies. The variability of companies' values within industries is measured as the range of the market value of large companies in the industry over two decades (Lambson and Jensen 1998). As discussed previously, this measure is a proxy for the variation in the company's future prospects and therefore, indirectly, for its financial well-being.

Table 6 shows the bivariate correlations between NSWAs and industry variability, while table 7 shows multiple regressions of NSWAs on industry variability, controlling for the characteristics of the labor force in that industry that affect supply of labor to NSWAs.[16] These analyses indicate that in industries with companies experiencing considerable variability in market value, the proportion of NSWAs increased considerably between 1995 and 1997.[17] However, the *level* of NSWA#1—either previous or subsequent—is not correlated with variability. Thus, similar to productivity, the recently adopted NSWAs have different roles than did historical NSWAs. The results suggest that in the mid-1990s, a strategy of hiring nonstandard workers is being used to address an industry's inherent volatility in both sales and market value.

TABLE 6

Bivariate Correlation between Industry Variability
of Market Values and NSWAs

	Correlation with variability	Correlation with variability[a]
Average 1995-1997 levels		
NSWA#1	-.002	.030
	(.993)	(.865)
NSWA#2	-.288°	-.279°
	(.088)	(.105)
NSWA#3	-.267	-.257
	(.115)	(.136)
Changes between 1995 and 1997		
NSWA#1	.323°	.344°
	(.054)	(.043)
NSWA#2	-.025	-.040
	(.885)	(.818)
NSWA#3	.156	.160
	(.364)	(.359)

Note: Refer to text for definitions. p values in parentheses.
[a] Excludes household services and business services.
° Correlations with p values greater than or equal to .10.

TABLE 7
Regression Results: Variability of market values and NSWAs
(standard errors in parentheses)

	NSWA#1	NSWA#1 excl. 2 inds°°	NSWA#2	NSWA#2 excl. 2 inds°°	NSWA#2	NSWA#2 excl. 2 inds°°
Dependent Variable: Average of 95, 96, and 97 levels						
Industry variability	-2.31×10^{-4} (2.01×10^{-3})	3.96×10^{-4} (1.91×10^{-3})	$-1.71 \times 10^{-2*}$ (8.75×10^{-3})	$-1.60 \times 10^{-2*}$ (8.90×10^{-3})	1.39×10^{-2} (8.72×10^{-3})	1.33×10^{-2} (8.87×10^{-3})
Average proportion clerical	-.075 (.051)	-.085* (.049)	.056 (.224)	.039 (.226)	.153 (.226)	.136 (.229)
Average proportion young (<30)	.064 (.043)	.048 (.041)	.296 (.188)	.267 (.192)	.318* (.183)	.294 (.189)
Average proportion high school degree or less	-.068* (.023)	-.062* (.021)	-.102 (.098)	-.092 (.100)	-.059 (.100)	-.053 (.101)
Average proportion covered by collective bargaining	2.308* (1.017)	2.294* (.957)	-4.419 (4.423)	-4.443 (4.447)	-3.880 (4.320)	-3.923 (4.361)
Average profit rate					-.238 (.146)	-.227 (.148)
Adj. R^2	.24	.24	.11	.07	.16	.11
Dependent Variable: Changes (Δ) between 1995 and 97						
Industry variability	$2.44 \times 10^{-3*}$ (1.40×10^{-3})	$2.79 \times 10^{-3*}$ (1.37×10^{-3})	-2.61×10^{-4} (1.75×10^{-3})	-5.47×10^{-4} (1.76×10^{-3})	-6.97×10^{-4} (1.81×10^{-3})	-9.28×10^{-4} (1.82×10^{-3})
95 Proportion clerical	-.009 (.034)	-.013 (.033)	-.002 (.042)	.002 (.042)	-.014 (.044)	-.009 (.044)

TABLE 7 (*Continued*)

Regression Results: Variability of market values and NSWAs
(standard errors in parentheses)

	NSWA#1	NSWA#1 excl. 2 inds°°	NSWA#2	NSWA#2 excl. 2 inds°°	NSWA#2	NSWA#2 excl. 2 inds°°
95 Proportion young (<30)	-.048	-.056°	-.003	.004	-.007	-.0008
	(.029)	(.028)	(.036)	(.036)	(.036)	(.037)
95 Proportion high school degree or less	.0009	.004	-.003	-.006	-.008	-.011
	(.015)	(.015)	(.019)	(.019)	(.019)	(.020)
95 Proportion covered by collective bargaining	.186	.221	-.021	-.007	-.154	-.165
	(.565)	(.547)	(.707)	(.705)	(.731)	(.729)
95 Profit rate					.028	.025
					(.029)	(.028)
Adj. R^2	.07	.13	-.16	-.16	-.17	-.17

Refer to text for definitions.

All averages are for the years 1995, 1996, and 1997.

° Coefficients with p values greater than or equal to .10.

°° Excludes household services and business services.

Once again, results for independent contracting (NSWA#2) are completely different from results for NSWA#1 (see tables 6 and 7). In contrast to NSWA#1, there is no relationship between *first differences* in independent contracting and variability but a significant negative relationship between *levels* of independent contracting and variability.[18] Industries with highly variable companies[19] tend to have less independent contracting. This is the same general pattern we saw between profitability and independent contracting.

Summary and Implications

The two parts of this paper use very different methods to learn more about the reasons for and effects of hiring nonstandard workers: in the first section, in-depth interviews with HR executives and, in the second, statistical analysis of relationships between NSWAs and firm performance across industries. Quite strikingly, the two approaches lead to some of the same implications.

The interviews indicate that most large companies analyze the pros and cons of using NSWAs and identify the level and features of NSWA use that are most profitable for them. Important factors weighed are direct costs, added flexibility, impact on productivity, improvements in recruiting, ease of discharge, and legal risks. Companies have identified the kinds of jobs where NSWAs can be most advantageous. Line managers typically have the primary role in making the daily choices between temps and regular employees, but central management determines corporate policies intended to guide NSWA use to its most profitable level. The level of sophistication in evaluating the bottom-line impact clearly improved between 1996 and 1999, as companies had more time to analyze the new national NSWA phenomenon.

The statistical analysis confirms that the NSWAs adopted in the mid-1990s do seem to have a positive impact on firms' productivity. Recent changes in NSWA#1 are positively correlated with productivity, while the historical use of NSWA#1 had a negative impact, if any. Thus, newly added NSWAs signal strategic uses of flexible staffing alternatives that tend to have positive financial implications. In addition, both the empirical analysis and the interviews imply that in the mid- to late 1990s, NSWAs were adopted as a conscious strategy to help companies adapt to variability in their financial performance.

The interpretation that newly added NSWAs have positive financial impacts implies a direction of causality; yet it needs be repeated that there are no clear clues in the statistical analysis to suggest the direction of causality or even whether these relationships are causal at all. We must keep in mind other possible interpretations of the empirical relationship between productivity and recent NSWA growth besides the suggestion that NSWAs increase productivity. For instance, it may be that the most productive, efficient companies have increased their NSWAs because their executives believe it will improve efficiency even more, whether or not it actually does.

The positive relationship between the 1995–1997 changes in NSWA#1 and productivity does not, however, carry over to profit rates, which are shown to have no statistical relationship with changes or levels of NSWA#1. This anomalous set of results opens up the much more general question of the correlation between productivity and profitability. Typically, the two are not related when differences in labor intensity create the productivity variations. Yet NSWA use is high in labor-intensive service industries, which, *ceteris paribus,* should lead to lower productivity rather than the higher productivity observed here. Thus, labor intensity cannot explain the disparate results for profitability and productivity. The insignificant relationships between profits and NSWAs may simply be due to the fact that profitability is an extremely noisy measure. However, further research is called for to confirm and illuminate these disparate results concerning productivity and profitability.

Independent contracting was not addressed separately in the interviews, but in the statistical analysis, independent contracting appears to be quite different from NSWA#1. The level of independent contracting is consistently negatively related to *levels* of profitability but not productivity, although first differences of profits are unrelated. The negative relationship with profitability could indicate that independent contractors may have been historically hired in times of financial distress, perhaps to replace laid-off workers. For companies that cannot provide the needed services themselves, independent contractors may impose high costs because they tend to receive higher wages than other nonstandard workers, controlling for other factors (see Belman and Golden, this volume; Polivka, Cohany, and Hipple, this volume).[20] This interpretation is buttressed by the fact that productivity has no relationship with independent contracting, despite the fact that we would expect a positive relationship if workforce was underestimated in the productivity data. In contrast, the new independent contracting of the mid-1990s appears to be the result of a strategic plan to employ a flexible workforce that may not have yet produced greater profits (insofar as the relationship to profits and to variability has fallen to zero) but at least does not signal a company in distress.

Notes

[1] More precisely, this result requires some randomness of diffusion.

[2] The 1996 interviews are also discussed in Kahn, Foulkes, and Heisler (forthcoming).

[3] In the single 1999 exception, the company used NSWAs for temporary replacements but in response to my query about whether they ever considered using NSWAs more broadly the HR executive replied, "No one ever did that analysis." The respondent, however, had been at the company for only six months. It is quite likely that someone *had* previously done that analysis but that she was unaware of it.

[4] Accompanying this sophistication came a sense of disinterest in the interview. HR executives who widely used NSWAs in 1996 found it an exciting new development that they were happy to brag about; by 1999 it seemed to have become run of the mill.

[5] Companies concerned about co-employment have adopted other policies as well to limit their exposure. They use third-party temporary agencies, channel all instructions and messages through these agencies, differentiate temps by requiring them to wear badges, and exclude them from fitness programs, company childcare, holiday parties, and bonuses. These policies often create low morale among temps. One senior HR VP bemoaned that "you want to make the temps feel good about working at [company], but you have to keep remembering they aren't your employees. For instance, if there is an employee relations problem, it is sometimes hard to remember that we should call Kelly to take care of it, not deal with it directly."

[6] Neither profitability nor variability was available for the private household industry. Variability was also unavailable for social services and the professional service industries subcategories.

[7] It would have been preferable to have productivity figures directly from the BLS. While the BLS does calculate some productivity figures, they cover a very incomplete group of industries.

[8] The authors provided these data, derived from Compustat files.

[9] Permanent components of profits smooth out transitory items such as lumpy capital expenditures.

[10] See Polivka (1996) for the algorithm identifying this latter group from CPS data.

[11] Conducting Granger or other formal statistical tests of causality would require substantially more years of NSWA data.

[12] Many additional specifications were run whose qualitative results were similar to those presented. For instance, while the analysis reported is based on unweighted micro-observations of individuals aggregated into industries, the same analysis was performed using various weighting systems. One variant used the CPS weight for the contingent sample to create the proportion NSWA in each industry; another multiplied these CPS weights by hours to get the proportion of FTE (full-time equivalent) employment in NSWAs in each industry. Finally, all analysis was redone using weighted least squares, where weights were industry size. All results were similar to those reported.

[13] Profitability figures were not available for the private household industry. All analysis was duplicated excluding the business services industry, but none of the results changed qualitatively. Profitability analysis included the 1995–1997 percentage growth of industry gross product as a control.

[14] As a result, profitability is also inversely correlated with NSWA#3 when independent contracting (NSWA#2) is not simultaneously controlled for.

[15] In the bivariate analysis of table 4, the significance level falls from .94 to .84. In the regression analysis of table 4, significance falls from .96 to .80.

[16] Labor force characteristics include the proportion of workers (1) in clerical jobs, (2) less than 30 years old, (3) with a high school degree or less, and (4) covered by collective bargaining agreements. Results are unchanged when 1995 to 1997 industry growth rates are included as an additional control.

[17] Note that this result is particularly striking given our expectations of high random measurement error in first-difference data. In additional regressions (available from author), first differences in NSWA#1 were regressed on the *first differences* of demographic variables as well as on variability, with similar results on variability.

[18] We see this both in the bivariate correlation coefficients of table 6 ($p = .088$ or $p = .105$) and in the regression analysis of table 7 ($p = .061$ to $p = .144$). The last two columns of table 7 add profit rates as regressors since profitability was shown to have a significant correlation with the level of independent contracting.

[19] In terms of market value and, by extension, present and expected sales and profits.

[20] Note that financially healthy companies operating strategically would hire high-cost independent contractors only if, *ceteris paribus*, these hires improved bottom-line results.

References

Abraham, Katharine G. 1988. "Flexible Staffing Arrangement and Employers' Short-Term Adjustment Strategies." In Robert A. Hart, ed., *Employment, Unemployment and Labor Utilization,* Boston: Unwin Hyman, pp. 288–311.

Abraham, Katharine G. 1990. "Restructuring the Employment Relationship: The Growth of Market-Mediated Arrangements." In Katharine Abraham and Robert McKersie, eds., *New Developments in the Labor Market: Toward a New Institutional Paradigm,* Cambridge, MA: MIT Press, pp. 85–120.

Golden, Lonnie. 1996. "The Expansion of Temporary Help Employment in the US, 1982–1992: A Test of Alternative Economic Explanations." *Applied Economics,* Vol. 28, no. 9, pp. 1127–1141.

Houseman, Susan N. 1996. "Temporary, Part-Time, and Contract Employment in the United States: A Report on the W. E. Upjohn Institute's Employer Survey on Flexible Staffing Policies." Report prepared for the U.S. Department of Labor, Office of the Assistant Secretary for Policy.

Kahn, Shulamit, Fred Foulkes, and Jeffrey Heisler. Forthcoming. "Changes in Large Companies' Use of Temporary Workers and Their Impacts on Financial Measures of Performance." In S. Houseman and G. Wong, eds., *Changes in Working*

Time in Canada and the United States [working title], Kalamazoo, MI: Upjohn Institute.

Laird, Karylee, and Nicholas Williams. 1996. "Employment Growth in the Temporary Help Supply Industry." *Journal of Labor Research,* Vol. 17, no. 4 (Fall), pp. 663–681.

Lambson, Val Eugene, and Farrell E. Jensen. 1998. "Sunk Costs and Firm Value Variability: Theory and Evidence." *American Economic Review,* Vol. 88, no. 1 (March), pp. 307–313.

Polivka, Anne E. 1996. "Contingent and Alternative Work Arrangements, Defined." *Monthly Labor Review,* Vol. 119, no. 10 (October), pp. 3–9.

Segal, Lewis M., and Daniel G. Sullivan. 1997. "The Growth of Temporary Services Work." *Journal of Economic Perspectives,* Vol. 11, no. 2 (Spring), pp. 117–136.

Chapter 9

HR Strategy and Nonstandard Work: Dualism versus True Mobility

Charles Heckscher

Rutgers University

Introduction

Human resources (HR) managers and scholars are caught in a strangely contradictory set of forces around the changing employment relationship. On one side is the widespread celebration of entrepreneurship, flexible teaming, and labor market mobility; on the other side is a set of powerful forces and arguments pulling toward traditional stability. The HR function stands uneasily at the center of this conflict.

The HR literature on the employment relationship is fragmented and piecemeal and generally avoids coming to grips with its internal inconsistencies. The basic themes can be summarized as follows:

- Contingency is a liberating advance for employees and businesses.

- All employees should develop their marketability and mobility.

- Most nonstandard workers do poorly.

- There is substantial worker insecurity and mistrust even under very favorable economic conditions.

- Retention is one of the biggest HR problems.

- There are often tensions between standard and nonstandard employees.

- Government policies and the legal system are hopelessly out of touch with the changes.

- After all, observable changes are not as dramatic as often suggested.

Each of these themes makes sense in itself, but they do not fit together. The clearest contradiction is between the widespread image of radical change and the reality of relatively small increments. But there is also the problem that managers are seeking to discourage mobility among some employees while at the same time they encourage it in general. The "best" employees are deluged with advice and enticements to look around for something better, while their companies, struggling to keep them in the fold, appeal to their loyalty; the rest flounder, unable to find the support they need to build flexible careers. Thus, the most desired employees are the least loyal—and vice versa.

These inconsistencies result from the conflict between two ways of organizing economic activity: the old way, which relied on building firms into large and stable organizations, and a new way based on *networks*, aiming for fluidity and strategic flexibility, encouraging constant reinvention and recombination. Today, the latter has rhetorical momentum, but the former still holds the institutional power. So far the new pattern has not made much progress against the tremendous inertia of the existing order. Nor is it clear that the new approach would actually increase efficiency and growth, as opposed to just sounding good.

In the meantime, the contest between the two approaches is producing a series of social and economic distortions—and also, incidentally, putting HR managers in a serious bind. It creates a free-agent mentality among some employees, which is highly disruptive to managers seeking consistency and predictability, and at the same time creates a deep moral resentment of free agency among others. Further, it generates misunderstanding and mistrust, which undermine the collaboration vital to a healthy knowledge-based economy.

The most practical way out, which most HR managers in fact pursue, even if not always intentionally, seems to be to divide the workforce into "first-class" and "second-class" employees with very different expectations. This dualism has always existed but seems to be growing. The end of that road, however, is not the land of flexibility and innovation that so many seek but rather a place of conflict and confusion. This is therefore a time for reflection on what is needed to build a new system.

The Logic of Firms and the Logic of Networks

The rationale behind the firm was developed in Max Weber's theory of bureaucracy a century ago and applied to private corporations by Alfred Sloan at General Motors in the 1920s. The basic idea was to create an organization to solve a problem—breaking the overall goal down into pieces so that hundreds or thousands of people, each pursuing one segment, would nevertheless come up with a coherent product. This produced the familiar hierarchy of offices with functional divisions.

Inside the firm there arose a structure of tightly interlocking elements. For example, compensation was relatively uniform within each level in order to prevent envy among peers and to avoid overlaps between levels;

rewards were expected to come through promotions, not pay differentials. Elaborate internal training organizations took over from the educational system to provide company-specific skills beyond the entry level. Strong norms of loyalty developed to anchor a lifetime commitment, with reciprocal obligations from the company. Equally strong norms have prevented people from going over their bosses' heads or transgressing onto others' turf. These norms, and many more, were found to be necessary to smoothly functioning bureaucratic organizations.

The logic of networks turns most of this on its head. The basic idea of networks is to create for a given problem not an organization but a team—a constellation of exactly those people who have the right knowledge and resources for that particular problem; their mission is not to create routinized answers that can be used over and over but to analyze the particular issues and respond to them. This destroys the idea that people should be attached to particular jobs: the measure of value is no longer how well you do your job but how well you contribute to the team's mission. In a hierarchical organization, those who go beyond their defined job functions are viewed as threats to the order of the whole; in a network-based system, they are vital to responsiveness and innovation.

In a world of networks, traditional career paths are disrupted. No longer is good performance rewarded with upward movement in a fixed structure; now individuals build reputations that gain them access to larger and more interesting teams. They need to impress not so much their bosses as the community of people who collaborate with them and who may have input into recruiting for the next team.

The network approach has also undercut the traditional compensation system. When high-performing individuals expected to be rewarded by big promotions within the hierarchy, they did not mind waiting a while. But when that expectation disappears, they want their reward now. Such demands destroy the advancement rules within the hierarchy (Kanter 1977).

Nonstandard employment clearly makes sense within the logic of networks. There is no imperative for internal development of talent; it can be bought from the network. The stability and predictability of a group of loyal employees become liabilities when the main competitive challenges are innovation and responsiveness to change.

In the abstract, the network logic even appears to make sense from the employees' point of view: it offers them a chance for variety and independence, for self-development and choice, for an escape from the "iron cage" of conformity and the overweening personal demands of large bureaucracies.[1] And indeed, many employees, especially younger ones with few obligations and great optimism, embrace this vision of freedom.

But this picture of an economy that offers mobility and independence to workers, whatever its conceptual merits, runs into serious problems when it collides with the existing pattern of a society organized around large firms. First, most institutions are adapted to the old system:

- For the most part, our educational system is geared to taking people up to their entry to the labor market but not beyond. A network logic would require that people return intermittently throughout their careers to educational institutions rather than getting their training from inside the firm. Though there has been a small boom in continuing and adult education in recent years, our institutions of lifelong learning remain inadequate to the tasks required of them in a network economy.

- Career development is likewise assumed to be taken care of by the firm: internal evaluations and postings are thought to be sufficient to select and guide employees. A network, on the other hand, requires that reputations be independent of particular organizations and that there be open information about opportunities so that people can move quickly and efficiently to the "right place" in the complex network. Again, there has been some recent creation of new institutions—especially the use of the Internet to publicize job opportunities and the growth of head-hunting firms—but nothing approaching the scale needed to solve the problem.

- Then there are health and retirement benefits: firms took these on largely as a way to sustain lifetime loyalty from their employees—to "lock them in" to single-firm careers.[2] A network requires a social infrastructure for these benefits to support more mobile careers. There has been a little movement in that direction in the retirement area with the development of 401(k) plans but practically none with respect to health care.

- Cultural norms have not caught up with the shift to network arrangements. The reciprocal obligations of employers and employees, for instance, are still largely defined by the old concept of loyalty: employees owe complete deference, and the company is supposed to take care of them. And social status is still largely determined by the size of your company and the level you have achieved in it.

In all these ways and more, society still acts as if it expects people to move through "traditional" careers and therefore makes it much harder for those who do not.

The continuing hold of the old system means, furthermore, that there is little incentive for organizations to create institutions that would facilitate the mobility they advocate. The reason may be that even if it were good for the *whole* to have a system of true mobility, it is not in the interest of most of the *parts,* so it does not get done. In particular, every organizational unit—from a shop-floor group of four to a company of thousands—is interested in keeping its good people. Therefore, all organizational leaders, from supervisors to CEOs, act in ways intended to lock in their best employees and to reduce mobility. They may want to get rid of some of their lower performers and to get some better ones, but their interest in the stability of their own organizations means that they put no energy into creating a *system* of mobility.

The Literature: Fractured Analysis

A review of the HR literature reveals this fragmented picture:

Mobility as a Virtue

Those who celebrate mobility and entrepreneurship see themselves as being "on the right side of history"—they express ideas that will shape the future, while ideas linked with the old system are "outdated." The network enthusiasts' view, repeated in very similar terms in numerous publications and memos, starts with this premise: "The 21st century will be characterized by innovation rather than pure production as the principal source of wealth creation. The environment for innovation to prosper requires motivated individuals, dynamic small companies and flexible corporations" (Edelstein and Paul 1998).

Then follows praise for reforms that have increased corporate flexibility since the early 1980s, including hard-headed restructuring of businesses and raising of performance standards. This view is frequently accompanied by criticism of Germany, Japan, and other industrial economies for attempting to regulate labor markets in order to protect workers. Finally, the most consistent exponents of these views argue that good employees welcome these changes and embrace the new opportunities. They further contend that

> Anybody who is in an organization today has a place, an opportunity to contribute—there's no deadwood. . . . The extra

responsibility makes people feel important and appreciated
. . . even though workloads may be heavier. . . . The people
who remain face a challenge, but it's one that a great many are
eager to confront. (Graham 1997)

From this perspective, contingency is an unalloyed good, opening up
new options for both employers and employees, and its advocates see it
sweeping triumphantly through the economy, breaking down outmoded
barriers and paternalistic obligations, bringing about a "paradigm shift"
in relations.[3]

Rarely do writers who hold such views deal with the real problems
of resistance, loss, and destruction of social bonds. Nor do they generally recognize the need for institutional reforms to support the new mobility. Sometimes they even forget what they once knew. Peter Drucker,
for example—a perennial harbinger of new trends—wrote in 1988 of
the danger of mistrust resulting from managerial layoffs and recommended the reestablishment of the job as a property right. By 1992,
however, he was celebrating continual change and flexibility with hardly
a nod to the losers or the potential for chaos.[4]

"Pack Your Own Parachute"[5]

Consistent with this ideal of flexibility is a large set of writings offering advice to mobile and nonstandard workers. The consistent theme of
this bookshelf-breaking pile of works—some of it written by former HR
managers—is that all employees should consider themselves mobile and
independent: "going to work for You, Inc." (Gieseking and Plawin,
1993). Generally, the authors are enthusiastic about the new opportunities opened up by this independence and exhort readers to break the
bonds of psychological servitude to corporations. Rarely, however, do
they consider anything beyond the narrow problem of getting a new job:
they do not have much to say about health insurance or family dynamics
or other potential side effects of intermittent joblessness.

The Cost to Employees

Another group of authors argues to the contrary that the new mobility is harmful to employees. A substantial number of books with titles
like *The Judas Economy* (Wolman and Colamosca 1997) bemoan the loss
of security in highly charged terms. Clinical studies such as *Falling from
Grace* (Newman 1988) are heart-rending, even terrifying, in their de-
pictions of people sliding into pits of self-blame and loss of identity, and
of families falling apart. More quantitative researchers are less dramatic

but provide few grounds for optimism. They show almost uniformly that nonstandard workers have far fewer benefits than "regular" employees. Beyond that, the data show considerable differences among groups: independent contractors do relatively well, but temporary workers and on-call employees—a larger group—have substantially lower wages and less favorable working conditions than standard employees (Hipple and Stewart 1996).

Mistrust and Stress

Poll data suggest that most people are unconvinced of the benefits of mobility and show a high and widespread sense of insecurity despite the economic boom of the 1990s. Alan Greenspan (1999), chair of the Federal Reserve, has cited surveys showing that only 12% of people in 1981, in the depth of a recession, feared losing their jobs, while in 1999, in "the tightest labor market in two generations," the number was 30%.[6]

Mistrust and cynicism are now at a rather high level in the workforce as a whole, despite the good economic times. A 1996 Towers Perrin poll ("Towers Perrin" 1997), for example, found that in the previous year, employee attitudes have grown more negative in several key areas:

- the belief that management considers employees' interests in decisions affecting them
- the belief that ability and performance are fairly rewarded and recognized
- the belief that workplace policies are fairly administered

"Basically, our data suggest employees see less evidence of the partnership employers have said they want to build with their workers," said Steve Bookbinder, principal and leader of the Towers Perrin Workplace Index research organization.[7]

The Problem of Retention

For HR professionals, the glories of mobility show up mainly as a major pain: trying to find ways to retain valued employees.

Every day, the calls pour in to a bank of telephone lines here at the Society for Human Resource Management. On the phone are personnel directors, and the big question they ask their trade group is this: How do we keep talent from jumping to competitors?

The "retention" issue has swiftly become the hottest topic among the society's 86,000 members. . . . ("The Outlook" 1997)

This problem is certainly one of the main drivers of the "pay-for-performance" trend sweeping through corporations since the 1980s (Baker 1990; O'Dell 1987; Kanter 1987). The evidence that this system actually helps firm performance is very weak,[8] but managers clearly believe that they have to raise the pay of their top performers to keep them from leaving.

At the same time, the heavy use of pay for performance has some problematic side effects. It necessarily—indeed, deliberately—increases pay inequality[9] and thereby tears the fabric of community, which was one of the important "retention" forces in the traditional order. It also undermines the incentive power of promotions and may even undermine the hierarchy of authority when subordinates are paid more than their bosses (Kanter 1987). In short, pay for performance runs contrary to the development of long-term identification with the company.

Other retention strategies have moved in a contrary direction, back toward the insulation of employees from the market characteristic of the old welfare capitalism. For example, Kingston Memories (a small maker of memory chips) achieves great success in retention by sharing bonuses among all employees, providing catered lunches every Friday, and promising that they will take care of their "family" of employees no matter what happens. Michael Jensen, a Harvard Business School professor who is one of the chief advocates of individualism and dynamic mobility, is of course critical of the Kingston approach for stifling the ability of the economy to "release resources on the downside" (Miller 1996).

The Problem of Managing Integration

Those who *manage* nonstandard workers run into a persistent problem: how to integrate them with the regular workforce. Some experts advocate letting the two groups work together closely and freely; but there is often tension when people work side by side at similar tasks with completely different levels of pay and security. Others go to the opposite extreme, advocating avoidance of all communication between the two groups; but this multiplies management problems, increases costs, and makes the smooth flow of information and ideas all but impossible (Kochan et al. 1994).

The problem of integration is further exacerbated by existing law and policy. The tax code creates strong incentives for employers to push employees off the regular rolls to avoid paying taxes, which can amount to 35% of a contractor's payroll. The IRS therefore tries to prevent companies from doing this by sharply bounding the definition of *nonemployee*

(McKenzie 1996; Burns and Freeman 1996). The legal system similarly seeks to draw as clear a line as possible to determine jurisdiction for such laws as OSHA and the Americans with Disabilities Act (Krawczyk, Wright, and Sawyers 1996). These conflicting pressures produce further strong reasons for companies to separate nonstandard workers as sharply as possible from the regular workforce.

The Modest Evidence for Change

Given the conflicting pressures, it is not surprising that the overall picture reveals not a dramatic movement toward greater mobility and flexibility but a halting and unsteady one. Most economists were skeptical until the mid-1990s that any trend toward mobility existed at all. In the last few years, however, even some of the skeptics have begun to detect a slight decrease in job tenure. (For a review of job tenure debates, see Bernhardt and Marcotte, this volume.) The proportion of nonstandard workers has almost certainly grown, though perhaps by only a few percentage points.[10] The scholarly consensus is beginning to move toward acceptance that a real shift is occurring—but there is room for disagreement about how significant it will be in the end.

To be sure, some things have changed sharply. There seems to be little doubt that layoffs, especially of white-collar and managerial employees, have increased to a level consistently higher than in the past. Sustained prosperity has not slowed the willingness of companies to get rid of businesses as well as employees who are no longer seen as performing essential duties (i.e., contributing to the distinctive competitive strength or "core competencies" of the corporation).[11] Executives of many companies feel that since the 1980s they have been doing something that they had never done before—breaking a long-standing implicit agreement with their exempt employees. This has caused a great deal of turmoil within those companies, even when the extent of the layoffs was rather small, and it undoubtedly has contributed heavily to the public perception of an overturning of the old order.

Yet what is most evident so far is the gap between perception and reality: though there is general movement toward increased contingency and flux, it runs far behind the public perception of dramatic change. Existing levels of mistrust and insecurity reflect not the *real* numbers, which are not large, but the powerful *ideology* of change that has swept the nation.

The announced layoff of 40,000 managers at AT&T in 1996 is often seen as a watershed, leading to a spate of articles including the searching

New York Times series, "The Downsizing of America" (1996). But it turned out to be emblematic in a quite unexpected sense: after all the trauma and the turmoil, AT&T ended up eliminating a much smaller number of jobs, and those were more than offset by new job creation. One might interpret this as a great deal of churning but little fundamental change. Nonetheless, the episode reinforced the perception among the public that no job is really permanent.

An Incomplete Change: Resistance, Inconsistency, and Vicious Circles

This incongruous picture makes sense as a snapshot not of a stable system but of one in transition. The new model of mobility and entrepreneurship is attractive to many in a hazy sort of way, but it does not provide all the support to employees provided by the old order.

There is little question that the values people are willing to accept and argue for have changed sharply over the last 30 years. "Bureaucracy" was once not a bad word but, on the contrary, often had positive connotations: it suggested reliability, focus, stability, and efficiency. General Motors was the image of how well capitalism could do. Almost no one, certainly not those in the mainstream, thought of questioning the value of loyalty. For whatever reasons, all of this has been turned on its head, with bureaucracy as a synonym for rigidity and inefficiency, GM as the epitome of bad management, and loyalty as a highly questionable value. It is not that everyone believes fervently in the new image of a flexible, entrepreneurial economy but that most of those who question it no longer have much confidence in alternatives.

If one goes inside firms and talks to employees and managers, however, one finds that while most people at all levels talk the language of flexibility and entrepreneurship, they generally do not act it. Most employees feel that the situation is frightening and out of control; most managers are just trying to "protect their people."[12] For the former, the thought of being cast out into the open labor market is a fearful one: they believe that it would leave them completely adrift, without support or clear prospects for the future. Dreading the knock on the door, they cling tightly to their existing jobs—even though they "know" this is a defensive and perhaps slightly unprincipled thing to do.[13] Those who are already "out on their own" usually seek to get *into* the relative security of traditional jobs in large companies. Even younger employees, who have always been more prone to move than older ones, appear (according to polls) to have become more focused on landing steady, lifetime jobs.[14]

From the managers' standpoint as well, the old bureaucratic ethic remains largely in force: most feel responsible for "their" subordinates and try hard to protect them. As one typical manager told me: "It's a family type of thing, where you look at the people that look up to you for the leadership and the guidance, and that's probably all part of what turns us on as managers." Similarly, a second one said: "Managers are fighting tooth and nail to protect their people, and this encourages real loyalty" (Heckscher 1995, p. 101).

These reactions are entirely sensible, from the point of view of both self-interest and value commitments. For the vast majority of employees, the open labor market *is* a fearful place. It is hard to get training, it is hard to get placement, it is hard to get health care, and it is hard to explain to your family and friends—and to yourself—why you are not working. For managers, the turbulence caused by employee turnover is far more dangerous than the possible gain from getting better people. Managers are better off working with what they have, which is at least predictable, than taking a wildly uncertain bet on the labor market.

On the plane of values, both sides feel caught in an insoluble dilemma. On one side is the old virtue of loyalty, which now seems rather quaint, outdated, and for many not really legitimate; on the other is the ethic of free agency, which just about everyone abhors. For free agency is essentially an absence of moral obligation: everyone is expected simply to seek the best deal. Only the most die-hard of free-market ideologues—and in hundreds of interviews with managers, I have not met more than two or three of these—thinks that such pure self-interest is a *good* thing.[15] Many people feel that is what they are being reduced to by the new order, and they hate it; they continue to cling to obligations of loyalty as the only moral compass they have.

At present, the underdeveloped labor market institutions beyond the firm fail to support smooth mobility. We might assume that the advocates of the new order would advocate building such institutions. But in fact, only the most consistent and far-seeing do advocate such reforms, and they have been unable to build much support.

Here an emblematic story is that of the Talent Alliance. After the announced 1996 layoff, AT&T proposed to a group of peer corporations that they form a network to help laid-off employees find work more easily and conversely to help the companies find the right talent quickly. It seemed an exciting idea at the time: 14 large companies jumped quickly on the bandwagon, including leaders such as DuPont, Johnson & Johnson, and UPS. One observer called the alliance's approach "groundbreaking in that they're working for the greater good of all the companies and individuals rather than being narrow in their thinking" (John Epperheimer, director of corporate services for Cupertino-based Career Action Center, quoted in Silverstein 1997).

In fact, the broader approach has never really gotten off the ground. No new companies have been added to the consortium since its founding, and at least one has dropped off. Only a small handful of people—fewer than 10—have actually been placed through the network. The reason for this sluggish performance is that, as suggested earlier, managers' interest in keeping their talent has overwhelmed their longer-term interest in building the institutions for greater flexibility. Most of the Talent Alliance's member companies, for example, have refused to allow their employees access to the consortium's job bank information; only people already designated for layoff have been given passwords to this part of the service.[16]

The societal and legal context is even more negative in terms of the set of obligations and values suited to a more mobile economy. Employment law continues to be patterned essentially on the template of master–servant relationship: employees owe absolute loyalty to their master and are in turn owed basic protection.[17] Employers are obligated to fulfill a set of protective commitments, including payment of "fair" wages and unemployment insurance, which fit this paternalistic relationship. Entirely different laws have developed around "professional" employment relations outside the hierarchy of the firm: mandated benefits do not apply in that situation (Hylton 1996).

This has the perverse effect of making employers want to keep nonstandard workers at a long arm's length in order to avoid the paternalistic obligations; most legal advice is to keep them *entirely* separate from any "internal" relations—to treat them, in effect, as pure free agents or "hired hands." Any attempt at supervision, to say nothing of collaboration or teamwork, it is feared, will trigger scrutiny by the IRS and other government agencies (Lyncheski and Andrykovitch 1996; Ma 1997).

Thus, the effect of the legal structure is paradoxical but typical of a transitional period. At the very moment when the boundaries between the primary and secondary parts of the workforce are weakening, the legal and policy systems work to divide the workforce into two sharply distinguished parts: one inside the firm, with employer obligations and a presumption of loyalty from the workers, and the other clearly outside, with no link beyond the formal contract. This further reinforces the habitual tendencies of HR and other managers to keep their "inside" and "outside" people in distinctly different statuses rather than opening the boundaries of the corporation as a truly flexible system would require.[18]

At the firm level, these inconsistencies and contradictions seem to lead not toward a network model but rather toward what might be called a "churning firm": an organization with a nominally stable form and job structure but with a lot of workers entering and leaving, as well as a modest increase in outsourcing. This is in effect an attempt—not as a conscious strategy but as the outcome of conflicting pulls—to maintain organizational control while achieving the benefits of network flexibility. But while this approach may appear to be logical in the short run, it leads to instability and ineffectiveness, because it fails to resolve deep tensions over internal dualism, compensation, retention, and motivation.

In the final analysis, then, we are in a historical period in which the dominant values—the ideologies of entrepreneurship and individualism—do not match real behaviors very well. The result is the relatively high level of mistrust on the part of employees, which keeps surprising analysts who expect that a good economy will produce happy workers. Despite the good economy, employees floundering between conflicting expectations are uncertain that any commitment can be counted on. They feel less sure about their jobs than they used to and equally unsure about their future. As one middle manager put it:

> I want to feel that the company is loyal to me and I do, to some degree, but I also know intellectually that they will only remain loyal for as long as they need me. When it comes time for them to make a choice if there is someone better, I'm out and they are in.

This sort of mistrust makes it very difficult to achieve the vision of teamwork that is widely seen as key to the growth of a "postindustrial" economy.

All of this also explains why the research literature on the effects of corporate downsizing and restructuring finds remarkably little in the way of positive effects for firm performance.[19] The problem is not necessarily that the idea is wrong but that it has not really been tested: the new approach cannot work unless new institutions, currently not even seriously considered in the United States, are developed. The transition process, with its conflicting crosscurrents, has produced a turbulence in which everyone responds to local rather than systemic pressures and which has therefore failed to coalesce into a grand flow toward a flexible and mobile society.

Possibilities for the Future

Faced with these tensions, many people wish that they could go back to the past—to the culture of loyalty and stability, which, while never universal, was at least more dominant through the 1960s. Yet few are willing to advocate that explicitly: it collides with too many real changes. Setting that option aside, there are really two major possibilities:

Performance-Based Dualism

Many managers talk and think as if the way out of these dilemmas is to be ruthlessly consistent about a true performance-based culture, with no guarantees. According to this view, you should deal with both high performers and low performers as they deserve: you retain the former by paying them a lot; you get rid of the latter by not rewarding them and thus maintain pressure on everyone. It appears to be elegant and consistent.

The trouble is that it does not work very well even in the short run—and its effectiveness promises to spiral downward in the future. On the high end, you get people who are highly marketable and constantly enticed by the lure of something better, leading to a kind of compensation "arms race." This is clearly manifested in the extraordinary escalation of CEO salaries[20] but is just as true further down in the ranks of investment banking, high technology, and other "hot" industries.[21] Other people, however, are stuck where they are because they cannot generate competing offers. The gap between the former and the latter inevitably develops into a sharpening dualism.

Since the compensation race for retention of superstars is potentially endless, companies quickly find that it does not really work, so they turn to other mechanisms that mimic the old loyalty bargain in order to tie superstars' interests more broadly to a single company. They use such devices as stock options that are not immediately redeemable and benefits for their spouses and families; they also try to restrict rather than encourage information about other opportunities. These mechanisms differ in detail but not in essence from the ways in which "traditional" companies sought stability by locking in their employees through long-term interests. Meanwhile, the non-superstars need no such incentives—they are already frightened enough of being thrown out the door. So the dualism is extended not only to pay but also to many other formal and informal benefits.

No one really *advocates* this dualistic solution; it creates obvious value problems and does not fit the explicit image of an entrepreneurial, participatory, mobile order. But most managers—especially HR managers—*in practice* pursue it because it is the only way to get through the day. It is the inevitable result of a pure performance-based model but also a response to a number of further problems: it responds to the pressures from the IRS and government regulatory bodies to make a clear distinction between nonstandard and standard employees; it enables businesses to build a culture of teamwork and commitment at the core without "polluting" it with people who are outside the community.

But the resulting problems are practical as well as ideological. The more the gap between valued and nonvalued employees grows, the more a vicious paradox develops: the people you most *want* to keep are the ones who have no particular interest in staying; they can easily get another deal. Meanwhile, the ones you *don't* particularly want to keep are desperate to stay. This latter group naturally engages in narrow organizational politics to reduce their vulnerability, and they are also resentful because it is increasingly obvious that the company does not value them.[22] The end of the road is an organization to which no one is really committed.

True Mobility

To develop a system of true mobility would require at least two major components: institutions that support mobility for the whole workforce and a "social contract" of reciprocal obligations that the parties could rely on.

Neither is a trivial undertaking. The institutional infrastructure would need to include a whole set of major items, including effective systems providing information about job opportunities, institutions offering continuing training and adult education outside of firms, portability of benefits such as health care and retirement funds, career counseling, and adequate safety nets for periods of transition and unemployment. Although corporate management often acknowledges the importance of such institutions in theory, it has (as we have seen) little incentive to create them in practice. The other obvious source for many of these institutions is, of course, government, yet there is little evidence that government is able or willing to shoulder the major burden of creating them, whether the administration be Democratic or Republican.

That leaves one set of actors that has played only a minor role so far: *employee* organizations, including unions, professional groups, and other associations. Unions have not been a major factor in this debate because they are in large measure still linked to the system of stable lifetime employment. Collective bargaining (at least in industrial unions) is built around companies and jobs rather than around employees; those who do not have stable and permanent jobs are not easily dealt with in this framework. The major unions have therefore generally tried to *limit* nonstandard employment rather than to represent people affected by it; they have been among the forces resisting the model of mobility, but they—like others— have been unable to win widespread support for alternatives.

A few employee organizations, however, have taken the other approach, accepting the reality of mobility and trying to make it compatible with good working conditions.

- In this volume is a piece by Sara Horowitz, executive director of an organization called Working Today, which has started by creating a portable health care and pension fund and offering financial advice, and which aims over time to develop much of the infrastructure needed for mobility by organizing networks of employee associations.

- Another approach, quite different in detail yet closely related in concept, is the Wisconsin Regional Training Partnership, which has organized a consortium of employers and unions to do what the purely employer-based Talent Alliance has failed to do: provide a network of job opportunities, information, and training to maximize employment throughout a region (Dresser, this volume; Parker 1998; McNerney 1995).

- Around the country there has sprung up a whole set of nascent worker-owned temporary agencies, that is, placement agencies with the explicit goal of helping workers rather than being profit-making intermediaries. A number of these, such as the Bergen Organizing Project in New Jersey, want to become "hiring halls" for the nonstandard sector of the workforce, improving working conditions through a tactic long used by craft unions: controlling the labor pool.

- The Carolina Alliance for Fair Employment tries to exert pressure on existing temporary agencies to improve conditions by threatening legal action in case of violations of the Fair Labor Standards Act and the Americans with Disabilities Act (Nixon 1997).

- Finally, in at least two cases, unions have negotiated with their employers for support of independent training organizations to prepare workers for new careers, inside or outside their current companies. The first, to my knowledge, was the General Motors–UAW "Paid Education Leave" agreement in the early 1980s; it was followed by the establishment of several "alliances" in telecommunications. Like the Talent Alliance, these efforts have been somewhat hampered by management's reluctance to promote true mobility and by the fact that unions also are committed to preserving jobs rather than supporting careers. Nevertheless, the interplay between the actors has produced more progress than the Talent Alliance has with only management support.

These efforts could be bellwethers in a process of reconstructing a system of employee representation on the basis of turning mobility into a good thing for workers rather than trying to stop it. So far they have only begun to diminish some of the disadvantages—by making it less painful for workers to move from job to job. There remains much to be done in order to realize the potential *benefits:* the independence, diversity, participation, and self-development that are potentially a part of network systems.

The final, vital element of a system of true mobility would be a set of accepted norms about the obligations of the players in the labor market. The norms of the old core market, as previously noted, involved unquestioning loyalty from the employees and high levels of protection and security from the employer. There have been a number of attempts at a conceptual level to redefine the "social contract" for the new era (Rousseau 1995; Work In America Institute 1992; Schein 1980). My own view is based on discussions with employees and employers in which they wrestled with what they themselves think their obligations are and then tried to reach agreement. The parties in such discussions generally come to center on something like a "professional" relationship:

- They believe that there should be a real commitment to a relationship but not a permanent one. The commitment is framed by a *mission* rather than by "eternal vows." A "mission" is in effect a large project requiring complicated cooperation—not a short task on the one hand, nor an unchanging set of values on the other, but a major strategic project of the firm. It helps to think of a mission as bound by a *time frame* of three to five years—enough time to plan and carry out something meaningful but not so long as to lock the parties into a "permanent" relationship.

- Such a commitment means, among other things, that employers have obligations not to lay the employee off within the term of the mission, or at least to provide major support if such a layoff becomes necessary, and that the employee has an obligation not to leave during that period, or at least to provide transitional time and support if leaving does become necessary so that the mission is not harmed.

- There is also general agreement on the obligation of both sides to provide full disclosure: on the company side, disclosure of business information and strategic intent; on the employee side, disclosure of career aims and competing commitments. In this way the parties can make informed decisions about exactly what they are getting into.

- Most participants in these sessions also agreed to something like an obligation of "reasonable accommodation": that the employer and employee both need to be flexible in order to accommodate legitimate
needs of the other side, for example, about overtime work or childcare.

This is just an initial sketch of a complex subject, but it shows, I
think, that there is the basis for agreement on a new social contract. In
my experience, some firms have begun in informal ways to "negotiate"
such "contracts" with their managerial employees, usually through discussions in the appraisal process, allowing considerable variation depending on the personal needs of the employee and the changing needs
of the business. But to my knowledge, none have set up clear and regular
ways of defining the obligations and making sure they are honored.[23]

Conclusion

Caught between strong images of a new order and strong institutions of an old one, managers and employees are floundering. The gap
produces defensive behavior as well as confusion. Many wish to go back
to what is remembered as a more secure and simpler era, but they have
no real program or vision of how to do so; there appears to be a general
sense (which I have not analyzed) that the basic forces pushing for more
mobility are irresistible.

But if we cannot go back, how can we go forward? The practical,
incremental steps available to real actors seem to be leading to a dualism that tears itself apart—one in which the core does not want to be
core and the contingent periphery does not want to be peripheral, while
all the time the gap between the two groups grows.

That has led me to consider whether the image of mobility can be
made a reality. What the ideological proponents of this model have not
come to grips with is that the social changes required are huge: the
entire set of institutions supporting careers needs to be recast and the
social obligations of employers and employees redefined. Only small
steps have been taken so far in this direction.

I have so far not made explicit one of the most important implications of the recent shift: if the problem is essentially one of a new world
of networks colliding with the old structures of the firm, then the very
nature of the firm is put in question. We are used to thinking of firms as
seeking immortality; almost every management text uses company survival as its key criterion of success. But if we are stumbling toward a
more flexible and mobile economy, companies cannot be such fixed

points within it: they also need to be structures focused on time-bound missions. As long as firms seek permanence, they will try to lock in key employees, thus producing the vicious circle of dualism I have outlined; only when they see the value of *encouraging true mobility* will they be able to tie into networks in a way that truly creates the flexibility and responsiveness that business is so confusedly seeking.

Notes

[1] The "iron cage" is, of course, Max Weber's pessimistic image of bureaucracy. The imprisoning side of life in the large corporation has been vividly documented by many writers, including C. Wright Mills (1951), William H. Whyte (1956), and Rosabeth Moss Kanter (1977).

[2] I am not forgetting, of course, that unions played a substantial part in forcing companies to maintain these benefits, especially for the blue-collar ranks. Nevertheless, the internalization of these benefits also fits with the basic managerial logic of the firm, which is why they spread even in nonunion companies and in management ranks.

[3] A good deal of this literature is condescending about our economic peers, especially Japan and Germany, for their insistence on clinging to the outmoded view that jobs should be stable. See, for example, "Japan's Cushioned 'Air Bag Economy' Spawns Leaders Who Will Tinker Not Innovate" (1998).

[4] I do recall being impressed in the late 1980s by a speech by Frank Doyle, then director of HR for General Electric, in which he took the argument to its conclusion—proposing that if management wants a more mobile workforce, it should take responsibility for portability of benefits, improvements in unemployment insurance, and the removal of other societal obstacles to mobility.

[5] This memorable phrase comes, of course, from Paul Hirsch (1987).

[6] See also a large-scale poll by the International Survey Research Corp. ("With All the Advice for Reducing Stress, Why Is Stress Rising?" 1996). It found substantial changes in the proportion of employees who agreed with the following statements:

- Frequently worry about being laid off: 1988, 22%; 1995, 46%
- Worry a lot about company's future: 1988, 36%; 1995, 55%
- Feel sure job is secure if perform well: 1988, 73%; 1995, 50%

[7] A 1996 Peter Hart poll (unpublished, prepared for the AFL-CIO) found that 83% agreed (59% strongly) that "average working families have less economic security today, because corporations have become too greedy and care more about profits than about being fair and loyal to their employees." See also Schmidt (1999), "Survey Finds" (1995), and Kepner-Tregoe (1994).

[8] Brian Becker and Mark Huselid (e.g., Becker and Huselid 1998) have recently made this case, though their studies have troubling methodological flaws, such as low response rates. In any case, this evidence far postdates, rather than drives, the phenomenon.

[9] Indeed, Baker, Jensen, and Murphy (1988) express shock at the small differentials they find in real companies and advocate a much larger spread of pay according to performance.

[10] This is the conclusion of Nollen and Axel's (1995) review of the literature. Interestingly, there are some hints that there may have been significant jumps in nonstandard, and especially part-time, work much *earlier*—during the 1960s and 1970s; but if anything, they leveled off in the 1980s. Part of the story in debates about job stability is that there has always been less stability than the popular image suggested. A study based on Census Bureau data concluded that between 1972 and 1988 37% of the labor force changed its employment status *every year* (Davis, Haltiwanger, and Schuh 1996). It does, however, seem plausible that in the earlier period this instability was confined to a smaller part of the workforce than it is now—that is, there was a more clearly defined "secondary sector" of unstable employees.

[11] See, for example, "New Calculation Shows Steady Rate of Layoffs" (1996) and "U.S. Companies Stepped Up Job Creation" (1996).

[12] Usually, of course, managers are also employees in this sense; how they respond depends on whether they are looking "up" or "down" at the particular moment.

[13] These comments, and much of this section, are based on my interviews in the early 1990s with over 250 middle managers in large companies, reported in *White-Collar Blues* (Heckscher 1995).

[14] According to polls by the Survey Research Center (Johnson, Bachman, and O'Malley 1987), the percentage of high school seniors saying they want "to stay in the same job for most of my adult life" *increased* from 1975 to 1985 from 51% to 57%. Robinson (1996) also indicates that young people's expectations of lifetime jobs have not significantly declined.

[15] Such ideologues often think they are acting according to a pure Adam Smith type of market picture, in which the "invisible hand" of the market will create good for all while every individual follows individual self-interest. One trouble with the argument is that Smith himself was strongly opposed to it, expressing a clear view that "moral sentiments" are needed to stabilize the system (Smith 1751).

[16] Bencivenga (1997) points to a few company programs that encourage mobility, but the effect of the whole article is the opposite of his intention: there is very little real evidence of effective employer efforts of this type.

[17] This is complicated by a strand of legal thought from the 1880s—the "employment-at-will" doctrine—which says that the government should not interfere at all in employer decisions. But the government has in fact intervened sufficiently to mandate coverage of certain benefits that fit the paternalistic master–servant model.

[18] Edward L. Gubman, HR practice leader at Hewitt Associates, is explicit: companies must acknowledge that they are offering employees different deals and that there is "no one employment relationship, even in the same company." At some point management has to tell employees who is "core" and who is not (Bencivenga 1997).

[19] Here is a sampling of the evidence that corporate restructuring produces little performance gain:

- A 1997 Wharton study shows little benefit from downsizing (Koretz 1997).
- A study of Fortune 500 firms finds no evidence that downsizing leads to improved financial performance—though it does lead to higher stock prices (Cascio, Young, and Morris 1997).
- A series of reports from Kepner-Tregoe in New Jersey has documented the limitations of reengineering and total quality management (see, for example, Kepner-Tregoe 1995).
- Appelbaum and Batt (1994, p. 23) and Van Horn (1996, p. 103) cite a substantial further series of studies with the same thrust.

[20] The AFL-CIO, in a report released in April 1999, calculated that the average salary of chief executive officers of the nation's major corporations in 1997 was 326 times more than that of the average factory worker. While the data are not strictly comparable, Verba and Orren (1985) found the ratio of CEO pay to auto assembly line workers' pay 15 to 20 years ago to be just 22:1.

[21] Vinod Khosla, the cofounder of Sun Microsystems, recounted recently that he had offered a software engineer a package worth a million dollars in the first year— and was turned down for a better offer (speech at Wharton Conference on New Organization Forms, March 19, 1999).

[22] Sue Cobble has pointed out to me another dynamic that reinforces the pattern: in the past, women formed a group of employees who generally accepted a "contingent," second-class status because they were secondary wage earners both in fact and in self-image. As that has changed, a huge new group has pushed to get into the stable core.

[23] These issues are explored a bit further in Heckscher (1995, chapter 8).

References

Appelbaum, Eileen, and Rosemary Batt. 1994. *The New American Workplace: Transforming Work Systems in the United States.* Ithaca, NY: ILR Press.

Baker, George P. 1990. *Pay-for-Performance: Causes and Consequences.* Boston: Harvard Business School.

Baker, George P., Michael C. Jensen, and Kevin J. Murphy. 1988. "Compensation and Incentives: Practice vs. Theory." *Journal of Finance,* Vol. 43, pp. 593–616.

Becker, Brian E., and Mark A. Huselid. 1998. "High Performance Work Systems and Firm Performance: A Synthesis of Research and Managerial Implications." *Research in Personnel and Human Resources Management,* Vol. 16, pp. 53–101.

Bencivenga, Dominic. 1997. "Employers & Workers Come to Terms." *HRMagazine,* Vol. 42, no. 6 (June), pp. 90–93+.

Burns, Jane O., and Tracy A. Freeman. 1996. "Avoiding IRS Reclassification of Workers as Employees." *Tax Adviser,* Vol. 27, no. 2 (February), pp. 102–109.

Cascio, W. F., C. E. Young, and J. R. Morris. 1997. "Financial Consequences of Employment-Change Decisions in Major U.S. Corporations." *Academy of Management Journal,* Vol. 40, no. 5, pp. 1175–1189.

Davis, Steven, John Haltiwanger, and Scott Schuh. 1996. *Gross Job Flows in U.S. Manufacturing.* Cambridge, MA: MIT Press.

"The Downsizing of America" [series]. 1996. *New York Times,* March 3–March 9.

Drucker, Peter F. 1988. "Managing in the '90s: Tomorrow's Restless Managers." *Industry Week,* Vol. 236, no. 8 (April 18), pp. 25–27.

Drucker, Peter F. 1992. "The New Society of Organizations." *Harvard Business Review,* September–October, pp. 95–102.

Edelstein, Robert, and Jean-Michel Paul. 1998. "Japan's Broken Employment Escalator." *Wall Street Journal Interactive Edition* <http://interactive.wsj.com>, June 19.

Gieseking, Hal, and Paul Plawin. 1993. *30 Days to a Good Job.* New York: Simon and Schuster.

Graham, Ellen. 1997. "Work May Be a Rat Race, But It's Not a Daily Grind: Job Morale Is Buoyant Despite Cutbacks and Constant Change." *Wall Street Journal Interactive Edition* <http://interactive.wsj.com>, September 19.

Greenspan, Alan. 1999. Semiannual economic testimony to Congress, February 16.

Heckscher, Charles. 1995. *White-Collar Blues: Management Loyalties in an Age of Corporate Restructuring.* New York: Basic Books.

Hipple, Steven, and Jay Stewart. 1996. "Earnings and Benefits of Workers in Alternative Work Arrangements." *Monthly Labor Review,* Vol. 10 (October), pp. 46–54.

Hirsch, Paul. 1987. *Pack Your Own Parachute: How to Survive Mergers, Takeovers, and Other Corporate Disasters.* Reading, MA: Addison-Wesley.

Hylton, Maria O'Brien. 1996. "Legal and Policy Implications of the Flexible Employment Relationship." *Journal of Labor Research,* Vol. 17, no. 4 (Fall), pp. 583–593.

"Japan's Cushioned 'Air Bag Economy' Spawns Leaders Who Will Tinker Not Innovate." 1998. *New York Times,* June 19.

Johnson, Lloyd D., Jerald G. Bachman, and Patrick M. O'Malley. 1987. *Surveys by Monitoring the Future.* Ann Arbor: Survey Research Center, Institute for Social Research, University of Michigan. [Collection of poll results, latest 1985, reported in *Public Opinion,* May/June 1987: p. 35.]

Kanter, Rosabeth Moss. 1987. "From Status to Contribution: Some Organizational Implications of the Changing Basis for Pay." *Personnel,* January, pp. 12–37.

Kanter, Rosabeth Moss. 1977. *Men and Women of the Corporation.* New York: Basic Books.

Kepner-Tregoe. 1994. *House Divided: Views on Change from Top Management—and Their Employees.* Skillman, NJ: Kepner-Tregoe.

Kepner-Tregoe. 1995. *People and Their Jobs: What's Real, What's Rhetoric?* Princeton, NJ: Kepner-Tregoe.

Kochan, Thomas A., Michal Smith, John C. Wells, and James B. Rebitzer. 1994. "Human Resource Strategies and Contingent Workers: The Case of Safety and Health in the Petrochemical Industry." *Human Resource Management,* Vol. 33, no. 1 (Spring), pp. 55–77.

Koretz, Gene. 1997. "The Downside of Downsizing." *Business Week, Industrial/Technology Edition,* Vol. 3524 (April 28), p. 26.

Krawczyk, Kathy, Lorraine M. Wright, and Roby B. Sawyers. 1996. "Independent Contractors: The Consequences of Reclassification." *Journal of Accountancy,* Vol. 181, no. 1 (January), pp. 47–51.

Lyncheski, John E., and Ronald J. Andrykovitch. 1996. "Leased Employees and Joint Employer Status." *Getting Results,* Vol. 41, no. 5 (May), p. 7.

Ma, Beverly. 1997. "Independent Contractor Pitfalls: Lessons from Microsoft." *HR Focus,* Vol. 74, no. 5 (May), p. 13.

McKenzie, Robert S. 1996. "Avoiding Tax Liabilities Resulting from an Independent Contractor/Employee Examination Program." *Journal of Asset Protection,* Vol. 2, no. 2 (November/December), pp. 30–37.

McNerney, Donald J. 1995. "Wisconsin Employers Join Forces." *HR Focus,* Vol. 72, no. 7 (July), pp. 7+.

Miller, Greg. 1996. "Kingston Employees Take Bonus in Stride." *Los Angeles Times,* December 16.

Mills, C. Wright. 1951. *White Collar: The American Middle Classes.* London: Oxford University Press.

"New Calculation Shows Steady Rate of Layoffs." 1996. *New York Times,* October 26.

Newman, Katherine S. 1988. *Falling from Grace: The Experience of Downward Mobility in the American Middle Class.* New York: Free Press.

Nixon, Ron. 1997. "Organizing Temps." *Progressive,* Vol. 61, no. 7 (July), p. 16.

Nollen, Stanley, and Helen Axel. 1995. *Managing Contingent Workers.* N.p.: AMACOM.

O'Dell, Carla. 1987. *People, Performance, and Pay.* N.p.: American Productivity Center.

"The Outlook." 1997. *Wall Street Journal Interactive Edition* <http://interactive.wsj.com>, September 8.

Parker, Eric. 1998. "High Road Regional Partnerships: A Labor-Based Strategy for Workforce Development." Paper presented to Cornell University Conference on the Revival of the American Labor Movement, October.

Robinson, Sandra L. 1996. "Trust and Breach of the Psychological Contract." *Administrative Science Quarterly,* Vol. 41, no. 4 (December), pp. 574–599.

Rousseau, Denise M. 1995. *Psychological Contracts in Organizations.* Thousand Oaks, CA: Sage.

Schein, Edgar. 1980. *Organizational Psychology,* 3rd ed. Englewood Cliffs, NJ: Prentice Hall.

Schmidt, Stefanie R. 1999. "Long-Run Trends in Workers' Beliefs about Their Own Job Security: Evidence from the General Social Survey." *Journal of Labor Economics,* Vol. 17, no. 4 (October, pt. 2), pp. S127–S141.

Silverstein, Stuart. 1997. "Corporations Ally to Get a Handle on the Turbulent Labor Market." *Los Angeles Times,* March 9.

Smith, Adam. 1751. *The Theory of Moral Sentiments.* London: Millar.

"Survey Finds That Employees View Lack of Trust as a Problem in Their Organizations." 1995. *Quality Progress,* Vol. 28, no. 10 (October), pp. 21–22.

"Towers Perrin 1997 Workplace Index Reveals Growing Concerns in Employer Delivery on the New Deal Contract." 1997. *Los Angeles Times,* September 15.

"U.S. Companies Stepped up Job Creation: Management Survey." 1996. *Dow Jones Business News,* October 20.

Van Horn, Carl E. 1996. *No One Left Behind: The Report of the Twentieth Century Fund Task Force on Retraining America's Workforce.* New York: Twentieth Century Fund Press.

Verba, Sidney, and Gary R. Orren. 1985. *Equality in America: The View from the Top.* Cambridge, MA: Harvard University Press.

Whyte, William H., Jr. 1956. *The Organization Man.* New York: Simon and Schuster.

"With All the Advice for Reducing Stress, Why Is Stress Rising?" 1996. *Wall Street Journal Interactive Edition* <http://interactive.wsj.com>, October 2.

Wolman, William, and Anne Colamosca. 1997. *The Judas Economy: The Triumph of Capital and the Betrayal of Work.* Reading, MA: Addison-Wesley.

Work In America Institute. 1992. *Toward a New Social Contract: Employment Security for Managers and Professionals.* Scarsdale, NY: Work In America Institute.

Chapter 10

Historical Perspectives on Representing Nonstandard Workers

Dorothy Sue Cobble
Rutgers University

Leah F. Vosko
McMaster University

"The reports of my death are greatly exaggerated," Mark Twain once quipped. So too are the reports of the rise of a new contingent workforce. Contingent work may be increasing if the standard of comparison is the work world of the decades following World War II. But a comparison with the pre–New Deal era reveals as much continuity as discontinuity. The majority of jobs before the New Deal exhibited many of the characteristics now associated with contingent and other nonstandard employment today: part-time and temporary work, lack of guaranteed income and benefits, and a loose and/or triangulated relationship between employer and employee. In short, contingent and other nonstandard work was as much the norm as the exception before the New Deal (Morse 1969).

Even if the historical perspective is short-term—that is, in relation to the golden or "wonder years"[1] after World War II—contingency is a *new* phenomenon primarily for white, middle-aged male workers. This group, whether unionized blue-collar workers or white-collar middle managers, now feels rising anxiety about job security. Further, although average U.S. job tenure (length of time with one employer) has changed little in the last few decades (falling slightly for men and actually *increasing* for women), unionized and white-collar male workers have experienced layoffs in ever-increasing numbers (Medoff 1993; Cappelli et al. 1997). In contrast, women and nonwhite men have always faced a labor market dominated by contingent jobs (Morse 1969; Kessler-Harris 1982).

The real change today is the greater job insecurity experienced by unionized blue-collar workers and white-collar middle managers, and the greater frequency with which these privileged segments of the labor force experience other features of the nonstandard work arrangement (low wages, lack of benefits, part-time employment, agency and contract labor). Granted, those formerly in long-term, stable employment relationships are generally the elite of the nonstandard workforce, receiving the highest pay and best benefits, and women and nonwhite men continue to be disproportionately represented among nonstandard workers (Kalleberg et al. 1997). Nevertheless, this "feminization of employment relationships"—a phenomenon whereby a growing proportion of work arrangements carries wages, benefits, and terms and conditions of employment resembling those historically associated with women and other marginalized workers (Vosko 2000a)—is an important impetus for the new attention to nonstandard work.

Moreover, contingency and the poor working conditions generally associated with nonstandard employment have become increasing sources of public concern because the conventional gender division of labor has, at least to some extent, been disrupted. A growing misfit exists between so-called secondary workers and the secondary jobs that these workers occupy. Of course, most workers relegated to the low-wage, dead-end, and insecure world of peripheral employment never took these jobs by preference. Yet, particularly in the postwar decades, as white, married, middle-class women flooded the labor market, the slotting of secondary workers into secondary jobs was perceived and experienced as less of a social problem than it is today. Many (though not all) of the new middle-class, married, female workforce saw themselves as secondary wage earners, and many gained security, status, and fulfillment as much through family and community as through paid employment. Today, women are still the majority of nonstandard workers (Spalter-Roth and Hartmann 1998), but increasingly they resist placement in secondary jobs. Like men, most women seek jobs that offer career advancement, benefits, and an income that will allow them to support themselves and their families.

A historical perspective thus suggests that nonstandard work is not atypical or new. Including gender as a category in the analysis also helps explain the recent emergence of contingency as a research focus and a social problem. In this article, we rely on a historical perspective not only to better understand the ways in which work is changing and for whom but also to learn more about how workers organized to improve nonstandard jobs. Our assumption is that working conditions can be improved through state intervention and regulation but that workers through their own self-organization have done as much to advance their interests as has the regulatory apparatus of the state.

In the following sections, we first detail the changes in the work world that we see as particularly troubling because of their correlation with declining income, working conditions, and worker representation. Here our emphasis is not on job insecurity per se but on other aspects of nonstandard work arrangements: the increasing looseness or ambiguity of the employer–employee relationship, the unraveling of the very notion of *employee* and *employer*, and the heightened mobility of workers. We then turn to the past to explore how workers themselves addressed these problematic aspects of nonstandard work. First, we look at occupational unionism, the most common form of worker representation in the pre–New Deal era. How effective was it in representing nonstandard workers? How can we account for its decline over the course of the 20th century? Second, we explore how unions resolved the problem of representing those who were neither "employees" nor "employers." Here, the focus is on contract and subcontracted workers in manufacturing trades as well as the owner-operators in the transportation industry who formed the bulk of membership in the early International Brotherhood of Teamsters (IBT). We see these case studies as contributing to the creation of new and viable forms of collective representation for today's workforce, as well as helping to determine the proper mix of regulatory and voluntary solutions appropriate in today's economy.

Current Workforce Transformations

If recent employment trends continue, a large proportion of the 21st-century workforce will move from job site to job site, and their loyalties will be more to other members of their occupation or profession than to a single company or industry. These mobile workers will derive their compensation and security more from their access to multiple employment opportunities than from their prospects at a single firm. Although such a mobile workforce is not new and may not be growing as fast as many proclaim, it will be a critical component of the 21st-century work world and, as such, deserves more attention than it has received heretofore.

An even more fundamental challenge to current worker representational practices and employment policy is not mobility per se but the erosion of a clear demarcation between the categories of "employee" and "employer." Increasingly, the lines between employee and employer are blurred as less work is organized on older Taylorist[2] principles of a dichotomous divide between the functions of workers and managers. The growth of knowledge and interactive service work fuels this erosion, because relational and mental labor are not and never were amenable to the Taylorist principles of microsupervision and centralized hierarchical command (Zuboff 1988; Benson 1986). Moreover, many manufacturing work systems have reorganized along post-Taylorist lines in the face of the imperatives of new flexible technology and the global marketplace (Piore and Sabel 1984; Appelbaum and Batt 1994).[3]

The decentralization of business and the breakdown of once dominant vertically integrated bureaucratic structures also are undermining the traditional roles of employee and employer (Chandler 1977; Cappelli 1995). Like the shift away from Taylorist work organization, decentralization means that workers take on more managerial responsibilities and develop a looser or more tenuous (even virtual) relationship to their employer. Many work in teams that are self-regulating and formed around particular projects or tasks (Jackson 1999; Rubenstein, Bennett, and Kochan 1993). Many, both professional and nonprofessional, are direct contract workers categorized as self-employed or independent contractors. They may also work for a temporary agency, a labor contractor, or a contracting firm, thus existing in a triangulated employment relationship rather than a dualistic one (Vosko 1997). Many arguably should nonetheless be classified as employees (Linder 1992; Dunlop 1994) rather than as independent contractors, managers, or self-employed. Others, however, are indeed no longer employees in the traditional sense of the word. They control their own work processes. They are paid a price for a labor service or product rather than a wage for their labor. They may own their own equipment or business. Some may hire and supervise others. The issue, then, is not simply ensuring that those who work as traditional employees are classified appropriately under the law. Rather, the current transformations open other more fundamental questions: Who should be considered an employee? Who should have state-guaranteed rights to organize collectively? How should the labor movement change to accommodate the new realities of nonstandard work? It is with these questions in mind that we turn to the past.

Occupational Unionism: Representing the Mobile Workforce

The majority of workers who organized successfully before the New Deal practiced a very different form of unionism than the one that became dominant with the rise of the Congress of Industrial Organizations (CIO). Virtually every trade that successfully organized workers before the Rooseveltian reforms relied on some elements of occupational unionism. Occupational unionism is not work site or firm based, nor are wages, benefits, and job security dependent on organizing workers employed by an individual firm. Rather, these unionists organized the labor supply for an occupation (Cobble 1991a, 1994).

Classic craft unionists such as printers and construction workers, as well as other craft-identified workers such as waiters and waitresses, bartenders, teamsters, and garment workers, all recruited and gained recognition on an occupational basis. Even longshoremen, agricultural workers, and other casual laborers relied on aspects of occupational unionism. Benefits and union membership were portable, and in the rhetoric of human resource professionals, occupational unions offered employment or career security rather than job security. The issue was not fighting for tenure at an individual work site but increasing the overall supply of good, well-paying jobs and providing workers with the skills to perform those jobs (Cobble 1991a, 1994).

Occupational unions strove for control over hiring through closed shops, hiring halls, and worker-run employment bureaus; they also provided training—what would now be seen as professional development—and job placement (Cobble 1991a). The union took over the function of labor recruitment and deployment. In construction and agriculture, for example, the union-operated hiring hall was an alternative to the labor contractor system (Milkman and Wong 2000; Edid 1994). In maritime work, the hiring hall replaced the "shape-up" system of job procurement, in which foremen chose day laborers from among the unemployed gathered on the docks (Nelson 1988).

Occupational unions took over other management functions as well. Many embraced peer discipline or self-management instead of the industrial union norm common by the 1930s and 1940s, in which the employer disciplines and the union grieves. They preferred to write their own workplace rules and regulations rather than react to those created by management. Together, workers decided upon acceptable performance standards, how to divide up work time, and many other work organization and quality questions. What we now think of as management rights or personnel matters were subject to peer control; unions saw this approach as exercising their craft prerogatives—not unlike what persists today among some professional groups that determine and monitor the standards for their profession.

Occupational unionism flourished because it met the needs of workers and employers outside of mass-production settings. In local labor markets populated by numerous small employers, the unionization of construction workers, garment workers, restaurant employees, and teamsters brought stability and predictability as well as inhibited cutthroat competition. Employers gained a steady supply of skilled, responsible labor: an outside agency (the union) ensured the competence and job performance of the workers who were its members. In many cases, the union took responsibility for expanding the customer base for unionized enterprises. Garment unions, for example, encouraged the purchase of goods made with the union label; the hotel and restaurant unions urged the patronage of retail establishments that displayed the union house card in their window (Fraser 1991; Cobble 1991a). Further, a floor for minimum wages and acceptable working conditions was established. Workers gained not long-term job tenure but the opportunity to invest in their own "human capital" through training and experience at a variety of work sites. As long as employers in the unionized sector remained competitive—a goal to which both labor and management were committed—unionized workers gained real employment security because the union helped make them more employable individually and helped ensure a supply of high-wage, "good" jobs. In contrast to industrial unionism, occupational unions never developed rigid seniority rules at individual work sites; they were committed to maintaining employee productivity, providing high-quality service and production, and ensuring the viability of unionized firms (Cobble 1991a, 1994).

With the increasing tendency in recent years for workers once again to identify primarily with their occupation rather than their employer, a unionism emphasizing cross-firm structures and occupational identity appears viable once again. A union that provides portable benefits and training, emphasizes occupational identity, and shoulders responsibility for upgrading and monitoring occupational standards would appeal to today's new workforce. Many nonprofessional as well as professional employees would welcome membership in an organization that would enhance their job security while also assisting them in improving the image of their occupation and in performing their work to the best of their abilities (Cobble 1991b).

Worker-run employment agencies could presumably offer important services to today's mobile workforce—high-quality benefits and higher wages than those offered by temporary agencies run for profit—and do so without penalizing workforce intermittence. Many workers desire mobility among employers, a variety of work experiences, and flexible scheduling. Well-run agencies could provide such job variety and flexibility. Finally, reviving hiring halls would help reverse the "re-casualization" of work that is occurring in such sectors as construction, agriculture, and maritime (Milkman and Wong 2000; Edid 1994).[4]

Yet few of the practices once common among occupational unionists can be easily achieved or sustained today. How can this be explained? Occupational unionism declined dramatically in the postwar era as unions embraced the industrial model, one designed to fit the realities of factory work and large bureaucratic workplaces. Occupational practices such as peer management or union control over training, benefits, and job referral fell into disfavor and were discarded.

Legislative and legal decisions also hampered the ability of occupational unionism to function effectively. Ironically, the industrial union paradigm in labor law spread in the postwar era, even as the number of workers for whom it was appropriate declined. Closed-shop, top-down organizing, secondary boycotts, the removal of members from the job for noncompliance with union bylaws and work rules, and union membership for supervisors and other managerial workers became illegal. Many of these practices were banned in 1947 when the Taft-Hartley Amendments to the National Labor Relations Act (NLRA) were passed over Truman's veto. Additional restrictions came into play in the 1950s as smaller establishments came under the interstate commerce provision of the NLRA and Congress passed the 1959 Landrum-Griffin Amendments. Unions lost their ability to organize new shops, to enforce current bargaining agreements, to maintain multi-employer bargaining structures, to set entrance requirements for the trade, to oversee job performance, and to punish recalcitrant members (Cobble 1991a, 1991b, 1994).

By the 1960s, occupational unionism was but a shadow of its former robust self. Only the building and construction trades (which obtained special legislative language exempting them from some of the new legal restrictions on unions) along with certain highly specialized professional crafts (such as the performing arts) retained a degree of power and influence (Mills 1980; Gray and Seeber 1996). And, in the 1970s and 1980s, even those few remaining occupational union outposts reeled under the continuing assault of the National Labor Relations Board (NLRB) and court rulings that appeared blind to the needs of workers outside the standard employment relationship (Grebelsky 1999).

A fuller account of the institutional and policy reforms that would allow occupational unionism once again to flourish is provided elsewhere (Cobble 1994, 1997). Suffice it to say here that a new legal framework—albeit one based on fundamentally different premises and norms than those derived from the standard employment arrangements typical of the post-WWII decades—is essential for the organization of a mobile workforce. Mobile workers, whether full- or part-time, do not stay with one employer long enough to utilize the conventional election procedures associated with NLRB work-site-based organizing. Employees at small, individual work sites have minimal economic leverage against a multinational corporate employer or a chain-style enterprise. Decentralized, work-site-based bargaining also is simply too labor intensive: consider the thousands of small restaurants or retail establishments in even one metropolitan area. Therefore, marketwide, multi-employer bargaining needs to be encouraged (Fudge 1993; Cobble 1994).

Of equal importance, if a mobile workforce is to have effective representational rights, unions must once again have the ability to act as professional organizations do: to set performance standards and to enforce them by removing members from an individual work site or even from employment eligibility. Further, they must be able to exert many of the economic pressures on employers that were once legal. The millions of nonstandard workers who successfully organized before the 1950s relied on mass picketing, recognitional picketing, secondary boycotts, "hot cargo" agreements (assurances from employers that they will not handle or use the products of nonunion or substandard employers), and prehire agreements (contracts covering future as well as current employees)—all tactics now illegal under current labor law (Cobble 1991a, 1994; Gordon 1999).

Will the Real Worker Please Stand Up?

Today, close to one third of private-sector workers are no longer defined as employees under the NLRA, and the number of so-called nonemployees is growing every day (Cobble 1994, Table 20.1: 290). An old episode of the *Seinfeld* TV series makes the point well. Elaine is telling Jerry that she's just been made an associate at the publishing house where she works. At which point, the waitress serving them coffee pipes in with, "Oh. So have I." In the following section of this paper, we return to an earlier world in which associates were common. How did unions draw membership lines before the world of dichotomous, rigid demarcations between employees and employers more fully emerged? Also, what implications does this history have for a current reform agenda that would meet the needs of nonstandard workers?

First, we turn to the 19th-century manufacturing trades and look at the ways in which unions addressed the contract labor system that was so ubiquitous in the factory before the triumph of bureaucratic mass production in the early 20th century. Second, we move forward in time and follow the debate among the teamsters over where the boundaries of union membership should be. What characteristics distinguished workers from entrepreneurs and employers? In an era devoid of extensive federal regulations delimiting who and how they could organize, workers themselves debated the meanings of these terms and drew their own lines of eligibility.

Unions and the Contracting System in Manufacturing

Nineteenth-century manufacturing was largely dependent on a nonbureaucratic, loosely coupled system of production that utilized skilled craft workers and their helpers (Montgomery 1979; Nelson 1995; Clawson 1980). Not only did a substantial number of workers contract for the production of a specific product rather than sell their labor by the hour or the day but many skilled craftspeople hired and supervised their own helpers and moved with their team from shop to shop. This system varied enormously depending on, among other factors, the nature of the industry, the degree of unionization, and management's competitive strategy. Montgomery (1979) offers a view of the highly unionized settings and emphasizes the control that craft workers gained through union work rules and economic action (strikes, picketing, and boycotts). Nelson (1995) focuses more on the unorganized sectors, detailing the rise of the contracting system inside manufacturing, the power of individual contractors in relation to their employees and to owners, and the replacement of the contract system by wage laborers and salaried managers. Scholars disagree over the inevitability of the rise and ultimate dominance of bureaucratic and Taylorist mass production by the early 20th century, but a general consensus exists about the widespread nature of nonbureaucratic work arrangements in 19th-century manufacturing.

How did unions view this contract system? What methods did they use to regulate it and prevent "sweating" (the deterioration of pay and the speedup of the work pace)? Probably the most famous example of a union's attempt to regulate the contract system in the 19th century involved the journeyman molders in the iron foundries. In its founding constitution in the late 1850s, the Iron Molders Union forbade any journeyman molder to hire and pay a "helper" or "berk," unless the helper was the journeyman's own son. Later, the molders limited the kinds of tasks a helper could perform and made it a union rule that any employer who insisted upon journeymen's hiring and paying their own helpers (the berkshire system) would be blacklisted (Ashworth 1915: 67–68). As a self-regulating, voluntaristic organization, the molders relied upon the individual actions of their members to honor the union rules to which they had each voluntarily agreed. Each member should refuse work where owners insisted upon the berkshire system, and any member who violated these rules would be fined and denied access to union jobs. The struggle against the berkshire system lasted over half a century, involving numerous strikes and lockouts, and gradually the system was eliminated (Ashworth 1915: 68–71; Nelson 1995: 41).

Other unions pursued a different strategy in the face of the contract system. The puddlers and rollers in the iron and steel mills (who formed the largest and most powerful union in the 19th century), as well as other manufacturing trades such as the glassblowers, potters, and blacksmiths, were more amenable to the contract system. Rather than oppose the hiring and payment of helpers by journeymen, they used union rules to ensure that the strong did not exploit the weak by limiting the number of helpers, the work that helpers could do, and the pay that they would receive (Ashworth 1915; Clawson 1980; Montgomery 1979).

The puddlers, for example, favored allowing every man the "privilege of selecting his own assistant without dictation from management." Yet union rules collectively set the wages of helpers at "one-third and five percent" of the payment received by the journeyman (Ashworth 1915: 72–77). According to Montgomery (1979: 11–15), at the Columbia Iron Works in the 1870s, management provided raw materials, a place to work, and sold the finished product. The rest was up to the workers. The iron rollers organized themselves into 12-man teams. They negotiated a rate for each rolling job, and workers decided collectively how payments would be distributed among team members and how the supervisory function would be executed.

As Ashworth (1915) explains, the contract system was not opposed by the puddlers in steel in part because of the nature of the production process.[5] In a capital-intensive industry such as steel, output varied little when additional workers were added or work pace increased. In other words, in part because of the context in which the contract system existed, it did not tend toward sweating (Clawson 1980).

In contrast, the garment industry, in which the contract system also proliferated, was plagued by sweating, partly because of its labor-intensive production processes and partly because it required little capital to enter and thus was highly competitive. Garment unions initially pushed for an end to contracting in the pre-WWI era. But unable to abolish the system, they instead sought government regulation of the wages and hours of contract workers, and they attempted to police the behavior of contractors by putting pressure on the owners. At various historical junctures, unions had enough economic power to hold owners responsible for the wages, benefits, and working conditions in contractors' shops and to force owners to award contracts only to firms that were unionized (Mazur 1994; Fraser 1991).[6]

The building trades were even more successful in limiting the exploitative aspects of the contract system. Practicing a classic form of occupational unionism, they gained the loyalty of the workforce through control over training and access to good jobs. And, as in the garment trades, they exerted economic pressure on the general contractor to use only unionized contractors or contractors who met certain minimum standards in their employment practices (Mills 1980).

Teamsters and the Debate over Union Membership

Manufacturing unions differed among themselves in their responses to contracting and in their views of whether or not the contracting journeyman should be a member of the union. The majority appears to have thought that taking on certain managerial functions per se did not disqualify one as a worker. What was determining, however, was the number of helpers the journeyman employed, whether the journeyman continued to do the work of the craft, and whether or not the journeyman's managerial function was permanent (Clawson 1980: 86–90).

The same issues surfaced in the transportation industry. The historical records of the IBT provide one of the fuller accounts of the debate over union boundaries and the criteria workers devised to determine who was a worker. The first national organization of team drivers, founded in 1899, affiliated with the American Federation of Labor (AFL). Nevertheless, many of the locals that gathered to form the Team Drivers' International Union (TDIU) had earlier been linked, either formally or informally, with the Knights of Labor, the AFL's rival and the largest labor federation of the 19th century (Witwer 1994). The Knights' admission policy reflected a "producerist" consciousness that was rooted in moral as well as economic views on how economic value was created. All producers of commodities and services were welcome to join, including housewives, small farmers, employers, and others. Only financiers, lawyers, bartenders, large manufacturers, and others deemed nonproducers were excluded (Fink 1983; Cobble 1997).

Not surprisingly, then, the first national organization of teamsters included not only team drivers but also those who owned teams, even when they employed other team drivers. In its constitution, the TDIU opened membership to "any Teamster engaged in driving a truck, wagon, hack or [other] vehicle, who does not own or operate more than five teams" (TDIU Constitution and Bylaws 1899: 4). This membership clause, which was rooted in an ideology compatible with the principles of the Knights of Labor, allowed two categories of teamsters to coexist in the union, namely, "employee-drivers" (i.e., drivers employed by owner-operators or employers) and "owner-operators" (i.e., drivers owning and operating up to five teams of horses).

This clause became the focus of considerable debate inside the union as early as 1901. A sizable segment of teamsters criticized the union as a "bosses" organization, dominated by "owner-operators" who were really "employers" and not "workers." They feared exploitation of drivers by owner-operators. Their concerns also reflected a growing trend in the early 20th century labor movement to formalize the distinction between workers and employers and to admit only wage earners into union membership. AFL President Samuel Gompers, for example, proclaimed there was "a deep-seated conviction among team drivers that employers of labor have no right to become members of any local union." And, he continued, "that conviction is fully shared by the members of the Executive Council of the AFL as well as the AFL itself." The teamsters' leadership, he added, should "make the TDIU what it was destined to be, that is, an organization of the workers, by the workers, and for the workers" (letter to George Innis, August 28, 1902, in *Proceedings of the Fifth Annual Convention of the TDIU* 1902: 15).

The opposition to including owner-operators in the union boiled over in April 1902, when a group of Chicago teamsters seceded and formed the Teamsters' National Union (TNU). The TNU vehemently objected to the TDIU because it believed that the TDIU's General Executive Board was dominated by men who owned "five to fifteen" teams of horses. Such men, it thought, should more appropriately be grouped with the owners of the means of production (i.e., the capitalist class) and excluded from union membership. The interests of these owner-operators, it argued, inevitably conflicted with the interests of the average driver whose income derived solely from his labor (*Team Drivers' Journal*, March 1902: 1–2, 13).

At the TDIU convention in 1903, a compromise was reached between the two factions, facilitated by the intervention of the AFL. The factions reunited and founded the International Brotherhood of Teamsters, Chauffeurs, Stablemen and Helpers of America (IBT). Membership in the IBT was now limited to teamsters or helpers who do not "own, operate or control more than one team or vehicle." Moreover, "should any member become an employer [i.e., own more than one team], he shall be given an honorable withdrawal card" (IBT Constitution and Bylaws, October 1, 1903: 4).

In spite of its controversial nature, the constitutional amendment temporarily resolved a complicated question about who did and did not belong to the working class, at least from the perspective of teamsters. The majority of drivers thought that the number of teams one owned was crucial in determining class and craft allegiance because it was the best predictor of how one's time was spent and how one's income was derived (be it from capital—the team, truck, or equipment—or from labor). Those who owned more than one team were indeed employers, but those owning only one team were not—despite their ownership of the means of production and their taking on the employerlike functions of hiring and supervision.[7] The IBT thus rejected a narrow notion of worker that would preclude self-management and supervisory functions, but they also limited the extent to which members could be "capitalists" and employ others. They declared all who spent the majority of their time driving as members of the craft, even if they also derived income from capital and "employed" other team drivers. They recognized that many in their craft were not entirely either employee or employer, and they adjusted their policy accordingly. Like the Knights of Labor, their membership was not restricted to wage earners. Yet unlike the Knights, they had moved beyond the essentially moralistic categories of the 19th-century "producerist" world view.

In the 1920s and 1930s, IBT membership policies came under scrutiny once again. Not only was the issue of operators who owned more than one team reopened, but questions also were raised about union membership for the growing number of self-employed drivers who were engaged in sales ("vender-drivers"). Dan Tobin, the IBT president, initially opposed membership for both. But with the onslaught of the Depression, the rise of cutthroat competition for transport jobs, and the changing nature of delivery work, the IBT adjusted its membership policies dramatically. In 1940, the union amended its constitution to include "vender-drivers" in its membership, defining *vender* as "a person who purchases products and sells the same on his own behalf" (IBT Constitution and Bylaws 1940: 5). In addition, the IBT opened up its membership to drivers who owned *more* than one team or vehicle and to "owner-equipment operators," or drivers who owned other equipment (IBT Constitution and Bylaws 1940: 5).

Tellingly, however, some restrictions were placed on the admission of venders and owners. For example, the IBT president could exclude them if their joining the union were deemed detrimental to the members in existing local unions. Of equal importance, the constitution denied them the right to hold office and to vote on wage and hour scales, unless their local was composed only of owners and venders. In both these instances, the primary concern (like that of the manufacturing workers in the 19th century discussed previously) was to protect the working conditions of those who derived their livelihood *solely* from the sale of their labor.

Nonetheless, these changes amounted to a significant expansion of the definition of membership, which helped the IBT add close to a million new members to its rolls, including many from the groups Tobin had earlier been reluctant to admit (Estey 1976: 10). From the postwar decades forward, the IBT retained its expansive definition of membership[8] and, in the case of trucking, negotiated master freight agreements that covered "regular" employees as well as owner-operators, vender-drivers, and owner-equipment operators.

The IBT, however, was increasingly precluded from acting on its own evolving definition of "community of interest" by changes in the labor law. The 1935 Wagner Act did not define "employee" explicitly or narrowly (Linder 1989: 558), but its passage made the state rather than the unions the principal arbiter of eligibility for collective representation. In 1947, the Taft-Hartley Amendments to the Wagner Act narrowed the definition of "employee" considerably, explicitly excluding "independent contractors" and similar groups from coverage.

The debate over Taft-Hartley in the Republican-dominated Congress revealed the degree to which employment relations were still mired in outmoded common-law assumptions premised on the master–servant relationship. As the 1947 report by the House Committee on Education and Labor put it, "[T]here has always been a difference, and a substantial one, between 'employees' and 'independent contractors.' 'Employees' work for wages and salaries under direct supervision." Those who "decide how their work will be done" or who "undertake to do a job for a price" rather than a wage or who hire others were termed "independent contractors" and hence were not employees (House of Representatives, 80th Cong., 1st sess., 1947, H. Doc. 245, 18, cited in Linder 1989: 567). Congress thus assumed a clearly divided world "in which 'almost everyone' would know an employee when he saw one" (Linder 1989: 566–568).

The courts, for their part, continued to recognize "the existence of gray areas where line-drawing would be difficult," but they gradually also came to embrace a narrower and more dichotomous world view. Increasingly, the courts have relied upon what have been termed the "common-law agency criteria" (which emphasize a worker's lack of control) for determining who is an employee rather than the "economic reality of dependence test" (which emphasizes more the economic character of the employment relationship) (Linder 1989: 567).[9]

The Two-Edged Character of Contracting

What can be learned about present-day approaches to upgrading nonstandard work from these historical accounts of workers' responses to nonstandard work arrangements? These cases suggest that an analysis of the larger context in which contracting arrangements exist is crucial for devising strategic responses. The exploitative potential of contracting appears to be as much a function of the larger technological and market context in which it is situated as it is of the system of contracting per se. For example, in situations where the technological process itself or the nature of the market limited or even precluded speedup, workers did not resist the contract system. They found that it offered as many advantages as disadvantages. They gained some measure of flexibility, autonomy, and opportunity; and through their union rules they were able to inhibit the tendencies in the system toward exploitation, or sweating. In other settings, however, the contract system devolved into sweating, pushed by a labor-intensive production process or the pressures of a competitive market. Here, the "competitive menace," to use John Commons's phrase, was exacerbated by the contract system and could be restrained only through a combination of union power and state regulation (Commons 1909).

Current policy proposals need to recognize the malleable character of contract work: its ability to enhance as well as to degrade working conditions. Workers may use it to reestablish control over production, but employers can use it to bolster their own power. And the balance between exploitation and freedom can shift, depending on the larger context.

In addition, however, the history of workers' responses to contract work suggests that one of the greatest weaknesses in current policy debates over how to improve nonstandard work is the almost exclusive focus on state regulatory solutions. As Eileen Boris (1993) and others have shown, attempts to end sweating (or even to regulate it) solely through government fiat have been failures, particularly in sectors characterized by labor-intensive, small, mobile enterprises that can easily escape government scrutiny. Thus, it is important to move beyond protective state policies and explore ways that worker self-organization and self-protection can be strengthened. Workers and their voluntary organizations need to be empowered if the potentially exploitative structural imperatives of the contract system are to be avoided.

The Limits of Seeking to Define an Employee

Similarly, the question arises as to what a historical perspective offers those trying to resolve the vexing dilemma of who is an "employee" and who is an "employer." Many policy analysts, including those on the Dunlop Commission, now recommend placing economic realities at the center of any legal definition of "employee" and classifying workers as "employees" if they depend on a single firm or another individual for their livelihood. This standard would displace the current reliance on the control test, in which workers who exercise independent judgment and control are defined as "independent contractors" and hence not "employees."

The history sketched here certainly supports this proposition in many respects. The majority of workers in the 19th and early 20th centuries successfully combined self-management, peer management, and team work with collective representation. Why should worker autonomy and independent judgment be thought incompatible with the right to collective representation? Why should the common law of master and servant dominate employment policy in the very era that celebrates discarding paternalism and loyalty?

Increased reliance on the economic realities test in defining who is an employee is necessary for progress. Yet it is not sufficient. Tests of employee status that focus on economic dependence fail to provide a principled or coherent distinction between independent contractors and employees, and in arguing for this approach, advocates may simply be replacing one narrow test with another (Vosko and Fudge 2000). Another problem with the economic realities test is its reliance on dependency rhetoric. This emphasis is at odds with the historic goals of workers to increase their control and autonomy at work.

In view of the limitations of the control test and the economic realities test, one alternative is to abandon the distinction between independent contractors and employees altogether and to recognize a general category of "contracts for the performance of work," whereby social benefits and labor protections would be provided independent of specific employment relationships. Instead, standard protections would be provided by all contracts in which work is performed (Brooks 1988).

The world of work has changed dramatically since the New Deal era, and the notion of formulating any one criterion that can divide employees from employers is no longer tenable. Policy analysts and the courts need to reject a dichotomous approach to the work world and acknowledge that a growing number of workers are neither fish nor fowl, neither employees nor employers.

Indeed, why should the state limit the rights to representation a priori? The 1994 Dunlop Commission, for example, recommended including supervisors and professionals in NLRA coverage in the private sector but held the line on managers, although managers in the public sector may organize. How can such a distinction be justified, especially in view of the fact that managers are successfully organized throughout Europe? Why not shift the burden of proof and assume that all workers have the right to organize unless it can be shown that their organization will be destructive and harmful to the social good?

Moving Workers to the Center of Reform Strategy

Ultimately, it is important to question the narrow parameters of a policy debate that focuses so exclusively on how the state should determine who qualifies for labor protections rather than on how to return more agency and responsibility for self-definition to workers themselves. Before the New Deal, workers defined their own community of interest and insisted upon their right to set their own criteria for union membership. Workers' loss of their right to self-definition has weakened not only the labor movement but also the efforts of social reformers to achieve a rational system of employment protections.

The historical cases presented here suggest that workers in some ways have been better at facing ambiguity and acknowledging the evolving realities of work than has the state. Nineteenth-century unionists did not insist that only those without capital, power, or autonomy could join their movement; rather, they embraced those who needed or wanted collective representation, including many who would today be labeled managers, contractors, or self-employed and hence denied representational rights. These early unionists acknowledged that many in the labor force had supervisory responsibilities, made a living from profit as well as wages, and saw themselves as "independent." Yet these characteristics did not automatically signal exclusion from the ranks of organized labor.

Today, as the functions of buyer, seller, and producer once more increasingly overlap, we need to be able to acknowledge these multiple identities without losing sight of how to distinguish which of these is the primary identity in a given context. The key, as the early teamsters argued, is to focus on how the balance is struck between labor and capital. The critical issue, according to the IBT, was not ownership or selling or even economic independence but rather a realistic assessment of where the person's primary allegiance lay: Did their income primarily result from the work they did or from the capital they invested? How was their time spent (both short term and long term)? Was it primarily spent supervising others? Would it remain so in the long run?

Last, the question of who is a capitalist was just as important to workers historically as who is a worker. Today, that question deserves revisiting as much as, if not more than, the definition of employee. After all, it is the rhetorical ground marked off by conservatives, and in fact, it may be the redefinition and expansion of the concept of entrepreneurs by conservatives that has so eroded and narrowed the definition of employee. One can hardly pick up a business magazine without encountering the argument that we are now all entrepreneurs and hence free from exploitation by employers or the market. We are entering the world of "Me, Inc.," as one article puts it, a strange new world in which everyone can define themselves as "independent economic entities" and sell themselves as products on the market (Porter, Porter, and Bennett 1999).

Drawing on historical understandings of how workers organized themselves before the New Deal helps pierce the veil of this troubling rhetoric of entrepreneurial independence (Linder 1989: 598). Workers understood that even many of those who owned capital, employed others, and sold a product or a service were still in need of protection from the market, just as were those paid wages for their labor. And they understood that for them the only real freedom in the market came not through autonomy but through greater equality of bargaining power—a bargaining power based on the most expansive definition of *worker.*

Acknowledgments

The authors would like to thank Michael Merrill, Gerald Kernerman, Mike Belzer, Francoise Carré, Marianne Ferber, Ruth Milkman, Paula Voos, and David Witwer for their advice and encouragement.

Notes

[1] The term is from Herzenberg, Alic, and Wial (1998), but a certain nostalgia for the so-called golden era of the 1940s and 1950s is widespread in the industrial relations literature. One issue not addressed in this literature is "golden" for whom?

[2] *Taylorist* refers to the ideas of Frederick Winslow Taylor. His system of management, called Taylorism, was originally described and publicized in his book *The*

Principles of Scientific Management (1911). It quickly became the dominant managerial philosophy of its time.

[3] At the same time, Taylorist techniques are by no means becoming entirely obsolete. In the case of electronics assembly, garment work, and even auto-parts manufacturing, "hyper-Taylorism"—that is, an extreme fragmentation and deskilling of jobs—is perhaps the more dominant trend (MacDonald 1991; Graham 1995).

[4] Despite many obstacles, various initiatives are under way to introduce worker- and union-run hiring halls, the most successful of which operate in a well-defined geographical area and confine themselves to a single sector, such as farm labor or telecommunications. For examples, see Vosko (2000b, ch. 8).

[5] Indeed, as Stone (1975) argues, the contract system among puddlers, unlike that among iron molders, was ended primarily at the behest of employers. The Homestead Strike of 1892, for example, a lockout initiated by the Carnegie Steel Works under the supervision of Henry Clay Frick, resulted in a disastrous decline of union power in steel and the replacement of the inside contract system with foremen and waged day labor.

[6] Like the construction unions, garment unions until recently enjoyed certain exemptions from both the Taft-Hartley Act and the Landrum-Griffin Act. These exemptions allowed the unions greater freedom to engage in concerted activities against employers and to fine and discipline their own members.

[7] There were those who argued that employers (those owning more than one team) should remain in the union for the sake of controlling the labor market and permitting "a thorough unification of our branch of industry" (*Proceedings of the Fifth Annual Convention of the TDIU* 1902: 15).

[8] To date, the IBT continues to include owner-operators, vender-drivers, and owner-equipment drivers in its membership, based on a membership clause reminiscent of that adopted in 1940 (IBT Constitution and Bylaws 1991: 6–7).

[9] See Justice Souter's majority opinion in the recent Supreme Court decision *Nationwide Mutual Insurance Co. v. Darden,* 503 US 318 (1992).

References

Appelbaum, Eileen, and Rosemary Batt. 1994. *The New American Workplace: Transforming Work Systems in the United States.* Ithaca, NY: Cornell University Press.

Ashworth, John H. 1915. *The Helper and American Trade Unions.* Baltimore: Johns Hopkins Press.

Benson, Susan Porter. 1986. *Counter Cultures: Saleswomen, Managers, and Customers in American Department Stores, 1890–1940.* Urbana: University of Illinois Press.

Boris, Eileen. 1993. "Organization or Prohibition? A Historical Perspective on Trade Unions and Homework." In Dorothy Sue Cobble, ed., *Women and Unions: Forging a Partnership.* Ithaca, NY: Cornell University Press, ILR Press, pp. 207–225.

Brooks, Adrian. 1988. "Myth and Muddle: An Examination of Contracts for the Performance of Work." *University of New South Wales Law Journal,* Vol. 11, no. 2, pp. 49–101.

Cappelli, Peter. 1995. "Rethinking Employment." *British Journal of Industrial Relations,* Vol. 33, no. 2, pp. 563–602.

Cappelli, Peter, L. Bassi, H. Katz, D. Knoke, P. Osterman, and M. Useem. 1997. *Change at Work.* New York: Oxford University Press.

Chandler, Alfred. 1977. *The Visible Hand: The Managerial Revolution in America.* Cambridge, MA: Harvard University Press.

Clawson, Dan. 1980. *Bureaucracy and the Labor Process: Transformation of US Industry, 1860–1920.* New York: Monthly Review Press.

Cobble, Dorothy Sue. 1991a. *Dishing It Out: Waitresses and Their Unions in the Twentieth Century.* Urbana: University of Illinois Press.

Cobble, Dorothy Sue. 1991b. "Organizing the Postindustrial Work Force: Lessons from the History of Waitress Unionism." *Industrial and Labor Relations Review,* Vol. 44, no. 3 (April), pp. 419–436.

Cobble, Dorothy Sue. 1994. "Making Postindustrial Unionism Possible." In Sheldon Friedman et al., eds., *Restoring the Promise of American Labor Law.* Ithaca, NY: Cornell University Press, ILR Press, pp. 285–302.

Cobble, Dorothy Sue. 1997. "Lost Ways of Organizing: Reviving the AFL's Direct Affiliate Strategy." *Industrial Relations,* Vol. 36, no. 3 (July), pp. 278–301.

Commons, John. 1909. "American Shoemakers, 1648–1895." *Quarterly Journal of Economics,* Vol. 24 (November), pp. 39–81.

Dunlop, John T. 1994. *Report and Recommendations: Commission on the Future of Worker–Management Relations.* Washington, DC: U.S. Department of Labor.

Edid, Maralyn. 1994. *Farm Labor Organizing: Trends and Prospects.* Ithaca, NY: Cornell University Press, ILR Press.

Estey, Marten. 1976. *The Unions: Structure, Development, and Management,* 2nd ed. New York: Harcourt Brace Jovanovich.

Fink, Leon. 1983. *Workingman's Democracy: The Knights of Labor and American Politics.* Urbana: University of Illinois Press.

Fraser, Steven. 1991. *Labor Will Rule: Sidney Hillman and the Rise of American Labor.* New York: Free Press.

Fudge, Judy. 1993. "The Gendered Dimension of Labour Law: Why Women Need Inclusive Unionism and Broader-Based Bargaining." In Linda Briskin and Patricia McDermott, eds., *Women Challenging Unions: Feminism, Militancy, and Democracy.* Toronto: University of Toronto Press, pp. 231–248.

Gordon, Colin. 1999. *The Lost City of Solidarity: Metropolitan Unionism in Historical Perspective.* Center for Labor Studies, Working Paper No. 8 (March). Seattle: University of Washington.

Graham, Laurie. 1995. *On the Line at Subaru-Isuzu: The Japanese Model and the American Worker.* Ithaca, NY: Cornell University Press, ILR Press.

Gray, Lois, and Ronald Seeber, eds. 1996. *Under the Stars: Essays on Labor Relations in Arts and Entertainment.* Ithaca, NY: Cornell University Press, ILR Press.

Grebelsky, Jeff. 1999. "Building Trades." Paper presented at the Symposium on Changing Employment Relations and New Institutions of Representation, Cambridge, MA, May 26.

Herzenberg, Stephen, John Alic, and Howard Wial. 1998. *New Rules for a New Economy: Employment and Opportunity in Postindustrial America.* Ithaca, NY: Cornell University Press, ILR Press.

Jackson, Susan. 1999. "Work in the 21st Century." *Rutgers Focus,* April 16, p. 8.

Kalleberg, Arne, E. Rasell, K. Hudson, D. Webster, B. Reskin, N. Cassirer, and E. Appelbaum. 1997. *Nonstandard Work, Substandard Jobs: Flexible Work Arrangements in the U.S.* Washington, DC: Economic Policy Institute.

Kessler-Harris, Alice. 1982. *Out to Work: A History of Wage-Earning Women in the United States.* New York: Oxford University Press.

Linder, Marc. 1989. "Towards Universal Worker Coverage under the National Labor Relations Act: Making Room for Uncontrolled Employees, Dependent Contractors, and Employee-like Persons." *University of Detroit Law Review,* Vol. 66, no. 4 (Summer), pp. 555–602.

Linder, Marc. 1992. *Farewell to the Self-Employed: Deconstructing a Socio-economic and Legal Solipsism.* New York: Greenwood Press.

MacDonald, M. 1991. "Post-Fordism and the Flexibility Debate." *Studies in Political Economy,* Vol. 14, no. 2 (Autumn), pp. 177–200.

Mazur, Jay. 1994. Testimony of the ILGWU before the Commission on the Future of Worker–Management Relations, July 25.

Medoff, James. 1993. "Middle Aged and Out of Work: Growing Unemployment Due to Job Loss among Middle Aged Americans." Washington, DC: National Study Center.

Milkman, Ruth, and Kent Wong. 2000. "Organizing the Wicked City: The 1992 Southern California Drywall Strike." In Ruth Milkman, ed., *Organizing Immigrants: The Challenge for Unions in Contemporary California.* Ithaca, NY: Cornell University Press.

Mills, D. Quinn. 1980. "Construction." In Gerald G. Somers, ed., *Collective Bargaining: Contemporary American Experience.* Madison, WI: Industrial Relations Research Association, pp. 49–98.

Montgomery, David. 1979. *Workers Control in America.* Cambridge: Cambridge University Press.

Morse, Dean. 1969. *The Peripheral Worker.* New York: Columbia University Press.

Nelson, Bruce. 1988. *Workers on the Waterfront: Seamen, Longshoremen, and Unionism in the 1930s.* Urbana: University of Illinois Press.

Nelson, Daniel. 1995. *Managers and Workers,* 2nd ed. Madison: University of Wisconsin.

Piore, Michael, and Charles Sabel. 1984. *The Second Industrial Divide: Possibilities for Prosperity.* New York: Basic Books.

Porter, Shirley, Keith Porter, and Christine Bennett. 1999. "Be Your Own Boss." *National Business Employment Weekly,* May 2–8, pp. 11–12.

Rubenstein, Saul, Michael Bennett, and Thomas Kochan. 1993. "The Saturn Partnership: Co-management and the Reinvention of the Local Union." In Bruce Kaufman and Morris M. Kleiner, eds., *Employee Representation: Alternatives and Future Directions.* Madison, WI: Industrial Relations Research Association, pp. 339–369.

Spalter-Roth, Roberta, and Heidi Hartmann. 1998. "Gauging the Consequences for Gender Relations, Pay Equity, and the Public Purse." In Kathleen Barker and Kathleen Christensen, eds., *Contingent Work: American Employment Relations in Transition.* Ithaca, NY: Cornell University Press, pp. 69–103.

Stone, Katherine. 1975. "The Origins of Job Structures in the Steel Industry." In Richard C. Edwards et al., eds., *Labor Market Segmentation.* Lexington, MA: Lexington Books.

Vosko, Leah F. 1997. "Legitimizing the Triangular Employment Relationship: Emerging International Labour Standards from a Comparative Perspective." *Comparative Labor Law and Policy Journal*, Vol. 19, no. 1 (Fall), pp. 43–77.

Vosko, Leah F. 2000a. "Gender Differentiation and the Standard/Non-standard Employment Distinction: A Genealogy of Policy Interventions, Post World War II–Present." In Danielle Juteau, ed., *Social Differentiation in Canada*. Montreal and Toronto: University of Toronto Press, University of Montreal Press.

Vosko, Leah F. 2000b. *Temporary Work: The Gendered Rise of a Precarious Employment Relationship*. Toronto: University of Toronto Press.

Vosko, Leah F., and Judy Fudge. 2000. "Prospects for the Current Legal and Legislative Framework." In R. Chaykowski and A. Starkman, eds., *Labour Policy in the New Millennium*. Toronto: University of Toronto Press.

Witwer, David Scott. 1994. "Corruption and Reform in the Teamsters Union, 1898–1991." Diss., Brown University.

Zuboff, Shoshana. 1988. *In the Age of the Smart Machine: The Future of Work and Power*. New York: Basic Books.

CHAPTER 11

Looking for Leverage
in a Fluid World: Innovative Responses
to Temporary and Contracted Work

FRANÇOISE CARRÉ
Radcliffe Public Policy Center, Harvard University

PAMELA JOSHI
Brandeis University

Introduction

The U.S. labor market now includes many workers in nonstandard employment arrangements. In this paper, we explore how to facilitate job transitions, earnings maintenance and stability, access to protection under labor and social regulations, and access to representation for workers who experience instability in their employment relationships. We draw on case studies of 31 institutional innovations designed to meet the needs of nonstandard workers. Using telephone and in-person interviews, as well as documentary and literature searches, we prepared reports on each of these innovations. We developed typologies for the wide range of organizations initiating innovations as well as of the primary and secondary strategies they have devised. To the extent that workers in "standard" employment relationships increasingly experience employment instability, the innovations we consider have relevance that goes beyond "nonstandard" arrangements.

Two Groups of Workers with Related Needs

This paper focuses primarily on two groups of workers in need of increased economic security, opportunity, and representation. The *first* group includes workers in temporary and short-term employment arrangements that entail

- a tenuous relationship between the worker and the employer on whose site the work is performed;

313

- the presence, in many cases, of an intermediary firm (a temporary-staffing firm or placement service); and

- as a corollary, a separation between the nominal employer (or "employer of record"), who meets the payroll, and the employer at the work site, who controls conditions of employment (e.g., compensation and duration of assignment).

These workers may have either low or high skills and little or significant bargaining power in the labor market. Accordingly, their fortunes vary substantially.

The *second* group consists of workers who provide labor-intensive services to other businesses or public institutions (e.g., janitorial services) and to individual households (e.g., home health care). These services are usually low-skill, low-wage activities. Workers in these sectors are affected by

- competition based on contract price and, because labor costs are a high proportion of total costs and thus prices, intense pressure to keep wages and benefits low;

- low barriers to entry that result in employer inability to capture a surplus to reinvest in workforce training, benefits, or other expenditures toward improving retention; and

- small establishments, either because the firm is small or, when it is a large company, because employment is dispersed across small workplaces. These conditions make monitoring of employment conditions and worker access to union representation difficult.

We include this second group of workers in the discussion, even though they often are standard payroll employees, because many of their employment conditions parallel those of workers in temporary and short-term arrangements. Often the employer is a contractor to a public agency or a large private firm that sets contract levels that tightly limit workforce compensation. In some other cases, the employer provides contract services to households with limited resources, such as home health care services to Medicaid recipients.

There is a great deal of heterogeneity in the arrangements and experiences of workers in these two broad groups, but there are also shared experiences in terms of job instability, lack of mobility opportunities, limited—or nonexistent—benefits coverage, and frequently low wages. These adverse conditions underscore the limitations of the current system of employer-based social protection and work-site-based worker representation that are premised on the standard employment relationship.

What should be the goals of efforts to improve the conditions that these workers confront? Solutions are needed to reduce the risks to workers and to eliminate egregious abuses. At their best, solutions could reinforce the potential advantages offered by nonstandard arrangements, such as the possibility of exposure to a broader range of work settings and to a greater range of skills, as well as a reduction in dependence on the fate of a single employer. An added challenge for policy makers, unionists, and activists is to devise solutions in a political environment in which significant changes are unlikely in federal laws governing either systems of employment, social protection, or worker representation.

Workers in these two groups need labor market and social institutions that span employer boundaries and are not predicated on stable attachment to a single employer. Workers must find substitutes for the functions that regular employment and internal labor markets have performed and for the protection that related social insurance programs (e.g., unemployment insurance, health insurance, and pension) have provided to standard workers in the postwar period.

Workers in temporary and contracted-out arrangements are most likely to have the following needs:

1. Access to mechanisms for assessing their skills and experience that enable them to find other jobs. Information on job location and employer quality is also crucial, particularly for workers who experience repeated job changes. Over time, workers need mechanisms for skill recognition in order to be able to move across industries and occupations and to gain access to career ladders.

2. Access to training and skill development either on the job or during periods in between jobs. Currently, employers and client or user firms have little incentive to provide training to workers in temporary arrangements, although a few do offer training.

3. Improved benefits coverage, such as health insurance, pension, and access to childcare, in addition to higher wages.

4. Portability of benefits.

5. A voice in the negotiations of their conditions of employment.

6. A community of shared social, economic, and political experiences. The lack of community can be particularly acute for temporary workers

with shifting assignments and for private contract workers who provide services in isolation.

7. Additional support structures when their jobs are temporary or entail shifting assignments. For example, when the schedule or location of assignments change, people tend to have difficulty meeting their family responsibilities. This is particularly important because women are heavily represented in these arrangements (Polivka, Cohany, and Hipple, this volume).

Although these needs are shared by many workers in standard arrangements, they are particularly acute for temporary and contract workers.[1] Earnings and regular work hours are of special concern to contract workers in low-skill services. To meet these needs, new organizations and structures must span the boundaries of individual firms. For workers in regular arrangements, efforts to build industry-wide and geographically based training opportunities, skill recognition mechanisms, and job ladders are already under way (Dresser, this volume). For temporary, transient, and contract workers, innovative institutions are emerging as well.

The Study of Innovative Responses

At the Radcliffe Public Policy Center, we conducted exploratory research on emerging innovations that span firm boundaries and aim to meet some of the workers' needs outlined previously. During 1996–97, we identified and prepared case studies of 31 innovative labor market intermediaries (Carré and Joshi 1997).[2] We identified these innovations based on in-depth reviews of research, academic publications, and popular press articles, as well as recommendations of personal contacts and colleagues. We focused on innovations devised by a wide range of organizations in order to broaden the known repertoire of responses. These included, for example, community-based organizations, which often address the needs of temporary workers along with those of other workers. The nature of the innovations studied also generated new insights about problems faced by subgroups of workers in temporary and contracted work.

In open-ended interviews, we sought answers to two questions about each innovation: (1) How does the organization identify and define workers' needs? (2) What functions does it perform? The extensive use of multiple data sources enabled us to weigh claims, hopes, excessive optimism, and political insights. By design, the study struck a balance between breadth and depth. By gathering a broad range of innovations, we are able to illustrate the range of problems faced by this heterogeneous group of workers as well as the value of eclectic and mixed strategies for solving them. We did, however, focus on cases that were far enough along that we could document and evaluate the approach used.

To guide the reader through our case study findings, we developed typologies of organizations and of strategies (tables 1 and 2). The organizations that engage in these innovations include (1) for-profit firms, (2) unions and worker associations, (3) community organizations, (4) worker cooperatives, (5) public–private partnerships, and (6) information and organizing networks. As we shall see, these diverse organizations often adopt strategies that go beyond their traditional purview to address the labor market and representation problems of workers in temporary and contracted work. A corollary of this is that widely different institutions are acting in ways that are rather similar. For example, when unions build new placement services or "employment centers," they look like temporary-staffing services and aim to substitute their job-placement system for that of conventional companies. Similarly, when community organizations devise ways to improve job access, they also perform one of the functions of temporary placement services.

1. **For-profit firms** (see table 1): Some temporary-staffing firms have taken steps to go beyond the traditional activities of their industry. For example, they offer workers better terms of employment, sometimes providing health insurance. Additionally, a few temporary-staffing companies have developed business alliances with outplacement firms to provide temporary employment for job seekers while those individuals search for more permanent employment. The workers targeted by this strategy are usually mid-level managers, physicians, and other technical and paraprofessional workers who have been displaced from long-term jobs.

2. **Union-run innovations:** Unions operate in their traditional realm of action but also move beyond it to protect nonstandard workers. Sometimes they extend existing collective bargaining conditions to temporary, part-time, and contract workers (SEIU 1993). They may also negotiate new contractual terms for temporary workers along with provisions that allow temporary workers to access the benefits of regular employment.

Unions also have sought to form labor market intermediaries because of their long history of operating in sectors where employment is short-term or seasonal and employers may be small (e.g., construction,

TABLE 1a

Typology 1a: Innovations by Organizational Structure

Typology 1a Innovation	Private initiatives		Public–private partnerships	Union-based initiatives			
	Private corp.	Private co-op		Union/ conventional bargaining unit (company-based)	Multiemployer employee assoc.	Organizing efforts (not fully formed)	Community-labor coalitions
Adia–L. H. Harrison	X						
Atlanta Union of the Homeless						X	
BUILD–AFSCME					X		X
CAFE						X	
N.E. Campaign on Contingent Work–NECARC/UAW local							X
Childspace		X					
Co-Counsel	X						
Columbus Works–EP and Interim°	Alliance						
Cooperative Health Care Network		X					
CWA Employment Centers			Employment center				
CWA–AT&T AI program				X			
CWA–Bell South Utilities Operations				Union/mgt. subcontractor			
DARE							
HR only	X						

MacTemps	X				
Manpower–Drake Beam Morin					
Manpower–State of Wisconsin					
Michigan Works! Agency–Kelly Services				X	
New Hope Project					
New Ways to Work					
Osborne Group	X				
SEIU Local 100					
SEIU Local 509			X		
Campaign°			Goal°		
SE Regional Justice Network					
Southerners for Economic Justice					
Suburban Job-Link					X
TIRN					X
Working Partnerships		X			X
Working Today		X			
Worksource Staffing Partnerships	Goal°				
9to5	X		Goal°	X (Local ofc.)	

° No field report; categorization based on research in Seavey (1998) and Carré and Dougherty (1995).

TABLE 1b

Typology 1b: Innovations by Organizational Structure

Typology 1b Innovation	Community			Networks	
	Community organizations (multiple funding)	Community/ publicly funded programs	Individual-based employee associations	Information networks	Organizing networks
Adia–L. H. Harrison					
Atlanta Union of the Homeless				X	
BUILD–AFSCME		X		X	X
CAFE				X	X
N.E. Campaign on Contingent Work–NECARC/UAW local				X	X
Childspace	X				
Co-Counsel					
Columbus Works–EP and Interim*		X			
Cooperative Health Care Network	X				
CWA Employment Centers					
CWA–AT&T AI program					
CWA–Bell South Utilities Operations					
DARE	X				
HR Only					X
MacTemps					
Manpower–Drake Beam Morin				X	
Manpower–State of Wisconsin		X			

Michigan Works!Agency–Kelly Services					
New Hope Project			X		
New Ways to Work	X		X		
Osborne Group					
SEIU Local 100					
SEIU Local 509 Campaign°					
SE Regional Justice Network					
Southerners for Economic Justice		X	X		
Suburban Job-Link		X	X		X
TIRN		X	X		
Working Partnerships		X	X		
Working Today		X	X	X	
Worksource Staffing Partnerships		X			
9to5		X (national)	X (national)		

° No field report; categorization based on research in Seavey (1998) and Carré and Dougherty (1995).

garment, and food service sectors). Outside the realm of traditional collective bargaining, unions have sought to displace temporary employment firms or traditional subcontractors by opening their own "employment centers" or operating subsidiary firms jointly with management.

Mainly to lessen the pressure in labor-intensive services for firms to
compete by keeping compensation low, unions have also established
bargaining units that represent workers at multiple work sites or workers whose employers operate under contract to a single, larger corporate
or public entity. As another approach to raising labor standards in temporary and contracted work, unions have entered into coalitions with
community-based organizations to create information-sharing networks
and run public information campaigns or to work on living wage campaigns.

3. **Innovations by community organizations:** Some community
organizations from inner-city, minority neighborhoods run temporary
job placement businesses that provide access to jobs and may lead to
slightly improved wages and benefits. Also, some community organizations join with labor unions to form coalitions to bring about legislative
change.

4. **Worker-owned enterprises:** Worker-owned (for-profit) firms
have developed as "model employers" not only to improve wages, benefits, and training but also to provide steady work in sectors such as home
health care and childcare.

5. **Public–private partnerships:** Partnerships between temporary-
staffing companies and public agencies also have been formed. These
make use of the brokering capabilities that the private temporary-
staffing companies have because of their detailed knowledge of the skill
requirements of jobs and their experience assessing workers' skills, providing brush-up training, and matching workers with clients. Such partnerships have grown as states have implemented welfare reform. In
such cases, public agencies cooperate with private operators who find
jobs for recipients of public assistance who are subject to work requirements and time limits on benefits.

6. **Information and organizing networks:** Many organizations
(e.g., unions, community groups, policy groups, churches) use networks
to assist and mobilize workers in temporary and contracted employment. Multiple organizations gather into networks to develop common
analyses and consider joint action around a particular issue. The networks have been spearheaded by organizations as diverse as New Ways
to Work (a public policy information and consulting organization),

Atlanta Union for the Homeless (a community organization that focuses on mobilizing homeless day laborers), 9to5 (National Association of Working Women), unions and associations such as the Tennessee Industrial Renewal Network, Working Partnerships in San Jose, Southeast Regional Economic Justice Network, and Working Today (see table 1). Their scope may be regional or national.

Strategies

The strategies followed by these organizations are wide ranging. Many of them use more than one approach to identify worker needs and to meet those needs. In this section, we identify a few key strategies and provide some examples.[3] (Table 2 reports primary strategies.)

Job Brokering

By definition, temporary-staffing companies deliver "brokering" services to workers and firms, mostly for low-skill and middle-skill work. These services can shorten the time spent between jobs, for example, for word processing and light manufacturing assembly work. However, temporary agencies ordinarily offer, at the most, limited access to benefits and only restricted choice of assignments. The innovations described later seek to move beyond these traditional functions.

A number of unions, community groups, and temporary-staffing services now seek to become the temporary service of choice for both workers and client firms. In Southern California and Ohio, for example, the Communications Workers of America (CWA) operates "employment centers" that aim to provide better-trained workers and better matches of workers to jobs (duRivage, this volume). The centers find employment for displaced union members and for new workforce entrants. As part of their activities, the centers provide job referrals, skill assessment, and some training, as well as union representation, collective bargaining coverage, and therefore access to benefits for members who work a certain number of hours per year.

Community organizations also have established temporary-staffing services to enable low-skill workers from a particular community (often an inner-city, minority community) to get better wages, more regular employment, and more opportunity to advance (whether through new skills or access to a "good" employer with some permanent jobs) than is available through ordinary temporary services. One example is the temporary service run by Suburban Job-Link, a community-based organization in the Chicago area (best known for its "reverse commuting" program).

TABLE 2a

Typology 2a: Innovations by Primary Organizational Strategy/Action

Typology 2a Innovation	Compensation		Job matching		Sectoral			Legislative	
	Increasing wages	Improving benefit coverage	Job placement	Target poverty populations	Skills access	Access to career ladder	Job training	Living wage	Policy
Adia–L. H. Harrison Atlanta Union of the Homeless			T						
BUILD–AFSCME	X	X						X	X
CAFE									X
N.E. Campaign on Contingent Work–NECARC/UAW local			Goal°						X
Childspace	X	X							
Co-Counsel			T						
Columbus Works–EP and Interim°			T	X	X		X		
Cooperative Health Care Network	X		P	X	X		X		X
CWA Employment Centers		X	T/P		X		X		
CWA–AT&T AI program	X	X	T/P		X		X		
CWA–Bell South Utilities Operations	X	X				X			
DARE		X						X	X
HR Only			T						

MacTemps				T	X	
Manpower–Drake Beam Morin				T	X	
Manpower–State of Wisconsin			X	T		
Michigan Works!			X			
Agency–Kelly Services		Access	X	X	T	X
New Hope Project		Access	X	X	T/P	
New Ways to Work	X				T	
Osborne Group					T	
SEIU Local 100						X	Goal°
SEIU Local 509						Goal°	Goal°
Campaign°	X	Goal°				Goal°	Goal°
SE Regional Justice Network		Goal°					
Southerners for Economic Justice	X		X				
Suburban Job-Link	X		X		T/P		
TIRN	X			X			
Working Partnerships	X			X			
Working Today						X	Goal°
Worksource Staffing Partnerships		Access		X	T		
9to5	X						

° No field report; categorization based on Seavey (1998) and Carré and Dougherty (1995).

T = Temporary placement

P = Permanent placement

TABLE 2b

Typology 2b: Innovations by Primary Organizational Strategy/Action

Typology 2b Innovation	Provide worker voice				Public education		Influence employer	
	Union coverage/ worker assoc.	Worker ownership	Building coalitions	Info. sharing	Outreach projects	Document workers' experiences	Promote code of conduct	Develop list of model firms
Adia–L. H. Harrison								
Atlanta Union of the Homeless			X	X				
BUILD–AFSCME	X		X	X				
CAFE			X	Temp school	X	X	X	
N.E. Campaign on Contingent Work– NECARC/UAW local	Goal*							
Childspace		X	X	X			X	
Co-Counsel								
Columbus Works–EP and Interim*				X				
Cooperative Health Care Network		X						
CWA Employment Centers	X							
CWA–AT&T AI program	X							
CWA–Bell South Utilities Operations	X							
DARE								
HR Only								

	Goal°					
MacTemps						
Manpower–Drake Beam Morin						
Manpower–State of Wisconsin						
Michigan Works! Agency–Kelly Services						
New Hope Project						
New Ways to Work	X	X	X		X	
Osborne Group						
SEIU Local 100	X					
SEIU Local 509						
Campaign°						
SE Regional Justice Network						
Southerners for Economic Justice	X	X		X	X	
Suburban Job-Link	X					
TIRN	X	X	X	X	X	
Working Partnerships	X	X	X			
Working Today	X				X	
Worksource Staffing Partnerships						
9to5	X	X	X	X	X	X

° No field report; categorization based on Seavey (1998) and Carré and Dougherty (1995).

Another example is Columbus Works, Inc., an employment training and job placement program for disadvantaged young adults, which developed partnerships with two temporary firms (Express Personnel and Interim Personnel) to provide training and temporary employment (Seavey 1998). What these temporary firms bring to the partnership is their past experience with developing job access and with running skill assessment and training programs.

Some alliances between temporary-staffing services and outplacement firms provide temporary assignments to mid-level management and technical workers who lost their jobs because of downsizing, while they search for another long-term job. For example, the temporary firm Adia/Adecco established closer cooperation between its main temporary-staffing unit and Lee Hecht Harrison, its outplacement subsidiary, to provide integrated job search and temporary placement services to mid-level managers. These alliances operate on the premises that job searches for "long-term" jobs last longer than in the past and that a temporary assignment offers middle managers not only a source of income but exposure to new industries and occupations and the proverbial "foot in the door."

Some temporary-staffing services also provide brokering services to the welfare-to-work population. For example, Michigan Works!, a state agency, has collaborated with Kelly Services to assist job seekers making the transition from public assistance. Also, from 1994 to early 1997, Manpower provided lists of available jobs and employer contacts as part of a partnership with the Wisconsin Employment Service to facilitate job matches.

Higher Wages and Better Benefits Coverage

The most direct and effective, albeit often inaccessible, way for temporary and contract workers to gain improved wages and benefits is through union representation. Representation can be achieved through inclusion in an existing bargaining unit or forming a nontraditional, multiemployer unit. Examples of extending an existing collective bargaining agreement to temporary workers include two CWA experiments. The AT&T Administrative Intern program brings interns who rotate across temporary clerical assignments back on the company payroll and into the CWA bargaining unit. Thus, the program, which places about 180 interns yearly, is an alternative to the company's using outside temporary services. Temporary workers in this program also gain access to skill screening, training, and job-bidding rights, as well as to benefits and higher wages. The CWA–Bell South Utilities Operations is a jointly (union–company) managed subsidiary set up to substitute for external cable-drop subcontractors. The workers of this jointly managed subcontractor are now covered by a collective bargaining agreement, albeit with less generous wages and benefits than those for Bell South employees.[4]

When unable to include temporary and contract workers in a regular bargaining unit, some unions have sought to organize new, nontraditional bargaining units. Particularly with contract workers whose payroll employer has little market power (e.g., janitorial contractors), unions may seek leverage with the contracting customer. The customer may be a public entity (a state or locality awarding contracts) or a private company (e.g., a building owner who contracts out janitorial services). In one instance, garbage collectors employed by private operators who had a service contract with the city of New Orleans gained union representation with SEIU. They obtained wage increases as part of a multiemployer bargaining unit. The uniform wage levels achieved under these multiemployer bargaining agreements eliminate the tendency toward underbidding contracts, which is common when multiple companies seek to win contract awards away from their competitors.

Another strategy is to organize to raise the wage floor or to gain benefits in a geographic area through changes in public policy, such as the implementation of living wage ordinances at the city or county level. Such ordinances require government contractors and, in some cases, recipients of subsidies and tax abatements to pay a "living wage" well above the minimum wage. The best-known living wage campaign occurred in Baltimore, through the cooperation of the American Federation of State, County, and Municipal Employees (AFSCME) and Baltimoreans United in Leadership Development (BUILD), an Industrial Areas Foundation (IAF) affiliate. In addition to achieving passage of a city ordinance establishing a gradually increasing living wage level that private contractors must pay, the Baltimore effort has led to the formation of a multiemployer association of workers who get the living wage, AFSCME Local 1711, which includes the employees of many city contractors. Through this association, workers gain portable, albeit limited, benefits (coverage for drugs, eyeglasses, and some dental care as well as life insurance). The local union is also exploring the possibility of negotiating access for its members to training and opportunities to advance to better-paying employers.[5] Overall, this strategy has entailed making the fate of private contract workers who provide services under city contracts a matter of public policy. Living wage laws have passed in about 35 localities, including Boston, Los Angeles, San Francisco, San Jose, and Santa Monica; few, if any, besides Baltimore involve the formation of a worker association.

To raise compensation, unions have sometimes succeeded in enlisting limited cooperation from private firms that provide services under public contract. Unions seek voluntary recognition by these employers and aim to collaborate with them on lobbying efforts in order to achieve increases in public contract awards. In human service work in particular, employers and organized workers can lobby together for more funding designed to raise wages, lower turnover, and increase the quality of the service.[6] For example, SEIU in Massachusetts has sought since 1995 to join with private mental health and mental retardation service providers to lobby the state legislature for more money. The argument put forth by the union and its employer allies is that a collective bargaining agreement ensures that increases in state contract awards go toward wage increases, which have been shown to improve quality of care (Carré and Dougherty 1995). In Philadelphia, a recently initiated campaign spearheaded by AFSCME's United Child Care Workers Union seeks to organize childcare workers into a union and childcare providers into an employer association. Organized employers and workers could then make a case to the public and the legislature to raise public investment in childcare for working families.

A third approach to raising compensation, used by a few high-end temporary-staffing services, begins with the identification of market niches where clients will pay a premium for more-skilled and reliable workers. To attract and retain such workers, the temporary companies provide comparatively higher wages, better assignments, and access to group plans for benefits after a probationary period. The best-known case of this strategy is MacTemps, which primarily places workers with specialized software skills such as desktop publishing or editing. Other specialized high-end temporary-staffing companies are beginning to move in the same direction as a way of competing for workers with companies that offer standard employment arrangements. HR Only, specializing in the placement of human resource professionals, offers workers access to a group health insurance plan after they work 1,000 hours; the company pays 75% of the premium.

A fourth strategy for raising compensation is to offer affordable benefits to workers who pay for the benefits themselves because, as independent contractors, they cannot lay claim on any employer or end customer. This is the strategy adopted by Working Today, an association of independent contractors and freelancers. Working Today has formed alliances with professional associations of freelancers in several fields in order to build a portable benefit pool for a larger number of workers, bargain on their behalf for better deals with insurers, and build the political clout to influence policy (Horowitz, this volume).

Sectoral Strategy

Innovations that we call *sectoral strategies* provide job brokering and aim to improve benefits as well as wages for a targeted market subsegment, a specific occupation within an industry (Clark et al. 1995). Moreover, they combine this targeted approach with the provision of significant skill assessment and training not only at the start of employment but in an ongoing way. In the broadest sense, innovations that follow a sectoral strategy not only address labor supply issues but also aim to shape labor demand—how employers in the sector hire, compensate, and deploy workers. Some innovations aim to change low-quality jobs by operating as a "model business player" in a market segment. In so doing, they strive to establish industry standards for job performance, employment conditions, and product quality.

One type of sectoral strategy seeks to transform low-wage human service work by improving benefits, offering training, and facilitating worker ownership. In home health care and childcare, model worker-owned enterprises seek to demonstrate that they can be viable in these low-wage, labor-intensive service sectors while providing better jobs and delivering higher-quality care. Workers are often recruited from welfare-to-work training and job readiness programs, and their training is partially subsidized by public funds and charitable grants. The strategy aims to "stabilize" the workforce in a sector known for high turnover. One example from human services is the Cooperative Health Care Network (CHCN), a group of home health care, worker-owned cooperative companies including Cooperative Home Care Associates of the Bronx, New York. CHCN generates higher-quality jobs through relative stability in assignments and hours, benefit provision, counseling, continuous skill training, and worker ownership.

Another type of sectoral strategy entails providing intensive training for specific occupations that already pay higher wages and offer benefit coverage. For example, Focus:Hope, a Detroit-based project, targets technical occupations in engineering. This project relies on partnerships between community-based organizations and corporations to provide apprenticeships (in conjunction with college-level courses) and build career ladders to higher-paying occupations for young workers.

*Educating and Raising Awareness among Transient Workers
and the Public*

Information sharing is a key part of the activities of the wide range of community–labor networks and of the worker centers that have sprung up in recent years. Networks and worker centers document the problems faced by workers, as well as employer practices. They also run public education campaigns to reach workers in transient employment and to raise awareness among policy makers, legislators, regulators, media, and the general public about the difficulties these workers face. Their efforts may support specific campaigns, for example, a living wage campaign or unionization effort. One community–labor coalition, the Carolina Alliance for Fair Employment (CAFE), ran temporary-worker schools in 1994 to document temporary workers' experiences in the region and begin an organizing process. The public outreach efforts of Working Partnerships, a community–labor coalition spearheaded by the South Bay Labor Council of San Jose, California, helped to pass a law requiring companies that receive targeted tax breaks to disclose the wage levels and benefits of newly created jobs (Benner and Dean, this volume).

The sharing of information—research, policy options, innovative approaches—across organizations seeking to assist, and organize, transient and low-wage contract workers is also one of the goals of these networks. For example, national networks such as the one run by the National Campaign on Contingent Work (in 1999 renamed the National Alliance for Fair Employment, a coalition of community, labor, and policy groups) and a contingent worker project run by New Ways to Work from 1996 to 1998 have disseminated information about organizing, policy options, and legislative reforms under consideration.

Efforts to build multiemployer, geographically based career ladders for incumbent workers, such as those undertaken by labor, business, and community groups in the Milwaukee and San Francisco areas, also began with information sharing (Dresser, this volume). This step is important to the building of geographically based career ladders, which requires the systematic gathering of information about which occupations have shortages and about skill requirements of jobs. Such career ladders make possible enhanced mobility and improve the prospects for individual workers to remain steadily employed.

Raising Employment Standards

Some networks of unions and community groups have sought to raise employment standards through voluntary employer compliance, if

possible, or public pressure, if necessary. They have developed and publicized "employer codes of conduct" as well as lists of "model employers" in their regions. In New Jersey, the Temp Worker Task Force of the
United Labor Agency of Bergen County developed a voluntary *Temp
Agency Code of Conduct* and was successful in getting about 30 temporary-staffing agencies to agree to comply. Agencies that, in addition,
meet two other requirements gain recognition as "Best Practice Temp
Agencies" in a *Consumers' Guide*. Over 6,000 copies of the 1999 guide
were distributed. In a tight labor market, such a recognition makes it
easier to recruit temporary workers. The task force also reports temporary-staffing agencies that operate without mandatory county registra-
tion to the Consumer Affairs and Disability Insurance Court. Members
of the New England Campaign on Contingent Work have explored the
development and publicizing of a national code of conduct in collaboration with other groups in the National Alliance for Fair Employment.
The organization 9to5 (National Organization of Working Women) has
provided information to some temporary-staffing companies on how to
handle and turn down discriminatory requests—veiled or not—from
customer firms.

Other networks and organizations undertake employer "audits" of
the kind piloted by civil rights and research groups for employment and
housing. Volunteers affiliated with a member organization apply and go
to work for local temporary-staffing services and report any cases of
noncompliance with state or federal laws to appropriate public regulatory authorities. For instance, the Carolina Alliance for Fair Employment has been using this strategy to document violations of a state law
mandating employers to post or to notify workers in some other formal
way of the wage levels for job assignments. The Urban League has
explored the use of such audits in some large cities. Similarly, the
Workplace Project on Long Island calls attention to violations of the
Fair Labor Standards Act and to the nonpayment of wages to immigrant
workers in domestic work, landscaping, and day labor pools. It has
worked to compel state authorities to enforce the law.[7]

Expanding Worker Voice

Many of the innovations studied provide for, and strengthen, worker
voice. The representation structures in the cases in this study are diverse. They include Working Today, Direct Action for Rights and Equality (DARE, an organization of family daycare providers that pressured
the state of Rhode Island into paying for health insurance for providers

that deliver publicly subsidized childcare), union locals, and the Cooperative Health Care Network and Childspace, respectively home health care and childcare providers, both worker owned (see table 2).

Sometimes, providing worker voice is as elementary as furnishing a room where workers' stories about transient employment can be heard and documented, thus helping to identify patterns of transient employment in a region. The Temp Worker School run by the Carolina Alliance for Fair Employment helped workers to document their experiences and the difficulties they encountered in union organizing. In 1997–98, the "Temporary Employee Meeting Place" started by the United Auto Workers (UAW) and the New England Citizen Action Resource Center (NECARC) in the Boston area operated as a drop-in center, call-in service, and meeting place. Since 1998, this joint project has led to the New England Campaign on Contingent Work, a member of the National Alliance for Fair Employment.

Organizations and Strategies

The diverse organizations we have discussed do not all deal with the same worker populations. Innovations by for-profit companies as well as those by established unions tend to target higher-skill workers, while community organizations and alternative business structures such as worker-owned cooperatives tend to target workers lower down the job scale. Also, different types of organizations gravitate toward different strategies. Private for-profit temporary-staffing firms do not mobilize public opinion around the difficulties of nonstandard workers, nor do they actively seek to increase workers' voice. Yet all these organizations pursue strategies with shared elements such as job brokering or creating benefit pools. They all engage in some form of compensation improvement strategies. All, except for the organizing and information networks, pursue a sectoral strategy that relies upon knowledge about the market structure for an industry-occupation cluster. All engage in policy advocacy. Information and organizing networks as well as unions (whether fully formed collective bargaining units or associations) engage in developing mechanisms for worker voice, public information, and influencing employer behavior.

Research and Policy Implications

Our analysis of institutional responses to temporary and short-term arrangements points to several challenges for future research but also has some policy implications. One challenge future researchers will face, as we did, is to find proper boundaries for the subject. The forms that transient and temporary employment takes and its consequences for workers are in flux. The ways in which user firms deploy temporary workers have changed over time, as have the ways in which state and local governments use private contractors. Categories of work arrangements considered to be nonstandard tend to shift according to changing employer practices and employee needs. Researchers need to reevaluate how they define nonstandard work when designing a research project on responses to it and cannot rely exclusively on BLS definitions.

We see three areas that require exploration. First, many of the innovations previously described are relatively new. Some will fail; many will change over time. A fruitful research strategy would be to select a small number of enduring innovations, each involving a particular type of organization and strategy, and to conduct in-depth analysis of the evolution of that strategy. Second, the strength and breadth of networks developed as part of these innovations need to be explored. In recent years, much attention has focused on the formation of networks of community organizations in the community development and service delivery fields. These organizations also participate in more- or less-developed networks and, to a great extent, need to pool their limited resources. Comparison across these two fields may be fruitful.

Third, the outcomes of these innovations for workers need to be studied further and more rigorously. Questions exist about the capacity of these innovations to support different kinds of workers. Particularly important questions are: How well do they serve low-income populations in transient employment? Do they adequately address changing family needs? Do they take into account that needs vary for male and female workers and for different types of households? Innovations that ignore these issues are likely to be less successful. For example, we learned that the Cooperative Health Care Network found that providing help to their employees with handling clients is critical for service quality and job retention but that support in case of family difficulties such as childcare crises is crucial as well. One research strategy might be to study the families of workers involved with one or two of the most stable innovative programs, to learn how they handle job and hour fluctuations, care giving, and income needs.

This study of innovative labor market intermediaries also has immediate policy implications. Policy action should address the needs of short-term, temporary, and contract workers, such as the need for information about job assessment and job matching, access to training, portability of benefits, in some cases higher wages, and a sense of workplace community. Some observers question whether the intermediary organizations we studied can address these needs in a systematic manner. Clearly, a system of mandated and universal benefits and a fully formed and operational national employment service would go a long way toward resolving many of the labor market difficulties and the lack of protection experienced by nonstandard workers. However, the odds of such systems being seriously considered, let alone implemented, in the United States in the foreseeable future are small. In the absence of such national policies, the innovative approaches examined in this study point toward possible useful mechanisms for meeting workers' needs and deserve serious consideration. We also believe that, at a minimum, appropriate policy action can enable these organizations to act or remove regulatory barriers to their activities.

Areas for concerted policy attention include:

Modifying existing regulations that penalize some nonstandard workers. A regulatory framework that hinges on stable attachment between workers and firms penalizes temporary and contract workers. Regulations could be changed to allow portability of benefits within an employer-provided system but also to enable the formation of alternate benefit structures through unions and employee associations. Existing regulations concerning the roles of unions in hiring and training as well as the tax code regarding health and pension benefits should be altered. Independent contractors would benefit from the removal of the differential treatment in the tax code of their health insurance premiums, pension savings, and Social Security contribution. The unemployment insurance system, as implemented by states, tends to underserve workers with multiple assignments and variable hours. Ultimately, regulatory change will be needed to foster the formation and survival of risk-pooling mechanisms that are not employer specific nor, in some cases, even industry specific.

Encouraging the development of information-sharing networks and collaboration across organizations. Collaboration within and between organizations in different sectors can foster policy change through government and public support. Also, in the absence of labor market protection for transient workers, some will need protection from abuses of basic employment and safety standards. The enforcement of existing labor standards is more difficult when employment relationships are more tenuous. Access to networks will help workers gain information about employer practices, keep the public informed of egregious abuses, and help compel policy change. Federal and state governments can also foster labor–management collaborations for the formation of industry-wide, geographically based career ladders and of benefit and training pools.

Government support of workers in low-wage, transient employment. Such support could take the form of wage subsidies and access to most benefits such as health insurance and childcare. As welfare reform compels mothers to enter and remain in the labor market, many will find themselves in temporary or short-term employment. Difficulties with gaining access to childcare support and health benefits will be significant if not insurmountable in the absence of policy intervention. These difficulties are compounded by the irregular assignments that are common in low-wage work. As public policy moves from facilitating job access toward enhancing job retention, these concerns become salient.

Setting a floor on industry standards. There is a limit to the stability that organizations and firms involved in temporary and contract employment (such as worker-owned home health care and childcare) can create when they must continue to operate as "quality service providers" in low-wage sectors where most operators still compete based on low wages. Temporary and contract workers in some industries may benefit from barriers to entry to protect employment standards (e.g., bonding and other insurance requirements that protect worker compensation in case of bankruptcy and thus make it difficult for marginal companies to enter the industry). They would also be helped by government-mandated standards for compensation and working conditions and by stronger enforcement of such rules.

Policy action in these four areas would help meet some of the needs of workers most disadvantaged under nonstandard work arrangements. Some of these proposals have been implemented in part in other countries. All of these proposals would support, rather than compete with, the innovations we have analyzed here.

Acknowledgments

We thank Marianne Ferber, Lonnie Golden, Steve Herzenberg, Sandra Gleason, and the MIT Institute for Work and Employment Research seminar participants for their thoughtful comments. The research on which this paper is based was initially funded by a Russell Sage Foundation grant to the Radcliffe Public Policy Center.

Notes

[1] There is some consensus on these needs, broadly defined; see, for example, Benner (1996), Bernhardt and Bailey (1998), Freedman (1996), and Ontario Ministry of Education and Training (1996).

[2] Since we conducted this research, other innovations have come to our attention that are useful examples. They have been incorporated in the narrative but not in the attached typologies because the latter are derived from extensive case studies.

[3] Full details on the activities of these groups and businesses are reported in Carré and Joshi (1997).

[4] This statement was informed by in-depth case studies prepared by duRivage of CWA as background materials for Carré and Joshi (1997).

[5] See also Fine (1997).

[6] The goal of these efforts is to build cross-firm collaboration and thus cross-employer job ladders and training pools.

[7] See Gordon (1999).

References

Benner, C. 1996. *Shock Absorbers in the Flexible Economy: The Rise of Contingent Employment in Silicon Valley*. San Jose, CA: Working Partnerships USA.

Bernhardt, A., and T. Bailey. 1998. *Making Careers out of Jobs: Policies to Address the New Employment Relationship*. New York: Institute on Education and the Economy.

Carré, F., and L. Dougherty. 1995. "Improving Employment Conditions for Contingent Workers: The Massachusetts Community Care Workers' Campaign." Unpublished paper, University of Massachusetts at Boston.

Carré, F., and P. Joshi. 1997. *Building Stability for Transient Workforces: Exploring the Possibilities of Intermediary Institutions Helping Workers Cope with Labor Market Instability*. Working Paper No. 1. Cambridge, MA: Radcliffe Public Policy Institute.

Clark, P., S. L. Dawson, A. J. Kays, F. Molina, and R. Surpin. 1995. *Jobs and the Urban Poor: Privately Initiated Sectoral Strategies*. Washington, DC: Aspen Institute.

Fine, J. 1997. *Moving Innovation from the Margins to the Center for a New American Labor Movement*. Working Paper No. 97-001. Cambridge, MA: Industrial Performance Center, Massachusetts Institute of Technology.

Freedman, A. 1996. "Contingent Work and the Role of Labor Market Intermediaries." In G. Mangum and S. Mangum, eds., *Of Heart and Mind: Social Policy Essays in Honor of Sar A. Levitan*. Kalamazoo, MI: W. E. Upjohn Institute for Employment Research, pp. 177–199.

Gordon, J. 1999. *The Campaign for the Unpaid Wages Prohibition Act: Latino Immigrants Change New York Wage Law*. International Migration Policy Program Working Paper No. 4. New York: Carnegie Endowment for International Peace.

Ontario Ministry of Education and Training. 1996. *Contingent Workers and Their Adjustment Needs*. Ontario, CA: Ontario Ministry of Education and Training.

SEIU Research Department. 1993. *Part-Time, Temporary, and Contracted Work: Coping with the Growing Contingent Workforce.* Washington, DC: SEIU.

Seavey, D. 1998. *New Avenues into Jobs: Early Lessons from Nonprofit Temp Agencies and Employment Brokers.* Washington, DC: Center for Community Change.

Chapter 12

Building "Jobs with a Future" in Wisconsin: Lessons from Dane County

Laura Dresser

University of Wisconsin–Madison

In the mid-1990s, despite low unemployment, many young Dane County workers were stuck in dead-end jobs in small service establishments. To address this problem, the Dane County Economic Summit Council asked the Center on Wisconsin Strategy (COWS) at the University of Wisconsin–Madison to conduct an analysis of the regional economy and labor market. Based on its analysis, COWS recommended building industry training partnerships and career ladders in three leading sectors (manufacturing, health care, and finance and insurance). Efforts to build industry partnerships began with the identification of common needs, followed by attempts to fill those needs. In addition to improving the labor market for low-wage workers, organizers in Dane County hoped that firms would come to see that industry partnerships would help solve training and skill development problems. Drawing on the author's experience as research director of COWS and an active participant in building the Dane County partnerships, this paper assesses the potential and sustainability of industry partnerships in light of their ability to attract attention to industry needs from educators and trainers and in view of the weakness of unions.

Dane County, Wisconsin (population 400,000), stands out as one of the strongest economies in the nation. In the 1990s, the unemployment rate never rose above 2.5% (figure 1). For the last five years, it has been below 2%. With Madison at the county's center, the state capitol and flagship public university anchor the economy and provide a buffer from economic fluctuations. However, recent growth in Dane County has been driven by the private sector, especially high-tech services and manufacturing, health care, and business services.

Even with low unemployment, as the following examples illustrate, thousands of workers find themselves stuck in low-wage service jobs, with little hope of moving forward on the basis of skill or seniority. Take Mary, a 24-year-old single mother, who has been steadily employed as a clerical worker at a local company.[1] She still relies on Food Stamps, Child Care Assistance, and housing subsidies to make ends meet. She spends more than three hours getting to and from her job on public transit each day. Leila has a customer service job that pays less than $7.00 per hour and offers no benefits. She likes her co-workers and the skills she's learning on the job, but the wage is simply too small to support her and her family. Katie is a food service worker placed through a temporary agency. She works day shifts so that she can be home with her three children in the evenings but gets no health benefits on the job and brings in about $8.00 per hour. Mira has worked full time in childcare, and with a wage around $6.00 per hour, she can't make ends meet. Each of these women wants to find a better job and is looking for help to move up.

This is the underside of one of the hottest economies in the nation. Despite consistently low unemployment rates, earnings have been stagnant at up to the 70th percentile of the earnings distribution (COWS 1998; see figure 2). Perhaps more important, an analysis of state unemployment insurance data reveals that more than 40% of workers who start with very low earnings (below the poverty line for a family of three) still have very low earnings three years later.[2]

FIGURE 1

Dane County Unemployment, 1989-99

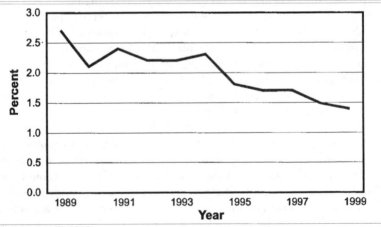

FIGURE 2

Quarterly Earnings in Dane County, 30th, 50th, and 70th Percentiles

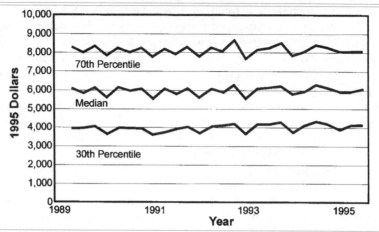

Source: COWS 1998

In the mid-1990s, Dane County leaders, especially the county executive, became concerned that prosperity was not being shared by all residents of the county. In response, they formed the Dane County Economic Summit Council. A blue-ribbon commission comprising leading public- and private-sector representatives, the council is seeking to improve opportunities for entry-level and low-wage workers. The council sought the support of COWS to help build systems to do that. Starting with a base of labor market and industry analyses, Jobs with a Future partnerships have been founded in each of three industries. These partnerships bring employers, labor, public educators, and human service providers together to discuss and act on common industry problems and collectively work to increase opportunities for entry-level and low-wage workers in those industries. This is the story of what has been built in Dane County over the last three years and an analysis of the lessons of that experience.

Solving Labor Market Problems

Even before COWS was involved in the project, civic leaders set their eyes on building "jobs with a future for all Dane County residents." They envisioned a "community career ladder" system that would lead to more orderly upward progression through tiers of employment. People on the lower rungs of the ladder would be able to look to a future of better jobs. Workers would move from entry-level employers (such as fast-food restaurants) to better jobs, increasing their wages and building skills as they advanced. This vision aspired to deliver to low-wage workers what many formally gained within large-firm internal labor markets: predictable routes of advancement to better jobs.

In working with employers, however, it became clear that such an orderly and logical progression was very hard to sell. Focus groups and discussions with them made it clear that, regardless of interest in such a system, few firms could really imagine themselves as the bottom rung of the ladder. Employers worried that the project's intent was to "take your best workers and give them to someone else." While in some other regions pilot programs with cross-firm ladder schemes continue, Dane County employers have yet to show much openness to the idea.[3] Given these difficulties, COWS and the Economic Summit Council began to refer to the "jobs with a future project" and dropped the "community career ladders" language altogether.

Moreover, from the start, COWS suggested that improving the opportunities for advancement of Dane County's working poor would require stakeholder partnerships organized on an industry basis to identify training needs and skill requirements. The advocacy for this structure grew out of experience in Milwaukee, where COWS had built the Wisconsin Regional Training Partnership (WRTP), a manufacturing training consortium. The WRTP's success suggested that industry partnerships could substantially improve labor market functioning and opportunities for workers. Additionally, simply linking jobs across sectors—for example, fast food to packing to machining jobs—does nothing to raise investment in training or encourage improvements in the organization of work. Improving labor market opportunity for low-wage workers requires attention to training and work organization as well as to transitions.

Industry partnerships are intended to build an infrastructure that improves labor market information and increases training opportunities consistent with industry demand. Improved labor market information can be used by public agencies to prepare workers for good jobs in the economy. Workers gain if the partnerships can produce a general increase in training, and firms gain if that training is more closely tied to actual skill shortages. The partnerships are intended to provide collective capacity to manage skills and workforce issues on an ongoing basis. They should help workers to learn where the jobs are and the payoff to different levels of skill. They should also help labor market entrants to find predictable routes to jobs that will enable them to support a family. Further, if successful, industry partnerships should help incumbent workers acquire training that leads to advancement.

The WRTP, which served as a model for efforts in Dane County, is a partnership in the Milwaukee area's durable manufacturing sector. To build it, beginning in the early 1990s, COWS worked with labor and management leaders in the area to identify industry problems and suggest collective solutions to those problems. The WRTP is now a consortium of some 46 firms employing nearly 50,000 workers in the Milwaukee area, with active committees overseeing incumbent worker training, workplace modernization, and future workforce development. The WRTP has built an infrastructure of workplace education centers in the industry, connected more than 300 central city residents to jobs in member firms, and worked on numerous modernization projects.[4] Led by labor and management representatives, the WRTP works closely with the public sector to ensure that the industry's needs are met. By presenting a unified voice regarding skills shortages, training requirements, and technology needs, the WRTP contributes to and improves the administration of public programs such as "school to work," the Workforce Investment Act (WIA), and manufacturing extension in the Milwaukee area.

In Dane County, COWS set out to build industry partnerships akin to the WRTP not only in manufacturing—where the high-productivity, high-wage path, if not always taken, is at least better documented and understood—but also in the service sector. Given low union density in Dane County, partnerships could not be built on a foundation of labor–management partnership within member companies. After quantitative analysis of local labor market conditions and focus groups and interviews with business and labor leaders, in the fall of 1996, three promising sectors were identified: health care, manufacturing, and finance and insurance.

The Dane County Jobs with a Future Partnerships

The health, manufacturing, and finance and insurance sectors together account for about 30% of Dane County employment.[5] To get information on current practices and needs in each industry, the COWS research team conducted two- to three-hour interviews with 12 to 15 human resource and training experts from the area's leading firms and issued reports at partnership kickoff conferences in the spring of 1997. The conferences highlighted shared problems in the industry and suggested that a partnership of industry leaders could be the first step toward building solutions. For these meetings, those who had participated in the survey were brought together with others from each sector to discuss the results of the investigations. This led to a series of discussions with industry leaders about shared industry recruitment, training, and retention problems and the potential of collectively solving those problems. After a summer of meetings, three Jobs with a Future partnerships formed. These have been meeting once a month ever since. They have focused on identifying occupational shortages and developing training so that incumbent workers can move into better jobs. Recently, all three partnerships have begun to concentrate on recruiting new workers and finding new ways to work with the Job Center to reach out to the area's working poor.

The Health Care Partnership includes three of Dane County's four hospitals, two clinics, three nursing care facilities, three home health organizations, and five unions. Together, these organizations represent around 10,000 workers. Currently, partnership activities focus on overcoming a countywide Certified Nursing Assistant (CNA) shortage and changing training systems in response to occupational shortages and industry restructuring.

Frontline caregivers do some of the industry's most difficult and poorly paid work. The job has traditionally been disconnected from pathways to more skilled work. While some CNAs may make their way to higher-skilled nursing positions, the schooling required makes this goal unattainable for most. The Health Care Partnership has been working to identify other occupational shortages, often in hospitals, in jobs that build on nursing assistant skills. These jobs can provide a pathway for frontline caregivers into better-paying work. The first success was achieved by working with the technical college to develop and offer condensed training in phlebotomy for CNAs (formerly, blood drawing was a part of the yearlong lab technician curriculum). Already three classes of 15 students each have graduated, graduates' wages and skill are up, and the area's hospitals and clinics are able to fill positions that used to go empty for months. Presently, new training programs for restorative aides and health unit clerks are being developed.

The partnership hopes that the success of these short courses will encourage the modularization of health care curricula at the Madison Area Technical College (MATC).[6] Industry representatives from the partnership have worked with leaders in the health division of the technical college, writing letters of support for programs and identifying supervisors and workers to help with curriculum development and serve as instructors.

The Health Care Partnership is also pursuing strategies to improve the quality of frontline caregiver jobs. As a first step, modeling an analysis of Pennsylvania nursing homes (Eaton 1997), COWS and the Health Care Partnership released a document on the high turnover of nurse's aides and some examples of best local practice to reduce that turnover (Dresser, Lange, and Sirkus 1999). The report shows that good wages and benefits, respect for CNAs, workplace teamwork, and two-way communication with supervisors correlate with lower turnover. Using the report, partnership members are reaching out to regional nursing homes and home health agencies to promote improvements in job quality for frontline caregivers.

The Finance and Insurance Partnership, representing approximately 6,000 workers, includes seven insurance companies, three financial institutions, and two finance-related organizations, with two unions participating informally. Its most noteworthy work to date has been the development of a training program that allows clerical workers and others an internal career ladder to programming and computer systems positions.

To date, students in two classes of 15 have been sponsored by their employers to become programmer trainees. The companies pay the cost of both the training and students' time in class. Most trainees are clerical and customer service workers that have topped out in their present occupations. They are selected on the basis of programming aptitude (not seniority). After a 16-week intensive course designed and taught by the local technical college, trainees move into their employers' programming department. This "grow-your-own programmer" approach appeals to companies that have to fill programming positions in a tight technical market in which companies are fighting over an insufficient pool of qualified candidates. Not only does this program develop a new source of workers, but the firms expect these trainees to prove more loyal than programmers hired on the external labor market.

In response to employer demand for additional training, MATC has also developed a Phase 2 program, in which Phase 1 program graduates will continue to upgrade their skills at an accelerated pace. In these courses, students also receive credit toward their associate's degree at MATC.

The programmer trainee project was the Finance and Insurance Partnership's earliest success, but local demand for programmers is now waning. So, too, is demand for the course, and the one planned for the fall of 1999 was canceled due to lack of enrollment. On the other hand, there is considerable interest among partnership companies in developing other new technical training modules for emerging technical fields.

More recently, the Finance and Insurance Partnership has worked with the Dane County Job Center to recruit and prepare workers for customer service positions. For the first class, candidates were recruited from the welfare and Food Stamps recipient pool. Companies and the public sector shared the costs of the 25 hours of training, and graduates were guaranteed interviews at sponsoring companies. This class was a learning experience for everyone concerned. Of 15 students who started, 10 completed it, and only 3 were offered customer service positions. Of the others, some are still looking for work in the industry, and some have chosen to pursue other jobs. There is, nonetheless, interest in repeating the class but with much clearer understanding between the industry and the Job Center on prerequisites for the class and better orientation to the nature of customer service jobs for prospective participants.

The Manufacturing Partnership consists of more than 15 area manufacturers and two unions. In its first years of operation, it devoted considerable resources to visits to the plants of participating companies, during which members of the partnership learned about one another's training and production processes. During one visit, the host plant highlighted its on-site ESL (English as a Second Language) classes for Latino and Hmong workers.

While the on-site ESL class inspired many firms, most partnership members are simply too small to be able to offer ongoing ESL training for immigrant workers. As a result, the partnership began to work on one shared ESL class, which was filled by three firms. The curriculum built upon the existing program with input from bilingual staff in participating companies. A fourth company participated in program development but found that it had enough students to run its own on-site course. Graduates from the shared training are already requesting more advanced manufacturing ESL, and co-workers are asking when the next introductory course will be offered.

Additionally, industry representatives have worked to more clearly describe their entry-level jobs and are collaborating with the Job Center to reach new groups of prospective workers. More than 25 prospective job seekers recently attended an orientation at the center, which emphasized the experience of frontline women workers at partnership firms. Each participating company brought one human resource representative and one current employee with shop-floor experience. Participants asked questions of incumbent workers, met the human resource managers of prospective employers, and filled out applications. One of the companies received 10 applications and made three offers at the event itself. Participating managers said the evening was much more effective than running an ad in the paper.

Lessons Learned: Filling Occupational Shortages

Industry leaders and the technical college have worked within the partnerships to develop new ways of addressing occupational labor shortages. Often, a fairly simple problem drives cooperation: smaller firms do not have the human or financial resources to support an entire class for training. They are therefore likely to be willing to develop a shared curriculum and send a few of their workers to the class. About 100 students—from programmer trainees to phlebotomists—have participated in training designed in response to needs identified by the partnerships. A number of lessons from this Dane County program may be useful to others considering building industry partnerships and career advancement programs in their own communities.

- Proponents of career ladders need to be clearly focused on solving pressing business problems. While the goal of project developers is worker well-being, the appeal to business must be based on a good understanding of the problems in the industry. An industry partnership is not the place to count on civic interest to motivate participation, though it can provide a nudge. Compelling solutions can be developed only out of real understanding of firms and jobs—skills required, occupational shortages, advancement possibilities, and problems shared by multiple firms. Unless outsiders quickly develop this knowledge, they will not elicit respect and trust from managers, who often face competitive and time pressures. Nor will managers take the time to consider how to improve the project. Without understanding different jobs and skills, it is difficult to make creative suggestions about career transitions. This lesson is important for community organizations, labor unions, and policy makers. Such outsiders often relate to managers in essentially naive ways, asking managers to make social or moral commitments that have no clear link to employers' bottom line. In Dane County, COWS continuously seeks bottom-line problems that can be solved through programs that advance workers.

- Partnerships can provide the infrastructure of relationships and trust that is required for building training programs. Simply networking with colleagues from other firms can build trust; managers often find it a relief to learn that others confront similar problems, that they are not alone. They appreciate the opportunity to think in new ways and learn from others' experiences. The partnerships have built relationships with and among firms so that new ideas can be developed and then "owned" by the group as a whole. Getting firms to try something new (such as building new career advancement systems) requires confidence in the people suggesting that new strategy and some confidence that a competitive firm pursuing it will not be "suckered."

• Trust among firms and between firms and public-sector partners, especially the technical college, has been another outcome of the partnership building process. The first time that classes are offered, confusion can ensue: when will the class start, who is sending students, what are the costs?[7] Given these problems, the fact that all classes to date have been offered at least twice (and have run much more smoothly the second time) is evidence of the growing relationship between the firms and the technical college.

• Once career advancement proponents have developed a good understanding of the industry, they must develop practical ideas on how workers currently without options (but with relevant skills) could be prepared to move into higher-level occupations that are experiencing shortages. Because of the pressure managers are under, they typically spend little time thinking about ways to increase the value of lower-end employees. They tend to concentrate on those with greater market or production leverage and seek to fill existing gaps in higher-end jobs through external recruitment rather than "growing their own." To promote career advancement opportunities for those in low-wage jobs, it is necessary to show concrete ways to accomplish this.

• Close collaboration with the technical college to support curriculum development and provide training has been absolutely essential. The contract training division of MATC was willing to develop curricula with industry representatives, prepare new courses, allow multiple companies to be served by a single contract, and become more flexible about delivery of training. Technical colleges do have quite a bit to gain from working with such partnerships, including connections and new means of marketing to smaller firms. At the same time, such projects do challenge institutional rigidities. If you are looking to build an industry partnership that will be an advocate for students and send them to classes, you need allies inside the key training institutions.

• Partnerships that are building career ladders can also provide the public sector with a more legitimate and informed employer voice in the governance of public employment and training programs. Individual employers who historically sat on regional and state governance bodies for training programs (for instance, private industry councils) tended to be ill-informed and have idiosyncratic interests. The establishment of training partnerships in major regional industries gives the public sector the opportunity to engage with more informed employers that truly represent the labor market. Those who set out to build partnerships in a regional labor market should seek to find ways to have information flow back from the partnerships into public systems.

The work on Dane County's partnerships has also provided a few lessons on balancing the interests of workers with those of employers and achieving short-term successes while pursuing larger, long-term goals. Such tensions are common, and there are no simple solutions. Worker advocates are generally concerned primarily with employee advancement and skill upgrading. They are usually interested in profits to the extent that they motivate managers to be interested in worker advancement. By including union representatives and nonprofit employers, it is easier to keep worker concerns on the table. So far, in Dane County, achieving this balance has not proven particularly difficult, but to the extent that the partnerships build their own identities and programs, the goals of founding advocates could receive less emphasis.

An issue of balance also occurs with respect to implementation. While COWS was needed to push the process forward, further progress requires that employers buy in to the program. At the end of partnership kickoff conferences, for example, COWS conducted a roll call of employers and asked whether they were willing to participate in a series of four meetings over the summer, given what they had learned at the conference. At the end of those meetings, COWS again called on employers to say whether they were in or out. In the partnerships, COWS has consistently tried to push projects forward, but it is the employers who initiate them. One human resources representative reported that what he liked most about the partnership was that these were the first meetings where industry was part of the process of building a shared solution. Getting business to lead on these issues required intensive external facilitation, nudging, listening, and writing.

The focus on short-term success (which motivates participation, builds a positive reputation, and keeps people interested) must be combined with a long-term focus on the health of the partnership. In the Finance and Insurance Partnership, a great deal of attention focused on the programmer trainee project, but the partnership was never intended to take on only information technology issues, and those without programmer shortages became alienated. Subcommittees and work groups are now used to keep the computer projects going, and the partnership has moved on to new issues, but some company representatives who found the original focus irrelevant have not come back.

Lessons Learned: Improving Recruitment for Partnership Firms

With unemployment under 2%, firms are constantly looking for entry-level workers. The partnerships work with the Dane County Job Center (Dane County's "one-stop" agency for employment and training services) to build pathways out of poverty-wage employment. Partnership firms offer higher-paying positions, more benefits, and more opportunities for advancement than the current retail and food service positions that many of the county's working poor hold.

Using surplus dollars from welfare programs, the county has funded the Job Center's Upward Mobility Program. County staff identify working poor adults, often Food Stamp and Medical Assistant recipients, many of whom were formerly on welfare. Counselors work with these clients on identification of skills and interest, career planning, and résumé development. Employer-services staff canvas firms for job openings and work on retention with their placements. When the project was just nine months old, it had successfully placed more than 80 Dane County residents in better jobs. The average wage increase for the new jobs is just over $1.00 per hour. Increases in health care coverage on the job are even more dramatic; only one third of participants had employer-provided health care before the program, but nearly all do on their new jobs.

It is still too early to judge the full potential of this program, but the response of participants and firms is promising, and a few lessons have been derived from this work:

- Moving people out of poverty-wage jobs requires information on where the better entry-level jobs are and how they are typically reached. Most policy makers and administrators lack good data on patterns of job transition, typical career paths, sectoral variation in wage and benefit structures, and so on. Furthermore, many workers have little idea of job requirements and wages, the ranking of employers on different scales of worker friendliness, or availability and quality of training. Partnerships can help gather such information (which usually requires supplementing government data with inside information from employer surveys and focus groups) and work with others to get the information to those who need it.

  The *Jobs with a Future Resource Book* has been one tool for overcoming the information deficiency in the labor market. This book provides industry overviews, worker profiles, and descriptions of companies that are partnership members. Released in January 1999, it has been widely distributed through a broad network in Dane County.

The copy at the public library is dog-eared from use. Schools use the information it provides about industries in school-to-work courses. Career counselors use it to show the range of employment options to their clients. Employers are asking how to get a page in it. COWS pulled together the first edition of the book, but employer-services staff at the Job Center are updating the next edition. A fairly simple document, it appears to be quite useful for job seekers, career counselors, and the participating employers.

- Information alone is not enough, however. Promoting mobility out of dead-end jobs requires targeting trapped workers and reaching out to them. Such people typically want to deal with somebody they know and trust.

  Staff from the Upward Mobility Program reach into the community through community centers and through caseworkers at the Job Center. When clients recertify for Food Stamps, county caseworkers provide information on the Upward Mobility Program. In a focus group, successfully placed Upward Mobility participants credited their success to support from these caseworkers. Unlike conventional program-funded staff, the Upward Mobility caseworkers can work in a very individualized way with each participant. For some workers, a lead on a job provides the solution. More commonly, however, they lack the confidence necessary to make a transition. The caseworkers encourage program participants but allow them to identify opportunities and move up at their own speed.

- Even with good information and strong relationships, workers may not really understand the opportunities in the labor market. Upward Mobility clients regularly come to the program with unrealistic notions about their abilities and the nature of various jobs. To counteract this, the Job Center and the partnerships have been conducting industry orientations for Upward Mobility. Additionally, the caseworkers are arranging "job-shadowing" experiences at partnership companies so that their clients can better understand their opportunities.

Participation in the Dane County partnerships has helped both the Madison Area Technical College and the Dane County Job Center redesign their services to better respond to employer demand. In the partnerships, the private sector is not treated simply as a potential recipient of services such as training or recruitment. Instead, the private sector works along with the public sector to craft new solutions.

The Shortfall of the Partnerships: Stuck outside the Firm

The work in Dane County models positive approaches for community colleges, job centers, and industries seeking new solutions to recruitment and skill development problems. A limitation has been that the main focus remains *outside* of firms. Negotiations focus on coordinating training resources, not redesigning jobs. In some instances, the partnerships have developed an internal solution (e.g., training current workers for occupations with vacancies), but filling current vacancies by training current employees for open positions is a far cry from actually increasing skill requirements across the board. For the most part, the partnerships have avoided getting into discussions of work reorganization, production modernization, or advancing work processes.

To have a real effect on the way companies deploy labor and on the opportunity structure throughout the economy, it is necessary to increase the general level of skills demanded inside firms, to build systems that increase incumbent worker training at all levels, and to modernize work processes. Though COWS has tried to facilitate work by various companies on such projects—within nursing homes and manufacturing firms, especially—there has been less progress on this front.

This stands in direct contrast to experience at the WRTP. It has three active committees—incumbent worker training, modernization (which deals with new technology and its effects on work organization), and future workforce development (which takes on school-to-work issues, as well as projects to connect disadvantaged workers with entry-level jobs)—with labor and management chairs for each. From the start, the committee for training incumbent workers has been one of the partnership's most active committees. Members are assisted as they develop workplace training centers and can learn about best practices in the region for designing and implementing workplace training. Labor and management teams learn from peers about critical elements and pitfalls concerning the training offered by and the administration of the center. The committee has also developed a curriculum for training peer advisors—shop-floor workers who inform and encourage their co-workers to take training at the centers.

The modernization committee works with the state's manufacturing extension partnership to ensure that area firms receive and effectively use state and federal support for technology upgrades and other productivity improvements. Two WRTP staff members serve as labor–management specialists for this program, working with management and workforce on the interface of work reorganization and technology transfer inside the plant. This depth of labor participation in the program is unique to manufacturing extension programs and a critical ingredient for success, for new technology always affects the organization of work and workers are often in the best position to know the specifics that can improve plant layout and job flow. In many WRTP firms, modernization and incumbent training advance together. The plant cannot change work processes without workers who can learn and adapt to new systems.

As previously noted, the Dane County partnerships have not reached inside firms so directly. Instead, their work has focused on cross-firm issues and training for jobs as currently organized. This has clearly improved the lot of some workers and increased investment in incumbent worker training in participating firms. It has had less direct effect, however, on the organization of work.

A number of differences between the capital-intensive manufacturing companies that make up the WRTP and Dane County partnerships' members may help explain their different outcomes. The WRTP has been operating since the early 1990s and has staff devoted to each of its committees. The Dane County partnerships have been operating more modestly and for just two years, and two of them are in the service sector, where the emphasis on work reorganization and incumbent worker training is more limited and the effects of such training on the bottom line less well documented.[8] Additionally, the Dane County manufacturing firms in the partnership are, in general, smaller and less capital intensive than the metalworking shops that predominate in Milwaukee and the WRTP.

Another important feature that has limited the Dane County partnerships to external problems and solutions is that unions are not a full partner of the project. Without labor union leadership at the partnership level and within participating firms, it is almost impossible to get inside firms and to initiate broad incumbent worker training projects. Such projects require an economic incentive or source of pressure that makes firms willing to invest in upgrading the skills of workers. Some union firms have an incentive because high, contractually negotiated wages generate a need for equivalently high productivity. Other firms and unions find worker training an issue on which they can start discussions of interest to both parties. In these ways, unions can increase firm commitment to worker training.

Effective incumbent worker training also requires good information from shop-floor workers. They have the most intimate knowledge of the content of work, wasted steps, and process problems. Without independently elected workforce representatives, companies must rely on their chosen informants for these details. Such informants may not feel safe to offer criticism. Because unions provide independent workforce representation and, often, greater security, they can contribute to making workforce training and modernization efforts more effective.

In Dane County, unions have participated in discussions and have in some cases worked actively on specific projects. However, unions have not been equal partners within firms and within the partnerships to the extent they are in the WRTP. As a result, the focus of partnership activities has been determined by business priorities. This has had some payoffs for a subset of workers and actually may have broader systematic effects in terms of curricular reform at the technical college. However, the fundamental problem of training and skill development for incumbent workers will not be solved without more leverage inside firms.

Can Career Ladders Be Built Anywhere?

New economic realities and the discouraging situation for many at the bottom of the labor market require consideration of new models for building training and skills. The partnerships provide some solutions to key problems in regional labor markets, especially the lack of training for workers and lack of good labor market information. In large part, this approach works because managers can come to realize that remedying these problems is critical not only for workers but for firms as well. The partnerships have attempted to find solutions that could meet business needs while also improving opportunities and wages for the workforce.

The models constructed in Dane County may be applicable elsewhere. Regions tend to have leading sectors that employ a considerable share of all workers and firms in those sectors that tend to confront a number of skill and training problems, whether they need more entry-level workers or are facing a shortage in a particular occupation. With some attention to detail and some creative ideas, those firms can likely be convinced that joint action to solve existing and future problems is in their interest. As long as firms have shared needs and are willing to search for innovative responses together, there should be some support for developing partnerships.

It is also important to note that even very small interventions can make considerable contributions, particularly in the realm of labor market information. For example, announcing the release of the *Jobs with a Future Resource Book*—which provided detailed industry, job, and firm opportunity profiles—brought a flood of calls, in part because workers are looking for more-detailed labor market information than they can find from reading job descriptions. Developing such a book is a relatively straightforward process, and doing so can help build interest in partnerships and systems of outreach.

At the same time, the tight labor market has contributed substantially to the success of the work in Dane County. Obviously, sustained unemployment levels below 2% push employers to seek out new solutions. If the economy were in recession, the interest in developing or sustaining joint programs for recruiting and investing in training would fade. Even in labor market slumps, however, occupational shortages tend to emerge, so some firms are likely to be looking for more effective ways to relate to public programs that can help solve the shortages. Thus, while interest in partnerships might fade as the economy slows, it probably would not disappear.

A further limitation of this approach is that in many sectors there are few jobs requiring higher skills and paying higher wages that could be linked with entry-level jobs. In food service, for example, there have never been many opportunities for advancement. In other sectors, such as health care, opportunities on the first rung of the ladder (e.g., home health aides) are increasingly abundant, while restructuring is eliminating midrange hospital jobs and thus some potential upward mobility paths.

None of these limitations render partnership development pointless. Partnerships should focus on sectors where leverage is high and at least some significant share of jobs pays well. At the same time, in the long run, countering the growth of inequality and improving outcomes for workers generally will take more than a series of regional industry partnerships. As long as business can readily hire low-wage workers, many will do so, and work reorganization to upgrade skills, wages, and opportunity will take place in only parts of the economy. Nonetheless, partnerships can demonstrate that improving jobs and training opportunities in local industries is possible and desirable. They can also help change the way the public sector responds to industry and, in so doing, improve the efficiency of training and support services. Last, but not least, if public policy shifts the incentives firms face away from low-wage strategies, partnerships may even be able to lay the foundation for larger-scale changes.

Acknowledgments

Thanks to Stephen Herzenberg and Marianne Ferber for their comments on earlier drafts of the paper.

Notes

[1] These cases come from a survey of working Food Stamp recipients conducted by COWS and the Dane County Job Center. Those who received the survey were invited to respond if they were interested in better work. All names are fictitious.

[2] These data come from unpublished COWS analysis of a 5% sample of the Wisconsin Unemployment Insurance wage record file.

[3] There is, for example, a Burger King in Michigan that refers its employees to an area manufacturing firm and is also seeking to partner with other manufacturers. Another example is a newly established Job Ladder program in Detroit. In it, participants move from tier 1 employers (often fast food) to tier 2 employers (banking and health care).

[4] For more on the WRTP, see Parker and Rogers (1996) and Neuenfeldt and Parker (1996).

[5] For more details on the process COWS used to develop the partnerships, see State of Wisconsin Department of Workforce Development (1999).

[6] The focus on training and advancement through the health care industry builds on some of the principles developed at the Cape Cod Hospital, where SEIU Local 767 and hospital managers have developed an institution-wide career ladder program. In fact, Bill Pastreich, a union leader at the hospital, presented the model at the partnership kickoff conference. While the work in Dane County does not exactly follow that model, it does mirror the principle of making incremental training and advancement possible within the industry.

[7] To varying degrees, the question of when the class should start can be most difficult. The technical college will not want to guarantee a class until they have secured enough students. Companies have a difficult time recruiting students for a program that has no clear start date. This is quite obviously a problem that is not insurmountable—the technical college can offer a contingent start date (e.g., given 15 students by date 1, the course will start on date 2)—but on the first run of each course it is always a problem.

[8] For other studies of service-sector projects, see Abrams et al. (1998).

References

Abrams, Jan, Dennis Bellafiore, Stephen A. Herzenberg, and Howard Wial. 1998. *Delaware's Financial Services Network: Case Study and Replication Guide.* Keystone Research for the Delaware Economic Development Report under contract #110-300-3071. Harrisburg, PA: Keystone Research Center.

Center on Wisconsin Strategy. 1998. *Dane County Labor Market Indicators Report.* Madison: University of Wisconsin, Center on Wisconsin Strategy.

Dresser, Laura, Dori Lange, and Alison Sirkus. 1999. *Improving Retention of Frontline Caregivers in Dane County.* Center on Wisconsin Strategy Briefing Paper. Madison: University of Wisconsin, Center on Wisconsin Strategy.

Eaton, Susan. 1997. *Pennsylvania's Nursing Homes: Promoting Quality Care and Quality Jobs.* Keystone Research Center High Road Industry Series, No. 1. Harrisburg, PA: Keystone Research Center.

Neuenfeldt, Phil, and Eric Parker. 1996. *Wisconsin Regional Training Partnership: Building the Infrastructure for Workplace Change and Skill Development*. AFL-CIO Human Resource Development Institute Briefing Paper No. 96-01. Washington, DC: AFL-CIO Working for America Institute.

Parker, Eric, and Joel Rogers. 1996. *The Wisconsin Regional Training Partnership: Lessons for National Policy*. National Center for the Workplace Working Paper No. 3. Berkeley: Institute of Industrial Relations, University of California.

State of Wisconsin Department of Workforce Development. 1999. *High Performance Partnerships: Winning Solutions for Employers and Workers*. Madison: State of Wisconsin Department of Workforce Development.

CHAPTER 13

Labor in the New Economy: Lessons from Labor Organizing in Silicon Valley

CHRIS BENNER
University of California, Berkeley, and Working Partnerships USA

AMY DEAN
*Working Partnerships USA and South Bay AFL-CIO
Central Labor Council*

Introduction

Workers today face significant challenges in finding and maintaining decent employment in a context of insecurity and rapid change, and this is particularly true of those in nonstandard employment relations. The rise in nonstandard employment reflects more fundamental changes in employment relations that are creating greater insecurity for workers in both nonstandard and standard employment (Cappelli 1999; Bertrand 1999). In the present environment of rapid change and complex outsourcing arrangements, the dominant forms of employee representation, which are based on the post–World War II industrial relations system, are increasingly ineffective. Hence, there is an urgent need to develop new models of representation that are more appropriate for our altered economic structure.

Silicon Valley, widely hailed as the leading global center of new information technology industries (Saxenian 1994; Castells and Hall 1994), provides an important context for examining possible new forms of employee representation. This region is at the cutting edge of innovation in technological and economic change and is seen as the harbinger of a new economy. New technologies and the management processes associated with them are often first developed and used in Silicon Valley and then extend into world markets or other economic sectors. Silicon Valley is thus a key laboratory for the development of emerging paradigms in work and employment practices.

Given such innovations in labor market arrangements, it is not surprising that new forms of flexible work—including networking, heightened mobility, and nonstandard employment—are prominent features of industrial organization in the region. The Silicon Valley region has two times the national percentage of the workforce employed by temporary agencies, with up to 40% of the region's workforce involved in nonstandard employment relationships. Rapid turnover has become the norm, even for people classified as having "permanent" employment (Carnoy, Castells, and Benner 1997; Saxenian 1996; Gregory 1984). Traditional forms of industrial unionism are poorly suited to this type of economic structure. Though unions are strong in traditional sectors in the region, they have almost no presence in the high-tech industry. The continued decline in wages for workers in some sectors of the high-tech industry, along with continued insecurity at all income levels, suggests a need for more effective models.

In recent years, the South Bay AFL-CIO Central Labor Council has played a crucial part in developing new roles for labor organizations in the region and exploring new models of employee representation. These new roles are centered around shaping regional economic development strategies to improve the economic circumstances of all workers while building strong coalitions with various other constituencies in the region (e.g., community organizations, small businesses, religious communities, environmental groups, etc.). The new models of employee representation are being built first to assist temporary clerical workers through creating an organizational structure that combines advocacy with training and placement services to improve their career prospects. Although still in their early stages, these strategies have potential applications in a wide range of occupations and industry sectors.

In the first part of this chapter, we present data about the pervasiveness of tenuous employment throughout the region, documenting the rise in nonstandard employment relations and the insecurity in more permanent employment as well. The second part of the chapter discusses the implications for employee representation and organizing. We briefly summarize the experience and lessons from both union and nonunion efforts to represent employees in the region. We then move on to discuss the role of the Central Labor Council in building the presence of labor in the region and in exploring new forms of employee representation.

Silicon Valley Labor Markets and Employment Relations

Silicon Valley labor markets are characterized by high levels of turnover and by complex subcontracting. Such a high percentage of the workforce is involved in nonstandard employment relations that such relations have become "standard." Even people in standard employment relations face rapidly changing skill demands, resulting in high levels of insecurity and stress. They frequently move from firm to firm and thus have relatively short-term ties with any single employer. These "open" labor markets are an essential component of the region's economy and of its economic success (Saxenian 1994, 1996). Some workers thrive in this environment—essentially trading increased risk for increased returns for their highly valued skills—but, as already noted, many workers face declining wages, uncertain career opportunities, and high levels of stress.

Nonstandard Employment

The extent of employment insecurity in this region is significant. Statistics on nonstandard employment there are particularly striking (Benner 1996, 1999).

Temporary employment. Between 1984 and 1998, employment in temporary agencies in the region grew 170%, while total employment grew 25%. Between 1984 and 1998, employment in temporary agencies grew from a yearly average of 12,340 to 33,850, growing from 1.6% of the workforce to 3.5% of the workforce. This is a rate that is close to two times the national average.

Self-employed workers. According to the U.S. Census, in 1990 a total of 52,000 people, or approximately 6.5% of the employed workforce of Santa Clara County, were self-employed—up from 5.9% in the 1980 census. This share is estimated to have increased further to over 7% by 1997 (Joint Venture Silicon Valley 1999), not including people who are classified as wage/salary workers but who are the sole employees of their own incorporated firms (see Bregger 1996). In Silicon Valley, adding the latter category would most likely increase the number of self-employed people substantially. The fact that in the four largest cities in Silicon Valley the number of single-employee business licenses increased 44% between 1989 and 1996, from 19,600 to 28,400, shows the extent to which such arrangements have proliferated recently.

Part-time employment. There are no specific estimates of part-time workers for Silicon Valley, but in California as a whole, 17.6% of the workforce was employed in regular part-time work in 1997, up from 14.9% in 1990. This is slightly less than the national average, but the pattern of growth and decline over time parallels the national figures closely.

Outsourcing. As already mentioned, the rise in outsourcing is one of the most significant trends in employment in Silicon Valley. By the mid-1980s, most high-tech firms had already outsourced most of their peripheral operations, such as building services and landscaping operations. In the 1990s, there was further rapid expansion in outsourcing a more diverse array of functions, including everything from payroll and human resource administration to manufacturing. The contract manufacturing services industry, for example, is one of the most rapidly growing segments of the high-tech sector, as original equipment "manufacturers" like Hewlett-Packard, Cisco Systems, and Sun Microsystems increasingly outsource their manufacturing functions to companies like Solectron and Flextronics (Sturgeon 1997). Thus, for a typical PC company, expenditures for components, software, and services purchased from outside have increased from less than 60% of total production costs in the mid-1980s to more than 80% (Ernst 1997). One proxy that has been used to estimate total employment in outsourced services is employment in the category "business services."[1] This covers a range of diverse companies that perform a large number of subcontracting services, including advertising; computer and data processing; consumer credit reporting and collection; and protective, building, and personnel services. In Santa Clara County, employment in business services has risen from 48,500 in 1984 to 132,100 in 1998, from 6.3% to 13.7% of civilian employment (Benner 1996).

Including all of these categories of nonstandard employment, between 254,080 and 389,770 people[2] in Santa Clara County in 1997—as much as 42% of the labor force—were in some form of nonstandard employment (table 1). During these years, up to 80% of the net job growth in the county was in nonstandard employment.

Other Signs of Insecurity and Volatility

As previously suggested, even people in standard employment in Silicon Valley face high rates of change in employment. Turnover rates in the range of 15–25% annually are not uncommon in large, stable high-tech firms, and the rates are much higher in the region's many small start-up companies (Gregory 1984; Saxenian 1996; Carnoy, Castells, and Benner 1997). While there are no accurate turnover data at the local level, we know that almost half of California's workers have been with their current employer for only two years or less, with the overall median job tenure no more than three years. Only 21% of employed adults in California had been with their current employer 10 years or more in 1998, compared with 35.4% for the country as a whole (Yelin 1998).

TABLE 1

Growth of the Nonstandard Workforce in Santa Clara County, 1984-1997

	Workers		Increase	
	1984	1997	%	No.
Temporary workers	12,340	33,230	159	20,890
Part-time workers	136,200	164,240	21	28,040
Business services	48,500	122,400	152	73,900
Self-employed	45,700	69,900	53	24,200
Contingent workforce, upper estimate	242,700	389,770	51	147,070
Contingent workforce, lower estimate	189,300	254,080	34	64,780
Total civilian employment	761,200	933,200	23	172,000

Source: Analysis of California Employment Development Department data.[3]

Similarly, there is also a good deal of insecurity among people who have not experienced rapid change in employment and who may stay within the same firm for a long time. The rapid pace of technological change requires constant skill development and learning, with fears of obsolescence ever present. Human resource managers describe skill "half-lives" of 18 months for skilled positions. Even employees who stay with the same employer for long periods of time face pressure and insecurity associated with rapidly changing requirements and pressures from external labor markets. In Peter Cappelli's words (1999, 33), "The fundamental characteristic of the real deal between employees and employers is that the relationship is no longer defined inside the company or described by internal development policies such as training, compensation, and promotion practices. It is now much closer to a market relationship in which the governance is outside the firm, in the market."

While many highly skilled workers thrive in this context of volatility, large numbers of workers who lack appropriate skills and social networks do not. An analysis of wage trends in Silicon Valley shows growing inequality because of significant wage declines at lower levels of the labor market. During the recession of the early 1990s, wages in the Valley dropped by over 10% across all but the highest part of the labor market (table 2). Despite some recent growth, wages in most of the lower half of the labor market remain below their prerecession levels when adjusted for inflation.

These declines are not limited to wages in low-paid service jobs but include those for production workers in core high-tech industries as well.

TABLE 2

Real Hourly Wage Rates: San Jose, CA, 1989-98 (1998 $)

Wage percentile	1989	1994	1998	Change (%)	
				1989-94	1989-98
90th	$32.84	$31.47	$37.05	-4.2	12.8
70th	22.49	19.77	24.20	-12.1	7.6
Median	15.52	13.94	17.01	-10.2	9.6
30th	11.82	10.09	10.54	-14.6	-10.8
10th	7.44	6.39	6.88	-14.1	-7.5

Source: Analysis of Current Population Survey (CPS) data.

Overall, earnings for nonsupervisory workers in nearly all manufacturing industries in the region have declined significantly since 1990, with wages in the industrial machinery (computers) and electronic equipment industries being below the average for the region (table 3).

TABLE 3

Industries with Declining Real Average Hourly Earnings, Santa Clara County, 1990-1998 (1998 $)

	1990	1998	Change (%)
Manufacturing	$17.07	$16.70	-2.2
Durable goods	17.22	16.89	-1.9
Fabricated metal products	14.07	12.87	-8.5
Industrial machinery	17.78	16.52	-7.1
Electronic equipment	16.96	16.19	-4.5
Transportation equipment	24.76	21.53	-13.0
Nondurable goods	16.19	15.30	-5.5
Printing and publishing	20.80	17.27	-17.0

Source: Bureau of Labor Statistics Annual Report on Employment, Hours and Earnings.

Thus, the picture that emerges from a review of employment trends in Silicon Valley is of high levels of insecurity and volatility across the labor market, with growing levels of inequality as well.

Worker Organization in the New Economy

How can the interests of workers be protected in an environment of such rapid change, and such temporary or tenuous ties between employers and employees? What is the role for labor and community organizations in this context? It is clear that our current system of industrial relations—which assumes a stable, relatively long-term relationship between employer and employees—is inadequate in this climate.

Therefore, while San Jose has relatively high union density in the public sector and more traditional industries, union representation in Silicon Valley's high-tech industry is relatively limited. Efforts to organize high-tech workers using traditional, work-site-based organizing methods have been largely unsuccessful. For example, in the 1980s, campaigns at Atari, Siliconix, and National Semiconductor failed to get enough support to have elections, while campaigns at Xidex and Raytheon failed to win a majority of votes when they did have elections. A combination of company intimidation and strong-arm tactics together with the threat (and in some cases the reality) of moving operations overseas contributed to the insecurity employees felt and consequently the difficulties in gaining collective representation (see Benner 1997–98 for details).

Although traditional organizing efforts have failed, some examples of more innovative strategies have achieved a level of collective representation for workers in the high-tech sector. Between 1989 and the early 1990s, for example, the Justice for Janitors Campaign of the Service Employees' International Union (SEIU) succeeded in getting the majority of janitors in the high-tech industry unionized through a campaign that depended largely on public events and media outreach and largely ignored the standard National Labor Relations Board election process (Martinez-Saldana 1993). A number of small guild-like unions—the Sign, Display and Allied Craft Union, the Graphic Artists Guild, the Tech Writers Group of the National Writers Union, and the Graphic Communications Industrial Union—have achieved a significant presence through improving members' skills and providing placement services or networking opportunities to increase their employment prospects. Employers are happy to work with these union members—in some cases without any collective bargaining agreement—because of their desire for a skilled workforce.

Outside of the union context, there is also a wide array of employee organizations and professional associations that provide some lessons for how to gain effective representation. The HTML[4] Writers Guild, the System Administrators Guild, and the Society for Technical Communication are just some examples of professional organizations that go beyond their traditional role of maintaining standards in a profession. They play an active role in shaping the region's labor markets by educating members about strategies for negotiating their own contracts, sharing salary information, networking with employers to provide improved career opportunities, and even providing legal assistance for grievances (Benner

2000). These employee associations, however, primarily focus on middle-
and upper-level professional occupations. They are also isolated and fragmented; therefore, while they may provide improved career opportunities for their members, they have had little impact in shaping the industry as a whole.

Thus, the lesson from the existing situation is that there is clearly a
need for organizations that can represent workers' interests across multiple work sites and help to build career opportunities for people. There
is also a need to connect workers across constituencies, linking concerns
about workplace issues with other concerns in their lives, such as the
high cost of housing, lack of good childcare, or poor transportation in
the area. This is essentially the strategy that the Central Labor Council
has recently been pursuing: building the role of unions in shaping the
regional economy and body politic on the one hand, and exploring new
forms of employee representation on the other.

Building a Union City

Starting in the early 1990s, the AFL-CIO Central Labor Council
(CLC) in San Jose began to build a broad program to increase the presence of the labor movement in the city as a whole. The central goal of
these efforts has been to position the CLC as a vital force by promoting
organizing among local unions, educating the community, mobilizing
community support for workers' rights, and building a stronger voice for
labor in the political arena. These initiatives have played an important
role in shaping the development of the AFL-CIO's Union City campaign (Dean 1998).

To reach out in these new directions, the CLC launched a new kind
of coalition—Working Partnerships USA—intended to build bridges
between organized labor and nonunion workers in the new economy.
This nonprofit research, education, and policy institute was established
in 1995 by the CLC in collaboration with a range of community organizations. It was an attempt to bring a wider range of voices to the table on
questions of regional economic development and to develop effective
responses to the changing structure of production in information technology industries. The overarching goal was "reinventing" the local labor
movement with an eye toward offering high-tech workers the representation and services they truly need. It has proved to be an effective vehicle for enabling organized labor to develop a more relevant voice—one
that resonates with working families as a whole, not just their own institutional base.

The activities of Working Partnerships USA break down into three broad areas: research and policy development, education and training, and developing new models of employee representation. The first two areas have played a key role in building broad support for working families. The third is beginning to make progress in developing innovative models of employee representation that can have an impact in the regional economy.

Research and Policy Development

Research efforts have focused on identifying and documenting issues that working families in the area are facing, ranging from high levels of insecure employment to growing inequality and a declining standard of living for large sectors of the region's workforce. This research has played an important role in changing public discussion in the region, shifting debates away from simply celebrating the economic success of the region toward addressing urgent social problems. The most important point about this agenda, however, is that it is integrally linked with action. Research and action are strategically connected in all activities of the organization, ensuring that the research findings have an immediate connection on the public-policy front. Specific campaigns were developed around challenging corporate subsidies (see LeRoy 1994), obtaining a living wage for city contractors (see Pollin and Luce 1998), redirecting redevelopment money toward poor neighborhoods, and developing a "Community Economic Blueprint" to guide regional public policy. The policy initiatives have helped to increase the visibility of the labor movement as a strong voice for *all* working families. They have helped to build coalitions and deeper political relationships with a variety of other constituencies, to give the labor movement a significant role in shaping the political direction in the region, and to represent the interests of working families as a whole.

Education and Leadership Development

The education and leadership development component of Working Partnerships includes a number of specific programs: (1) a nine-week leadership institute that provides participants with a deeper understanding of economic changes in the region and the political institutions that help shape the region's development; (2) an intensive leadership training program for members of neighborhood associations in San Jose, developed in cooperation with the Community Foundation of San Jose; and (3) labor–management partnership training, aimed at empowering frontline workers in their work sites and increasing the capacity and level of activism of local unions in the area. The courses are all run in an active, participatory manner, using the principles of popular education (e.g., Freire 1973). Together, these programs help to build long-term collaborations with a range of constituencies, by building a common vision of social justice and a deeper mutual understanding of the problems facing community residents. Simultaneously, they build the skills and capacity of community members to be effective leaders in a wide range of organizations.

New Models of Employee Representation

The Temporary Worker Employment Project is the Working Partnerships' activity that is most directly geared toward confronting the growth in nonstandard employment and creating new models of employee representation. It includes a placement agency and a professional association that brings temporary employees together to work on a variety of issues in which they share a common interest. These are the elements of the program:

- *Membership-based organization.* The Working Partnerships Membership Association affords people the opportunity to share experiences and strategies for improving their employment conditions. It helps break through the isolation that temporary workers face on the job and creates a sense of belonging in an organization of people with similar experiences in the workplace.

- *Advocacy agenda.* The purpose of this crucial component is twofold. One goal is to upgrade conditions in the temporary help industry as a whole by developing a code of conduct for temporary help agencies and monitoring its success through selective testing. The second purpose is to help create market niches in the industry for the Working Partnerships Staffing Group.

- *Placement services.* Working Partnerships Staffing Group is a worker-centered alternative to for-profit temporary agencies. As a nonprofit organization, it is able to charge employers competitive rates while paying workers a higher hourly wage. It also gives priority to working with employers who have demonstrated a willingness to move temporary workers into more permanent positions.

- *Benefits provision.* This program provides access to inexpensive health insurance, pension coverage, and financial services. People placed by the Working Partnerships Staffing Group have access to a $50-per-month health insurance program for families provided by Kaiser Permanente. Kaiser subsidizes this program and agreed to the terms because it gains experience in serving a population with no long-term connections with employers, which Kaiser sees as a growing market.

- *Training.* This initiative is guided by a regionally defined set of skills standards for clerical and administrative occupations, developed by a council of employers working closely with Mission Community College, one of the most highly regarded community colleges in the Valley. People can enter and leave the program as needed, so that workers have the flexibility to get training as needed and to take advantage of employment opportunities when they become available. An additional goal of the program is to develop a joint council of employees and employers to help review and modify the training standards.

The placement service targets particular occupations that have opportunities at the entry level with clear prospects for real advancement. The main focus is on clerical, administrative, and other office skills, though there are plans to expand to include health care workers or assembly workers and technicians within the next two years. In the clerical field, as workers gain skills, there will be opportunities for advancement from basic administrative and computer tasks to more sophisticated software manipulation; Web page design; HTML skills; and even programming, depending on the participants' abilities and interests. The goal is to create authentic advancement opportunities even for participants who start at the very bottom of the labor market. Many of the participants never graduated from high school and often lack basic skills needed to survive in the job market, while others had successful work experience and good jobs but were laid off.

Other programs include training in financial planning and legal rights as well as providing information about access to legal assistance and ergonomics. They also include regular monthly meetings, which provide an opportunity for networking and more information gathering. Such "secondary" training, information gathering, and networking are often essential for people to be successful in the labor market in the long term.

Another important function of the placement agency is the development of relationships with strategic employers in the region. The goal of this activity is to provide well-trained and motivated workers with in-depth support services to improve their retention and to help both employers and employees be successful in the long term. Further, this agency gives employers an additional incentive to provide decent benefits and to improve the chances for long-term employment of their temporary workers, because the agency will not work with employers unless they do so. Initial agreements have been obtained with over 80 private-sector employers who recognize both the value of the employees that are being placed and the social benefit of a nonprofit, worker-friendly placement service.

Given the experience of working with these employers, the goal is to continue to expand both to other employers and eventually to other occupations, relying heavily on the advocacy component of the project. Advocacy strategies will be used to discourage "low-road" competitive strategies—by both temporary agencies and their clients—while providing a realistic, worker-friendly alternative, at least in particular niche markets in the Valley, and rewarding employers who use this union-friendly alternative. The focus of this effort is to develop a code of conduct for both temporary agencies and their clients that provides basic protections for workers who would otherwise be extremely vulnerable. Agencies that endorse this code will be acknowledged in a guide to good temporary agencies, while those that refuse may become targets of public media campaigns.

The process used to develop the code of conduct is as important as its content. The initial draft was developed through consultation with a national network of organizations concerned with temporary employment. However, the final version was developed in consultation with a wide range of local organizations and an advisory board that includes a broad cross section of leaders from local labor, business, religious, and community-based organizations. Again, this participatory process is important for building in-depth support for the initiative.

A New Model of Employee Representation?

In sum, the Temporary Worker Employment Project has the elements of a new model of employee representation. Its significant components include

- *Focus on the regional labor market.* Organizations that can play a significant role on a regional scale help break through fragmentation and isolation of individualized employment relations while providing more flexibility and more opportunities for face-to-face interaction than national structures. This is important for building solidarity among members while developing sophisticated knowledge of labor markets.

- *Occupation- and sector-specific organizations.* These are structures that are not based in a single work site or a single employer but rather cut across multiple employers within an industry while coalescing around an occupational or sector identity. Such organizations provide a basis for solidarity among workers and improve their situation, even in the absence of collective bargaining, although that may be an eventual goal.

- *Membership-based structures not limited to workers who have a collective bargaining agreement.* Workers benefit from membership through access to useful training and other services as well as a sense of solidarity.

- *Strong focus on training and career development.* The aim is to improve workers' conditions by helping them move from dead-end jobs to better positions, often in other firms (see Herzenberg, Alic, and Wial 1998).

- *Combining advocacy and services.* Organizing and service provision go hand in hand. The advocacy agenda helps build workers' presence and power in the industry, while basic services such as placement and inexpensive health insurance are offered to workers who need them.

- *Social movement approach.* These initiatives are linked with a broader, unified movement to support working families in the region and to create prosperity for all.

At present, it is too early to fully evaluate the effectiveness of this model in Silicon Valley. The Temporary Worker Employment Project only began in 1998 and was not formally launched until the beginning of 1999. Nonetheless, within five months, the Staffing Group was placing four to six people a week in jobs that paid at least $10 an hour, and the association had more than 80 members. This initial interest suggests a strong potential for growth, and the project aims to have 200 active members and to have placed 250 people in jobs by the end of 2000. The ultimate success of the effort, however, will depend on the extent to which it can improve wage levels, employment security for temporary workers, the cost of health insurance and pension coverage, and employment practices of other temporary agencies.

In any case, it is already clear that this approach of positioning labor organizations as valued intermediaries within the labor market and moving beyond narrow work-site-based organizing and bargaining is a valuable strategy that holds significant promise for the future.

Notes

[1] This approach was used by Belous (1989). It clearly overestimates nonstandard employment in some ways since it includes people in the software industry, which is classified as a business service. However, it also clearly underestimates nonstandard employment since it includes none of the people in the contract manufacturing sector.

[2] Depending on the method for dealing with possible double-counting.

[3] Following Belous's methodology, the lower estimate does not count business services at all since it assumes that all business service workers are already counted in one of the other groups, and it counts only 60% of the temporary workers since survey data suggest that 40% of temporary workers are part-timers.

[4] Hypertext mark-up language (HTML) is the set of codes inserted in a file to allow it to be displayed on the World Wide Web.

References

Belous, Richard. 1989. *The Contingent Economy: The Growth of the Temporary, Part-Time, and Subcontracted Workforce*. Washington, DC: National Planning Association.

Benner, Chris. 1996. *Shock Absorbers in the Flexible Economy: The Rise of Contingent Employment in Silicon Valley*. San Jose, CA: Working Partnerships USA.

Benner, Chris. 1997–98. "Win the Lottery or Organize: Traditional and Non-Traditional Labor Organizing in Silicon Valley." *Berkeley Planning Journal*, Vol. 12.

Benner, Chris. 1999. *Silicon Valley Labor Markets: Overview of Structure, Dynamics and Outcomes for Workers*. Task Force Working Paper No. WP 07. Cambridge, MA: MIT Institute for Work and Employment Research, Task Force on Reconstructing America's Labor Market Institutions.

Benner, Chris. 2000. "Navigating Flexibility: Labor Markets and Intermediaries in Silicon Valley." Diss., University of California, Berkeley.

Bertrand, Marianne. 1999. *From the Invisible Handshake to the Invisible Hand? How Import Competition Changes the Employment Relationship*. National Bureau of Economic Research Working Paper No. 6900 (January). Cambridge, MA: National Bureau of Economic Research.

Bregger, John. 1996. "Measuring Self-Employment in the United States." *Monthly Labor Review*, Vol. 119, nos. 1–2 (January/February), pp. 3–9.

Cappelli, Peter. 1999. *The New Deal at Work: Managing the Market-Driven Workforce*. Boston: Harvard Business School Press.

Carnoy, Martin, Manuel Castells, and Chris Benner. 1997. "Labour Markets and Employment Practices in the Age of Flexibility: A Case Study of Silicon Valley." *International Labour Review*, Vol. 136, no. 1 (Spring), pp. 27–48.

Castells, Manuel, and Peter Hall. 1994. *Technopoles of the World: The Making of Twenty-First-Century Industrial Complexes*. London: Routledge.

Dean, Amy. 1998. "On the Road to Union City." In Jo-Ann Mort, ed., *Not Your Father's Union Movement: Inside the AFL-CIO*. London: Verso Books.

Ernst, Dieter. 1997. *From Partial to Systemic Globalization: International Production Networks in the Electronics Industry*. BRIE Working Paper No. 98. Berkeley: Berkeley Roundtable on the International Economy, University of California.

Freire, Paulo. 1973. *Education for Critical Consciousness*. New York: Seabury Press.

Gregory, Kathleen. 1984. "Signing-Up: The Culture and Careers of Silicon Valley Computer People." Diss., University of California, Berkeley.

Herzenberg, Stephen, John Alic, and Howard Wial. 1998. *New Rules for a New Economy: Employment and Opportunity in Postindustrial America.* Ithaca, NY: Cornell University Press, ILR Press.

Joint Venture Silicon Valley. 1999. *1999 Index of Silicon Valley: Measuring Progress Toward Silicon Valley 2010.* San Jose: Joint Venture Silicon Valley Network.

LeRoy, Greg. 1994. *No More Candy Store: State and Cities Making Job Subsidies Accountable.* Washington, DC: Institute on Taxation and Economic Policy.

Martinez-Saldana, Jesus. 1993. "At the Periphery of Democracy: The Binational Politics of Mexican Immigrants in Silicon Valley." Diss., University of California, Berkeley.

Pollin, Robert, and Stephanie Luce. 1998. *The Living Wage: Building a Fair Economy.* New York: New Press.

Saxenian, AnnaLee. 1994. *Regional Advantage: Culture and Competition in Silicon Valley and Route 128.* Cambridge, MA: Harvard University Press.

Saxenian, AnnaLee. 1996. "Beyond Boundaries: Open Labor Markets and Learning in Silicon Valley." In Michael Arthur and Denise Rousseau, eds., *The Boundaryless Career.* New York: Oxford University Press.

Sturgeon, Tim. 1997. *Turnkey Production Networks: A New American Model of Industrial Organization?* BRIE Working Paper No. 92A. Berkeley: Berkeley Roundtable on the International Economy, University of California.

Yelin, Ed. 1998. *California Work and Health Survey—1998.* San Francisco: University of California Institute for Health Policy Studies.

CHAPTER 14

CWA's Organizing Strategies: Transforming Contract Work into Union Jobs

VIRGINIA L. DURIVAGE
United Food and Commercial Workers Union

The Communications Workers of America (CWA) currently represents nearly 630,000 workers in telecommunications, printing and publishing, the media, passenger service, and the public sector. Within these industries, mergers, converging technologies, and deregulation have unraveled traditional employment relationships between information workers and their employers and ushered in the growth of nonunion and nonstandard employment. In response, CWA has fashioned a variety of strategies to organize and represent contingent workers in the information industries.

The employment center concept is one of several strategies employed by the CWA, along with negotiating new contract language to bring subcontracted workers back into the bargaining unit and increasing the CWA's efforts to organize new sectors, to improve the working conditions of nonstandard workers and to increase CWA's union representation within the information services industries. This paper examines two particular efforts within CWA to improve nonstandard work: (1) CWA's experiments with employment centers and (2) organizing high-tech temporary workers at Microsoft.

The Growth of Nonstandard Work within the Information Sector

Where once there were four distinct information industries of voice, data, text, and video with union representation centered within an individual company, these same industries today are converging and delivering services through wire, wireless, and/or cable networks. Over the past two years alone, as a result of further deregulation within the telecommunications industry, there has been more than 400 billion dollars' worth of mergers and acquisitions involving American telecommunications firms. Telephone companies that were 80% unionized are brokering deals with cable companies with fewer than 5% unionized workers and wireless companies with less than a 1% unionization rate. As a result, union power within the industry has been diluted. For example, in 1984, about 65% of AT&T's 300,000 employees were unionized. By 1995, after a decade of deregulation, the percentage of unionized employees had dropped to 43%. While job loss in unionized sectors often explains changes in the percentage of union-represented workers within a company, at AT&T, job loss within the traditionally unionized sector has been replaced with "look-alike" job growth in AT&T's nonunion subsidiaries, subcontractors, and temporary agencies. In addition, management in these nonrepresented sectors has often adopted an anti-union attitude that has increased the difficulty of organizing workers in these new locations.

The combined effects of subcontracting, industry convergence, and competition have created a ring-and-core employment structure within telecommunications where an aging core of union workers is surrounded by a ring of nonunion, often temporary or contract workers who are employed in subsidiary firms owned by AT&T and the Regional Bell Operating Companies (RBOCs) or in small- to medium-sized firms that have been established since the AT&T breakup in 1984. In addition, the use of nonunion contractors and temporary and part-time help has increased in every sector represented by the union. While the traditional union response to nonstandard employment has been to negotiate contracts that limit the use of temporary or contract labor, the phenomenal growth of subcontracting and competition have weakened the effectiveness of these approaches. In addition, new workers joining CWA are employed as part-time, temporary, or contract employees in other sectors of the information industry. CWA recognizes that to maintain its presence in telecommunications and to represent new information workers employed in nonstandard work schedules, the union must develop organizing and representation models that protect these employees and improve their employment relationships (Carré and Joshi 1997).

CWA Employment Centers

While pursuing organizing and collective bargaining strategies to unionize contract work, the introduction of CWA Employment Centers (ECs) is an innovative approach to improving nonstandard employment by providing employers with highly qualified, productive, CWA-affiliated (as opposed to nonunion) contractors. Equally important to the EC mission is to reemploy "surplused" or displaced workers formerly represented by the CWA.

During 1994, the CWA Executive Board approved two pilot projects to develop employment centers in CWA locals in Ohio and California. A third pilot, approved, but not yet fully developed, involved working with the National Association of Broadcast and Entertainment Technicians (NABET), an affiliate of CWA, to develop a national database for freelance employment within the broadcast industry. The goals of CWA Employment Centers are to offer workers displaced from permanent full-time jobs in the telecommunications industry and also people just entering the field the following benefits: (1) a dependable resource for locating employment, either part-time or full-time, regular or temporary; (2) a portable benefit package that includes medical and dental coverage, retirement savings, and training (apprenticeships); and (3) the opportunity to be union members. The benefits for employers include (1) a dependable resource for locating qualified workers, (2) relief from having to administer benefit plans, and (3) access to training programs for their employees.

Workers who find employment through the EC join existing CWA locals but may pay a different rate for union membership in recognition of their intermittent work status. Wage rates are determined by the local's collective bargaining agreement and depend upon the title classification of the particular employee. Unlike contractors employed by nonunion firms, EC workers receive pay equal to that of persons performing the same job under a regular union contract. For each employee dispatched by the center, the signatory employer contributes to a CWA benefits fund and an education and training fund.

Employment Center Locations

Each of the Employment Center pilots has been customized to fit the specific market conditions in which it is located and the particular needs of the local union and employer. For example, the center in Southern California involves collective bargaining with employers and referral of workers directly to the firm that hires them. This center has operated a modest program, with 5 to 20 workers who have been dispatched by the center employed at any given time. Some of these assignments have turned into full-time work. Recently, the TeleCore Company, based in Los Angeles, has also contracted with the California EC to locate skilled telecommunications workers for nationwide assignments.

A different model was adopted in Cleveland because employers did not want to carry CWA workers on their payrolls. As a result, CWA has entered a partnership with an employment agency, which is the employer of record. When the agency needs telecom workers, it is understood that CWA will furnish them. The collective bargaining agreement between CWA and the agency, although not as detailed as a traditional agreement, covers wages and other expense items as well as some grievance procedures, but it does not extensively cover job postings, job bidding, or vacations. Benefits have been structured so that funds are paid into a trust and a person's amount of employment drives the individual benefit level. Although some of the placements are clerical, most are technical, ranging in skills required from simple "wire pulling" to installing and maintaining sophisticated equipment, both residential and commercial. For example, the Department of Labor brought in 400 to 500 people for a short, one-time assignment to act as tellers for a Teamsters election. And a major telecom firm used the center to backfill positions left open by workers who transferred to other jobs as a result of an operator office's closing.

The recent merger with NABET has involved CWA in a field where there are a growing number of daily hires and temporary workers. Only some of these jobs have union representation. CWA is working with one of the larger NABET locals based in California to develop an employment center that can provide assignments and help to improve wages and working conditions for these workers. Currently, if a production firm does not have a collective bargaining agreement in place, CWA tries to secure a basic agreement that at least covers workers for the duration of their employment. Although this is only a modest advance, CWA's long-range hope is to represent all such workers, and it is currently trying to sell this idea to trade and industry associations.

EC activities may well expand further. Interest in the EC concept has been expressed by CWA locals representing workers at Bell South and by corporate personnel at telecommunications companies represented by CWA, including Ameritech and GTE. In addition, a New York CWA local that represents public employees has explored developing an employment center for white-collar and pink-collar workers in Manhattan that would offer office-support workers to both the public and private sectors.

The Need for State-of-the-Art Training

The employment function of the ECs has had only limited success. For example, a pilot EC launched in Seattle, Washington, in 1998 by U S

WEST and CWA, was shut down in 1999. U S WEST had planned to hire residential installation and maintenance technicians through the center for operations in Denver and Colorado Springs. One of the obstacles to providing needed workers on a supplemental basis is a scarcity of technicians with the requisite advanced skills. Employers want contract labor but want them to have state-of-the-art skills. And, in an effort to reduce employment costs, they are increasingly abandoning internal training. The CWA ECs hope to meet these needs through a joint labor and management effort that merges apprenticeship and training center functions with the dispatch and referral functions.

In Seattle, CWA and U S WEST have established such a joint apprenticeship program for about 200 apprentices from Washington state, with plans to expand the program from Washington into Arizona and Colorado. Initially, the program offered apprenticeships to existing U S WEST workers who did not possess adequate technical skills. However, few workers were interested, perhaps because climbing poles or laboring underground may not have seemed desirable to people not accustomed to that kind of work or possibly because starting an apprenticeship from scratch appeared attractive only to relatively young people. To make this option more attractive to in-house workers, the union is experimenting with bringing older workers and displaced workers into the training program at the appropriate level so that they can upgrade their existing skills. CWA is also exploring the possibility of offering ongoing training that will enable workers to keep up with technical changes in the industry.

In California, the union has set up a multiemployer program with approximately 40 apprentices. The 12 employers involved pay for part of the costs. Training is conducted at the EC site in Fremont. A similar CWA multiemployer apprenticeship program in Cleveland is now in operation. The union is talking with other employers where CWA is represented, including PacBell, Bell South, Bell Atlantic–New York, and the New Jersey State Public Workers, regarding the possibility of establishing additional apprenticeship programs.

In January 1999, CWA and Cisco Systems announced a new partnership to provide high-tech skills training to military veterans as part of a "military-to-work" program funded by the U.S. Department of Labor. Through online assessment testing developed by Cisco and CWA, veterans who qualify are matched with jobs at major telecommunications firms and other high-tech companies. Those who do not qualify are referred to appropriate organizations for training, which may include CWA's pre-apprenticeship programs and the Cisco Academy Certification program. Employers currently using this military-to-work program include AT&T, Bell Atlantic, SBC, U S WEST, Bell South, and Lucent Technologies. These companies report a desperate need for qualified technicians, both entry level and experienced.

CWA foresees a need to retrain and upgrade the skills of thousands of telecommunications workers to keep up with new technologies, and the union will start using Cisco training to meet these needs. Similarly, CWA has signed on with the International Brotherhood of Electrical Workers (IBEW) and other unionized telecommunications firms such as U S WEST, Bell Atlantic, and AT&T to develop a two-year, online, distance-learning course in telecommunications that will certify technicians for employment in this industry. The union has a dual purpose for this participation: to provide a means for CWA members to upgrade their skills and thus improve their employment opportunities and to attract new union members from the beneficiaries of these programs.

CWA is also involved in school-to-work programs, particularly in the state of Washington. As a member of the South King County Tech-Prep Consortium, CWA and the consortium received a $500,000 grant from the Department of Labor to teach high school students technical and other skills needed to make them employable and to meet eligibility requirements for apprenticeships. In addition, the CWA director of apprenticeship is building alliances with community groups that are trying to provide alternatives to gang life, unemployment, and poverty (interview with Paul Anderson, February 1999). Further, CWA is exploring the possibility of establishing links between apprenticeship graduates and the employment centers. At the same time, they are looking at school-to-work programs for the purpose of recruiting new union members. Part of this vision is informed by the aging of the current network technician workforce and the need to establish a new labor pool from which to draw future technicians.

Challenges to Expanding CWA Employment Centers

Organizational Pressure

For the union, working with the contingent workforce is a particularly sensitive issue. CWA has fought subcontracting and now is trying, in a sense, to become the subcontractor of choice. The notion of the union's providing the means for employers to use an incidental workforce has been difficult to accept for some leaders of CWA and for many of its members. This tension persists, and internal debates on the ECs continue.

Training and Skills Validation

Technical advances in telecommunications mean that many capable people are likely to become unmarketable unless they can update their skills. For ECs, important questions related to this issue include skills evaluation, validation to ensure a match between workers and available jobs, and training for both new entrants and experienced workers.

Validating the skills of experienced workers has proven to be a particular stumbling block in operating the existing sites. Even after the CWA negotiated favorable "buyouts" for workers with employers such as AT&T, PACTEL, and General Tel, there were still workers who needed or wanted to work to augment their pensions. As CWA Employment Centers evaluated credentials and dispatched workers when a job request matched skills on a résumé, it became clear that in some cases workers did not have the up-to-date skills required in that job today. This jeopardized CWA's credibility with employers. Now the CWA is building into the EC models ways to validate and certify skills. The apprenticeship program, approved by the Department of Labor, establishes standards that can also be used for screening. Additionally, as already noted, to be more effective for older workers, employment centers need to develop training that does not require them to start from scratch but rather allows them to build on existing skills. The CWA is also working with Cisco Systems to develop assessment tools to be used in their joint military-to-work effort and in retraining of the current CWA-represented telecommunications workforce.

Corporate Collaboration and Market Conditions

Because CWA ECs rely on procuring and maintaining hiring agreements with telecommunications firms, their success depends not only on market conditions but also on maintaining a working relationship with the signatory firm. This is a challenge to the tradition of both labor and management and has been a matter of much debate in both camps. As a result, the collaboration between these traditional adversaries, which the nature of the ECs requires, tends to be rather fragile. The current shortfall of skilled workers, however, has helped them to transcend traditional hostilities. But market conditions fluctuate. Therefore, if joint agreements to train or hire CWA members are to work in the long run, there must be a commitment to collaborate at the highest levels. These commitments are affected by changes within the industry and the organization. As corporations merge and revamp their internal functions and as market conditions change, such joint agreements become vulnerable. When corporate personnel changes and government priorities shift, so does the level of corporate and public funding. The development of the joint apprenticeship program in Seattle, for example, has been repeatedly stalled because of personnel changes at U S WEST. Similarly, the extent to which the union pursues a joint employment and training relationship with employers depends on continuing support from union leaders.

New Forms of Organizing

While the CWA continues to support experiments with the EC concept, it has renewed its commitment to organizing as its fundamental and most enduring tool for increasing its membership and improving the work lives of nonstandard workers in the information industries. In 1997, the union approved an amendment to its constitution that increased the union's organizing budget to 10% of total outlays. It has embarked on aggressive campaigns to represent nonunion workers at telecommunications firms such as AT&T and SBC and to pursue organizing among the growing numbers of computer professionals. Two current campaigns are worthy of note: (1) organizing workers under a newly approved neutrality agreement and (2) building an employee association for computer temps at companies like Microsoft that combines traditional grassroots organizing with electronic tools and with community and political pressure.

Bargaining for Neutrality with AT&T

At the CWA 1999 annual convention, Executive Vice President and Director of Organizing Larry Cohen reported that the union's most dramatic current campaign was to organize nonunion cable and other workers who became AT&T employees as a result of corporate acquisitions, including those at Telecom, Inc. (TCI), Teleport Communications Group (TCG), and McCaw Cellular, which became AT&T Wireless.

According to CWA research, AT&T is now the largest provider of cable TV systems. These workers, along with those in AT&T and local services and AT&T Solutions, outnumber AT&T union members in long-distance services. Most of the nonunion employees are technical support or customer service workers, like many CWA members at AT&T. In May 1998, CWA won contract language at AT&T guaranteeing neutrality in organizing campaigns in companies that AT&T acquires and wholly owned subsidiaries. The provision became effective July 1, 1999, at AT&T Wireless, Local Service, and Internet Operations. In March 2000, AT&T cable operators from the former TCI were also covered by this agreement. Recent "experiments" with the neutrality provision are promising. In June 1999, 118 tech workers at AT&T Local Services in Mesa, Arizona, voted for CWA representation; another 16 workers at AT&T Local Services in Kansas City voted for CWA; and in July 1999, CWA successfully organized over 100 credit representatives at AT&T Wireless in West Palm Beach, Florida, under the neutrality provision.

CWA's WashTech Campaign: Developing an Employee Association to Represent High-Tech Agency Temps

In July 1998, former Microsoft contract workers Marcus Courtney and Mike Blain, with the support of CWA, created TNG-CWA Local 37083, the Washington Alliance of Technology Workers (WashTech). According to union representatives, out of the nearly 19,000 employees working for Microsoft in Seattle, an estimated 6,100, or 35%, are agency employees. And of this group, close to one third have been on the job for more than one year. Organizing efforts are aimed not just at Microsoft but at the temporary agencies that control their employment contracts (Bernstein 1999).

Dubbed by the popular media as "permatemps," these workers are recruited by Microsoft and then referred to a temporary agency that assigns them to Microsoft and processes their checks. The company dictates which agency most contractors must use based on their job category. Also, most of the employment agencies contracting with Microsoft, such as Volt and Kelly Services, refuse to disclose to their workers how much they are billing Microsoft for contractors' work, although agency rates can range from $20 per hour for software test engineers to $100 or more an hour for programmers and developers. In a survey of 500 Microsoft contractors conducted by WashTech in early 1999 (WashTech 1999), over 90% stated that Microsoft contractors should be able to choose the agency through which to work.

Microsoft permatemps are working side by side with regular Microsoft employees, performing the same work, but without benefits or stock options from Microsoft. In the WashTech contractor survey, 79% of the contractors reported that full-time Microsoft employees earn more total compensation than do full-time contractors performing similar work. Further, permatemps are required to wear orange badges, which set them apart from regular employees, whose ID badges are blue. Even their e-mail addresses are different. (Their addresses begin with an "a" after the @ sign to denote their temporary status.) And they are not permitted to attend company parties, picnics, and sports events or to play on any company teams.

Two recent legal developments have facilitated the high-tech organizing. The first is a ruling by a U.S. District Court judge in July 1998 (*Vizcaino v. Microsoft*)[1] who found that workers employed as independent contractors and subsequently forced to work through temporary agencies were in fact common-law employees of Microsoft while working at the company between 1987 and 1990. The ruling in the class-action suit clarified which workers would likely be part of the class but left open the possibility that potential class members not covered under this case could be a part of future litigation. The case is currently in appeal, pending a decision on just what the classification should cover. Meanwhile, another class-action suit was filed in 1998 by a new group of Microsoft temporary agency workers seeking a court ruling that would classify them as common-law employees and force Microsoft to pay millions of dollars in benefits, including gains from the employee stock purchase programs.

The second event that gave impetus to union organizing was a Washington state law implemented in January 1998 after heavy lobbying by the software alliance there. This law exempts any high-tech employee paid more than $27.63 an hour from overtime pay. High-tech agency temps who average $30 an hour and work 60 or more hours a week are adversely affected by the law. Over 900 agency temps lobbied the state legislature against the bill, and WashTech emerged from this pool of activists.

In response to organizing efforts and the court decision in *Vizcaino*, Microsoft has effected a number of policy changes to more clearly delineate contract workers and avoid any future employer responsibilities toward them. In June 1998, Microsoft instituted a break-in-service policy that forces long-term agency employees to leave the company for at least a month before they can begin a new contract assignment. This policy, effective as of July 1, 1998, requires that agency employees who have held one or more continuous assignments at Microsoft for 12 months or more must leave the company for at least 31 consecutive calendar days upon finishing an assignment or ending a contract. In November 1998, the Contingent Staffing Group (CSG) at Microsoft stated that it does not want any contractors at Microsoft for more than 12 months without their working somewhere else in between. Microsoft is contemplating extending the forced break to 90 days.

According to WashTech, these forced layoffs do not indicate that these jobs are disappearing or that there is no longer a need for workers to do the work. Rather, the people who have been doing these jobs are simply being forced to leave the company for a period of time, and new contractors are being hired to replace them. To more clearly delineate the temporary agency as the employer, Microsoft has followed the court's finding that a contract worker's real employer is determined by who awards raises and has shifted that responsibility to the temporary agencies. In addition, Microsoft managers are now forbidden from formally discussing job performance with agency temps. The company has taken these measures to separate itself from any employer responsibility. Microsoft has also tried to insert new language into temporary agency contracts that requires temps to forgo any benefits that might be awarded to them in a future employment-related lawsuit. However, a federal judge immediately quashed this last action.

Through its mix of media outreach, which has garnered both state-wide and national attention in the popular press, and through its political lobbying, WashTech has developed allies in the Washington state legislature. In January 1999, Senate Bill 5583 was introduced in the Washington State Senate to improve some of Microsoft's practices. SB 5583 would have prohibited employers from terminating employees, limiting their contracts, or taking other action solely to avoid providing employer-based benefits to which employees are entitled under state law or employer policies. For example, it would provide unpaid family and medical leave to temporary employees who work for more than a year and prohibit language in their vendor contracts with temporary agencies that prevents temps from receiving benefits. This bill failed in the senate in March 1999. A second legislative initiative to improve the working lives of contingent workers was more successful. In April 1999, the Washington State Senate passed SR 8402, the Contingent Work-force Study Bill, which created a bipartisan task force to study Washington state's growing contingent employment. The task force will (1) identify the size, rate of growth, and demographics of the contingent workforce in both the public and private sectors; (2) examine the impact of the growth of the contingent workforce on the state and local economies and social services and specifically on workers' families; (3) review federal and state employment laws that provide for a different level of employee benefits based on the number of hours worked and employment relationship; (4) evaluate state and federal proposals to address the issues of contingent work; and (5) make recommendations to the senate based upon the task force's findings. One of the factors that influenced the decision to fund this study was a recent finding that in 1998 neither Microsoft nor the temporary agencies claimed to be employers of the contract workers, thus cheating the city of Redmond, Washington, out of about $260,000 in annual city revenue ("Tech Workers Testify on Contingent Workforce Bill," WashTech Legislative Update, February 5, 1999).

In addition to mobilizing media and political support for its organizing efforts, WashTech is the first unit within CWA to organize using the Internet. The group's organizers, skilled in developing graphical interfaces for employers such as Microsoft and Adobe, have used these skills to create an attractive, interactive Web site (http://www.washtech.org) that allows permatemps at Microsoft and other "Silicon Forest" companies to join the organization online. So far, 1,000 people have signed up with the Web site's list server, and a significant number of this group have paid electronically to join WashTech. The Web site is a critical organizing tool for this new generation of workers, as many of the computer professionals are isolated in scattered workplaces or work at home. The Web site offers them a virtual community, thus helping them to learn about new developments that affect them, to share their experiences, and to develop strategies for improving their work and their futures.

WashTech's goals include (1) establishing a workers' voice in any policy decisions, public or corporate, that directly affect high-tech temps; (2) making sick pay, holiday pay, and medical coverage basic rights that should be expected by anybody working primarily full time in this industry, whether a temp, contractor, or regular employee; (3) educating workers about their legal rights to organize, negotiate contracts, and share employment information; (4) providing information to the press, the government, and others in order to get out their side of the story about contract work in the industry; and (5) challenging the unbalanced nature of the agency–employee relationship, such as "at-will" contracts, restrictions on agency choice, and "non-compete" clauses in contracts.

WashTech is currently trying to form a high-tech workers' cooperative that would contract out their own labor and operate similarly to the CWA Employment Centers. The goal is to empower computer professionals who are tired of working for temporary agencies that take an exorbitant fee out of their pay. This cooperative would compete with other temporary agencies but would be owned and operated by WashTech, with fees divided between higher wages for contract employees and operating expenses for the cooperative.

At present, staffing companies who contract out computer professionals to Microsoft do not disclose agency billing rates. Nondisclosure allows the temporary agencies to charge a premium on every hour worked. Therefore, WashTech is currently circulating a petition in Washington state that calls on staffing companies to voluntarily disclose the markup rates they charge for workers' labor. In its survey of 500 Microsoft contractors in early 1999 (WashTech 1999), as many as 80% reported that they would support the creation of a worker-owned co-op.

In June 1999, WashTech petitioned four different temporary agencies (Excell Data Corporation, Volt Accounting, Kelly Technical Services, and General Employment) for bargaining recognition on behalf of 18 Microsoft contractors. According to a report in BNA's *Labor Relations Week* ("Union Asks" 1999), the 18 workers, who earn between $15 and $30 per hour, all perform similar work at Microsoft and have similar education, experience, and background. They thus constitute a community of interest as required under the National Labor Relations Act for bargaining-unit formation. WashTech and CWA have argued that Microsoft and the temporary agencies are co-employers, but thus far the agencies have refused to recognize the group.

In response to high-tech workers' requests, WashTech began offering classes in January 1999. They are one month long and cover such topics as JavaScript, Web development, scripting, database design, Web–database connectivity, digital design and illustration, and also career planning. The fees for these classes are heavily discounted or waived for WashTech members. The intention is to provide training that will help fill the gaps in what is offered by clients, agencies, or university and community college programs and help WashTech members to get up to speed quickly in targeted technologies. In addition, while such courses will undoubtedly serve the employers' needs for higher-skilled workers, they will also serve as organizing opportunities for WashTech and CWA. As is the case with CWA Employment Centers' involvement in education and training, WashTech's involvement in direct training expands the role of unions in workers' lives beyond that of representatives who bargain over wages, hours, and working conditions to that of trainers and job brokers.

Conclusion

In the past few decades, employers have dramatically restructured the employment relationship between workers and the firm. Prior to the late 1970s, unionized information workers could expect a permanent relationship with their employer that promised growing wages, benefits, and an adequate pension. By loosening their relationship, and thus responsibility, to their employees, employers have significantly reduced labor costs, increased workforce flexibility, and weakened the ability of labor unions to represent these workers.

Strategies to represent nonstandard workers require unions to adopt a proactive rather than a reactive approach to labor management relations. Initially, the Communications Workers of America responded to the growing contingent workforce by negotiating collective bargaining agreements that restricted the growth of subcontracting. But despite strong contract language, the growth of nonstandard work appears unstoppable. Consequently, CWA has created more aggressive and strategic measures to protect this worker group. In the 1990s, the union resisted the worst effects of industrial convergence and employment restructuring by revitalizing its commitment to grassroots organizing and reinventing old forms of labor control such as union employment centers. This expanded role may serve to strengthen the ability of unions like CWA to organize nonstandard workers and increase their power to improve their employment conditions and future opportunities.

Note

[1] In 1990, the IRS determined that Microsoft had misclassified workers in various positions held by independent contractors. As a result, Microsoft offered some of the misclassified employees jobs as regular employees and converted some to temporary agency employees. The common-law definitions of *employee* relate to factors used by the IRS to determine who controls the location, scope, and content of an individual's work and examine how many clients an individual contracts work with. On appeal of this case, the U.S. Court of Appeals for the Ninth Circuit ruled that a federal district court erred in narrowing the class of contingent workers who may be entitled to participate in the company's stock purchase plan. In *Vizcaino*, the appeals court judge ruled that the independent contractors who worked in positions that were reclassified by the IRS or converted by Microsoft were entitled to participate in the stock purchase plan both before and after conversion. Citing the common law of agency, the judge emphasized that a worker's status as an employee of a temporary agency does not preclude a finding that the worker is also a common-law employee of Microsoft. The judge agreed that it should be presumed that any person in a position reclassified by the IRS and satisfying the stock requirements—five months of employment at half time or more—is an eligible common-law employee, regardless of being converted to a temporary (see "Union Asks" 1999).

References

Bernstein, Aaron. 1999. "Programmers of the World Unite." *Business Week*, December 7, p. 49.

Carré, Françoise, and Pamela Joshi. 1997. *Building Stability for Transient Workforces: Exploring the Possibility of Intermediary Institutions Helping Workers*

Cope with Labor Market Instability. Radcliffe Public Policy Institute Working Paper Series No. 1, August. Cambridge, MA: Radcliffe Public Policy Institute.

"Union Asks Temporary Employment Agencies for Recognition of Microsoft Bargaining Unit." 1999. *BNA Labor Relations Week,* June 16, pp. 649–650.

WashTech. 1999. "More Than 500 Microsoft Contractors Respond to WashTech Survey." WashTech Special Report
<http://www.washtech.org//roundup/contract/ms_survey_summary.html>, March 23.

Chapter 15

New Thinking on Worker Groups' Role in a Flexible Economy

Sara Horowitz
Working Today

Changes in the structure of the labor market and the terms of employment in the United States are having a profound effect on workers and their families. How can worker organizations best respond to the dislocation millions are experiencing as the economy changes and the laws and institutions that used to shape our work lives erode? This chapter describes Working Today, an effort to strengthen worker groups and bring the nonstandard workforce into the discussion concerning new approaches to health coverage, pensions, disability and unemployment insurance, and protections that humanize the workplace. One of our first projects will be a Portable Benefits Fund that provides health insurance and other services to workers who are not attached to a long-term employer. I believe labor could readily adapt to the recent changes and create a mirror image of the flexible, decentralized, and interconnected business world. Therefore, our approach builds on labor history but moves beyond nostalgia for the days of long-term employment.

A New Class of Labor

Current labor laws and the design of our social insurance programs are based on the large industrial workplace of the 1930s and the assumption that most workers have steady, full-time employment with a single employer. In the new economy—in which, according to some estimates, as many as 36% of Americans work in nonstandard employment as temporary, part-time, contract, and independent workers—this assumption is no longer valid (U.S. Department of Labor, unpublished estimate by Bureau of Labor Statistics based on data from the 1997 Current Population Survey Supplement).

Because nonstandard workers are often not considered employees under the law, many of them are excluded from protections afforded traditional workers in terms of pay, benefits, overtime premiums, unemployment and disability insurance, and legal protections regarding employment discrimination. Also, they have little expectation of job security, training, upward mobility, or benefits.

Even their access to private health insurance and pension systems is limited because they are not connected with an employer and therefore face substantially higher rates and significant tax disadvantages. As a result, the ongoing changes in the terms of employment are having a profound effect on the number of U.S. workers with health and pension coverage.

Warren Gebert

Who makes up this new workforce? The ranks of nonstandard workers include many young people and other new entrants into the workforce; older workers who have lost their jobs or chosen to leave them; a disproportionate number of female, black, and Hispanic workers at the low end of the wage scale for flexible work; and many self-employed professionals at the high end. On average, flexible workers tend to earn lower wages than traditional workers, particularly if they are men of color or women, but a significant segment of the independent workforce is also prospering (Kalleberg et al. 1997).

Despite this diversity, all nonstandard workers face some common problems. While the consequences of these are more severe for low-wage workers, their source remains the same for all nonstandard workers. This universality creates an opening for a broad cross-class constituency with common interests that join worker groups and individuals across industries and occupations—the same kind of universality that advanced Social Security and the GI Bill.

A New Organization for the New Workforce

Working Today was founded in 1995 to build this kind of constituency by linking institutions that support nonstandard workers in a network of associations that represents a broad spectrum of nonstandard workers and will have the political and economic clout to put issues of concern to them on the national agenda. Drawing on experiences from this country's history and the unusual diversity of mutual aid societies, this network is finding innovative, practical ways to support working people in the changing economy.

As most readers of this volume know, prior to the rise of industrial unions such as the auto and steel workers, labor organizations took a very different form in the United States. In the 1890s, guilds and craft unions such as the bricklayers and masons, the granges, and ethnic and religious mutual aid societies were the primary worker associations (Laubacher and Malone 1997, p. 2). Independent craftspeople formed these unions to gain control over training and entry into an occupation, exchange advice, secure good deals on tools and materials, ensure "fair" prices for their products, reduce their isolation, and build community. The craft unions were joined together across industry lines by the early American Federation of Labor (AFL), which increased the economic and political presence of working people.

Large bureaucratic industrial unions arose in the 1920s and 1930s to meet the challenges of the large industrial workplace. But as the manufacturing sector declined in later decades, so did the industrial unions, which are not well suited to the more flexible, decentralized structure of capital that is now coming to dominate our economy.

Even so, the news for labor is not all bad. A hundred years after the heyday of craft unions, an important variation on the craft model is emerging. For contingent and independent workers, voluntary associations now perform many of the social and economic functions of the preindustrial unions. In fact, I would argue that the recent growth of professional associations such as the New York New Media Association

(NYNMA) and some workforce development organizations has been largely due to the involvement of the growing ranks of independent workers, for whom these organizations play a vital role.

The problem is that, unlike unions and extended mutual aid societies such as the Masons, most of these modern associations are not linked together in any coherent way. Many do not have much labor consciousness or knowledge of the strategies that craft unions and guilds have used—some since the Middle Ages—to increase the economic security and solidarity of their members.

Working Today was created to address this problem. At its foundation are the many membership groups concerned with people's livelihoods. The organization aims to create a network that ties these disparate worker groups together around long-term common projects, such as the Portable Benefits Fund, that help support workers and their families. Groups join Working Today not only because they agree with our advocacy agenda on issues such as health insurance, pensions, and employment protections but also because we offer immediate support and practical tools to help their members solve common problems. And each of the autonomous groups gains a greater voice in the public debate by participating in a larger whole, as craft unions in the AFL did a century ago and continue to do today.

Building Infrastructure to Support and Connect Workers

As of fall 1999, 25 organizations representing nearly 92,000 workers, as well as over a thousand individual members, had joined Working Today. These groups represent the diversity of our constituency. They include guilds of freelancers that the Communications Workers of America, AFL-CIO, has brought under the union's umbrella; clerical temps represented by the Temp Task Force; older workers in Forty Plus who lost their jobs because of downsizing; skilled freelance professionals in Asian Women in Media; low-income microentrepreneurs supported by ACCION New York; and contingent workers supported by Alabama ARISE, a coalition of community, church, and labor groups.

All the groups in the network are organized around natural lines of affiliation—industry, professional community, neighborhood, or ethnic lines. The wide variety of bases around which the groups are organized reflects the evolution of both American political culture and the nature of work in the postindustrial economy.

When you consider the number of people who are connected with community, school, ethnic, church, and other associations concerned with work, the potential impact of a network of such associations is enormous. If these groups can build enough economic power to reduce their reliance on philanthropy or government, they can remain politically independent, advance the interests of members, and achieve long-term political solutions to seemingly intractable problems.

One goal of Working Today is to help worker associations learn from the labor movement how to get the most for their money when purchasing health insurance, pensions, and other products and services. Toward this end, we are developing projects that increase the security of worker associations and their members and that create ongoing incentives for groups to collaborate through our network. This is the role of our major demonstration project, the Portable Benefits Fund, which will act as a mutual aid organization to which associations commit themselves in order to solve a problem of great importance to their members: access to affordable health insurance.

This ambitious experiment is scheduled to be launched in late 2000 and has generated enormous interest in Working Today on the part of public health experts and policy makers. The Portable Benefits Fund will test the viability of a centralized fund for delivery of quality, portable health insurance at an affordable price. It will also create an ongoing incentive for associations and other groups to come together, thus building social capital and an enduring coalition of working partners. Members will join the fund either through affiliation with a worker association or union or through their employer.

In developing the fund, Working Today is collaborating with outside researchers to analyze existing benefit models for mobile workers, including those developed by the Screen Actors Guild and the Teachers Insurance and Annuity Association (TIAA-CREF). We are also working with employers and leaders of worker associations to find innovative ways to help manage risks, reduce turnover rates, and gain a position in the market that will enable the fund to substantially lower the benefit premiums workers face.

If the demonstration succeeds, Working Today will help its network of member organizations create similar funds. The idea is that the portable fund would be replicated by worker groups around the country to improve health coverage for workers. Groups as diverse as a taxi drivers' association in New York City, the American Association of University Professors, the American Federation of Teachers, and independent worker affiliates of the Communications Workers of America have already expressed interest in the idea of such a fund.

The Portable Benefits Fund—and in the future, others like it—will also help build a new set of structures that will offer contingent and independent workers greater security, community, and political presence. It does this in three ways. First, affordable health insurance is an essential service that will attract and build the constituency needed to mount an effective advocacy effort. Second, portable funds run by worker groups will generate income and help the groups become more financially self-sufficient and perhaps more ambitious. Finally, if the portable health experiment succeeds where other health insurance reform efforts failed, it will lend enormous credibility to arguments for a new safety net that serves the entire contemporary workforce.

The ultimate aim of all these efforts is to influence policy. In many cases, the best solution to a large-scale problem such as the growing number of working poor who are without health coverage will not be technical (like the portable fund) but political. The cost of any unsubsidized insurance will continue to be prohibitive for low-income families, regardless of improvements made in risk management and the delivery of the service.

By building a powerful alliance of organizations to work on long-term solutions, we can bring this workforce into the policy debate and mobilize middle-class and low-income groups around issues of mutual concern.

References

Kalleberg, Arne L., Edith Rasell, Ken Hudson, David Webster, Barbara F. Reskin, Naomi Cassirer, and Eileen Applebaum. 1997. *Nonstandard Work, Substandard Jobs: Flexible Work Arrangements in the U.S.* Washington, DC: Economic Policy Institute.

Laubacher, Robert, and Thomas Malone. 1997. *Flexible Work Arrangements and 21st Century Worker's Guilds.* Initiative on Inventing the Organizations of the 21st Century, Working Paper No. 004. Cambridge, MA: Sloan School of Management, Massachusetts Institute of Technology.

CHAPTER 16

Nonstandard Employment and the Structure of Postindustrial Labor Markets

STEPHEN A. HERZENBERG
The Keystone Research Center

JOHN A. ALIC
Johns Hopkins School of Advanced International Studies

HOWARD WIAL
General Accounting Office, United States Congress

Most of the essays in this volume share the view that Americans are increasingly likely to be working in nonstandard jobs at some time in their lives. This essay attempts to explain why this is so by situating the phenomenon of nonstandard employment within a new theory of the structure of the American labor market. The theory divides the labor market into four "work systems," which differ in how production is organized and task performance regulated. Our theory not only clarifies the reasons for increases in nonstandard employment, which we define in terms of limited job security and prospects for advancement. It also points to the changes in labor market institutions needed if workers generally are to enjoy security and upward mobility in the future. We use examples of innovative labor market institutions, several of them profiled in other chapters of this volume, to outline the necessary reconstruction. The chapter and the volume thus end on an optimistic note with the suggestion that it is possible to close the gap between workers' aspirations and opportunities by expanding the latter instead of diminishing the former. If this is to be accomplished, industrial relations researchers and practitioners in the years ahead will need to support the creation of a new labor market structure that can replace the one inherited from the old industrial economy.

The theory presented here is derived from extensive case study research on a wide range of service industries. The emphasis on service industries reflects the fact that they now employ about three quarters of

American workers. However, the theory is applicable to manufacturing and other industries as well as to services. (See Herzenberg, Alic, and Wial 1998 for details, including application of the theory to public policy analysis.)

Among the many characteristics that distinguish the four work systems we identify is the extent to which each requires standard employment relationships or is open to nonstandard ones. American workers are increasingly employed in nonstandard jobs for two reasons. First, the work systems that most readily accommodate nonstandard work account for a growing share of employment, while jobs in the work systems that are least open to nonstandard work make up a declining share. Second, the work systems that are least open to nonstandard work are losing key institutions that constrain the growth of nonstandard arrangements, such as labor unions. Thus our theory helps explain both the decline in standard employment as a share of total employment (Bernhardt and Marcotte, this volume) and the increasing movement of jobs back and forth across the standard–nonstandard boundary (Moss, Salzman, and Tilly, this volume).

Standard and Nonstandard Employment

Although nonstandard employment has generated a great deal of academic and public policy interest, there is no consensus on precisely how to distinguish it from standard work arrangements. Tilly (1996) notes Americans' fears about the growth of part-time as well as temporary employment, both of which are often considered nonstandard. The Bureau of Labor Statistics distinguishes "contingent work" and "alternative work arrangements" as different kinds of nonstandard work (U.S. Bureau of Labor Statistics 1995). "Contingent work" refers to jobs that employees expect to last for limited periods of time. "Alternative work arrangements" include on-call and day labor, independent contracting, contract employment, and employment by temporary help service agencies. Several of the authors in this volume (Bernhardt and Marcotte; Moss, Salzman, and Tilly; Heckscher) explicitly or implicitly associate standard employment with firm-specific internal labor markets. Among the most important features of internal labor markets are long-term employment relationships, employer-provided training, employer-provided benefits, standardized pathways of advancement within the firm, reciprocal loyalty between employer and employee as well as bureaucratic determination of wages and other job characteristics. Finally, American labor and employment laws can be said to draw distinctions between standard and nonstandard work by distinguishing between workers who are and are not entitled to statutory protections. For example, workers who do not have a long enough attachment to the workforce are ineligible to receive unemployment benefits. Those who do not have a long enough tenure with an individual employer are ineligible for federally mandated family and medical leave and can be denied the right to receive benefits from employer-sponsored pension plans. Many statutes also exclude workers employed by small firms.

Despite the lack of complete consensus, it is possible to use the aforementioned definitions of standard employment to identify policy-relevant values that, from the point of view of workers, are implicit in the idea of standard employment. Two of these values figure prominently in the analysis that follows: employment security and opportunities for economic advancement. We consider particular characteristics of standard employment, such as full-time or long-term jobs, as manifestations of these values.

Four Work Systems

Table 1 outlines the characteristics of the four work systems: tightly constrained, unrationalized labor-intensive, semiautonomous, and high-skill autonomous. The following sections expand on these descriptions, stressing the differences that matter most for employment security and advancement opportunity and, hence, for the prevalence of standard and nonstandard employment, as we use those terms. Table 2 summarizes that set of relationships.

The Tightly Constrained Work System

This work system is the realm of assembly lines and their service sector analogues, such as fast-food outlets and the back offices of banks. Its organizing principles are the separation of conception from execution, the standardization of tasks, and the embedding of much of the conception in single-purpose capital goods. In this work system, technology and organizational practice combine to control task performance within narrow bounds. Formal skill requirements are low, with training limited to assigned tasks (e.g., the location of keys on the McDonald's cash register). In many companies, computer monitoring has joined the close supervisory oversight inherited from scientific management.

Despite its prominence in the post–World War II literature of industrial relations and work organization, the tightly constrained work system is the smallest of the four. Table 3 shows that only about 10% of U.S.

TABLE 1
Work Systems Summarized

	Tightly constrained	Unrationalized labor-intensive	Semiautonomous	High-skill autonomous
Examples	Assembly-line and fast-food workers, telephone operators, check proofers	Custodians, hotel housekeepers, nurses' aides, some sales workers and truck drivers	Clerical and administrative jobs with relatively broad responsibilities, low-level managers, some sales workers, UPS truck drivers	Skilled craft workers, physicians, teachers, and other recognized professionals, high-level managers
Extent of organizational rationalization	High (jobs prescribed by management)	Low	Moderate	Low to moderate
Task supervision	Close	Loose	Moderate	Little
Output monitoring/ quantitative performance measurement	Machine pacing common	Quantitative measurement in some cases	Quantitative measurement in some cases	Quantitative measurement rare
Formal education/ credentials	Low to moderate	Low to moderate (skill often unrecognized)	Moderate	High
Formal, firm-specific training	Minimal	Minimal	Significant for those who climb internal job ladders	Varies

On-the-job training	Limited	Some informal, unrecognized OJT from other workers	Limited to moderate	Substantial
Pay	Often flat hourly; some bonuses linked to output or profits	Sometimes piece rate; sometimes flat hourly	Often flat hourly; some bonuses linked to output or profits	Usually salary; salary or profit share may be linked to billing, attracting clients
Mobility across firms	Lateral mobility in some cases	Lateral, no upward mobility	Most experience not portable	Lateral mobility; upward mobility in some professions

Source: Herzenberg, Alic, and Wial 1998, table 6, pp. 42–43.

TABLE 2

Work Systems Related to Features of Standard/Nonstandard Employment

	Tightly constrained	Unrationalized labor-intensive	Semiautonomous	High-skill autonomous
Employment security	Relatively high in parts of manufacturing (e.g., unionized firms in stable markets); generally low in services	Generally low	Generally high but declining because of restructuring (due to deregulation, technological change, etc.)	High; often rooted in occupation rather than employer
Advancement opportunities	Limited, though somewhat better in manufacturing than in services	Low	Moderate to good for many workers	Generally high, although wage compression affects many occupations, including some professions

manufacturing workers and 4% of service workers fill such jobs. As table 4 indicates, tightly constrained workers earn substantially less in services than in manufacturing, where unions continue to represent many better-paid, longer-tenured employees. In tightly constrained service jobs, low wages, together with the fast pace and high stress of the work, contribute to levels of turnover that exceed 100% annually in some jobs.

TABLE 3

Employment by Work System, 1979 and 1996

| | Percentage of U.S. employment | | | |
| | 1979 | 1996 | | |
	All industries	All industries	Services	Mfg.
Tightly constrained	6	5	4	10
Unrationalized labor-intensive	23	25	26	15
Semiautonomous	37	30	29	34
High-skill autonomous	34	41	40	40

Note: Totals may not add to 100 because of rounding. To arrive at the figures above, which should be viewed as rough approximations, we assigned each three-digit occupation from the Current Population Survey to one or more of the four work systems, based on job content. In some cases, all workers in a given occupation were placed in one work system; in other cases, we split the occupation between two or more work systems. For further explanation, see Herzenberg, Alic, and Wial 1998, Appendix B, pp. 185-189.

Source: Herzenberg, Alic, and Wial 1998, table 7, p. 45, and table 10, p. 77.

TABLE 4

Wages by Work System, 1996

| | Median hourly wage | |
	Services	Manufacturing
Tightly constrained	$5.75	$8.00
Unrationalized labor-intensive	6.00	6.40
Semiautonomous	10.00	11.55
High-skill autonomous	15.00	16.00

Source: Herzenberg, Alic, and Wial 1998, table 8, p. 46.

Skills generally do not transfer even to tightly constrained jobs in other industries, much less to other work systems, limiting opportunities for economic advancement via change of employer. Except in some unionized, durable-goods manufacturing jobs, there are few opportunities for economic advancement within a firm. When there are such opportunities, advancement typically involves movement into semiautonomous jobs because work processes in the tightly constrained system are not organized to provide for much skill progression. In the service sector, employees may change employers within an industry or subindustry (e.g., fast foods) in search of a few cents more per hour or a more congenial working environment.

Where employees are unionized, they typically enjoy formal guarantees of job security, including seniority-based layoff policies and just-cause requirements for discharge. Where production is highly capital intensive, the employer's incentive to keep capital fully employed translates into an incentive to provide some degree of employment security, since the employer could suffer lost productivity from having to train new workers frequently (cf. Piore 1990). In less capital-intensive production processes (such as back offices in financial services), this incentive is much smaller. In addition, the firm- or subfirm-specificity of worker skills limits the possibility of employment security at the occupation or industry level.

Thus, the tightly constrained work system allows for either standard or nonstandard work (defined in terms of employment security and advancement opportunities). Where production is capital intensive or unions are present, work is more likely to be standard. Declining union density has therefore removed one of the constraints that in the past curbed the spread of nonstandard employment within this work system. The shift of employment from (more-capital-intensive) manufacturing to (less-capital-intensive) services has had a similar effect. These changes have made the tightly constrained work system more open to nonstandard work arrangements compared with, say, five decades ago.

The Unrationalized Labor-Intensive Work System

As table 3 shows, many more Americans hold unrationalized labor-intensive jobs than tightly constrained ones. In the unrationalized labor-intensive work system, tasks vary irregularly, so they cannot be easily systematized or "rationalized." As the work system's name suggests, production processes are labor intensive. Workers do not have craft, professional, or other occupational attachments that provide them with scarce skills or other sources of labor market power. Employers with little capital invested and who are able to hire workers at low wages have few incentives to train their employees or to analyze work processes systematically in order to enhance performance. Workers are expected to figure out for themselves how to do what needs to be done, for example, care for residents in a nursing home, load or drive a truck, clean an office building.

Those who have never worked in an unrationalized labor-intensive job may perceive the skills required as modest and generic (e.g., cleaning, lifting, caregiving). Even so, furniture movers, uncredentialed short-order cooks, and many others in this work system develop skills that make them much more productive than novices. Employers, however, rarely provide substantive or problem-solving training that would help workers build on their informal knowledge. Nor do employers devote time and effort to asking how technology might improve performance. In interviews in nursing homes, for example, a number of managers flatly denied that common tasks could be performed in any other way than they had always been performed.

The quantity and quality of output in this work system are controlled in several ways. Where it is easy to measure output and reject low quality, as with hotel housekeepers, janitors, or long-distance truck drivers, employers often pay a fixed amount per unit of output (i.e., a piece rate) or require workers to complete a fixed set of tasks in the workday (e.g., 18 hotel rooms or two floors in a commercial building). Workers who do not meet basic standards of cleanliness or deliver the goods on time can be fired. In some unrationalized labor-intensive social service jobs, such as child- and elder care, workers may have formal responsibility for a set number of clients, but quantity and quality of work are difficult to measure and depend substantially on workers' sense of obligation to those they serve. In other jobs in which output cannot easily be measured, workers have substantial control over how well the job is accomplished. Examples include much of independent retailing, low-skill office work (including much temporary work), and casual labor and nonprofessional self-employment. In these settings, where employers believe (often incorrectly) that there is little potential to improve performance through technology or job redesign, performance varies widely and may depend on whether supervisors have incentives (short of the threat of dismissal) to motivate workers.

Economic advancement is difficult within the unrationalized labor-intensive system because workers have neither the opportunity to acquire scarce skills that employers recognize nor, in most cases, the collective economic power that comes with unionization. Advancement out of the work system is difficult because the skills acquired may not prepare workers for other jobs and, most critical, there are rarely any organizational or institutional linkages between unrationalized labor-intensive jobs and other jobs.

There is nothing in the logic of the unrationalized labor-intensive work system that either requires or precludes employment security at the firm level, but formal employment security guarantees do not exist except in the few unionized jobs. The absence of strong craft or industrial identities on the part of workers makes formal employment security provisions beyond the individual employer level difficult to create. However, the transferability of skills across employer boundaries gives workers a modicum of employment security at the occupational level, and occupational tenure in this work system is often high even though tenure with individual employers is typically low. Still, this occupation-based security is only a bare security of employment; it does not include security of income or benefits, which are often thought of as part of the concept of employment security.

Because of the absence of advancement opportunities and the limited extent of employment security, nonstandard jobs are common in the unrationalized labor-intensive work system. Unlike tightly constrained jobs, where capital intensity and union density are sometimes high, there are few limits on employers' ability to shift jobs from standard to nonstandard and, absent severe labor shortages, few incentives to convert nonstandard into standard jobs. The larger this work system, therefore, the more nonstandard jobs there are likely to be in the U.S. labor market.

The Semiautonomous Work System

Semiautonomous workers include, among others, many clerical and administrative employees, low-level managers, and airline flight attendants. The main organizing principles of this work system are skill specificity and bureaucracy. As in the unrationalized labor-intensive case, tasks cannot be closely monitored or technically controlled because of variety or complexity or because the movement of workers over wide areas makes close supervision difficult. But unlike in the unrationalized labor-intensive system, workers' skills are substantial, recognized by employers, and largely specific to a particular employer. Therefore, employers share an interest with workers in promoting long-term employment relationships. They use financial incentives, sometimes quite elaborate, along with organizational culture and peer pressure, to motivate workers and limit labor turnover. Among these incentives are the job ladders of internal labor markets. For such reasons, wages are substantially higher than in the tightly constrained and unrationalized labor-intensive work systems (table 4).

Firm-specific employment security and advancement opportunities, and hence standard employment, are thus part of the organizing logic of the semiautonomous system. For several generations, this work system offered good jobs to many Americans who entered the labor market without a college degree or specialized skills. Many of these jobs were linked to extensive career ladders, perhaps most developed at the old AT&T but also evident in the 1960s at the corner bank and the regional grocery chain. Aided by formal company-provided training and informal on-the-job training, workers could acquire substantial repertoires of skills.

The semiautonomous work system is now in some decline. Economic restructuring has combined with technological change to dissolve many long-standing employment relationships in this work system and to simplify, homogenize, and automate work, especially office work. On the other hand, some employers who previously abolished or curtailed internal labor markets are now establishing new ones (Moss, Salzman, and Tilly, this volume), and some semiautonomous jobs, such as those for package express drivers, are on the increase. Nonetheless, the work system as a whole is shrinking, as table 3 indicates. Other things equal, this implies a decline in the share of standard jobs in the U.S. labor market.

The High-Skill Autonomous Work System

Peer pressure and commitment to the job motivate many semiautonomous and some unrationalized labor-intensive workers. These forces are more widespread and powerful in the high-skill autonomous work system, which is based on occupational pride and expertise. In this system, people largely manage themselves, even if, like electricians, nurses, or teachers, they are formally subordinate to another professional or a manager. With expertise often recognized by professional, technical, or craft credentials, skills have value to many employers. The high-skill autonomous work system is the best paying, largest, and fastest growing of the four. Today, these "knowledge workers" make up about 40% of the workforce.

Unlike employers who rely on the tightly constrained and unrationalized labor-intensive work systems, employers of high-skill autonomous workers usually screen job candidates carefully and provide substantial formal and informal support for on-the-job learning and supplementary education and training. As in the unrationalized labor-intensive system, employers may have little understanding of what determines performance and how it could be measured or improved. Although employers may track output and quality—the number of lines of code generated by computer programmers, for example, or surgeons' mortality rates—performance evaluation has a large subjective element usually dependent on peer judgment. (Some blocks of code are "better" than others; some surgeons take harder cases.) Indeed, the complex, nonroutine, and intangible nature of much craft and professional work makes defining performance, never mind evaluating it, a task that is sometimes insurmountable.

High-skill autonomous workers enjoy opportunities for economic advancement within their occupations. These opportunities derive from the market power that scarce and transferable skills confer, as well as from the increase in skills that occurs as a worker gains experience and higher levels of competence in an occupation. Advancement opportunities may also exist at the level of the individual employer but, whether advancement occurs within a firm or via movement between firms, what is important is that it is based on the development of occupational skills.

The employment security of high-skill autonomous workers is likewise based on the continued scarcity of their occupational skills and may require interfirm movement on the part of the individual worker. As college degrees and specialized occupational credentials become more widely available and as high-skill autonomous occupational groups (such as unions in the construction trades) lose control of the supply of skilled labor, the employment security and advancement opportunities of some high-skill autonomous workers may be eroded.

On the whole, the high-skill autonomous work system presents a mixed picture in regard to standard versus nonstandard employment. Standard work predominates only to the extent that occupational skills remain scarce. If the scarcity of an occupation's skills declines, the occupation becomes more open to nonstandard employment.

* * *

Although work can be organized in an infinite variety of ways, these four work systems capture the essentials. Each could be subdivided, but none of the four could be folded into one of the others. Some jobs fit squarely in one of the four categories, others less neatly. The defining mechanisms of each work system, moreover, may be supplemented with mechanisms identified with one of the others. Self-motivation and self-management, for example, are present to some extent in all four, but only in high-skill autonomous work are they pivotal. Many jobs, moreover, include tasks that are incidental to the distinctive core of the work. Professionals, for example, may do their own filing and sneak away after jamming the copying machine; but it is the core tasks of the job that determine the work system with which it should be identified.

Some statistical categories and traditional occupational definitions span work systems. Sales workers, for instance, include clerks in low-wage, low-skill, high-turnover positions best categorized as unrationalized labor-intensive (e.g., in discount retailing). They also include tightly constrained telemarketers who must follow the script when a householder answers a computer-generated call. Other sales jobs fall into the semiautonomous work system. Sales personnel at a lumberyard we studied get substantial training, are responsible for negotiating $100,000+ deals with builders, can advance to yard manager or higher, and receive thousands of dollars in profit sharing in good years. Some of those who sell retail banking services likewise benefit from considerable training and may develop a commitment to the job not unlike that of professionals. Finally, stockbrokers and insurance agents are part of the high-skill autonomous work system.

The Four Work Systems Compared with Dual and Segmented Labor Markets

Readers familiar with theories of dual (or segmented) labor markets developed from the 1960s through the 1980s will notice similarities between those theories and the framework we have presented. Like the earlier theories, ours is a structural theory that remains relatively close to the level of description. Although it posits economic and social mechanisms that account for the functioning of the four work systems, it does not derive those systems from an abstract, unified theory of the entire labor market. There are rough correspondences between some of the market segments we define and those of dual labor market theory. However, our theory takes into account important features of the contemporary labor market that, although present throughout the earlier postwar period, were largely ignored in earlier representations.

The first formulations of dual labor market theory (e.g., Doeringer and Piore 1971) divided the labor market into a primary and a secondary sector. Primary jobs were characterized by most or all of the following: high wages, good working conditions, employment stability, advancement opportunities, and procedural fairness; secondary jobs lacked most of these features. In terms of our theory, the primary sector included what we call the high-skill autonomous and semiautonomous work systems, as well as the high-wage unionized and/or capital-inten-sive parts of the tightly constrained system. The secondary sector included unrationalized labor-intensive jobs and the remaining tightly constrained jobs. A later elaboration of dual labor market theory (Piore 1979) divided the primary sector into an upper tier, corresponding roughly to the high-skill autonomous work system, and a lower tier, cor-responding to the semiautonomous system and the high-wage portion of the tightly constrained system.

Our framework differs most notably from these earlier theories in distinguishing between the tightly constrained and semiautonomous work systems. In a manufacturing-centered economy in which many tightly constrained jobs were unionized and advancement to off-line semiautonomous jobs was based on seniority, considering both of these work systems as part of one labor market segment made sense. Their logics overlapped; bureaucratic incentives, for example, operated in both. In the service sector, by contrast, most of the tightly constrained jobs are low-wage, nonunion, and high turnover. There are few if any links to advancement opportunities within the firm, which was not the case in the old hierarchical manufacturing organizations. In other words, service industries exhibit a much more distinct separation between the tightly constrained and semiautonomous work systems. In addition, the distinction between the semiautonomous and tightly constrained systems is important to the analysis of nonstandard employment today, since the sources of employment security and advancement opportunities can now be seen to differ sharply between the two systems.

Our theory more closely resembles the segmented labor market the-ory of Edwards (1979), which distinguished between segments on the basis of the mechanism by which employers control the work process. In the secondary sector, employers simply told workers what to do and usu-ally let them figure out the details of how to do it, as in our unrational-ized labor-intensive work system. In the subordinate tier of the primary sector, employers relied on technology to subdivide work into tasks that could be performed by different categories of workers; this resembles our tightly constrained system. In the primary independent tier, employers motivated workers through bureaucratic incentives, as in our semiau-tonomous work system. However, Edwards's theory neglected the high-skill autonomous work system, failing to distinguish it from the semi-autonomous system. Once again, in the more manufacturing-centered economy about which Edwards wrote, the distinction between these two largely white-collar work systems may have seemed less important than in today's service-dominated economy. For the analysis of nonstandard work, on the other hand, the distinction between the semiautonomous and the high-skill autonomous work systems is crucial, because the sources of employment security and advancement opportunities differ so greatly between the two.

Osterman's (1987) theory of employment subsystems is the segmentation theory that bears the greatest resemblance to our own. Osterman distinguished between four subsystems on the basis of the ways in which jobs are classified and defined, the rules by which workers can be moved between jobs within an organization, the type of employment security offered to workers, and the rules by which wages are determined. The industrial subsystem, which corresponds roughly to our tightly constrained work system, is characterized by narrowly defined jobs with clear work rules and wages attached to each job and seniority as the main determinant of both promotions and layoffs. The salaried subsystem, which resembles our semiautonomous work system, features strong, firm-specific guarantees of employment security combined with substantial flexibility in job definition, job assignment, and wage setting within the firm. In the craft subsystem, Osterman's analogue to our high-skill autonomous work system, the occupation rather than the individual employer is the source of workers' skills, employment security, advancement opportunities, and wage bargaining power. Finally, the secondary subsystem, like our unrationalized labor-intensive work system, consists of "dead-end" jobs that lack clear linkages to other jobs within either a firm or occupation.

Although Osterman's job categories do not correspond precisely to our own, the most important difference between his theory and ours is not how particular jobs are classified but how job categories are defined. Our categories are defined by the way in which production is organized; we then derive other features of the categories, including labor market characteristics, from the core logic of each category's method of organizing production. Osterman's categories are defined by a more eclectic set of organizational and labor market characteristics. For him, employment security and advancement opportunities are among the defining features of job categories, while for us they are derived from the more fundamental dynamics of the different work systems. We believe that focusing on the underlying organization of production makes it possible to address a broader range of analytical and public policy issues using our framework (e.g., the implications of work systems for economic performance; see chapter 5 of Herzenberg, Alic, and Wial 1998).

Finally, our theory owes a debt to economic models that explain why, in some jobs, employers and employees share an interest in long-term employment relationships. Lazear (1995) explored the consequences of firm-specific skills for the nature of internal labor markets. His analysis can be regarded as an economic explanation of the logic of the semiautonomous work system. Bulow and Summers (1986) distinguished between primary and secondary jobs on the basis of whether they pay efficiency wages. Although efficiency wages do not figure in the scheme we present, our more comprehensive analysis (Herzenberg, Alic, and Wial 1998) attributes efficiency wage properties to the semiautonomous work system. The Lazear and Bulow–Summers theories, then, can be regarded as providing detailed economic analyses of this work system.

Nonstandard Employment and the Dynamics of Work Systems

To use the theory of work systems to analyze changes in the extent of nonstandard employment, it is necessary to know three things: the degree to which each work system requires standard employment relationships, changes that may be occurring in the openness of each work system to nonstandard employment, and changes in the relative sizes of the work systems. With regard to the first of these, we need only summarize the conclusions of the previous section. The semiautonomous work system requires standard employment to the greatest extent. At the other end of the spectrum, the unrationalized labor-intensive system is the most permissive of nonstandard arrangements. The other two work systems occupy intermediate positions. Tightly constrained jobs that are unionized or situated within capital-intensive production settings tend to be associated with standard work, while other tightly constrained jobs more readily tolerate nonstandard arrangements. In the high-skill autonomous work system, the extent to which work is standard depends in part on the scarcity of the relevant occupational skills.

Table 3 included our estimates, necessarily rough given the data limitations, of the shifts in size of the four work systems since 1979. The semiautonomous system, which is most resistant to nonstandard employment, has contracted substantially. In retailing, for example, employers have shifted many semiautonomous jobs into the unrationalized labor-intensive category. Department stores facing stiff competition from both discount and specialty outlets have transformed nonprofessional positions that once offered decent wages and benefits along with advancement opportunities—classic semiautonomous jobs—into low-paying, high-turnover positions that require little more than ringing up sales—classic dead-end jobs. Similarly, many banks have turned the teller job, once the first step on a career ladder, into a dead-end, often part-time position. Like department stores, banks now fill higher-level openings from the outside labor market and typically require a college degree.

The already small share of the tightly constrained work system, parts of which have built-in limits on nonstandard employment, is shrinking further. Most service jobs that can be easily rationalized and automated, such as those of telephone operators, have already been moved into the tightly constrained system. Even though many of the tasks in, say, health care are routine, they vary unpredictably in execution and in mix, making standardization, much less automation, difficult or impossible. At the same time, the high-skill autonomous work system, in which employment is usually standard but can in some occupations shift to nonstandard, has grown substantially.

Our estimates show a small increase in the employment share of unrationalized labor-intensive jobs, which can easily be either standard or nonstandard. Case studies, in addition, suggest not only that this work system has been expanding but that it will continue to do so. Employers facing cost-based competition (e.g., in retailing) may replace semiautonomous with unrationalized labor-intensive jobs in order to push down wages, even if this means sacrificing productivity and quality. In long-distance trucking, for example, government regulation and union influence checked low-wage competition before 1980. Deregulation changed this situation in part of the industry, especially for shipments of low-value goods, and drivers' jobs became more like unrationalized labor-intensive jobs (Belzer 2000). Finally, anytime there is substantial underemployment, the unrationalized labor-intensive work system will likely flourish, if only because displaced workers will seek to replace lost wages through casual labor.

Table 5 summarizes how jobs are shifting within each of the four work systems. There has been little recent overall change discernible in employment security or advancement opportunities in either the unrationalized labor-intensive or the high-skill autonomous work system. At the same time, some occupations in the high-skill autonomous system have experienced declines in security or advancement prospects, or both.

Both security and advancement opportunities (and hence standard work) have declined in the tightly constrained system. As union density and bargaining power have fallen and employment within this work system has continued to shift from more-capital-intensive manufacturing to less-capital-intensive services, the work system's constraints on nonstandard employment arrangements have loosened. Increased outsourcing has been one manifestation of this change.

TABLE 5
Work System Dynamics

Work system	Major forces of change	Likely impacts (within the work system)	Prospects for individual advancement	Job security
Tightly constrained	Continuing rationalization, computer-based automation	Declining number of jobs, relatively if not absolutely. Wages, benefits already low in most cases—little further change. Generally positive implications for productivity and service quality.	Poorer: more dead-end jobs with no prospect of internal advancement	Poorer: more outsourcing, permanent layoffs
Unrationalized labor-intensive	Spread of low-cost business strategies, wage-based competition	Growing number of jobs. Downward pressure on wages and benefits. Neutral or negative implications for productivity and service quality.	Still poor: low-wage jobs unconnected to better ones	Little change: some dead-end jobs are secure
Semiautonomous	Restructuring, continued spread and growing sophistication of information technologies	Declining share of jobs. Greater dispersion in wages and benefits as compensation rises for those with skills in high demand relative to those with more generic training. Employment instability tends to erode productivity and service quality.	Worse: skills valuable only to current employer firm-specific job ladders breaking down	Worse: more restructuring, permanent layoffs

| High-skill autonomous | Technological change permitting lower-skilled employees to replace some high-skill autonomous workers, accompanied by continued growth in demand for new types of skills (e.g., associated with electronic commerce) | Continued growth in number of jobs likely, but some high-skill autonomous jobs may come to resemble unrationalized labor-intensive work. Wages likely to rise for new and scarce skills, decline for some traditional professions (e.g., physicians). | Still good in most cases but may decline in some occupations as scarcity value of skills diminishes | Little change in most cases: skills widely recognized and valued by many employers, but may decline in some occupations with diminishing scarcity value |

Source: Adapted from Herzenberg, Alic, and Wial 1998, table 2, p. 13, and table 9, p. 76.

Similarly, advancement opportunities and employment security have declined within the semiautonomous work system. The truncation or elimination of internal labor markets has reduced rewards for firm-specific skills. Those semiautonomous workers whose employers provided them with training that substantially increased their general as well as their firm-specific skills have fared best in the current environment. (An example is clerical workers with experience in relatively sophisticated but nonetheless generic office software packages, e.g., database management or desktop publishing as opposed to simple word processing.) Other semiautonomous workers have been faced with reduced prospects for advancement with their current employers and have little chance of obtaining an equivalent or better position with another employer. Many of those who lost long-held jobs had to learn new skills in a lower-paying position at another firm. Even though some employers are beginning to rebuild internal labor markets for semiautonomous workers (Moss, Salzman, and Tilly, this volume), there is not yet any evidence that this countertrend is larger than the trend toward the erosion and elimination of internal labor markets.

It is likely, although not certain, that the combined effect of these changes has been to expand the share of jobs that can accommodate either standard or nonstandard employment and to reduce the share that must be standard. The share of the semiautonomous work system, which is least open to nonstandard employment, is shrinking, and the jobs that remain can increasingly be either standard or nonstandard. Much the same is true of the tightly constrained work system, which favored standard work more strongly in the past than today. At the opposite extreme, the employment share of the unrationalized labor-intensive system appears to be growing, although there is no evidence that this work system, which has always been open to nonstandard work, is becoming still more open. The only possible countertendency to an increase in the employment share of jobs that may be organized either as standard or as nonstandard is the expansion of the high-skill autonomous work system, where most jobs are standard (but with security and advancement opportunities tied primarily to occupations rather than employers). However, the constraints on nonstandard employment in this work system are weaker than those for semiautonomous jobs or in the unionized, capital-intensive part of the tightly constrained system. Further, our estimates of changes in the relative sizes of the work systems (table 3) are not accurate enough to reveal whether the growth of the high-skill autonomous work system outweighs the other trends mentioned previously.

Thus the theory of work systems, as applied to the question of nonstandard employment, is consistent with two major stylized facts about nonstandard employment presented elsewhere in this volume: a modest expansion in nonstandard work arrangements and the increasing tendency of jobs to migrate between the standard and nonstandard categories (Moss, Salzman, and Tilly, this volume). With more accurate classification of jobs into work systems as well as more careful operationalization of the core characteristics of nonstandard versus standard employment, it would be possible to determine with greater certainty whether the four work systems have the consequences for nonstandard employment described earlier.

Expanding Opportunity and Security in the Postindustrial Economy

Is it possible to reconstruct American labor market institutions so that the employment security and advancement opportunities once associated with standard work arrangements will again become more widely available in the future? The conceptual framework presented earlier suggests three strategies for accomplishing this goal (because different work systems demand different strategies). These strategies aim to (1) reorganize unrationalized labor-intensive jobs so that they more closely resemble semiautonomous or high-skill autonomous jobs, (2) create pathways along which workers can move out of dead-end jobs in the unrationalized labor-intensive and tightly constrained work systems, and (3) extend throughout the labor market the types of multiemployer institutions that provide security and advancement for high-skill autonomous workers. The idea behind all these strategies is that if too many Americans are mired in insecure, dead-end jobs, either pathways must be created out of those jobs or the work itself must be raised in status, compensation, and skill level.

While our focus is on economic opportunity, the changes discussed also have the potential to raise economic performance. Through investments in mentoring, in structured opportunities for workers to learn from one another (e.g., spanning multiple work sites and employers), and in classroom and other types of formal training, employees would become better at the tasks they perform and at communicating and working with others, thus yielding what we term "economies of depth" and "economies of coordination." Large gains in performance are possible in many services simply because little effort has gone into deliberate searching for these types of improvements in the past.

Reorganizing Unrationalized Labor-Intensive Work

It would be desirable for the unrationalized labor-intensive work system to shrink rather than grow, with jobs moving to the semiautonomous system or even the high-skill autonomous system. Higher wage and benefit standards would foster such a shift by deterring turnover and "shocking" some employers into reconsidering prevailing assumptions about "unskilled" work. Such changes also require training and career structures that deepen workers' knowledge. In services that depend partly on government financing, such as childcare, a final essential ingredient is to increase public funding. While these may seem like challenging preconditions, work-system transformation need not wait until they are satisfied nationally; rather, because human services (and many other services) are tied to the local markets where customers live, change can start in a single city or state.

In several places, efforts to reorganize sectors now dominated by the unrationalized labor-intensive work system are under way. In Philadelphia, the United Child Care Union (UCCU) seeks to bring all area center-based childcare workers and family childcare providers into a sector-wide organization with the power to raise compensation standards. A stakeholder group that includes center-based employers, family childcare providers, educators, professional associations, and the UCCU is seeking public support to create a regional consortium for recruitment, training, and career advancement. And a statewide coalition is pushing for increases in funding. Analogous efforts to promote changes in nursing home work systems are also emerging in several states, under the banner of the nursing home "culture change" movement.

Pathways out of Entry-Level Jobs. In fast foods, much of the rest of retail, and among food service contractors, work reorganization is not on the agenda, and the job structures of individual employers provide little possibility for advancement. Improving such jobs requires not only better wages and benefits but links with opportunities in other firms. While multiemployer linkages can sometimes be built within sectors, they are generally found in sectors with potential for work-system transformation, such as childcare and health care (on the latter, see Dresser, this volume). In other parts of the low-skill labor market, including at janitorial, food service, and security guard contract firms, and in "unskilled" temporary employment, job ladders must be built that lead out of the industry and occupation.